Hiking

Pennsylvania

Help Us Keep This Guide Up to Date

Every effort has been made by the author and editors to make this guide as accurate and useful as possible. However, many things can change after a guide is published—trails are rerouted, regulations change, techniques evolve, facilities come under new managment, etc.

We would love to hear from you concerning your experiences with this guide and how you feel it could be improved and kept up to date. While we may not be able to respond to all comments and suggestions, we'll take them to heart and we'll also make certain to share them with the authors. Please send your comments and suggestions to the following address:

The Globe Pequot Press
Reader Response/Editorial Department
P.O. Box 480
Guilford, CT 06437

Or you may e-mail us at:

editorial@globe-pequot.com

Thanks for your input, and happy travels!

A FALCON GUIDE®

Hiking
Pennsylvania

Second Edition

Rhonda and George Ostertag

FALCON®

GUILFORD, CONNECTICUT

AN IMPRINT OF THE GLOBE PEQUOT PRESS

Λ FALCON GUIDE®

Photo credits: George Ostertag

Library of Congress Cataloging-in-Publication Data is available.
ISBN 0-7627-2244-4

Manufactured in the United States of America
Second Edition/First Printing

Contents

Acknowledgments

We would like to acknowledge the trail associations and individual volunteers who help blaze and maintain the trails, the preservationists who work to save Pennsylvania's prized natural areas, and the landowners who have allowed the state trail system to grow. Most especially, we would like to salute the staffs of Pennsylvania's public agencies for their dedication to trails and their cooperation. They have been helpful every step of the way—from research to review—and we thank them. We would also like to thank the people we met along the way who volunteered their ideas or faces for the book, and we would like to thank our East and West Coast base camps for freeing us to do our work.

—Rhonda and George Ostertag

Map Legend

Interstate	(955)	Wetland	
U.S. Highway	(101)	Campground	
State or County Road	(222)	Picnic Area	
Paved Road		Trail Shelter	
Gravel Road		Bridge	
Unimproved Road		Building	
Trailhead/Parking	(P)	Cemetery	
Described Trail		Mine/Quarry	
Alternate Trail		Viewpoint	
Brook		Point of Interest	
River		Power Line	
Pier		Lookout Tower	
Body of Water		Railroad	
Dam			
Summit	2,477ft.	Scale	0 0.5 1 Miles
Waterfall		Spring	
Forest Road	7745	Boat Launch	

Overview Map

A. Lake Erie Region
B. Allegheny National Forest Region
C. Pocono Mountains Region
D. Valleys of the Susquehanna Region
E. Pittsburgh Region
F. Laurel Highlands Region
G. Hershey Dutch Region
H. Philadelphia Region

Introduction

The commonwealth of Pennsylvania rolls out like an intriguing canvas, with thousands of miles of trails leading the way to discovery. Hikes range from short nature walks to lengthy rail-trails to challenging mountain treks. Travel Penn's Woods and become immersed in its geological, cultural, and natural tales.

This guidebook samples the gamut of hiking opportunities found across the state. Here, find a collection of nature walks, day hikes, and backpack trips to challenge, excite, and engage you. The described trails explore many of the state's premier parks, forests, mountains, runs, swamps, and private reserves and sanctuaries.

Hikers travel past sparkling waterfalls and outcrop mazes, stand humbled by old-growth forests of white pine and eastern hemlock, traverse broad mountain summits, dip through valley floors, and walk in the footsteps of Native Americans, colonial soldiers, and the blue and the gray of the Civil War. Seasonally, they can stride through the splendor of a shower of colored leaves or a profusion of rhododendron and mountain laurel blooms. White-tailed deer seemingly lurk around each bend, while each fall, kettles of broad-winged hawks turn hikers' eyes skyward. Although some of this outdoor treasury is well known, great expanses remain little tapped.

Pennsylvania boasts a first-rate network of trails, responsive public agencies, and ardent groups of volunteers. For the most part, visitors will find the trails highly accessible and well designed, allowing passage without destroying the natural terrain and habitat. So lace on your boots and see what Pennsylvania really has to offer.

WEATHER

Overall, Pennsylvania offers three-season hiking. Winter hikes generally require you to strap on snowshoes or don cross-country skis. Spring and fall offer a preferred mix of mild temperatures and low humidity. Summers can bring extremes in both categories, as well as dramatic afternoon thunder-and-lightning storms. Come prepared for changeable weather, regardless of season.

Like much of the East, Pennsylvania can have a tormenting mosquito season. Carry insect repellent on spring and summer hikes, especially in the wet lowlands.

TERRAIN

From the Delaware Water Gap to the lowlands of Lake Erie and from the Allegheny Mountains to the arching Appalachian Mountains of the Valley and Ridge Province, Pennsylvania presents a varied tapestry. Much of the state is clad with hardwood forests, with rivers, creeks, and runs carving deep valleys through the mountain plateaus. The state flower—the mountain laurel—was aptly chosen, occurring across much of the state.

Amid Penn's Woods, naturally occurring vistas are treasured finds. Outcrops of flagstone, sandstone, shale, quartz, and schist invite exploration. A migrating peninsula; a wildflower prairie harking to those of the Midwest; swamps, potholes, and glacial lakes; abandoned fields and thickets; and a tidal freshwater marsh complement woods travel.

The historic presence of iron ore, oil, and coal did much to shape the development and present-day look of the state. The indiscriminate harvest of trees to make charcoal to fuel the iron furnaces (the pyramids of the Pennsylvania landscape) brought about the demise of native conifer forests and the rise of hardwoods.

LANDOWNERSHIP

While this book concentrates primarily on public land offerings, some trails do cross or occur on individual-, company-, or trust-held private lands. Hikers assume full responsibility for their own well-being when they cross onto these lands; they also consent to heed posted rules. Keep to the trail, leave gates as they were found, and police your own actions as well as those of less considerate hikers who may have passed before you. "Pack it in, pack it out."

The text will indicate if and where a trail traverses private land. Occasionally, though, landownership changes or a landowner may withdraw the privilege of thru-trail travel; respect such closures. Privately operated resorts or reserves may charge fees or suggest donations.

Trails traveling state or federally managed lands constitute the core of this book. Of the state-operated properties, *state parks* typically include developed recreation areas and visitor amenities, with networks of fine nature and hiking trails and often ties or spurs to the long-distance trails traversing the state. The day use is presently free.

Within state parks, overnight camping is restricted to designated, fee campgrounds; trail camping is prohibited. At Oil Creek and Laurel Ridge State Parks, where trail shelters are provided, hikers find first-rate lodging in the wild—well worth the modest maintenance fee charged.

The *state forests* account for large blocks of open space, where visitors can enjoy multiple-use recreation in the natural and planted woods. Typically, the developed facilities are more rustic. Trail camping is generally allowed; secure permits (free) from the district headquarters. Camping without a current camping permit issued by the district forester or a designee is prohibited. The lone exception: No permit is required for primitive backpack camping that is limited to one night per any one site. Leave no trace. At state forest *wild* areas and state forest *natural* areas, different rules may apply to camping and travel; inquire before visiting.

The *state game lands* primarily promote and sustain waterfowl and wildlife populations, and strive to make hunting, fishing, bird-watching, and hiking compatible recreations. Trail camping is prohibited in these areas, except along the Appalachian Trail. Learn and heed the restrictions that apply to the privilege.

TRAIL MARKINGS

Some manner of trail blazing—paint, diamond, or disk markers and/or junction signs—typically guides hikers along these routes. Often a double-blazing pattern warns of a change in direction, with the top blaze offset to the right or left to indicate the direction of the turn.

Because the intervals between blazes can vary greatly, familiarize yourself with the blazing frequency. An uncommonly long lapse between blazes may indicate that you have strayed off course. Autumn hikers need to be especially alert; leaves can conceal the tracked path. Cairns and stakes are other methods of marking a route.

Several fine long-distance routes crisscross the state, including the Appalachian Trail, the North Country Trail, the Laurel Highlands Hiking Trail, the Mid State Trail, and the Susquehannock and Tuscarora Trails.

THE VOLUNTEER COMPONENT

Devoted, energetic individual volunteers and established hiking organizations such as the Keystone Trails Association, the regional Appalachian Trail clubs, and other trail-specific clubs keep the Pennsylvania trail system maintained, promoted, and growing. Hikers should support these groups through membership and through the purchase of their maps and printed materials. Typically, maps produced and sold by volunteer organizations hold the most current information on the lay of the trail, landownership, shelters, facilities, and obstacles.

Hikers likewise owe thanks to private landowners who allow long-distance trails to cross their lands. Such trails would slip from existence without their cooperation.

How to Use This Guide

We have structured this book to aid in the trail selection process. First, we have grouped the trails according to eight commonly accepted geographical regions to ease page-flipping comparisons of the trails. Second, a trail summary presents a quick measure of each trail's overall interest.

Information bullets identify the trail, its general location, special features, length, elevation change, difficulty, maps, special concerns, and season. The key points and elevation profiles further help readers visualize a trail. Although the handful of key points allows a quick check on progress, the listing cannot replace the hike text for guiding you along the trail. At the end of each summary, you will find detailed directions to the site. For contact information, turn to appendix D for the complete address and phone number of each named source.

"The hike" component of the text describes the progress of the trail, drawing attention to special features and alerting readers to obstacles and potentially confusing junctions. Mentions of habitat changes, seasonal surprises, sidelights, and discoveries flesh out the tour descriptions. Where appropriate, we have mentioned flaws and disappointments.

The maps within the text are not intended to replace the more detailed agency maps, road maps, state atlases, and/or topographic maps, but they do indicate the lay of the trail and its attractions, helping readers visualize a tour.

AN EXPLANATION OF SUMMARY TABLE TERMS

Distance measures for the trails represent pedometer readings. Backpacking excursions—sometimes dictated by distance, sometimes by attraction—are left to the hiker's judgment and the rules of the appropriate managing agency, landowner, or private trust.

The subjective classification of "easy," "moderate," or "strenuous" takes into consideration overall distance, elevation change (the difference between elevation extremes), cumulative elevation (how rolling a trail is), trail surface, obstacles, ease of following, and its relative difficulty to the other hikes in the book.

We deliberately excluded estimated hiking times, because personal health and physical condition, party size, the interest of the trail, weather, and a trail's condition can all influence time on the trail. Gain a sense of your personal capabilities and hiking style and judge for yourself the time. Consider the distance, the elevation change, the difficulty rating, and what you glean from the text.

Customize the hikes to fit your needs; you need not continue just because a description does, nor must you stop where it stops. Interlocking loops, side trails, and alternative destinations await.

GLOSSARY

Car-shuttle hikes. Typically, these are linear routes that allow for a drop-off and pickup arrangement or for the spotting of a second vehicle at the trail's end, for one-way travel.

Corduroy. This side-by-side alignment of logs, boards, or branches provides dry passage over soggy trail segments or delicate meadow sites.

Forest lanes. These routes typically are narrower than a road yet wider than a trail, serving both foot and horse travelers.

Jeep trails. These two-track routes typically serve foot and horse travelers. Most are no longer drivable.

Service roads. These routes hold minimal traffic, allowing official vehicles only.

Woods roads. These dirt, grass, or rocky roads or faint road depressions represent old logging, mining, or farm routes that through time have fallen into disuse. Reclaimed for trails, most are closed to vehicle travel, although some may allow snowmobile or mountain bike use. We have attempted to alert readers when vehicle use may occur and when it is illegal.

Outdoor Primer

Whether wilderness trekking is a revitalizing experience or an ordeal depends largely on preparation. Nature does not come without some inherent risks and discomforts, but learning to anticipate and mitigate these clears the path to great outdoor fun.

PREPARATION

Ten Essentials. Outdoor experts have assembled a list of "Ten Essentials"—the cornerstone to safe backcountry travel. The essentials are (1) extra food, (2) extra clothing, (3) sunglasses, (4) knife, (5) candle or chemical fuel to ignite wet wood, (6) dry matches, (7) first-aid kit and manual, (8) flashlight with bulb and batteries, (9) maps for the trip, and (10) compass.

Dress. The amount and the types of clothing worn and carried on a hike depend on the length of the outing, the weather conditions, and your personal comfort. Layering is key to comfort; select items that can serve more than one purpose. A long-sleeve shirt may be layered for warmth, lends sun protection, hinders mosquitoes, and protects against ticks. A lightweight raincoat may double as a windbreaker. Choose wool for cold, wet, or changeable weather conditions; it retains heat even when wet. Choose cotton for dry summer days. For their weight, hats are invaluable for shielding eyes, face, and top of the head and for preserving body heat.

Footwear. While sneakers may be passable for nature walks, for long hikes and uneven terrain, wear boots for comfort and protection. Sock layering, with a light undersock worn next to the foot and a second wool sock worn atop, helps prevent rubbing, cushions the sole, and allows for the absorption of perspiration. Avoid socks with a large cotton content: they are cold when wet and slow to dry.

Food. Pack plenty—hiking demands a lot of energy—and pack foods that will not spoil, bruise, or break apart in the pack. Maximize the energy value for the weight, particularly when backpacking. Food fends off fatigue, a major contributor to accidents on the trail.

Equipment. The quantity and variety depend on the length and nature of the hike and on the season (appendix A offers a checklist of commonly carried items), but a good pack for transporting the gear is essential. A day pack with padded straps, a reinforced bottom, and side pockets for water bottles works for most short outings. For overnight outings, select a backpack that has a good frame and balance, and supports the weight without taxing hips, shoulders, or neck.

Because backpacks represent a major investment, newcomers should first try renting one. You cannot evaluate a pack in the store with only a few sandbags for weight. A trail test delivers a better comfort reading; it also demonstrates how well the unit packs with your personal gear. Most good backpacking stores with a rental program will allow the charge of one rental to be applied to the purchase price of a new pack; ask the manager.

Map and compass. All hikers should become familiar with maps and know how to read them in conjunction with a compass. Maps provide an orientation to an area, suggest alternative routes, and aid in the planning and preparation for the journey.

Become familiar with the United States Geological Survey (USGS) topographic maps. While most of the quads for Pennsylvania are too dated to show the lay of the trail, they still provide information about the steepness and flatness of the terrain, whether a site is treed or open, waterways, and the works of human hands. The USGS offers two sizes: the 7.5-minute and 15-minute series.

Remember that true north does not equal magnetic north. For Pennsylvania, the declination is between 9 and 12 degrees west. Search the map border for the exact declination.

TAKING TO THE TRAILS

Pacing yourself. Adopt a steady, comfortable hiking rhythm, take in the surroundings, and schedule short rests at regular intervals to guard against exhaustion.

Crossing streams. Cross at the widest part of a watercourse, where the current is slower and the water more shallow. Sandy bottoms suggest a barefoot crossing; fast, cold waters and rocky bottoms require the surer footing of boots.

Shed socks before mounting a boot-clad wade. That way, once you are across, you will have a dry-sock layer to help protect and warm your feet in the wet boots; wool socks show their thermal value. The discomfort of hiking in wet boots is minor compared to the alternative dunking. For frequent stream crossings or for hiking streambeds, lightweight sneakers earn their portage.

Hiking cross-country. For safe cross-country travel, you must have good map and compass skills, good survival skills, and good common sense. Steep terrain, heavy brush, and downfalls physically and mentally tax hikers, increasing the potential for injury. This of all hiking should not be attempted alone. Even know-how and preparation cannot fully overcome the unpredictability of nature and human fallibility.

Hiking with children. For young children, choose simple destinations, and do not insist on reaching any particular site. Allow for the difference in attention span and energy level. Enjoy the passing, and share and encourage children's natural curiosity, but come prepared for sun, mosquitoes, and poison ivy. Discuss what to do should you become separated. Be sure your child knows to "hug a tree," not wander, and even small ones should carry essential items: a sweater, water jug, and food.

A WILDERNESS ETHIC

Trails. Keep to the path. Shortcutting, skirting puddles, and walking two abreast all contribute to erosion and the degradation of trails. Report any damage.

Permits and registration. Generally, hikers must secure a current, free overnight camp permit from the appropriate district forester for stays exceeding one night at any one site. In special areas, permits are required in all cases to help monitor and manage the trails and minimize overuse. To protect the integrity of the wild, keep your party size small.

Be sure to use the trailhead registers: The gathered information helps secure funding for trail maintenance, improvements, and expansion.

Pets. Owners should strictly adhere to posted rules for pets. Controlling your animal on a leash is not just a courtesy reserved for times when other hikers are present; it is a responsibility to protect the wildlife and ground cover at all times.

Camping. No-trace camping should be everyone's goal. Select an established campsite and do not alter the ground cover, bring in logs for benches, bang nails into trees, or dig drainage channels around the tent. The clues that a hiker passed this way should be minimal.

Where no established campsite exists, select a site at least 200 feet from the water and well removed from any trail or road. Avoid delicate meadow environments, and do not degrade lakeshore, waterfall, overlook, or other prized sites with a camp.

Reduce comforts (as opposed to necessities). Carry a backpacker's stove for cooking; when a campfire is unavoidable, keep it small. Snags and live trees should never be cut.

Sanitation. For human waste disposal, select a site well away from the trail and at least 300 feet from any water body. There, dig a cat hole 8 inches deep in which to bury the waste. This biologically active layer of soil holds organisms that can quickly decompose organic matter. If the ground prohibits digging a hole of the specified size, dig as deep as possible and cover well with gravel, sticks, and leaves.

Use tissue sparingly, carrying a zipper-locked plastic bag for packing out soiled tissue. Burying results in the tissue becoming nest-building material for rodents or unsightly garbage scattered by salt-seeking deer.

Litter. "Pack it in, pack it out." This includes aluminum foil, cans, orange peels, peanut shells, cigarette butts, and disposable diapers. For nature to reclaim an orange peel takes six months; a filter-tip cigarette butt, ten to twelve years. Disposable diapers have become an incredible nuisance and a contaminant in the wild. Burying is not a solution.

Washing. Washing of self or dishes should be done well away from the lake or stream. Carry wash water to a rocky site, and use biodegradable suds sparingly.

Water. Water is the preferred refreshment; carry a safe quantity from home on all excursions, because wilderness sources dry up or may become fouled. Know that caffeine and alcohol are diuretics that dehydrate and weaken.

When taken from wilderness sources, drinking water and any water used to wash foods or eating utensils should be treated. *Giardia lamblia,* a waterborne organism causing stomach and intestinal discomfort, finds a home in even the most remote, clear streams. Water purification systems that remove both debris and harmful organisms offer the most convenient solution. But these filters come in varying degrees of sophistication, so make certain the selected system strains out harmful organisms. The traditional method of bringing the water to a full boil for at least five minutes still works. Iodine tablets offer less protection and no protection against *Giardia* and are not considered safe for pregnant women.

Getting lost. Prior to departure, notify a responsible party of your intended destination, route, and time of return. Then keep to it and notify them upon your return.

If lost, sit down and try to think calmly. No immediate danger exists as long as you have packed properly and followed the notification procedure. If hiking with a group, stay together. Short outward searches for the trail, returning to an agreed-upon, marked location if unsuccessful, are generally considered safe. If near a watercourse, following it downstream will typically lead you to a place of habitation or a roadway, where help may be sought. Aimless wandering is a mistake.

Blowing a whistle or making loud noises in sets of three may summon help. If you are lost late in the day, prepare for night by finding a means to stay warm and dry. Unless you have good cross-country navigational skills, your efforts are best spent conserving energy. Aid rescuers by staying put and hanging out bright-colored clothing as a signal.

Modern aids—global positioning system (GPS) receivers, cell phones, walkie-talkies, and the like—can reduce the risk of becoming lost or speed rescue.

Hypothermia. This dramatic cooling of the body occurs when heat loss surpasses body-heat generation. Cold, wet, and windy weather commands respect. Attending to the Ten Essentials, eating properly, avoiding fatigue, and being alert to the symptoms of sluggishness, clumsiness, and incoherence among party members remain the best protection. Should a party member display such symptoms, stop and get that member dry and warm. Dry clothing, shared body heat, and hot fluids all help.

Heat exhaustion. Strenuous exercise combined with summer sun can lead to heat exhaustion, an overtaxation of the body's heat regulatory system. Wearing a hat, drinking plenty of water, eating properly (including salty snacks), and avoiding fatigue are safeguards.

Poison ivy and poison sumac. The best way to avoid contact with these and other skin-irritating plants is to learn what they look like and in what environments they grow. Consult a good plant identification book. Vaccines and creams are beginning to come on the market, but science has yet to conquer these irritating plant oils. If you suspect you have come in contact with one of these plants, rinse off the affected area as soon as possible and avoid scratching, which spreads the oils.

Ticks, stings, and bites. Again, the best defense is knowledge. Learn about the habits and habitats of snakes, bees, wasps, ticks, and other "menaces" of the wild and how to deal with the injuries they may cause. Also become aware of any personal allergies and sensitivities you or a party member might have.

Lyme disease, transmitted by the tiny deer tick, has become a serious concern in the East, but it need not deter you from the outdoors. Hikers come into contact with these ticks amid grasses and shrubs; the ticks do not drop from trees. Wear light-colored long pants and long-sleeve shirts, and keep your layers tucked into one another. This will help you identify any ticks and keep them on the outside of your garments. While hiking, make frequent checks for the unwanted hitchhiker. When at home, shower and search skin surfaces thoroughly, and launder hiking clothing directly.

Should a tick become lodged in the skin, remove it by drawing evenly on the body, disinfect the site with alcohol, and monitor over the next few weeks. Look for a red bull's-eye swelling at the site of the bite; also be alert to inexplicable muscle pain and tiredness. Consult a physician immediately should any symptoms occur.

Bears. The black bears in the East represent more nuisance than threat. Use common sense: Do not store food near camp, and especially not in the tent. If clothes pick up cooking smells, suspend them, along with the food, from an isolated overhanging branch well away from camp. Sweet-smelling creams or lotions should be avoided.

Hunting. While most public lands open to hunters do not prohibit hiking during the hunting season, and few have any record of conflict, we would still advise fall hikers to point their boots toward lands and trails where hunting is not allowed. If you hike where hunting occurs, wear bright orange clothing and keep to the trail.

Trailhead precautions. Hikers' unattended vehicles are vulnerable to break-ins, but the following steps can minimize the risk:

- Whenever possible, park away from the trailhead at a nearby campground or other facility.

- Do not leave valuables. Place keys and wallet in a button-secured pocket or secure pack compartment where they will not be disturbed until your return.

- Stash everything in the trunk, and be sure any exposed item has no value.

- Be suspicious of loiterers, and do not volunteer the details of your outing.

- Also, be cautious about the information you supply at the trailhead register. Withhold information such as your license plate number until you are safely back at the trailhead.

Backcountry travel includes unavoidable risks that every traveler assumes and must be aware of and respect. The fact that a trail or an area is described in this book is not a representation that it will be safe for you. While this book attempts to alert users to safe methods and warns of potential dangers, it is limited. Time, nature, use, and abuse can quickly alter the face of a trail. Let independent judgment and common sense be your guides.

For more detailed information about outdoor preparedness, consult a good instructional book or enroll in a class on outdoor etiquette, procedure, and safety. Even the outdoor veteran can benefit from a refresher.

Lake Erie Region

While the trails are few in number, this region of Pennsylvania boasts a richness of features. Hikers travel a migrating isle; overlook the waters of Lake Erie; relive Commodore Perry's heroic naval battle that won the United States control over the Great Lakes; discover the birth of the petroleum industry; and explore creeks, canals, wetlands, and woods. Wildlife-watchers seldom walk away disappointed.

Lake Erie and the petroleum boom of the late 1800s gave rise to the region's towns, making the port city of Erie the third largest in the state. For the most part, you will find the terrain mild and the flavor rural. Many of the region's creeks fan into marshes.

Indian God Rock, Allegheny River Trail.

1 Presque Isle State Park: Beach Hike

Overview

This 3,200-acre state park protects a 7-mile-long peninsula jutting into Lake Erie. The curving finger of land represents a treasure trove of discovery. Within its 2-mile breadth, discover six biological habitats, ranging from open sand shore to climax forest, and discover a moving isle. In the past century, the actions of wind, wave, and current have brought about an eastward migration of nearly 0.5 mile. The isle holds national park service recognition as a national natural landmark and is recognized as one of the ten best birding sites in the United States.

General description: This hike travels along the bathing beaches and natural sands of Presque Isle's western shore, overlooking Lake Erie.

General location: 3 miles northwest of Erie.

Special attractions: Uninterrupted sandy strand, the beauty and power of Lake Erie, the abutting dune habitat, wildlife sightings, weather-watching, clues to migration, fishing, and the state's only surf swimming.

Length: Beach hike, 5.5 miles one-way.

Elevation: The hike is flat.

Difficulty: Moderate, due to leg-working sands.

Maps: State park brochure.

Special concerns: North of Beach 10, be alert for the posted special management area. From April 1 through November 30, the tip of the spit is closed to the public to protect critical habitat for nesting and migrating shorebirds; heed closure. In places, lake and wind erosion may steal the narrow strand.

Season and hours: Year-round, but expect blustery winter conditions. Sunrise to sunset. Swimming is restricted to guarded beaches: 10:00 A.M. to 8:00 P.M. from Memorial Day weekend to Labor Day, unless otherwise posted.

For information: Presque Isle State Park.

Key points:

0.0 Beach 1 access; hike north.

0.8 Stull Interpretive Center.

2.8 Lifeguard headquarters/Beach 7.

4.1 Presque Isle Lighthouse.

5.5 End at Beach 10/Budny Beach.

Finding the trailhead: Where Interstate 79 ends in the city of Erie, take exit 44B and go west on Pennsylvania 5, following signs. In 1.5 miles, turn

13

Presque Isle State Park: Beach Hike

north onto PA 832/Peninsula Drive. Enter the park in 1.2 miles, reach the interpretive center in 2 miles, and reach the park office in 3.3 miles. Marked beach accesses branch left off the divided park road.

The hike: On a south–north tour, begin at Beach 1 and turn north; the state beach also stretches south about 0.25 mile before reaching private homes. With swimming restricted to the immediate area of the lifeguard stations, hikers find the broad strand wide open for hiking.

Vegetated with cottonwood, locust, beach grass, honeysuckle, and wild grape, low dunes or mild ridges abut the beach. The gravelly sands then stretch to the lapping waters of Lake Erie, meeting it with a downward dip. Lingering tracks from the patrol vehicles steal from the pattern of the sand. Away from the bathing beaches, drift logs and sticks are more common, and the loose sand works the calf muscles.

Beach 1 marks the start of the regularly spaced white-rock breakers that form a dashed line 100 feet offshore. Together with some subsurface metal grates, the breakers are intended to slow migration and halt the loss of the isle's west-facing beaches. The result is a scalloped shore.

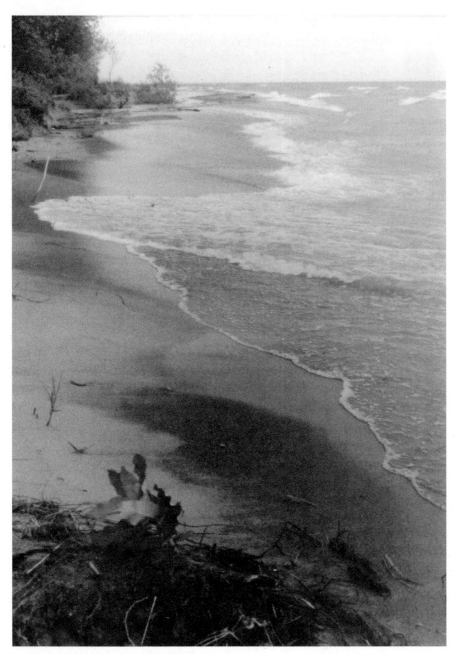

Beach near Gull Point, Presque Isle State Park.

Travelers along this sunset beach are treated to an oceanlike horizon. Songbirds, shorebirds, rabbit, deer, skunk, and raccoon may offer fleeting companionship. Off-season and cool, cloudy days promise less bustle, as do sunrise treks.

At 0.8 mile, an electricity-generating windmill towers above the upper edge of the beach, signaling the site of Stull Interpretive Center. Near it, find a covered picnic shelter, a native plant garden, and the start of the 0.2-mile Self-guided Interpretive Trail that travels north along the dune before looping back to the center. Signposts explain the process of succession and identify plant species. Beware of poison ivy in the cottonwood–shrub habitat.

To the north, find a longer stretch of unsupervised shoreline, with seedlings pushing up through the beach sands. At 2 miles, reach Beach 6. Where the beach narrows, the abutting bank becomes more pronounced. Breaches in the dune ease passage between shore and the developed beach facilities.

North of the lifeguard headquarters (Beach 7), pass a boardwalk and ramp that allows wheelchair users lake access for swimming, viewing, and picnicking. Enormous cottonwoods command notice. Winds transform the face of the beach, launch breakers, present a choppier inland sea, and energize treetops. The sand grows finer, losing some of its cobble.

Pass below Presque Isle Lighthouse, now a private residence semihidden by cottonwoods. The still active beacon recalls the past. A treed point and small jetty feature likewise mark the site. Northeast of the lighthouse, locate both a lighthouse exhibit and the Sidewalk Trail, spanning the breadth of the isle. Historically, the lightkeeper used this path to access his boat on Misery Bay.

The buffer between beach and roadway broadens as hikers pass into an ecological reservation. North of Beach 9, encounter a more exciting, untamed beach, with rolling, irregular shoreline, migrating sand, invading young trees, and more extensive beach grass. The tops of pines and cottonwoods overlook the beachward dune.

Where the terrain again flattens and opens up, find Sunset Point. Beach 10/Budny Beach then follows, for a temporary, although abrupt, interruption to the natural tour. Hikers may proceed along the northeast curving isle as far as beach real estate or the special management area restrictions allow.

For hikers with limited time, the shore between Beaches 9 and 10 encapsulates the story of the isle's migration and the human attempt to control nature. Here, view both natural and recreational strands.

2 Presque Isle State Park: Inland and Bay Trails

Overview

This state park encompasses a 7-mile-long Lake Erie spit, with unique environments and a tendency for walking. In the past century, the isle has migrated eastward nearly 0.5 mile. Recognized as a national natural landmark, the isle captivates with its beach and bay shores, its dune and woods habitats, and its history.

In the 1813 battle of Lake Erie, six of the nine ships in Commodore Perry's fleet were constructed on Presque Isle from native materials. After the battle, the fleet moored at Misery Bay. Battle casualties and those who died during the winter of 1813–1814 were laid to rest in what is now known as Graveyard Pond.

General description: More than 20 miles of trail introduce the isle's bay shore, inland ponds, reclaimed dunes, woodlands, and wetlands, and visit chapters from Presque Isle's past. The selected hikes represent the range of offerings.

General location: 3 miles northwest of Erie.

Special attractions: More than 300 bird species, with peak migration witnessed May 10 through May 25 and again in September; spring and summer wildflowers; habitat diversity; fishing; surf swimming; Perry Monument.

Length: Presque Isle Multi-purpose Trail, 5.8 miles one-way to Perry Monument; Gull Point Trail, 2.5-mile loop (including spur to Thompson Bay); Sidewalk Trail, 2.5 miles round trip; Dead Pond Trail, 4 miles round trip.

Elevation: Trails are virtually flat at an elevation of 580 feet.

Difficulty: Presque Isle Multi-purpose Trail and Sidewalk Trail, both easy; Gull Point and Dead Pond Trails are both easy to moderate, depending on the amount of standing water.

Maps: State park brochure.

Special concerns: Heed the posted special management area closure April 1 through November 30; this closure of the eastern tip of the spit protects critical habitat for nesting and migrating shorebirds. No collecting; no pets. Amid inland wetlands, standing water can turn back hikers. Carry insect repellent and take necessary precautions against ticks.

Season and hours: Year-round, with winter snowshoe and cross-country ski travel; sunrise to sunset.

For information: Presque Isle State Park.

Presque Isle State Park: Inland and Bay Trails

Key points:

Presque Isle Multi-purpose Trail:

- 0.0 Park entrance trailhead.
- 3.9 Marina Drive.
- 5.0 Return to bay shore.
- 5.8 Perry Monument.

Gull Point Trail:

- 0.0 Gull Point Trailhead.
- 0.3 Thompson Bay peninsula spur.
- 1.0 Observation platform; backtrack or add loop.

Sidewalk Trail:

- 0.0 Sidewalk Trailhead; hike east.
- 1.2 Thompson Drive; turn around.

Dead Pond Trail:

- 0.0 Sidewalk Trailhead; hike east.
- 0.1 Multiple junction; bear left.
- 2.0 Thompson Drive; turn around.

Finding the trailhead: Where Interstate 79 ends in Erie, take exit 44B and go west on Pennsylvania 5, following signs. In 1.5 miles, turn north onto PA 832/Peninsula Drive. Enter the park in 1.2 miles, reach the interpretive center in 2 miles, and reach the park office in 3.3 miles. Find marked beach and trail accesses off park roads.

The hikes: This 5.8-mile sampling of the 9.6-mile paved **Presque Isle Multi-purpose Trail** parallels the isle's eastern and southern shores, overlooking Presque Isle Bay and thrice crossing park roads to reach Perry Monument. Despite the trail's roadway proximity, naturalists find surprisingly good bird- and wildlife-watching, as well as modest habitat diversity. Hikers will share this bustling family-oriented corridor with cyclists, baby strollers, roller skaters, and joggers. Winter signals to strap on the cross-country skis.

Locate the trail's start east of the park entrance sign; the terminus for this hike is at Perry Monument on Misery Bay. Multiple developed parking sites allow travelers to vary starts and stops, customizing tour length. With 0.1-mile increments counted off and convenient access to rest rooms, picnic tables, and benches, the trail serves both the exercise-conscious and the casual stroller. Find off-season and midweek touring more tranquil.

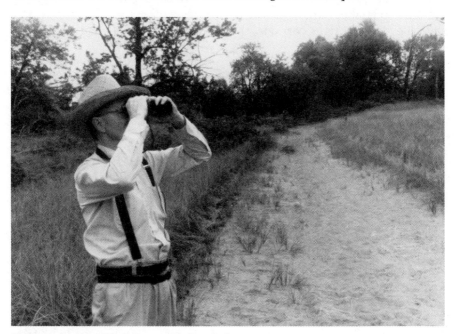

Birding on Dead Pond Trail, Presque Isle State Park.

Views include Presque Isle Bay, the Erie Bayfront, the curved profile of Presque Isle itself, wetlands, lily-capped inland ponds, and the watery neck between Marina Lake and Long Pond. Cottonwood, locust, alder, willow, and dogwood intermittently shade the route. In places, honeysuckle, wild grape, maple-leaved viburnum, Virginia creeper, and poison ivy knit a tanglewood. Look for sunfish, snapping turtle, cardinal, oriole, killdeer, heron, woodpecker, and rabbit. A few interpretive signs dot the way.

North past the Waterworks (2.8 miles), the trail drifts farther from the bay. At the first Marina Drive crossing (3.9 miles), proceed on the two-way stretch of trail to Perry Monument. On your left is the one-way return of the Multi-purpose Trail, if you opt for the full 9.6-mile tour. Silver and red maples now join the shade givers.

At 5 miles, the trail crosses back to the bay shore for the final leg to Perry Monument—an attractive stone-block tower and water fountain. Its metal crown rivals the treetops. Beyond Perry Monument, the Multi-purpose Trail is limited to one-way travel and becomes essentially a bike lane traveling side by side with the park road to complete the lasso back at the 3.9-mile junction.

Gull Point Trail leaves from the east end of Budny Beach (Beach 10), traveling a relatively new addition to the migrating spit—Gull Point, with its 319 acres of rare plants and animals. In 1903, Presque Isle ended at Budny Beach. The trail particularly appeals to birders. Sixty-seven acres at the eastern tip of Gull Point have been set aside as a special management area to protect critical shorebird habitat.

The mowed or sandy path threads between vine-entangled concentrations of bayberry, honeysuckle, dogwood, and willow. Watch out for poison ivy. Cottonwoods sit back from the immediate aisle; birch sometimes grow trailside. Beyond the tight corridor, spy wetlands of cattails and phragmites (plumed reeds).

At the 0.3-mile fork, a sign indicates that Gull Point is to the left. To the right stretches a 0.4-mile round-trip detour to a similarly vegetated Thompson Bay peninsula. This side path ends on the shore below an osprey nesting platform, with a cross-bay view of a beaver lodge; avoid the detour during nesting season.

En route to Gull Point, pass an unmarked connecting spur that heads left in 250 feet. This spur quickly meets up with a parallel return route. Proceed straight, still pursuing the attractive wooden signs to Gull Point. More freshwater pond/marsh habitat characterizes the trail.

At the 0.5-mile junction, reach a wooden-rail barrier and view of a large open-water pond. An arrow points hikers right to reach the observation platform. The left fork holds a loop return to the trailhead, touring amid dune grass and bayberry, but reserving Lake Erie views until the second half of its 0.6-mile distance.

Postpone the loop, bearing right to reach the observation platform. You will likely encounter a troublesome wet spot, aggravated by the tide. Planks and high ground generally allow for evasion, but sometimes soaked feet are unavoidable. Sightings along Gull Point may include a turtle burying its eggs (stay back), deer tracks in the loose sand, and monarch butterflies on milkweed. Beach pea, daisy, cinquefoil, yarrow, and fleabane sprinkle the sand.

By 0.8 mile, overlook Thompson Bay, where splashing fish and the noses of submerged turtles may draw attention. The observation platform rises to the left. Bypass the regularly spaced postings for the special management area to reach the single-story platform (1 mile).

Views sweep the cove curvature. You can see: Canada geese and gulls; the textured plain with its standing water, phragmites, young cottonwoods, beach scrub, and open sand; and the industrial skyline of Erie. Return as you came, or make a loop.

A sign marks the start of the historic **Sidewalk Trail,** which heads southeast across the peninsula to Misery Bay. Find its start across from the Presque Isle Lighthouse Exhibit, 0.4 mile west of Beach 9. The exhibit is the gateway to a short beach walk to a vista of the otherwise tree-masked lighthouse (now a private residence). The Sidewalk Trail gave the lightkeeper convenient access between the beacon and his boat. The present thin concrete walk (poured in 1925) replaced the original boardwalk.

The straight-arrow trail cuts a striking line framed by red and silver maples, cottonwoods, black cherry trees, and oaks. Baneberry, wild grape, honeysuckle, and poison ivy edge the trimmed corridor. Marking the multiple junction at 0.1 mile are artistic wooden signs pointing out side-trail options: The Fox Trail angles back to the right, the Marsh Trail heads due right, and Dead Pond Trail journeys left. Continue on the Sidewalk Trail.

Wetlands next border the tour, with sensitive fern and arrowhead growing in their midst. Bramble and bayberry form the trail's shoulder. Young

Mallard family, Presque Isle State Park.

trees and silver snags open the cathedral. At 0.5 mile, glimpse a matted water seasonally colored with yellow spatterdock blooms; elsewhere, view open water. This linear wetland is Ridge Pond. Red-winged blackbird, turtle, frog, heron, fox, or raccoon may share the area.

At 0.8 mile, look for a beaver-cut log in the marsh and a weathered beaver lodge across the way. A low ridge then builds to the right before the trail exits at Thompson Drive east of Graveyard Pond (1.25 miles). Closing views are of Misery Bay; return the way you came.

For **Dead Pond Trail,** retrace the first 0.1 mile of the Sidewalk Trail and bear left, traveling a trimmed track beneath a mostly maple canopy. Expanses of bayberry–grassland and stands of full-grown sassafras add variety. Soggy pockets can mar travel, at times turning back hikers. Here, highbush blueberry finds favorable growing conditions. Birds fill the air with musical notes and chatter.

Connector trails branch left to the park road, beginning at 0.5 mile; keep right. A vernal wetland often claims the A-Trail (the first of the connector trails). Mixed woods follow, with shrubs measuring shoulder- to head-high. Loose sands hint at the inland isle's dune past. At 0.7 mile, pass a stand of pine and tamarack, busy with squirrel and towhee.

Approaching the mile mark, ankle- to shin-deep waters may turn back hikers. When passable, continue bearing right. Again the trail overlooks an open bayberry–grassland, with distant pines off to the left. Birders proclaim that the isle rivals Point Pelee National Park in Canada for springtime sightings of warblers, flycatchers, rails, and shorebirds.

As the forest again builds, climb a 6-foot-high ridge to the right. Spurs top it for views of Niagara Pond. At 1.9 miles, a spur heads left for Thompson Circle; bear right to complete the trail. Views include an open cattail marsh. The main trail ends at Thompson Drive north of Beach 11.

3 Erie National Wildlife Refuge

Overview

Two isolated land parcels, the Sugar Lake Division and the less intensively controlled Seneca Division, make up this 8,777-acre national wildlife refuge named for an extinct lake tribe of Indians—the Erie. Wetlands, ponds, creeks, meadows, upland woods, cropland, and grassland contribute to the refuge mosaic. Naturalists encounter a diverse roster of amphibians, reptiles, birds, fish, and mammals. The three selected hikes explore the Sugar Lake Division. For hikers still in the mood to wander, a fourth trail tours the Seneca parcel.

General description:	Three trails and a short spur to an observation blind present the habitat diversity, welcoming wildlife and nature discovery.
General location:	35 miles south of Erie. Sugar Lake Division: 10 miles east of Meadville on the outskirts of the village of Guys Mills. Seneca Division: 10 miles to its north.
Special attractions:	2,500 acres of wetland; waterfowl migrations (March to early April, September to November); nesting wood ducks; screech owls, bald eagles, and ospreys; observation blind; a beaver-pond boardwalk; fox dens.
Length:	Deer Run Trail, 3-mile loop; Observation Blind Spur, 0.3 mile round trip; Tsuga Nature Trail, 1.6-mile loop, with option to shorten; Beaver Run Trail, 1.1 miles round trip.
Elevation:	Trails show minimal elevation change.
Difficulty:	All easy.
Maps:	Erie Refuge and Tsuga Nature Trail brochures.
Special concerns:	Expect wet conditions in spring; carry insect repellent. Winter visitors may cross-country ski or snowshoe the Tsuga Nature Trail and Deer Run Trail.
Season and hours:	Year-round, except during the firearms deer season. Grounds are open from half an hour before sunrise to sunset. Office, 8:00 A.M. to 4:30 P.M., Monday through Friday.
For information:	Erie National Wildlife Refuge.

Key points:

Deer Run Trail:

0.0 Boland Road trailhead; hike levee south.
1.2 Cross Fowler Road.
1.6 Cross Boland Road.
3.0 End at Boland Road trail parking.

Erie National Wildlife Refuge

Tsuga Nature Trail:
- 0.0 Headquarters trailhead.
- 0.4 Pool D.
- 1.0 Cutoff junction; bear right.
- 1.6 End at headquarters.

Beaver Run Trail:
- 0.0 Hanks Road trailhead.
- 0.2 Peninsular spur.
- 1.1 End at Hanks Road.

Finding the trailhead: Pennsylvania Highways 27, 198, and 173 all pass through the Sugar Lake Division. From Meadville, go east on PA 27 and State Route 2032 to Guys Mills. From there, continue east 0.8 mile on PA 198, and turn south for the headquarters.

The hikes: Start the **Deer Run Trail** off Boland Road: From the junction of PA 27 and dirt Boland Road (2 miles west of Mount Hope, 9 miles east of Meadville), go south on Boland Road for 1.1 miles. Find parking on the right, the trail on the left.

Hike south along the levee of Pool K, locating the trail sign past the fishing access for people with disabilities. Geese, ducks, and herons occupy shore, shallows, and the pool's small humped islands. A wooded east rim, silvered snags, mats of pond lily, and a cattail expanse contribute to pond views. To the west stretches an herb–forb flat secluding a smaller pond and wetland. Songbirds deliver a cheery address, while swallows dart for bugs.

By 0.2 mile, enter a thick mixed woodland, with oak, maple, birch, beech, ash, and black cherry. Hemlocks are but a hiccup in the otherwise deciduous woods. Small footbridges cross flowing, seasonal drainages. The trail rolls, topping a low wooded plateau. Admire fern, mayapple, and mayflower. Markers guide hikers and cross-country skiers.

During a slow descent, pass from planted pines to an open field of thigh-high grasses, peppered with daisy and clover. A mowed track advances travel. Atop the next low hill, scan the refuge mosaic and then descend to Fowler Road. Hike left along the road for 250 feet to pick up the trail on the right, passing through a shrub corridor.

Within the edge communities, find field vegetation intermingled with young aspen and maple. At 1.6 miles, cross Boland Road, skirting a field of waist-deep grasses to return to woods. Keep to the mowed track, passing between field and woods at the outskirts of Pool 9. Beyond a small wildlife pond at 2.75 miles, reach a two-track and follow it left to return to trail parking (3 miles).

While in this area, you may wish to hike the Observation Blind Spur. Drive south 0.5 mile on Boland Road, finding its parking on the right. This 0.3-mile round-trip spur leads to a wildlife-viewing blind. Travel through woods and past a large multitrunked black cherry to enter the peninsular shrub corridor that leads to the shelter. The three-sided, roofed structure has diagonal-slit windows for overlooking vegetated Reitz Pond. Spy waterfowl and observe their many behaviors.

For the **Tsuga Nature Trail,** start to the right of the headquarters building (pick up the interpretive brochure at headquarters or kiosk). Nine stations mark the tour; encounter all of them prior to the loop cutoff.

From the kiosk, hike a wide, wood-shavings lane entering a mixed hemlock–deciduous woods, edging a grassland. Mayapple and sensitive fern dress the floor. Next, pass from dense shoulder-high shrubs to a meadow's edge. Habitat changes occur in rapid succession. Soon follow a two-track overlooking an artificial pond (Pool D), coated by aquatic vegetation.

At 0.4 mile, turn left, touring transition habitat with dogwood and other flowering shrubs, to come to a boardwalk. Bullfrog, turtle, and red-winged blackbird enliven a stage of cattail and rush. In the wetland-bridging habitats, find aspen, hawthorn, apple, honeysuckle, and goldenrod.

At 0.6 mile, reach the more extensive boardwalk spanning a snag-riddled beaver pond, noisy with frogs and plied by geese. Duckweed and grasses dress the bases of snags. Dark glassy waters braid the vegetation.

Resume in a moist woodland with skunk cabbage, touring the unblazed but well-defined trail. Enormous old trees add to travel, including a trio of hemlocks (0.8 mile). *Tsuga,* the name for the trail, comes from the scientific name for eastern hemlock, *Tsuga canadensis*—the state tree.

Within a choked, dark hemlock grove, reach the cutoff junction, 1 mile. To shorten the loop, go straight, returning to the headquarters in 1,000 feet. For the full loop, bear right, crossing a footbridge over a small muddy drainage. Hemlocks continue to enfold the trail, with birch and beech among their ranks. At 1.5 miles, emerge from a young deciduous woods at a pair of benches to view pond and ridge. A left on the mowed grade returns to the headquarters (1.6 miles).

Tsuga Nature Trail boardwalk, Erie National Wildlife Refuge.

Reach the **Beaver Run Trail** by turning north off PA 198 onto Cooper Road, 0.4 mile west of the headquarters turnoff. Go 0.5 mile and bear left onto dirt Hanks Road to locate trailhead parking on the right in a little less than a mile.

Leave the southeast corner of trail parking, traveling a mowed path between aspen. Within 200 feet, overlook Beaver Run Pond with its open water and mats of lily. Sumac, maple, black cherry, hornbeam, and shrubs enclose the trail as it rims the pond basin. Beyond a skunk cabbage–sensitive fern wetland is the 0.25-mile junction: To the right lies the loop; straight holds a spur.

Proceed forward, still in woods, edging the floodplain; then push through a crush of bottomland vegetation. Aspen and dogwood rise amid the tangle. Cross Beaver Run, touring a low ridge separating Beaver Run Pond and an auxiliary wetland. Here, hornbeam and witch hazel provide the signature look; at the nose of the ridge, choked hemlocks reign. The trail halts at pond level (0.5 mile), with an overlook of the vegetated water.

Backtrack to the 0.25-mile junction (0.75 mile) and complete the clockwise loop (now a left) or retrace the first 0.25 mile of travel. The loop return visits young deciduous woods, ancient maples, and a few big black cherry trees before arriving at an open, but managed field of waist-deep grasses. Rim the right side, aiming for a hiker symbol. A second hiker symbol then points left to a gate at the foot of the slope. At Hanks Road, go right 100 feet to end at the trailhead (1.1 miles).

4 Oil Creek State Park

Overview

This 7,100-acre northwest Pennsylvania state park celebrates the oil boom and the birth of the petroleum industry, but its natural features equally stir visitors. Trails travel the steep-walled wooded canyon enfolding 13.5 miles of quiet-bending Oil Creek, along whose banks oil wells, boom towns, refineries, transportation centers, and cemeteries sprouted in the 1860s. To the north, the park adjoins Drake Well Museum, situated at the site of the first oil well, brought in by Colonel Edwin Drake in 1859.

General description: The linear routes that parallel Oil Creek (West Side Trail, East Side Trail, Bike Trail, and even the seasonally operating Oil Creek & Titusville Railroad) lend themselves to circuitous tours. The woods along the West Side Trail cradle artifacts from the petroleum era; the Bike Trail travels back in time via interpretive panels. With some 70 miles of hiking, theme, and interpretive trails in the park, the West Side Trail–Bike Trail Loop marks just the beginning.

General location: The park spans from the southern outskirts of Titusville to a point 4 miles north of Oil City.

Special attractions: Oil Creek; Petroleum Centre, with visitor information, depot, picnic area, and bike rental; dispersed petroleum-era artifacts; interpretive features; broadleaved forests, steep hollows, charming waterfalls, wildflowers, wildlife, and fall foliage.

Length: West Side Trail–Bike Trail Loop, 22-mile loop: West Side Trail, 12.5 miles one-way; Bike Trail, 9.5 miles one-way.

Elevation: West Side Trail, 500-foot elevation change; Bike Trail, 100-foot elevation change.

Difficulty: West Side Trail, moderate to strenuous; Bike Trail, easy to moderate.

Maps: State park brochure; Oil Creek hiking and bike trail flyers.

Special concerns: Two hike-in camp areas (one on each side of the creek) offer overnight Adirondack-style shelters. Each area holds six shelters available for single-night stays. Hikers must make advance reservations and pay a fee; contact the park office. The Drake Well Museum, the Oil Creek & Titusville Railroad, and bicycle rental concession are separate fee facilities; contact each for its season, hours, and rates. Find toilets at Petroleum Centre, hike-in camps, and Miller Farm Picnic Shelter.

Season and hours: Year-round, daylight hours.

For information: Oil Creek State Park.

Oil Creek State Park

To Titusville

East Bloss Street

Drake Well Museum and Train Depot

West Side Trail

Dutch Hill Road

0   1   2
Miles

N

Spring Run

Miller Run

Oil era artifacts

Oil Creek

Lower Miller Falls

Wolfkill Run

Miller Farm Road

Miller Farm Site

To 227

Shaffer Run

Pioneer Run

Pioneer Road

8

1009

Gregg Falls

Benninghoff Run

T617

To 227

Park office

Boardwalk Interpretive Trail and Train Depot

P

To Oil City

To 227

Key points:

  0.0   Jersey Bridge trailhead.
  2.1   Cross Spring Run bridge.
  3.2   Lower Miller Falls Bypass.
  4.6   Spur to Wolfkill Run Shelter Site.
  5.3   Miller Farm Picnic Shelter.
  9.0   Cross Pioneer Road.
  9.6   Gregg Falls.
12.3   Petroleum Centre.
14.0   Cross bicycle bridge over Oil Creek.
17.2   Miller Farm Picnic Shelter.
22.0   Jersey Bridge trailhead.

Finding the trailhead: Find Petroleum Centre (the main park entrance and southern terminus of the loop) off Pennsylvania 8, 1 mile north of the borough of Rouseville; signs mark the turn. Reach the northern-loop terminus out of Titusville: From the PA 89–PA 8 junction in Titusville, go south on PA 8 for 0.3 mile and turn left onto East Bloss Street at the sign for Drake Well Museum. Go 1 mile, reaching Jersey Bridge Parking.

The hikes: For this West Side Trail–Bike Trail Loop, start at Jersey Bridge Parking, passing through the gateway at the south end of the lot for the West Side Trail. A crush of riparian greenery enfolds the hiker path as it passes above Oil Creek. Yellow blazes mark the trail; white blazes signal side routes.

Ascend a boardwalk ramp from the floodplain, cross over the Bike Trail, and continue upslope, settling into a southbound contour at 0.3 mile. Maple, tulip, hemlock, big oak, and hickory contribute to the canopy; diverse ferns and wildflowers, the understory. Birdsongs raucous and sweet drift over the trail. Deer, squirrel, wild turkey, skunk, and even a black bear may be encountered. Oil Creek remains but a glare beyond the trees. Soggy spots commonly mark the tour.

At 1.1 miles, passage through a shrubby corridor allows downhill looks to Oil Creek. The trail rolls mainly along the upper slope, periodically topping wooded plateaus or dipping through hollows. At 2 miles, be alert for the double blaze signaling a switchback. Ahead is a signed junction; proceed right toward Miller Farm, crossing the Spring Run bridge. An old discarded barrel records the area's petroleum heritage.

At 3.25 miles, come to the white-blazed Lower Miller Falls Bypass, which later rejoins the West Side Trail. This route travels a more overgrown path, thrice crossing Miller Run. Discover rusting oil relics enmeshed with greenery (barrels, cables, rigging, compressors, and associated engines), and keep alert for the easy-to-miss 300-foot spur to Lower Miller Falls. This 15-foot broad, lacy falls skips engagingly through a dark hemlock hollow. A cable strung between trees warns travelers back from the precariously steep viewing slope. At 3.8 miles, rejoin the West Side Trail southbound. (During high water, delay taking the bypass until 3.8 miles, opting instead for a round-trip spur to the falls and oil-era relics, avoiding the need to wade.)

At 4.6 miles, find the 400-yard white-blazed detour to Wolfkill Run Shelter Site. Ahead, the West Side Trail follows Wolfkill Run downstream to a footbridge crossing. It then remains in the shade of the run, coming out near Miller Farm Picnic Shelter and the Bike Trail (5.3 miles). Here, the West Side Trail curves south back into woods. Hikers who wish to shorten the loop to 10 miles may return north via the bikeway to Jersey Bridge Parking.

Switchbacks lead southbound hikers back to the plateau; hemlocks shade the ascent. Soon after, find an artificially maintained opening to an upstream view at a long straightaway of Oil Creek with Miller Farm Bridge. On the tour ahead, stay alert as the blazed route passes back and forth between old road grades and trail. Shaffer Run and an area of gigantic rocks mark off distance. At 7.9 miles, reach a signed overlook.

At 9 miles, cross Pioneer Road for a pleasant woods stretch. On the ground, splashes of yellow paint warn hikers of protruding cables and pipes. At 9.4 miles is the next marked junction; stay on the West Side Trail southbound, pursuing Pioneer Run upstream to cross it just above charming Gregg Falls. From a pair of ledge overhangs, this falls spills in 20-foot streamers. Big beech trees and a ribbed and plated cliff add to the setting.

After 10 miles, encounter some corrugated tin buildings, a small tower, and slat-barrel tanks. In another mile, tour a shrubby regenerating woods—an area salvage-logged following the tornado of May 1985. Cross Benninghoff Run and State Route 1009 for a grassy wade and sunny travel. At 11.8 miles, find a stone-block foundation encircling gravestones dating to 1818. A 100-foot detour right on two-track finds more headstones semiburied in the tall grass.

Continue following blazes and wading the deep grasses, coming to a board-walk over a small wetland. Pass more rusting artifacts upon exiting at gravel Township Road 617. Here, turn left (east) for Petroleum Centre and the loop; the West Side Trail still proceeds south. The loop bypasses the Wetland Trail, the flag-stop train depot, and the Boardwalk Interpretive Trail (its pictorial and verbal panels relate the lay of the former town, Petroleum Centre).

At 12.5 miles, locate the Bike Trail on the east side of the Oil Creek bridge. The park office, picnic area, rest rooms, and drinking water all lie farther east (uphill) along the road. Bear left for the Bike Trail, which begins as a multiuse road.

The official 8.5-foot-wide asphalt bike path begins at 13 miles, with a modest grade, as it pursues Oil Creek upstream. Mileposts mark off distance; interpretive panels present the past. Aspen, sycamore, elm, birch, oak, silver maple, black and pin cherries, hemlock, and a tangle of vines shape the bordering woods. The route skirts wildlife ponds active with turtles, frogs, and dragonflies. Where the bikeway passes under the railroad bridge, find picnic tables.

Trail shelter, Oil Creek State Park.

Enjoy partial to full shade with looks at pretty Oil Creek, a slow, gently bending canoe water supporting rainbow and brown trout. Among the oil-history panels is information on the tornado of 1985. The rich riparian aisle, smooth trail surface, history panels, and occasional tables and benches welcome walkers. Despite the trail's popularity, hikers still enjoy solitude; naturalists, plant and wildlife discovery.

At 14 miles, cross the bicycle bridge over Oil Creek, taking time to admire the water. The trail now remains on the west shore; a soggy floodplain often distances the trail from the creek. At times, hikers may spy or hear the excursion train on the east shore. The bike path follows an old 1860 steam-engine grade. At 15.5 miles, overlook a bend of Oil Creek. A canoe, fly angler, or heron may add to the scene.

At 17.25 miles, reach the Miller Farm Picnic Shelter, and then cross Miller Farm Road (unpaved). More wetlands contribute to the tour, as do occasional creek views. This serene and richly wooded creek canyon little hints at its industrial past. Only a century ago, the hillsides were denuded, webbed by roads, dotted by wells, shrouded in smoke, and choked with oil fumes. Near the end of the tour, view the lawns, artifacts, and oil structures of the acclaimed Drake Well Museum. The trail then descends, entering Jersey Bridge Parking at 22 miles.

By starting at Jersey Bridge, hikers may opt to return by foot, bike, or train. Before starting an outing, investigate train schedules and times for the flag stop at Petroleum Centre Station. Or inquire about bike rentals and their return deadline. The East Side Trail offers yet another return option for foot travelers.

5 Allegheny River Trail

General description: This multiple-use rail-trail links Franklin and Brandon and strings past points of historical note and fine river views, while touring a mostly natural setting where wildlife can be spied.

General location: Along the Allegheny River between Franklin and Brandon.

Special attractions: Engaging Allegheny River impressions but limited access, Indian God Rock (a spiritual landmark and inscription rock), rich and varied second-growth forest and riparian growth, wildlife, wildflowers, fall foliage.

Length: 10 miles one-way, but additional access points allow the tour to be shortened. The Samuel Justus Recreational Trail, journeying upstream from Franklin to Oil City, offers the possibility for longer tours, as does the planned growth of this trail.

Elevation: Find a modest, sustained gradient passing between 990 feet at Franklin and 950 feet at Brandon.

Difficulty: Easy.

Maps: Brochure for bike rides in Venango County.

Special concerns: Due to the limited parking at Brandon, plan to hike round-trip from Franklin or prearrange a drop-off or pickup at Brandon for one-way touring. Camping is allowed in the developed campground 1 mile downstream of Franklin. Because the rail-trail is fully exposed, listen to weather reports about possible lightning storms or severe downpours, which could be dangerous or, at the very least, uncomfortable.

Season and hours: Year-round, with winter snow.

For information: Allegheny Valley Trails Association.

Key points:

0.0 Samuel Justus Recreational Trail Access; hike downstream.
1.1 Lower Two Mile Run Campsite.
1.4 Deep Hollow.
3.9 Riverfront picnic flat.
5.2 Pass below Belmar Bridge.
8.4 Indian God Rock.
10.0 Brandon.

Allegheny River Trail

Finding the trailhead: For the upper trailhead in Franklin, locate the shared-use parking for the Samuel Justus Recreational Trail, on the river 0.1 mile east of the Eighth Street Bridge off U.S. Highway 322. Chemical toilets are available at this site.

For the lower trailhead in Brandon, continue east on US 322 from the Franklin trailhead for 6.3 miles and turn right onto Rockland Road at Cranberry (directly opposite State Route 257). Proceed 4.2 miles and turn right onto Coal City Road, following it 6.3 miles to Brandon (the final 2.3 miles are unpaved). Locate the start of the trail by following the grade right 0.3 mile to the barrier. If you do park in the area, be sure not to block any drives or clog travel lanes.

The hike: At the Samuel Justus Recreational Trail Access, the paved route heading upstream under the Eighth Street bridge is the Justus Trail to Oil

City; the selected hike heads downstream (a left as you turn into the access). It rounds the barrier at the end of the parking lot; a trail mileage sign is at the start. The paved Allegheny River Trail explores a designated Wild and Scenic section of river. Along it, mileposts mark off 0.5-mile increments.

The start of the trail is the least wild and remote section of the entire journey, with US 322 sometimes audible or visible, cross-river views of residences, the telephone lines stretched overhead, and the passing of a quarry. Nonetheless, small creatures amuse and the river mesmerizes. Deer, rabbit, woodchuck, mouse, fox, heron, oriole, and hawk may number among the sightings.

Past milepost 1, reach the Lower Two Mile Run Campsite, a public recreational facility provided by the township of Cranberry. The attractive riverside flat consists of a couple of shelters, tent pads, tables, fire rings, and chemical toilets. The river trail, though, beckons. The grade shows long straightaways and gentle bends, mimicking the river course. Locust, hickory, sycamore, ash, and cucumber magnolia contribute to the riverside woods, with birch and hemlock sometimes adding to the mix on the canyon slope.

At the bridge crossing at Deep Hollow (Lower Two Mile Run) at 1.4 miles, discover a pleasing downstream view to the river confluence and a secondary access approaching the rail-trail. A divided river flow alters the sound and look of the Allegheny. Bench seats along the rail-trail invite a leisurely appreciation of the waterway and its canyon. The tour becomes more isolated.

Before milepost 4, a stairway descends to a riverfront plateau with its welcoming shade and picnic tables. Farther downstream, the floodplain woods are often indeed flooded. The leafy tangles reveal such species as wild grape, nettle, jewelweed, poison ivy, and Virginia creeper. The occasional angler path migrates to the river. Midway, Belmar Bridge adds to downstream views.

Where the rail-trail crosses the Sandy Creek span, the high steel walls of the bridge deny creek views. Overhead stretches the retired Belmar Bridge, which now carries the Sandy Creek Trail (an 8-mile trail through pristine Pennsylvania woodland that includes eight bridge spans and a tunnel). A woods road arrives on the left, signaling yet another secondary access; the mileage sign shows that Brandon is 4.8 miles farther.

The grade ahead is nicely isolated in its treed canyon, with its broad tracts of natural slope and shore. Keep to the corridor, because a few posted lands edge the route. Grassy islands, some dotted by trees, vary the river image. Glistening patterns of movement betray the current in the otherwise smooth green band.

An observation deck overlooking Indian God Rock, the historically and culturally significant sandstone at river's edge, precedes milepost 8.5. Although no longer visible, Indian art dating to A.D. 1200 once adorned this rock. Time, weathering, and the inscriptions left by later passersby all contributed to the demise of the ancient art. Some of the inscriptions visible today date to the mid-1800s. The rock also marks the spot where the French envoy placed a lead plate claiming the entire Ohio Valley for France, in 1749. The rock is recognized on the National Register of Historic Places; do not tamper with it.

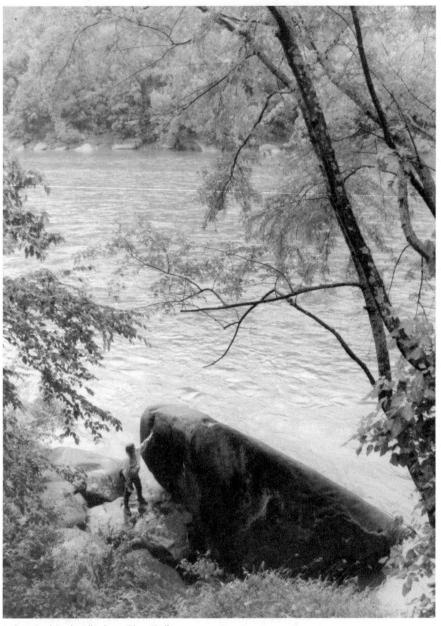

Indian God Rock, Allegheny River Trail.

A welcoming isolated rail stretch then carries the tour the remaining way to Brandon. The classic southern transition forest shows all its diversity, with red and silver maple, oak, sumac, sassafras, cherry, aspen, tulip poplar, basswood, and more. Cross-river views find unspoiled woods and mildly rolling hills and ridges. Reach the barrier at Brandon (10 miles). If a shuttle was not prearranged, return as you came.

Allegheny National Forest Region

This region holds the state's lone national forest and some of the state's few remaining roadless wild areas, clearing the way to some exceptional hiking. A stirring roster of discovery awaits: lush second-growth forests, intriguing rocky domains, steep hollows, cascading streams, bountiful swamps, Allegheny Reservoir, the largest intact old-growth forest remaining in the eastern United States south of Maine, and the belly and rim of the Grand Canyon of Pennsylvania—Pine Creek Gorge. Rhododendron and mountain laurel embroider the landscape. Small communities are interspersed throughout the area.

6 Tracy Ridge–Johnnycake Loop

General description:	This all-day or overnight hike within the Tracy Ridge Trail System strings together the Tracy Ridge segment, part of the North Country National Scenic Trail, and the Johnnycake Trail. Hikers tour a broad ridge plateau and visit Allegheny Reservoir before pursuing sparkling Johnnycake Run upstream. A network of interlocking loops allows the hike to be shortened, extended, or modified. Several add vistas. Junctions are numbered and correspond to the Tracy Ridge Trail System brochure. The brochure includes incremental mileages to aid in decisions.
General location:	18 miles west of Bradford.
Special attractions:	Rich and varied second-growth forest, a roadless wilderness, sterling runs, reservoir access, rock features, wildlife, fall foliage.
Length:	10.3 miles round trip.
Elevation:	Find a 900-foot elevation change, traveling between the ridge plateau at 2,245 feet and the reservoir at 1,328 feet.
Difficulty:	Moderate.
Maps:	Tracy Ridge Trail System brochure (sometimes stocked at the trailhead kiosk).
Special concerns:	Dispersed no-trace camping is allowed; pitch no camps within 1,500 feet of the reservoir's tree line. In late fall and spring, the trails serve hunters as well.
Season and hours:	Year-round, depending on winter snows.
For information:	Bradford Ranger District, Allegheny National Forest.

Tracy Ridge–Johnnycake Loop

Key points:

- 0.0   Pennsylvania 321–Tracy Ridge Trailhead.
- 0.9   Junction 2 (loop junction); bear right.
- 3.2   Descend from Tracy Ridge.
- 4.6   North Country Trail.
- 7.0   Johnnycake Trail.
- 9.4   Complete loop at Junction 2; backtrack to trailhead.

Finding the trailhead: From the junction of U.S. Highway 219 and PA 346 in Bradford, go west on PA 346, following the signs for Allegheny Reservoir through town. Go 13.7 miles and turn left (south) onto PA 321. In 2.6 miles, find Tracy Ridge Trailhead and its parking on the right. When it's open, Tracy Ridge Campground (0.4 mile south) offers an alternative start. Find its developed trailhead off the campground entrance road.

The hike: From the PA 321–Tracy Ridge Trailhead, hike west on the worn foot track parting a grassy lane. Birch, hickory, oak, and maple shape the aisle. In 1,000 feet, bear left at an arrow, entering a tight forest of silvered snags, young black cherry, and striped maple. The forest quickly transitions to tall oak and maple. Blue "i" blazes and white plastic markers show the way.

At 0.3 mile, bear right, continuing to tour the broad plateau of Tracy Ridge. Striped maple and young American chestnut dot the woods. Traverse an area of large outcrop slabs and boxy boulders—a network of vaults and short tunnels, decorated in moss and fern. Historically, Indian hunters used such rocks for shelter. Tracy Ridge Campground sits but 300 feet away. Where the trail crosses over a wooded lane descending from the campground, hikers may spy the green "i" blazes of the 2.5-mile Interpretive Trail.

Come to a Y-shaped loop junction at 0.9 mile (Junction 2). To the left travels Johnnycake Trail; to the right, Tracy Ridge Trail. Go right for a counterclockwise tour, initially keeping to the ridge plateau. Bear right at each junction until meeting the North Country Trail at Junction 11. The oak–maple forest remains spatially open, lacking a midstory. Enjoy penetrating looks into the forest; deer often steal away in the distance. The plateau welcomes carefree strolling. Rainy and humid days can bestow it with an aura of mystery.

After 3.2 miles, the trail veers off Tracy Ridge for a measured angling descent, passing through an oak–huckleberry woodland. Within sound of Tracy Run, at Junction 11 at 4.65 miles, meet the North Country Trail (NCT), marked by white "i" blazes and blue plastic diamonds. A brief detour to the right offers an open look at the vast, tree-rimmed Allegheny Reservoir and access to a deep drop-off for swimming. Bear left on the NCT to continue the loop.

Round the hillside, passing 100 feet above the reservoir, which is isolated by a steep forested slope. Springs give rise to skunk cabbage and muddy the trail, which progresses in rolls and spurts of climb. Where unnamed side

Allegheny Reservoir, Allegheny National Forest.

runs race across the path, stones provide dry crossings. By 6 miles, the slope gentles, and grasses dress the woods. Picturesque rocks precede the crossing of the cascading ribbons of Whisky Run.

Descend from Whisky Run, approaching the reservoir near the mouth of Johnnycake Run (6.9 miles). Here, view the green-hued bay and spy fish weaving through the water before hiking 0.1 mile upstream from the mouth of Johnnycake Run to Junction 10. A sign on the opposite shore indicates the fording that continues the NCT southbound. To conclude the loop, forgo crossing and instead proceed upstream on the Johnnycake Trail, once again following white "i" blazes and blue diamond markers. This leg of the loop follows Johnnycake Run the entire way, bearing right at Junction 17 and left at Junction 3 to close the loop back at Junction 2.

An old woods road degraded by runoffs forms the trail along the valley bottom for a comfortable, shady tour. Maple, ash, and hemlock favor the coolness beside fast-racing Johnnycake Run. To the left spans a meadowy young woods with apple, hornbeam, and hawthorn. Pockets of wet meadow and thick marsh grass are also seen.

By 7.6 miles, you will begin crossing the forked waters and runoff tributaries of Johnnycake Run, sometimes wading, still ascending. In another mile or so, gain a cross-canyon view through the woods at a waterfall on a Johnnycake side tributary. At 9.3 miles (Junction 3), the Interpretive Trail joins the Johnnycake Trail on the right. At 9.4 miles, end the loop at Junction 2 and bear right, retracing the initial 0.9 mile to the trailhead.

7 Morrison Trail

General description:	This circuitous tour travels through varied forest, effusive mountain laurel passages, and bouldered areas, with a side-trail visit to a shoreline camp on the Kinzua Creek Arm of Allegheny Reservoir.
General location:	16 miles east of Warren.
Special attractions:	Hike-in campground, Allegheny Reservoir, mixed second-growth forest, crystalline runs, unique rock features, wildlife sightings, mountain laurel blooms (mid- to late June), fall foliage.
Length:	12.4 miles round trip, with a spur to the Morrison Hike-in/Boat-in Campground.
Elevation:	Travel between a rim elevation of 2,000 feet and a reservoir elevation of 1,328 feet.
Difficulty:	Moderate.
Maps:	Morrison Trail brochure, sometimes stocked at the trailhead.
Special concerns:	Dispersed no-trace camping is allowed; pitch no camps within 1,500 feet of the reservoir's tree line, and do not camp at the trailhead parking lot. Beware—in late fall and spring, this trail serves hunters as well.
Season and hours:	Year-round, depending on winter snows.
For information:	Bradford Ranger District, Allegheny National Forest.

Key points:

0.0	Trailhead; hike south.
0.5	Loop junction; go right.
0.7	Cross upper Morrison Run.
3.2	Campbell Run.
6.3	Detour to Morrison Campground and Bay.
8.6	Pass cutoff and cross West Fork Morrison Run.
10.8	Top rim plateau.
11.9	Close loop; return to trailhead.

Finding the trailhead: Find the marked trailhead parking area on the south side of Pennsylvania 59, 16 miles east of Warren, 26 miles west of Smethport. A toilet is provided at the trailhead.

The hike: Follow the wide forest trail south for a slow descent through a tall maple–oak complex adorned with hay-scented fern. These ferns grow with abandon because the deer find them distasteful. Black cherry and small hemlock fill out the forest. At 0.5 mile, reach the Y-shaped loop junction near a large boulder; go right for a counterclockwise exploration. Blue "i" blazes and white diamond markers point the way.

Morrison Trail

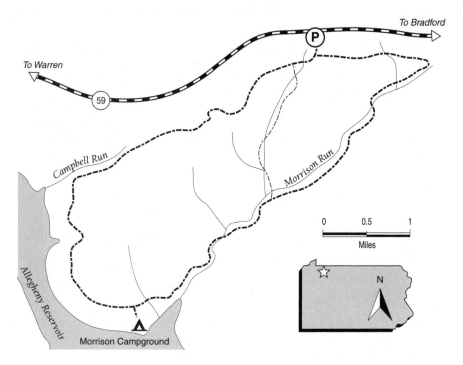

At 0.75 mile, stone-step across an upper fork of Morrison Run and bear right up the slope, avoiding an abandoned section of trail ahead. Follow the diamond-marked trail to encounter the first mountain laurel passage at 1 mile. A porcupine may waddle by, deer may flee, or a woodpecker may telegraph its location as the song of upper Morrison Run drifts through the forest. Laurel alternately disperses and crowds the trail. Seasonally, dogwoods add an umbrella of bloom.

Enjoy a rolling meander. Dark boulders contribute to the laurel-woodland enchantment. At the T-junction at 1.6 miles, follow the marked trail left along an abandoned woods road. At the Y-junction at 2.4 miles, bear left for 0.1 mile and then veer right, slowly descending.

The descent accelerates after the trail crosses the head of Campbell Run. It again travels fragments of woods roads as it pursues the run downstream. Iceberglike rocks rise in the forest, while birch, ash, and beech vary the ranks.

Near the bottom of the slope, look for the trail to turn left. Travel is in a dark second-growth hemlock–beech forest on a more difficult trailbed. The trail then rolls, touring a nose of a ridge. As the trail rounds toward Morrison Run, spy the glint of the Allegheny Reservoir. Afterward, pass through an area showing half a dozen elephant-size boulders to descend via a large grassy woods road. At 5.1 miles, the trail turns left off the descending grade to follow the slope, weaving through yet another rock field.

Where the slope flattens out, travel a habitat of hawthorn and highbush

White-tailed deer, Allegheny National Forest.

blueberry, with a meadow grass floor. Oozing mud, low branches, and thorny bushes can impede travel. At 6.3 miles, reach the signed junction for Morrison Campground. Proceed forward to hike the loop; detour right to visit the campground and Morrison Bay in 0.2 mile. Dispersed among the shoreline trees, find forty boat-to/hike-in campsites with vault toilets and a pump for drinking water. The view from camp is composed of the serial ridges that frame and descend to the shore of the reservoir.

To resume the loop at 6.7 miles, bear right, quickly cross the run near the campground, and pass through serene forest. Next, pursue Morrison Run upstream by hiking along either the woods lane or bank. During high water, the run becomes braided, and following the blazes may require several fordings. Keep to the north shore of the primary run.

At 8.6 miles, prior to the West Fork's confluence with the main stem, you will see the cut-off trail to shorten the loop heading uphill to the left. Proceed forward, crossing the West Fork, for the full 12.4-mile tour.

Enjoy a relaxing jaunt closely paired with scenic Morrison Run. Ferns contribute to the bank's beauty. At 9 miles comes the first of four main-stem crossings; wading may be necessary during high water. The trail still ascends. Boulders now contribute to the stream and woods.

At 10.5 miles, return to the north shore, touring a high-canopy forest with a fragrant fern floor. After a brief, steep ascent, claim the rim plateau (10.8 miles), crossing a side drainage. Maple and oak again rule. Seasonally, tulip poplar and cucumber magnolia trees shower their lofty blossoms onto the trail. Atop the next rim tier, close the loop at 11.9 miles. Bear right to return to the trailhead.

8 C. Lynn Keller Trail

General description:	Some 9 miles of interlocking foot trail explore 13,200-acre State Game Lands 37, which adjoins the Tioga–Hammond reservoir tract—a U.S. Army Corps of Engineers project. This relaxing circuit explores the Ives Run drainage, traveling the sometimes steep wooded slopes and traversing the summit plateau of Bald Hill.
General location:	13 miles northeast of Wellsboro.
Special attractions:	Mixed forest, meadow–shrub habitat, mountain laurel, berry bushes, a seasonal vista, wildlife sightings, and bird-watching along the nearby 2.6-mile Rail Trail (open September through March; take the gravel road heading west near the administration building).
Length:	C. Lynn Keller Trail, 8 miles round trip.
Elevation:	Travel from 1,100 feet near Hammond Lake to a summit elevation of 2,142 feet atop Bald Hill.
Difficulty:	Moderate.
Maps:	Trail flyer (generally stocked at the trailhead); or consult the trailhead mapboard.
Special concerns:	Following heavy rains, expect soggy stretches on the final leg of the loop. Although seldom seen, timber rattlesnakes are found in the area. Beware—in spring and fall, hunters share the state game land.
Season and hours:	Spring through fall, daylight hours. Ives Run Recreation Area, 8:00 A.M. to dusk for day use.
For information:	U.S. Army Corps of Engineers, Tioga–Hammond Lakes.

Key points:

- 0.0 Main Stephenhouse Road trailhead; hike east.
- 0.5 Loop junction; bear right.
- 2.0 Bald Hill.
- 5.2 Cross East Branch Ives Run.
- 7.1 Cross Ives Run.
- 7.5 Loop junction; return to parking.

Finding the trailhead: Follow Pennsylvania 287 North/U.S. Highway 6 West out of Wellsboro, remaining on PA 287 North. Go 11.8 miles and turn right for Ives Run Recreation Area. Proceed straight on Ives Run Access Road

C. Lynn Keller Trail

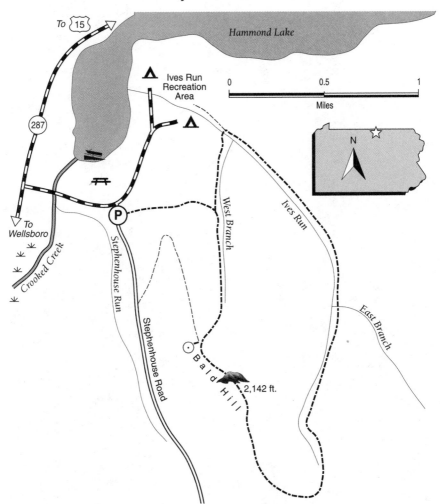

for 0.8 mile, meeting Stephenhouse Road. Locate the main trailhead and its parking area off Stephenhouse Road near the intersection. Find alternative accesses at Ives Run Campground and farther south off Stephenhouse Road.

The hike: Starting from the main trailhead, hike east following the orange circle blazes; elsewhere, remnant yellow blazes also signal the trail. With a steep 0.1-mile climb, enter an easier stretch beneath a varied umbrella of oak, maple, birch, beech, hemlock, and witch hazel. Green shoots pierce the leaf mat. Mountain laurel and fern pockets vary viewing.

Bypass a wooden lattice cylinder, and traverse a grassy wildflower clearing. An old jeep trail then continues the tour as it returns to woods and begins to climb. At 0.5 mile, come to a signed junction. To the left is the campground; bear right for the scenic vista and loop. Songbirds, red efts, turkeys, deer, grouse, and even a black bear may offer fleeting companionship.

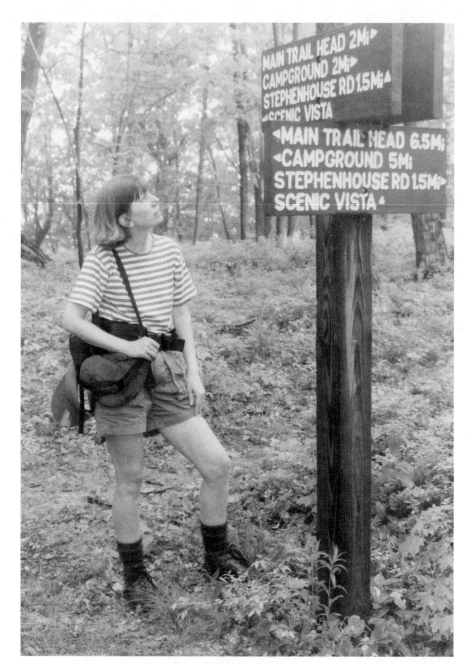

MAIN TRAIL HEAD 2Mi▶
CAMPGROUND 2Mi▶
STEPHENHOUSE RD 1.5Mi▲

◀SCENIC VISTA

◀MAIN TRAIL HEAD 6.5Mi
◀CAMPGROUND 5Mi
STEPHENHOUSE RD 1.5Mi
SCENIC VISTA▲

Lynn Keller trail junction, State Game Lands 37.

As you climb, you lose the background drone of PA 287. Tall mountain laurel congests the midstory, while planted pines pierce the forest canopy. By 1 mile, ascend beside the rocky, barely trickling West Branch Ives Run; here, the climb intensifies and becomes rocky. Be careful when the ground is wet or leafy. Look for the climb to ease above the drainage head.

At 2 miles, top Bald Hill, finding a junction. Straight now leads to the vista; a left continues the counterclockwise loop; and the right leads to the southern Stephenhouse Road access. Go straight, descending amid pine–oak woods and berry bushes, reaching the natural vista ledge in 250 feet. The ledge extends comfortable seating and seasonal views. Admire the immediate forest and backdrop ridge, the rimming bracken fern, and columbine color.

Resume the counterclockwise loop with a relaxing ridgetop stroll, passing through oak–maple woods. Berry bushes, laurel, witch hazel, and striped maple weave a rich midstory. Early-morning hikes often have an ethereal quality as sunbeams deflect through the morning mist. Travel a broad grassy track with attractive fern shoulders before turning left at 3.5 miles for a mild descent.

Cross the fern-clad head of Ives Run drainage, once again enjoying the classic beauty of gray birch and beech. A gnarly old multitrunked maple nudges the trail at the first of a series of springs abundant with jewelweed. After rains, expect to do some tricky stepping or outright slogging between 4.2 and 5.25 miles. The woods lend serenity, while Ives Run adds its steady, gentle voice.

At 5.25 miles, cross East Branch Ives Run; hemlocks precede the crossing. More sopping travel may follow, as a grassy lane or old jeep trail advances the hike through a wooded setting of small-diameter shad, hop hornbeam, and hornbeam. In places, apple and other fruit trees hint at an old orchard. Hickory and ash represent the big trees. Be on the lookout for wildlife.

With a slight rise, find dry footing (6.7 miles) just as the tour turns left off the jeep trail. Now follow the blazed path through transition meadow and hawthorn–elm woodland. Over-the-shoulder looks present the ridge of Bald Hill. Reach the next junction at 7 miles. A right leads to the campground; turn left to return to the main trailhead.

Explore an alder–shrub transition habitat to Ives Run, and then trace the cobble-bottomed run upstream to its crossing at 7.1 miles (sometimes a wading). Forest houses the trail as it ascends to close the loop at 7.5 miles. Turn right to return to the trailhead parking at 8 miles.

9 Hickory Creek Wilderness

Overview

This 8,663-acre roadless area in Allegheny National Forest represents the sole landlocked federal wilderness in all of Pennsylvania, New York, Ohio, Maryland, and New Jersey. Pennsylvania's only other designated wilderness consists of the seven Allegheny River islands. A loop trail bounded by East and Middle Hickory Creeks explores the gently rolling wilderness terrain of ridge plateaus and creek valleys. Traverse a quiet realm of hardwood–hemlock forests and broad meadows shared by deer, porcupine, raccoon, fox, pileated woodpecker, turkey, black bear, and more. Faint skid roads, woods roads, and an abandoned rail grade hint at former logging camps that predate the wilderness. The area was logged in 1837 and again after 1910.

General description: An all-day hike or backpack excursion celebrates the calm and beauty of Pennsylvania's prized wilderness.

General location: 15 miles southwest of Warren.

Special attractions: Mature second-growth forest, thick meadows, fish-supporting runs, wildlife sightings, fall foliage.

Length: Hickory Creek Trail, 12.1 miles round trip.

Elevation: Travel from a trailhead elevation of 1,900 feet to an elevation of 1,500 feet at both Jacks and Coon Runs.

Difficulty: Moderate.

Maps: Hickory Creek and Allegheny River Islands Wilderness brochure (seasonally available at the trail register).

Special concerns: In keeping with the wilderness spirit and to provide challenge, intentionally faint yellow blazes (sometimes spread far apart) mark the way. Parts of the hike may be difficult to follow after trees drop their leaves or when the trail first opens in spring. Once regular foot traffic begins, enjoy fairly easy travel. The blazes both ahead and behind you offer clues. Off-trail exploration requires a map and compass. As in any federal wilderness, no bikes and no motorized vehicles are allowed. Hikers may pitch dispersed no-trace campsites, but keep them 200 feet away from streams and trails. Limit stays to two days per site, and keep party size small. Hunting occurs October through December, and April and May.

Season and hours: Spring through fall for hiking, with winter cross-country skiing.

For information: Bradford Ranger District, Allegheny National Forest.

Hickory Creek Wilderness

Key points:

0.0   Trailhead.
0.5   Loop junction; go right.
1.7   Cross old logging grade.
5.3   Cross Jacks Run.
6.4   Saddle.
7.6   Cross Coon Run.
11.6 Close loop; return to trailhead.

Finding the trailhead: At the intersection of U.S. Highway 6 and Mohawk Avenue in Warren, go south on Pleasant Drive, following the signs for Hearts Content. In 10.7 miles, keep left on oiled State Route 2002, as the main road curves right. Go another 3.5 miles and turn left for Hearts Content Scenic Area. On the left is a large gravel parking lot with access to Hickory Creek Wilderness; no camping at the trailhead.

The hike: From the northeast corner of trail parking, enter a regimented red pine plantation, following the yellow "i" blazes on a diagonal course northwest to SR 2002. At 0.2 mile, cross the road and pass under a power line to travel through a mature second-growth forest of black cherry, beech, maple, ash, and oak. The wide path now allows easy strolling.

At 0.5 mile, come upon a trail register and map box, with the loop junction for Hickory Creek Trail 100 feet farther. To the right begins the north-side tour; straight is the south-side one. Go right (counterclockwise) for a rolling descent in deep woods of young hemlock and mixed deciduous trees. Mountain laurel grows at the grove's lighted outskirts. Where the trail returns to mature hardwoods, many of the trees show multiple trunks.

The wilderness extends a stress-erasing calm. At 1.3 and 1.7 miles, cross over faint logging roads. Rotting stumps recall the forest of old, and large mushrooms can pierce the forest duff. The rolling trail maintains its general downhill orientation.

At 2.7 miles, step over a rock, avoiding a tracked path that passes in front of it. Where the trail next descends, pass among mossy, solitary, or jumbled rocks. By 3.5 miles, snags create a more open cathedral. Along the rim, overlook the forested drainage of East Hickory Creek. Where the trail returns to fuller woods, the overhead leaf pattern engages.

Descend, passing along the foot of the slope, with its meadowy forest floor. At 5.3 miles, cross hemlock-shaded 5- to 10-foot-wide Jacks Run either by a fortuitous log or by wading. A previously used campsite sits near the crossing; avoid the paths branching from camp.

Upon crossing, follow a time-healed railroad grade pursuing Jacks Run up-

Mushroom, Hickory Creek Wilderness, Allegheny National Forest.

stream; a few rail ties remain in place. Skirt open meadows, duck under a multitrunked hornbeam, and cross back over Jacks Run, traversing a deep-grass meadow where does seclude their fawns. With a third crossing, ascend away from Jacks Run, reaching a saddle (6.4 miles).

Next, cross a broad, straight clearing recalling a onetime artillery range. Woods again bring shade. As the trail descends from the saddle, grapevines—both woody and fruit-bearing—entangle the trees. Tulip poplars find habitat on the moist lower slope.

At 7.5 miles, follow Coon Run downstream, cross, and parallel the waterway back upstream. Deep, narrow pools hold small fish. In the meadow-edge woods, springs can muddy the way. Cross a head fork of Coon Run at 8 miles to ascend along a scenic woods road for the next 0.4 mile. Stay alert for the blazes pointing hikers off the road and through a drainage dip. A fern understory complements the dark tree trunks. A more meandering ascent follows.

By 9.25 miles, travel the upper slope and rim above the Middle Hickory Creek drainage. More sunlight penetrates the forest, and the trail again rolls. At 10.6 miles, cross an old road grade and follow a side drainage upstream through hemlock forest, finding the first rocky stretch of the hike. Where the trail tops out, bear left, again crossing a woods road. Hemlocks once more create a deep-woods aura. At 11.6 miles, close the loop; bear right to return to the trailhead at 12.1 miles.

10 Hearts Content Interpretive Trail

General description: Two interlocking interpretive loops introduce the towering old-growth trees on a neck-craning journey. Signs identify tree species, compare bark, explain succession, and discuss forest evolution. The initial 0.25-mile loop offers wheelchair and stroller access. An audiotape may be checked out at the ranger district or, in summer, from the host at Hearts Content Campground.

General location: 15 miles southwest of Warren.

Special attractions: 121 acres of virgin forest, springs draining to the headwaters of West Branch Tionesta Creek, a logging display, ferns.

Length: Fully Accessible Loop, 0.25 mile; Long Loop, 1.25 miles.

Elevation: Trails show minimal grade, with the Long Loop having a 100-foot elevation change. Find less than a 5 percent grade on the Fully Accessible Loop.

Difficulty: Easy.

Maps: Hearts Content Scenic Area Interpretive Trail brochure.

Special concerns: During windstorms, beware of falling branches. Find a toilet and drinking water at the trailhead/picnic area. No camping or fires in the scenic area.

Season and hours: Spring through fall, with winter cross-country skiing.

For information: Bradford Ranger District, Allegheny National Forest.

Key points:

Fully Accessible Loop/Long Loop:

0.0   Trailhead; go left at loop junction.

0.1   Junction; Fully Accessible Loop turns right.

0.5   Lumber company tablet; cross stream.

1.2   End at picnic area or trailhead.

Finding the trailhead: At the intersection of U.S. Highway 6 and Mohawk Avenue in Warren, go south on Pleasant Drive, following the signs for Hearts Content. In 10.7 miles, keep left on oiled State Route 2002 as the main road curves right. Go another 3.5 miles and turn left for Hearts Content Scenic Area. On the left sits a large gravel parking lot; there is limited parking at the picnic area/trailhead at road's end.

The hike: This trail salutes a tiny but significant remnant grove of 300- to 400-year-old trees, including white pine, eastern hemlock, American beech, black cherry, and sugar maple. The scenic area won national natural landmark distinction in 1977. Trees tower 100 to 150 feet above the forest floor and boast diameters of 4 feet.

Hearts Content Interpretive Trail

Intriguing snags pierce the skyline, hinting at natural catastrophes that opened the stand for young white pines and other light-loving species to gain a foothold. A severe drought in 1644, followed by years of fire, gave the giant white pines of today their initial start. This grove is a looking glass to the past, predating the pioneers and the saws that came with them.

The wide, crushed-limestone trail starts at the east end of the picnic area. An information kiosk and a display on logging mark the start. Note the squaring of the exhibit pine; it shows how trees were readied for transportation and floated as river rafts to mills and markets. Giant beech and oak frame the trail's start. Beech bark disease steals the normally smooth skin of some of the beech trees. Biologists estimate the large beech in this grove will most likely disappear in twenty years.

Ahead 50 feet, at a sensory panel illustrating tree bark, sits the loop junction; bear left for a clockwise tour of the site's shallow basin and gallery of big trees. More logs and stumps open the forest cathedral. Respect the integrity of the ancient grove.

At a fence enclosure protecting the regenerating forest from deer, look for the 0.25-mile Fully Accessible Loop to turn right. Continue forward for the Long Loop, entering the heart of the big-tree area. Elsewhere, over-browsing deer have consumed the young shoots. Ferns, distasteful to the deer, thrive untouched.

A forked-top white pine joins the hemlock towers. By pacing off a tumbled giant stretched along the trail, hikers can better appreciate the tree's

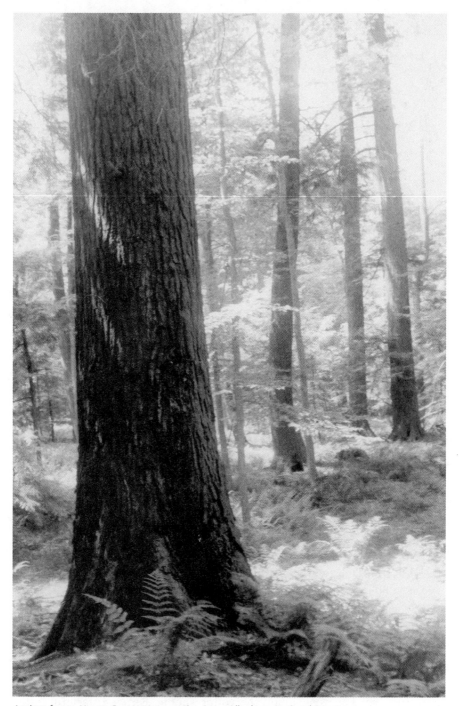

Ancient forest, Hearts Content Interpretive Area, Allegheny National Forest.

former standing height. This trail is one for slow touring, reflection, and appreciation. More pines fill out the cathedral as the trail descends.

At 0.5 mile, find a bench seat and the tablet honoring the lumber company founders who gave the government the first twenty acres of this celebrated grove. Close by, a spring bubbles forth feeding a small wetland. Cross the footbridge over the stream to begin the loop return.

The majesty of the big trees continues. Their lofty tops sway in the wind; more severe winds have stolen the crowns of some. Songbirds and squirrels visit the grove. Black-and-orange beetles favor the conches on gnarled trunks.

More footbridge crossings follow as the trail doubles back on itself. After the footbridge at 0.7 mile, look for a large beech tree snuggled into the trunk of an old-growth pine. The slow uphill return finds black cherry trees joining the mix. At 0.8 mile, big trees ring a bench. At the next pair of benches, view a woodpecker-drilled snag. At 1.2 miles, proceed either straight for the picnic area, or right and then left to close the loop and return to the trailhead.

11 Minister Creek Trail

General description:	This popular hiker circuit explores the woodland and rock features of Minister Creek drainage.
General location:	14.5 miles southwest of Sheffield.
Special attractions:	Attractive Minister Creek, boulder realms, vista, hike-in primitive camps, mountain laurel, fall foliage, access to North Country National Scenic Trail.
Length:	8.5 miles round trip, including a round-trip spur to Deer Lick Camp.
Elevation:	Travel between 1,240 feet at the trailhead and 1,700 feet at the overlook.
Difficulty:	Moderate.
Maps:	Minister Creek Trail brochure.
Special concerns:	In spring and late fall, hunters share the trail. There is no overnight camping at the trailhead parking lot, and hike-in camps have no amenities. On summer weekends, the parking lot can fill; find more tranquil visits midweek and off-season.
Season and hours:	Year-round, depending on winter snow.
For information:	Bradford Ranger District, Allegheny National Forest.

Key points:
- 0.0 Trailhead.
- 0.5 Loop junction; go right.
- 1.0 Cross Minister Creek footbridge.
- 1.8 Add spur to Deer Lick Camp.
- 4.6 Cross Minister Creek footbridge.

Minister Creek Trail

Triple Fork
Camp

North Country Trail

N

Deer Lick
Camp

Outcrop passage ★

Minister Valley
Overlook ⊙

Minister Creek

| 0 | 0.5 | 1 |

Miles

Minister Creek
Campground

P

To
Sheffield

To Tionesta ⟵ 666

Tionesta Creek

7.0   Minister Valley Overlook.

8.0   Close loop; backtrack to trailhead.

Finding the trailhead: From the village of Sheffield, follow Pennsylvania 666 west for 14.5 miles. There, find trail parking on the left, Minister Creek Campground on the right. The trail heads north off PA 666 just west of the campground entrance.

The hike: Hike a wide, ascending trail through beautiful, full forest, bearing right on a limited-access road at 0.1 mile. Maple, hemlock, black cherry, beech, and basswood continue to frame the way, but provide only scattered shade. White diamonds mark the route.

Ascend to road's end (0.5 mile), where a foot trail carries the hike. Conglomerate boulders add to the woods. Just ahead sits the signed loop junction; go right for a counterclockwise tour descending to the creek bottom. A left offers the quickest way to Minister Valley Overlook.

A fairly steep descent delivers hikers to the valley floor. At 0.7 mile, pass a mammoth boulder adorned in moss and ferns and wrapped by the snaking roots of a yellow birch. Previously used hike-in campsites dot the flat. Cross a footbridge over Minister Creek at 1 mile, admiring its beauty.

A steady, contouring ascent follows. Roots web and buckle the trail, while stones ease the crossings of routinely wet sites. Mayflower, oxalis, whorled aster, and partridgeberry contribute to the forest mat. Enjoy stolen looks at Minister Creek until 1.3 miles. In a field of boulders, admire the pebbly conglomerate and dressy fern caps.

After tagging a high point, descend to the Deer Lick Camp spur, marked by the yellow "i" blazes heading left. This 1-mile round-trip detour descends amid forest and grass–fern meadow, reaching a flat dotted by black cherry and used by overnight campers. Minister Creek courses nearby, flowing 15 feet wide and reflecting the hues of its rocky bed.

At 2.8 miles, resume the counterclockwise loop, crossing a drainage to ascend the opposite slope. Here, find boulder outcrops the size of barns. Ferns race to the boulders' feet; bigger black cherry and maple grow in their midst. Secondary paths wiggle away to the crest of imposing rock. Discover tiers, weathered ribs and hollows, and perhaps a fossil.

Cross several small side drainages, leaving the rocks behind at 3.6 miles. Upon crossing a slightly larger tributary, find the first of two junctions with the blue-diamond-marked North Country National Scenic Trail (4 miles). Hike left on a shared section of trail.

Descend, stepping across a beautiful, big spring feeding a clean-flowing stream. Next, spy a few apple trees before the bridge crossing of Minister Creek (4.6 miles). Triple Fork Camp occupies the flat on both shores. Cross the next headfork by bridge and part company with the North Country Trail, which ascends to the right.

Remain along the broad creek flat, touring meadowy plain and forest, following Minister Creek downstream. At 5 miles, an arrow points right. Enter a hemlock grove to cross a tributary bridge, pursue this last fork downstream to its confluence with the main stem, and then continue downstream along the main stem.

At 5.3 miles, ascend from the hemlock-shaded creek bottom, advancing via climbing spurts. Return to the now familiar broadleaved forest. At 6 miles,

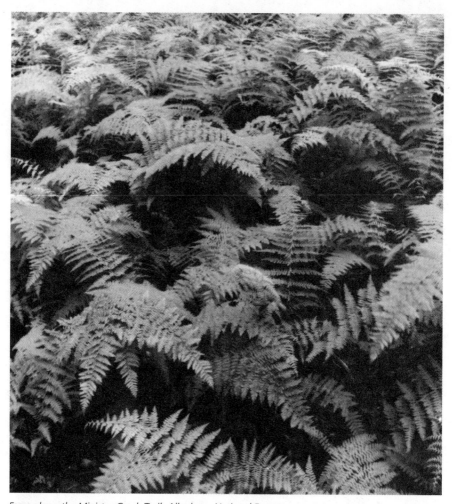

Ferns along the Minister Creek Trail, Allegheny National Forest.

traverse the upper reaches of the slope for a mountain laurel interlude. Dip and ascend through a drainage gouge to enter another impressive realm of boxy boulders, deep fissures, fern shelves, weeping mosses, and a 50-foot-high cliff.

Keep to the diamond-marked route, because side trails explore the area. At 6.8 miles, pass through a broadened mossy fissure, 8 to 10 feet wide and 100 feet long—an impressive natural funhouse. Next, admire the dizzying vertical drop of the overlook rock before ascending to its top (7 miles). The flat-topped rocky overlook serves up a natural view of the wooded ridges of the Minister Creek watershed. Mountain laurel dresses the edge of the rock. Songbirds serenade guests.

Hike past the overlook and descend stone steps, passing through an interesting collection of overhangs and dark grottos. Watch footing when rocks are wet; arrows help point the way. By 7.3 miles, return to woods for a lazy, switchbacking descent. Close the loop at 8 miles, and retrace the initial 0.5 mile to trailhead parking.

12 Susquehannock Trail System

Overview

This rolling, long-distance hiker trail swings an impressive oval through Susquehannock State Forest, visiting Ole Bull and Patterson State Parks, Hammersley Wild Area, and Cherry Springs Fire Tower. On this Allegheny Mountain tour, explore a terrain of moderate relief, with long, even-height ridges cut by sparkling runs that host native brook trout. Maple and beech dominate the second-growth hardwood forests, joined by impressive black cherry trees, stands of hemlock, and planted pine or Norway spruce. Oaks so familiar farther east are notably fewer here.

General description: This long-distance loop and its associated spurs offer comfortable travel, incorporating existing foot trails, old and new logging roads, and abandoned logging railroad grades. Although road crossings (mainly forest roads) come at regular intervals, minimal road travel is needed to complete the circuit. Allot at least a week to hike the entire loop; travel is mostly on public land. With multiple access points, shorter hikes and loops are possible. Be aware that side trails can vary in quality, and not all have markers.

General location: South of U.S. Highway 6, 8.5 miles east of Coudersport, 13.5 miles west of Galeton. The loop twice crosses Pennsylvania 44 and dips southeast of PA 144.

Special attractions: Full forests, a handful of views, Cherry Springs Fire Tower, access to the Donut Hole Trail and Black Forest Trail System, wildlife sightings, flagstone outcrops, mountain laurel, fall foliage.

Length: 84-mile loop.

Elevation: Find the high point, elevation 2,545 feet, between miles 82 and 83; the low point, elevation 1,050 feet, when crossing Kettle Creek at Cross Fork.

Difficulty: Easy to strenuous, depending on the length and section of the Susquehannock Trail System (STS) traveled.

Maps: Susquehannock State Forest; Susquehannock Trail Club's *Guide to the Susquehannock Trail System* (includes maps).

Special concerns: Respect private property, pitching no camps. For overnight camping on public land, thru-trail hikers must secure a free permit from Susquehannock State Forest. Thru-trail and overnight hikers starting at Ole Bull State Park (the southern gateway) must first contact the park office, supplying details of hike, name, address, and license plate number. No bikes; no horses. Pet owners should consider leaving dogs at home—porcupine incidents are common. Although rattlesnakes occur in the area, encounters are rare.

Season and hours: Year-round, depending on snow. District office, 8:00 A.M. to 4:00 P.M. daily.

For information: Susquehannock State Forest; Susquehannock Trail Club.

Susquehannock Trail System

Susquehannock State Forest District Office

Denton Hill State Park

Lyman Run Road

Lyman Run State Park

Galeton

Toe Road

Long

Patterson State Park

Prouty Place Picnic Area

44

Cherry Springs State Park

Cherry Springs Fire Tower

144

East Fork Road

McConnell Road

Proposed Hammersley Wild Area

The Pool

Oleona

44

Ole Bull State Park

144

N

Cross Fork

Greenlick Road

0   2   4

Miles

Key points:

0.0	Northern Gateway trailhead; hike east.
4.0	Jacobs Hollow.
6.6	Cross Lyman Run Road.
10.8	Sunken Branch Road.
13.7	Cherry Springs Fire Tower.
18.0	Cross Bolich Run.
26.5	Ole Bull State Park.
35.7	Junction with Donut Hole Trail.
49.0	Enter Cross Fork.
60.0	McConnell Road.
77.0	Patterson State Park at PA 44.
82.5	High point.
84.0	Complete loop at Northern Gateway.

Finding the trailhead: Find the Northern Gateway, south off US 6, 13.5 miles west of Galeton, 8.5 miles east of Coudersport. Take the turn for Susquehannock State Forest District Office; from the marked overnight parking area on the south side of the district office access road, hike east on a dirt road, locating the orange-blazed STS in 0.25 mile.

Find the Southern Gateway at Ole Bull State Park off PA 144, a couple of miles south of Oleona, 17.5 miles south of Galeton. Locate other main accesses at Cherry Springs Fire Tower, Prouty Place Picnic Area, and Patterson State Park (consult the state forest map).

The hike: For a clockwise tour of the STS (orange rectangle blazes), start at the Northern Gateway off US 6, following the orange blazes left (east) at the loop junction. The trail skirts the southern boundary of Denton Hill State Park as it explores the hardwood forest of the ridge plateau for its first 4 miles. At 2.3 miles, a short vista spur on the left offers a northern perspective. Be alert for the STS blazes where all-terrain vehicle trails cross the route.

The Susquehannock Trail Club does an admirable job in maintaining and blazing the STS. After 4 miles, Jacobs Hollow signals the first key descent, as the trail drops down to cross Lyman Run Road (6.6 miles) and, soon after, Lyman Run. A 1-mile detour east along the road leads to Lyman Run State Park and a lake. Striped maple, fern, and club moss commonly dress the forest, with bee balm and jewelweed coloring the drainages. In fall, the forest's impressive array of hardwoods showers a mosaic of colored leaves on the trail.

From Lyman Run, make a steep 0.5-mile ascent to return to ridge travel; another view sidetracks visitors on the uphill. Muddy and rocky sites periodically trouble hikers. Remain on the ridge until mile 10, then descend to cross Sunken Branch Road and West Branch Pine Creek. The next uphill roll leads to PA 44 and Cherry Springs Fire Tower (13.7 miles). Ascend the rickety eight-story tower at your own risk; the nearby attractive rock cabin is off-limits to the public. Hay-scented ferns create a fuzzy sea at the foot of the tower, while mountain laurel colors the hilltop.

A slow descent follows as the STS parallels Hogback Hollow and Bolich Run downstream; look for beaver sign. Deer, swallowtail butterfly, and grouse can steal attention, but the forest engages throughout. At 18 miles, cross Bolich Run and hike a stretch of road at Abbott before turning east back into forest at 21 miles to follow Cherry Run upstream.

Next, pass over the ridge and chase Ole Bull Run downstream to Ole Bull State Park (26.5 miles), where camping, a small lake, and amenities are available. Where the STS meets a dirt road upon entering the state park, a 0.2-mile side trail, Castle Vista Loop, leads to an interpretive sign and what remains of a "castle" foundation and its retaining wall. Here, in 1852, concert violinist Ole Bull had hoped to settle a colony of his fellow Norwegians, but years of hardship forced their disbandment. A bench seat offers a Kettle Creek overlook. Bluebirds sometimes visit the site.

Follow the STS through Ole Bull State Park, crossing an attractive footbridge over Kettle Creek. The STS then traverses the picnic area, crosses the park road north of Ole Bull Lodge, and ascends steps to PA 144.

On the opposite side of PA 144, the trail again rolls through mostly leafy forest, entering the gentle quiet of Spook Hollow (31 miles). Pine and spruce plantations vary views. At 32 miles and again at 34.2 miles, link trails branch away to the Black Forest Trail System; the latter (southern) link offers the shortest access.

Enjoy comfortable travel with a modest gradient. At 35.7 miles, reach the junction with the 56-mile Donut Hole Trail and bear right, hiking a 9-mile joint section of trail. Quickly enter a steep drop en route to Left Branch Young Woman's Creek. Next, cross the creek and forest road, pursuing Lone Hollow to a saddle passage (38 miles). As the trail rolls upward, laurel clad the ridge.

After Greenlick Run hosts the tour, look for the STS to cross Greenlick Road, travel a pipeline corridor, and descend along yet another run before the Donut Hole Trail departs left (downstream) at Porter Branch (44.5 miles). Remain with the STS, following Porter Branch upstream. Climb up and over a hill to enter Cross Fork for the next stretch of road travel and the crossing of Kettle Creek.

In Cross Fork, thru-trail hikers find stores and motels. Watch for blazes on signposts, guardrails, and rocks, pointing through the village and southwest along PA 144. Be alert for where the trail turns right off PA 144, swinging its way homeward.

Encounter more mountain laurel and chestnut oak atop the ridges as the trail enters the Proposed Hammersley Wild Area. Locate a vista at 51.2 miles; reach Hammersley Fork at 54 miles. A gradual ascent along the fork leads once more to the ridgetop, passing a popular deep basin dubbed "the Pool." Leave the proposed wild area at McConnell Road, 60 miles.

The trail then descends from the ridge, pursuing Gravel Lick Run downstream to East Fork Sinnemahoning Creek and the start of private lands (62.5 miles to 64 miles); pass respectfully. The STS parallels the creek before crossing the waterway and East Fork Road. Soon after, it leaves private land.

As the trail again climbs, reach an area of flagstone quarries and outcrops. More rolling adventure follows. After traveling along Stony Run, return to the ridge plateau (68 miles). The trail now stays along the ridge or upper drainage reaches. At 72 miles, a blue-blazed side trail leads to Prouty Place Picnic Area off Long Toe Road. Keep to the STS, locating a forest view at 73.5 miles.

Once more pass from hollow to ridge, reaching charming Patterson State Park, which borders both sides of PA 44 at 77 miles. Here, find a small pavilion, as well as open picnic tables, primitive toilets, and (seasonally) a water pump. The STS leaves the north end of the picnic area at a sign for the Plantation Trail, one of the former trails contributing to the greater STS.

Resume the ridge–run tour, completing the west side of the loop. Tag the high point at 82.5 miles, remaining on the ridge plateau to close the loop at the Northern Gateway at 84 miles.

Thru-trail hikers should consider purchasing the *Guide to the Susquehannock Trail System*, with its accompanying maps. It provides point-to-point description, identifies reroutes, and may help hikers navigate through areas where nature may have stolen the trail.

13 West Rim Trail

General description: This spectacular long-distance linear trail for the most part hugs the West Rim of Pine Creek Gorge— the Grand Canyon of Pennsylvania. The trail passes through relaxing woods and serves up striking views. Although thru-trail hiking is popular, day hikes can be sculpted that encapsulate the West Rim story.

General location: 8 miles southwest of Wellsboro.

Special attractions: Pine Creek Gorge vistas, varied woods with areas of impressive big trees, mountain laurel and fern, bird and wildlife sightings, colorful fall foliage.

Length: 16 miles one-way from the northern terminus to Bradley Wales State Forest Picnic Area; 24 miles to Steel Hollow Trailhead; or 30.5 miles to Pine Creek Trailhead/Pennsylvania 414.

Elevation: The West Rim Trail travels between 850 feet and 2,020 feet in elevation, with the segment to Bradley Wales showing a 600-foot elevation change; the segment to Steel Hollow has a 700-foot elevation change.

Difficulty: Moderate.

Maps: Tioga State Forest; West Rim Trail; Chuck Dillon's *Guide to the West Rim Trail.*

Special concerns: Salt-craving porcupines are a trailhead annoyance. Although scattering mothballs around the vehicle helps deter them from coolant hoses, thru-trail hikers may opt to use the shuttle services of Pine Creek Outfitters (see appendix D). Phone a few days in advance to discuss pickup/drop-off arrangements. Presently, thru-trail hikers may camp a single night per site without obtaining a permit. For stays exceeding a single night, contact Tioga State Forest. Camping is prohibited at the Bradley Wales State Forest Picnic Area, at either trail terminus, or within 100 yards of buildings.

Keep back from the rim, and stay off the rimrock. Toilets are located at each trail terminus and at Bradley Wales State Forest Picnic Area. Water is seasonally available at the picnic area.

Season and hours: Spring through fall for hiking.

For information: Tioga State Forest.

Key points:
0.0   Northern trailhead.
2.6   Barbour Rock Nature Way.
4.1   Cross Colton Road at Bear Run.
6.1   Cross Colton Road.

West Rim Trail

7.8	Reach Painter–Leetonia Road.
10.5	Cross Burdic Run.
14.1	Ice Break Vista.
16.0	Bradley Wales State Forest Picnic Area.
17.4	Meet West Rim Road.
23.4	Steel Hollow Trail junction.
26.5	Meet Mid State Trail.
28.1	Cross West Rim Road.
30.5	End at PA 414 trailhead.

Finding the trailhead: In Ansonia, turn south off U.S. Highway 6 onto Colton Road, finding the northern terminus in 0.5 mile; Barbour Rock Trailhead and day parking in 3 miles; and Bradley Wales State Forest Pic-

nic Area off West Rim Road in another 12.6 miles. (For Bradley Wales, go south on Colton Road, Painter–Leetonia Road, and West Rim Road before turning left onto Bradley Wales Road to reach the picnic area trailhead.)

To reach the Steel Hollow Trailhead, continue south on West Rim Road 5.6 miles from the Bradley Wales turnoff. Thru-trail hikers find the southern terminus and parking off PA 414, 2 miles south of Blackwell.

The hike: Orange blazes mark the West Rim Trail; blue blazes mark the access trails that pass between rim and forest roads.

Southbound, pass the trail register, entering a hemlock–hardwood forest with a few white pine, aspen, and striped maple. Avoid spurs branching right toward the road, which is fairly close but then pulls away and above the trail. After the bridge that spans often dry Strap Mill Hollow, the trail climbs.

At 0.5 mile, cross the road to Owassee Day Use Area at a sign for PINE CREEK GORGE NATURAL AREA. The trail continues to show a moderate incline, and hemlocks fade from the mix. The hike's excellent forest walk makes up for the early absence of Pine Creek images. Matson Spring (1.3 miles) and Owassee Slide Run (2 miles) sound off progress. Mosses, ferns, and mountain laurels vary understory viewing.

By 2.5 miles, the rim opens to views across the gorge and downstream. Pines hug the brink of the rim. At 2.6 miles, the blue-blazed Barbour Rock Nature Way, a popular day-hike approach, arrives from the west and briefly shares the West Rim Trail to lasso the prized Grand Canyon vantages preferred by photographers.

Wooden rails shape the two designated viewing spots, where classic views detain hikers. Overlook the twisting Grand Canyon of Pennsylvania, sculpted by Pine Creek and elegantly framed by steep, treed flanks. Areas of pinnacles and protruding red rock contribute to the wild persona of the canyon. Far below, an abandoned stretch of Penn Central Railroad hugs the east bank, forming a first-rate rail-trail (see hike 14).

Where the steep, eroding sedimentary cliffs create a natural window, view the bulging and cupping canyon walls. In summer, the canyon glories in green; in autumn, enjoy a multicolored palette. Continue south. The rim plateau offers flat forest travel, with abundant mountain laurel.

By 3.6 miles, the hike leaves the canyon rim to travel the rim of Bear Run, pursuing it upstream to where the run approaches trail level. Pass through pine plantation, cross Bear Run, and cross Colton Road (4.1 miles). Find parking for a handful of vehicles on the west side of Colton Road, suitable for spotting a vehicle or a drop-off/pickup arrangement.

From pine plantation, return to hardwood forest. The worn woods roads used by the trail form excellent paths. Again cross Bear Run, and in another 0.6 mile cross gravel Deadman Hollow Road (named for a trapper who fell victim to his own bear trap). The fern edge distances the trail from the forest and its desirable shade. Pass a cabin and gate (5.2 miles) and descend. Follow the blazed course on a sometimes vegetated route to cross Colton Road again at 6.1 miles (briefly go right on the road).

Immediately cross the span over Right Branch Four Mile Run for a steep ascent to a similar crossing of Painter–Leetonia Road. A patch of club moss may catch your attention. A canopy of maple and ash with a midstory of birch and beech enfolds the way. After crossing a logging road, the trail tops out (6.6 miles). Descend, finding more beech, before turning left onto gravel

Grand Canyon of Pennsylvania.

Thompson Hollow Road. Coming out at a curve on Painter–Leetonia Road, find the trail's continuation 100 feet to the right off the road. Climb through dark hemlock–birch forest.

At 7.8 miles, cross Painter–Leetonia Road and follow the grassy two-track uphill to the left. A shortcut to the Semans Trail is to the right. Beyond a small meadow, enter a setting of young forest. The trail descends. Where mature forest again hosts travel, hikers can detect beech trees failing with disease. At the T-junction with an old railroad grade (the blue-blazed Refuge Trail) at 9 miles, bear right for the West Rim Trail. Ahead, a manicured viewpoint confirms your return to the rim. Travel in cool, shady forest.

Descend and turn into the Burdic Run drainage. The trail briefly follows a leaf-covered woods road to the right before turning left to cross Burdic Run (10.5 miles). Ahead, meet the blue Semans Trail; to the right is Painter–Leetonia Road in 0.6 mile. The West Rim Trail heads left.

The next stretch of trail to Bradley Wales State Forest Picnic Area is vista-packed, with a mild gradient and splendid forest, but avoid the unstable rocky juts. A scenic area of big hemlocks precedes Horse Run. In an area of towering hardwoods, reach a campsite with a rustic backpacker table. A few strides downslope from camp is a view that whets anticipation for these ahead.

At a primary vantage atop a bald rim nose (the first of four main vistas), a few oaks partition the view. Admire a downstream bend, a fire tower atop East Rim, the bold treed flanks, and shimmering Pine Creek. At 11.8 miles, cross intermittent Tumbling Run. Along the rim, the young beech close ranks. The presence of fern, the absence of mountain laurel, and the occurrence of swampy pockets characterize travel on the mostly shaded trail.

Campsites dot the shore at Little Slate Run; cross its footbridge and pass another access trail at 13.1 miles. Toad, red eft, towhee, turkey, deer, and porcupine may share the sylvan splendor. The song of Pine Creek blends with lilting bird arias.

At 14.1 miles, a wooden railing defines Ice Break Vista. Atop this fast-plummeting point, find best views downstream. Just before the vista, a blue access trail heads west to Painter–Leetonia Road. Remain on the rim trail, crossing the rocky streambed of Ice Break Run (14.5 miles); jewelweed and nettles commonly line drainages.

At 14.9 miles, the trail traces the foot of a fern-clad slope below Pine Creek Vista on West Rim Road. At 15.6 miles, a lichen-stained flagstone outcrop rises next to the trail. Soon after, tag the third vista in this series, set off by rock and railing. This perch overlooks a shrub slope, with a gray birch rising center stage. Fog may reveal and conceal the canyon—nature's sleight of hand.

Track the orange blazes south for a gently rolling tour near the rim to find the rockwork and iron shaping the fourth overlook (the last in this series), with grand up- and downcanyon views. Admire a lazy-S bend on Pine Creek, treed islands and points, slow-water reflections, and the eastern cliffs. Continue south 30 yards and hike 0.1 mile west on dirt road to end at Bradley Wales Picnic Area (16 miles). Thru-trail hikers continue pursuing the orange blazes south.

The hike briefly follows an old railroad grade, passing at the outskirts of private land and crossing seasonal flows and Straight Creek. Mixed forest houses the trail as it climbs, replaced by spruce. Upon meeting West Rim Road (17.4 miles), follow the road left, past plantation and beaver meadow, before resuming on path in 0.5 mile.

Pass from settings of spruce and larch back to a hemlock–hardwood forest with aspen; keep alert, tracking blazes. As the West Rim Trail descends, it passes a blue spur to West Rim Road at 18.9 miles. At stream crossings, hikers might pause to search the rocks for seashell fossils. This section of trail travels the edge of a fern-filled meadow that was once farmed and twice crosses Good Springs Run before claiming a vista rise at 19.7 miles. Admire the steep canyon walls, detecting the geological strata of mudstone, shale, and sandstone.

Rolling travel follows, with stream crossings, a few notable trees, and teasing canyon glimpses. At 21.4 miles, reach the next meaningful view. Enjoy a cross-canyon look at the East Rim and rural hilltops, but the canyon bottom remains a mystery. The hike transitions into a mixed oak–mountain laurel complex. The mountain laurel is what sets the trek to Steel Hollow apart.

In 0.3 mile, reach the blue-blazed Gundigut Trail, which offers a 0.5-mile access to West Rim Road; it runs an attractive gauntlet of junglelike mountain laurel braided with witch hazel or chest-deep bracken ferns. The West Rim Trail rolls, tracing the contour of the slope, still in tall forest and abundant mountain laurel. Pass some unusual and inspiring trees. In places, striped maple drape the trail. The trunks of birch contrast with the abundant green.

Pass a campsite in an open flat at 22.3 miles and slowly descend, traversing an open woods and a sea of waist-high bracken fern. Beyond another camp, ascend a faint jeep trail before turning left. More light penetrates near the rim. At 22.7 miles, blue blazes mark a 100-foot spur to the next vista. Here, find an exciting tunnel view overlooking the laurel and wooded west flank to the reddish cliffs of the East Rim. A building afternoon thunderhead can bestow drama.

Resume the southbound journey, touring similar woods with brushing laurel and a few large-toothed aspen. Upon crossing the headwater springs of Steel Hollow, reach the junction post and blue blazes for the Steel Hollow access trail (23.4 miles). For hikers ending here, it's a 0.6-mile hike southwest (right) to West Rim Road; ascend through an open forest, wet with springs, coming out an old road for a gentle, winding stroll to West Rim Road.

Thru-trail hikers continue south, finding the next view in 0.2 mile. Here, peer across another mountain-laurel-covered slope at the folding canyon ridges, but the height of the laurel makes this a standing-room-only view. After the rolling trail turns west into Dillon Hollow, discover two rock slides reclaimed by lichen. Mountain laurel remains a key player. Find additional camping upon crossing Dillon Run, 24.5 miles.

Track the blazes, making more rock discoveries, finding attention-attracting tree specimens, and crossing runs. The hike intersects the Mid State Trail on the south side of Bohen Run (26.5 miles); head right (east), ascending on old skid road to remain on the West Rim Trail (both trails are orange-blazed). Past the vista at 27.4 miles that takes in Blackwell, Jerry Run, and the southern Pine Creek Canyon, the route becomes rocky. Remember, no camping within 100 yards of buildings.

Cross West Rim Road at 28.1 miles, edge an old cut, and pass among pines, eventually descending, at times steeply, to the PA 414 Trailhead in Pine Creek Valley (30.5 miles).

14 Pine Creek Rail Trail

General description: This outstanding segment of rail-trail follows the east bank of Pine Creek, exploring the belly of the Grand Canyon of Pennsylvania. This segment represents the flagship of an even greater proposed rail-trail that would span 62 miles between Wellsboro Junction (Pennsylvania 287) and the Jersey Shore.

General location: 7 miles southwest of Wellsboro.

Special attractions: Pristine Pine Creek and its canyon, part of which is recognized as a national natural landmark; fishing for trout and smallmouth bass; nesting bald eagles; wildlife sightings (perhaps even an elusive fisher, reintroduced to the area); ferns and wildflowers; seasonal cascades; colorful fall foliage.

Length: 20 miles one-way.

Elevation: The trail shows a 300-foot elevation change between its two trailheads.

Difficulty: Easy to moderate, depending on length and allotted time.

Maps: Tioga State Forest; West Rim Trail.

Special concerns: Dispersed primitive camping is allowed by permit only within an 8-mile stretch of the canyon between Burdic Run and Steel Hollow; secure permits in advance from the Tioga State Forest District Office. Thru-trail hikers may wish to use the shuttle services of Pine Creek Outfitters (see appendix D); phone a few days in advance to discuss pickup/drop-off arrangements.

Engage in no-trace travel, respect posted closures for eagles, and respect private property. Use utmost care with regard to sanitation to protect the integrity of the canyon and the scenic waterway. Find toilet facilities at the Darling Run Trailhead (northern terminus), Tiadaghton Primitive Campground, the Blackwell boater access, Rattlesnake Rock Trailhead (southern terminus), and the Hoffman Farm primitive camp area south of Blackwell.

Efforts are under way to improve the rail-trail south to the Jersey Shore, so look for this discovery to grow.

Season and hours: Year-round, with winter cross-country skiing.

For information: Tioga State Forest.

Pine Creek Rail Trail

Key points:

- 0.0   Darling Run trailhead; hike south.
- 2.2   Owassee Rapids.
- 4.0   Little Fourmile Run bridge/Turkey Path junction.
- 8.3   Tiadaghton Primitive Camp.
- 13.0   Pine Island Run.
- 18.0   Boater access in Blackwell.
- 20.0   End at PA 414 parking.

Finding the trailhead: Find the northern trailhead on Darling Run Road, southwest off PA 362, 1 mile south of Ansonia, 7.3 miles west of Wellsboro (take PA 660 west to PA 362). Find shared southern terminus parking for the Pine Creek Rail Trail and the West Rim Trail, 2 miles south of Blackwell, off PA 414. A boater access to Pine Creek sits on the east side of the PA 414 bridge in Blackwell, but avoid parking there.

The hike: North-central Pennsylvania boasts some of the most remote wilds in the state and, for that matter, in the entire eastern United States, with the Grand Canyon of Pennsylvania being the sterling prize. A superb lineup of trails explores these wilds. Look for this comfortable rail grade to assume a place at the roster's forefront.

Pine Creek Rail Trail follows an abandoned stretch of Penn Central Railroad, resurfaced in crushed limestone and open to foot and bike use. Sections of parallel trail serve horseback riders. For its total length, the railroad levee remains about 30 to 40 feet higher than the creek.

For a downstream journey from the northern (Darling Run) terminus, turn left upon descending the access ramp. A line of tall pines and an herbaceous floodplain initially isolate the trail from Pine Creek. The fuller woods on the left creates a buffer between the trail and PA 362. Goldfinch, towhee, and a glorious chaos of birdsongs accompany an early-morning start.

By 0.2 mile, view a broad, slow bend of Pine Creek as the floodplain narrows. Elsewhere, moderate whitewater stretches and lengthy quiet spells characterize the waterway. From the start, it is clear why Pine Creek won Pennsylvania Scenic Rivers System distinction.

Ahead, a sign cautions that no camping is allowed for the next 5 miles. Wildflowers dress the shoulders of the corridor, with poison ivy appearing in the mesh of Virginia creeper. With much of the tour open and sun-drenched, carry plenty of water and wear sun protection. Anglers on foot or bike are common passersby. Hawks and vultures ride the thermals, while a heron stealthily stalks its prey.

Closer to shore, find elm, ash, birch, and sycamore, with hemlocks and a different assortment of hardwoods claiming the canyon slope. Side drainages count off distance. By 1.9 miles, a few private residences dot both sides of Pine Creek; keep to the trail. At 2.2 miles, a sign along the creek warns canoeists and rafters of Owassee Rapids downstream. While out of view, the loudness of the rapids brings excitement.

A few concrete pillars, wooden posts, and rusted pins recall the railroading days. Deeper in the canyon, admire the red-rock palisades piercing the leafy and spired cathedral. At 3.2 miles, enter state park lands. At the rail bridge over cascading Little Fourmile Run (4 miles), look for the steep Turkey Path leading to Leonard Harrison State Park, atop the East Rim. Here, too, find an easy-access path to the rocky shore of Pine Creek—a satisfying turnaround for most day hikers. State park and private lands now claim the west shore. Exit the park at 4.7 miles.

Pine Creek flows broad over a rocky streambed. Generally, its waters barely top the knee, though a few 4-foot-deep pools entice anglers to dance their fly lines to them. Rich green grasses dress the shore. An upheaval of logs strewn across the floodplain hints at past floodwaters.

Throughout the hike, encounter tried access paths dipping to shore—some more sensible than others—and scenic shoreline changes, with wetlands enlivened by frogs and red-winged blackbirds. By 7.2 miles, the floodplain again broadens, with a built-up ridge now secluding the creek. Rock-ledge features, 25 to 40 feet high, frame the gently bending route; tulip poplars add their signature leaves. At 8.3 miles, cross a larger side drainage, reaching Tiadaghton Primitive Camp (permit required), with rest room, water pump, and a scenic camp flat.

Downstream, view more locust and box elder, and pass a few more residences at Tiadaghton. The rail corridor then narrows, losing the associated service road/horse trail. Over-the-shoulder looks present new perspectives on Pine Creek and better capture a sense of the canyon.

After 10 miles, taller ledges line the trail, with more woods spreading to shore. Here, too, view a West Rim cliff. Deer, porcupine, pileated woodpecker, bluebird, kingfisher, merganser, scarlet tanager, and bald eagle may make the list of sightings. The eagles are the pride of the canyon.

At 13 miles, cross the rail bridge over Pine Island Run. Maple, oak, and hickory remain familiar shade sources. Next, view a glassy straightaway on Pine Creek, where rainbow and brown trout, and rock and smallmouth bass slip through the water. After passing a NO CAMPING DOWNSTREAM sign, a tree border again alternately conceals and reveals the creek.

A side trail at 15.6 miles descends to a flat rock for admiring Pine Creek. Farther downstream, a grassy island adds to views. Dripping mosses cloak the cliffs. Private residences signal that Blackwell is just ahead; keep to the trail.

At 18 miles, reach the boater access in Blackwell. To reach the southern terminus, continue downstream 0.2 mile, cross the reclaimed railroad bridge over Pine Creek, and travel the west shore the remaining way. Find an open corridor of sumac, birch, locust, and box elder, with grassy meadow flowing to Pine Creek; trees later bring shade.

In the areas of sunken grade, admire the long straightaway of the rail-trail. The floodplain grasses virtually consume the deer wading in their midst. A planed overlook rock at 19.8 miles presents a scenic rocky point, attractive cove, and dark pools on Pine Creek for a first-rate sign-off to the tour. Take the spur angling uphill to the right at 20 miles (before the Lloyd Run bridge) to end at the PA 414 parking.

15 Beaver Meadows Recreation Area

Overview

The centerpiece of this Allegheny National Forest recreation area is thirty-four-acre Beaver Meadows Lake, created in 1936 as part of the Works Progress Administration (WPA). A network of five interlocking trails totaling 5.9 miles explores the natural woods, pine plantation, and grass–fern savanna of the lake periphery. An innovative floating boardwalk crosses the inlet for an up-close wetland/lake perspective—a sight generally reserved for canoeists.

General description:	Two short loop hikes encapsulate the recreation area, exploring quiet Beaver Meadows Lake and touring the gentle terrain above Salmon Creek, the lake's scenic meandering outlet.
General location:	25 miles north of Brookville.
Special attractions:	Diverse habitat, lake and creek fishing, bird- and wildlife-watching, boardwalk, flowering shrubs, protected blueberry patches.
Length:	Beaver Meadows Loop, 2.5-mile loop, with Lakeside Loop spur; Salmon Creek Loop, 1.5 miles round trip.
Elevation:	The trails show less than 100 feet of elevation change.
Difficulty:	Both easy.
Maps:	Beaver Meadows Hiking Trail System brochure.
Special concerns:	After heavy dew or rain, rain pants or chaps help keep your legs dry while hiking in the deep grasses of savanna and lakeshore. During the spring and late-fall hunting seasons, wear bright colors.
Season and hours:	Year-round, depending on snow.
For information:	Marienville Ranger District, Allegheny National Forest.

Key points:

Beaver Meadows Loop:
- 0.0 Dam Area trailhead.
- 0.4 Add Lakeside Loop.
- 1.0 Boardwalk.
- 2.5 End loop at day-use parking lot.

Beaver Meadows Recreation Area

Seldom Seen Trail

Beaver Meadows Loop

To Marienville

Beaver Meadows Lake

Lakeside Loop

Salmon Creek Loop

Salmon Creek

Penoke Path

N

0   0.25   0.5
Miles

Salmon Creek Loop:
- 0.0   Dam Area trailhead.
- 0.1   Loop junction; bear right.
- 1.4   Close loop; backtrack to trailhead.

FT

1,900 ── Close loop
1,800 ── Trailhead
1,700
1,600 ── Loop junction

Miles   1

Finding the trailhead: From central Marienville, turn north off Pennsylvania 66 onto North Forest Street/Forest Road 128. Go 3.8 miles and turn right onto FR 282 for Beaver Meadows Recreation Area. Find all trails starting near the dam in 0.8 mile; find a day-use parking area on the right (east) past the picnic area. A thirty-seven-site campground serves overnighters.

The hikes: Beaver Meadows Lake represents the heart of the recreation area; its companion trail, **Beaver Meadows Loop,** the heart of the hiking network. Although accessible from the day-use parking lot, start at the dam for early lake views and a counterclockwise tour. Because the trail system is laid out in a four-leaf-clover pattern, this hike may be extended by adding any one or all four of the other loops: Salmon Creek Loop, Lakeside Loop, Penoke Path, and Seldom Seen Trail. For this hike, the lone addition will be the Lakeside Loop.

75

Round the boulder barricade to traverse the grassy-topped dam. Flowering shrubs dress the right side of the route; Beaver Meadows Lake, the left side. Below the dam, the dark release waters of Salmon Creek meander through a textured wetland.

In its low, rolling terrain, this long east–west lake presents a scenic shrub-and-grass shore. Attractive mats of aquatic vegetation complement the dark water plied by ducks and geese. A heron may study the shallows. The lake's fish population is made up of bluegill, pumpkinseed, yellow perch, bullhead, and a few bass.

Upon crossing the spillway bridge, reach a four-way junction: Hiking left along the lakeshore advances the loop; the paths right and straight ahead form the Salmon Creek Loop. Proceed left, in pines with an understory of young maple, beech, hawthorn, serviceberry, fern, and bramble. White diamonds mark the way. Next, pass alternately between view-obstructing spruce and bracken fern clearings.

At 0.4 mile, detour left for the Lakeside Loop, making a clockwise tour, closer to shore. Blue arrows and disks help point the way. On a narrow footpath, wade through the thick grasses, ferns, and flowering shrubs to win an open lake view. At times, the vegetation overwhelms the trail, so be alert for arrows. Close the Lakeside Loop, bear left to return to Beaver Meadows Loop, and, once on it, resume the counterclockwise tour.

At 0.6 mile and again at 0.9 mile, meet the 0.8-mile Penoke Path, which swings southeast exploring more savanna. Forgo this side trip, remaining amid the fern meadows and stands of spruce and black cherry. At the second Penoke Path junction, encounter fenced blueberry plots—an effort to deter browsing deer (a larger plot lies along the Seldom Seen Trail). Ahead, reach the boardwalk at the east end of the lake.

The 0.1-mile-long boardwalk wins over visitors with the sights it affords and its innovative construction. Tall poles and vinyl palettes with water-release holes fashion the walk. When the lake and marsh waters rise, the boardwalk simply climbs the poles. The release holes handle the displaced water. Enjoy open lake views and a close look at the textured inlet marsh, including knee- to waist-high aquatic grasses and a mosaic of wildlife channels.

From the boardwalk, enter a more sheltered woods habitat, rolling farther from shore. Here, hikers may notice the harvest mound of a squirrel, the knocking of woodpeckers, or the serenade of songbirds. Be careful of wet roots. By 1.5 miles, return to a tree-dotted bracken fern expanse; ferns may attain shoulder height. Cross a footbridge over a hemlock-shaded inlet. Then slowly ascend; here, hay-scented ferns seasonally perfume the air.

After touring a pine plantation, bear left at 2 miles on a former logging railroad grade. A large meadow spans right. In another 0.1 mile, meet the 1-mile Seldom Seen Trail; it heads right, offering an alternative return to the trailhead. For the Beaver Meadows Loop, proceed straight on the railroad grade. Where the loop descends from the grade, cross several footbridges, weaving back toward the lake to complete the tour at the day-use parking lot (2.5 miles).

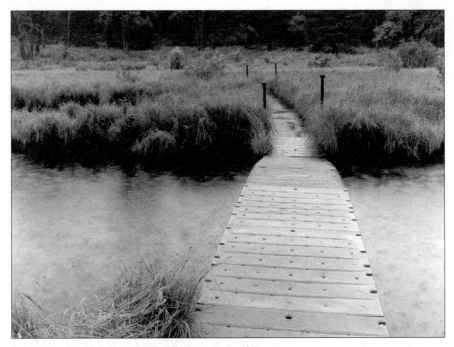

Beaver Meadows Lake boardwalk, Allegheny National Forest.

For **Salmon Creek Loop,** retrace the first 0.1 mile of Beaver Meadows Loop, but bear right upon crossing the dam for a counterclockwise tour along the lake outlet. Travel a piney woods interspersed with black cherry, overlooking the outlet-drained meadow. Blue diamonds mark the way.

At the trail split (0.2 mile), the right fork (the primary trail) passes closer to Salmon Creek, offering an overlook of the 8-foot-wide waterway and the grassy plain it parts before swinging left uphill. The path straight ahead explores the heart of the red pine plantation with its rhythmic array of trunks and tall bracken fern. Both paths merge at 0.4 mile, with a closing glance toward Salmon Creek—a waterway favored by beavers.

Continue the counterclockwise hike. Red pine needles beneath the green ferns vary the forest look. At 0.6 mile, swing left, still ascending in plantation. Hay-scented ferns replace the bracken ferns. Deer may bound away in flight. Before long, the loop again swings left, descending and meandering amid pines and a small alcove of spruce. Close the loop at 1.4 miles, and return to the trailhead at 1.5 miles.

16 Buzzard Swamp Trail System

Overview

At this Allegheny National Forest hiking and wildlife viewing area, closed roads, reseeded tracks, and foot trails introduce the site's gentle, mostly open terrain dotted by fifteen pond impoundments and numerous pothole wetlands. The site is a critical stopover for migrating waterfowl on the Atlantic Flyway. Porcupine, rabbit, deer, bear, coyote, beaver, snapping turtle, osprey, and bald eagle likewise find favorable habitat.

General description: Some 11.2 miles of trail explore Buzzard Swamp; the two selected hikes aptly present the wildlife area. The South Loop skirts the wooded thicket of the propagation area, journeys along and between ponds and wetlands, and tours levee and meadow, offering opportunities for wildlife viewing and fishing. The Songbird Sojourn Interpretive Trail concentrates travel within an attractive hardwood grove, with sightings of woodland creatures.

General location: 20 miles north of Brookville.

Special attractions: Wildlife viewing; fishing for bass, perch, crappie, catfish, and bluegill; meadows, ponds, thickets, and forest; wildflowers; forty-acre propagation area, providing vital nesting and rearing habitats for wildlife.

Length: South Loop, 3.9-mile loop; Songbird Sojourn Interpretive Trail, 1.5-mile loop.

Elevation: Both trails show minimal elevation change.

Difficulty: Both easy.

Maps: Buzzard Swamp Wildlife Viewing and Hiking Area brochure; Songbird Sojourn pamphlet (seasonally stocked at the trailhead; best to secure a copy from the Marienville Ranger Station, 2 miles north of Marienville on Pennsylvania 66).

Special concerns: Entering the forty-acre propagation area is forbidden; this area is well marked in the field and on maps. Because much of the travel is in open meadow, carry an area map with you. Hikers may port motorless boats to the ponds; find the nearest pond 1 mile from the trailhead. Allow wildlife a respectful safety margin. In spring and late fall, hunting occurs. Come prepared for insects. A vault toilet at the trailhead is the lone amenity.

Season and hours: Year-round, depending on snow.

For information: Marienville Ranger District, Allegheny National Forest.

Buzzard Swamp Trail System

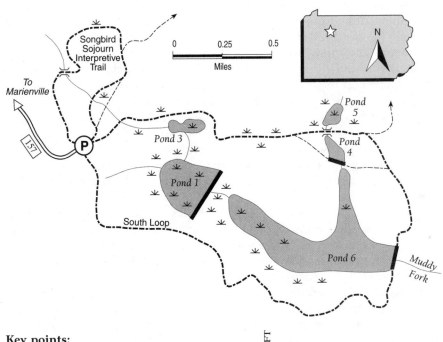

Key points:

South Loop:
- 0.0   Trailhead.
- 1.9   Spillway crossing at Pond 6.
- 2.2   Pond 4.
- 3.9   End loop at parking.

Songbird Sojourn Interpretive Trail:
- 0.0   Trailhead.
- 1.1   Cross footbridge.
- 1.5   End loop at parking.

Finding the trailhead: From PA 66 in Marienville, turn south onto South Forest Street/State Route 2005. Go 1.2 miles, turning left onto Forest Road 157 (an improved dirt road) opposite a National Forest Service/Pennsylvania Game Commission sign. Reach the graveled parking lot in 2.3 miles. Trails leave from the northwest and southwest corners and from the east end of the lot. For alternative hikes, a northern trailhead is 2.5 miles east of Marienville off Lamonaville Road.

The hikes: For a counterclockwise tour of the **South Loop,** begin at the southwest corner of the parking area, hiking gated FR 378 south. Black cherry, birch, maple, spruce, pine, apple, beech, honeysuckle, fern, and wild rose weave a thick, diverse protective habitat for wildlife; keep to the trail. A thin waterway weaves back and forth beneath the road, flowing through culverts. Red efts sometimes venture forth along the wetland shoulder.

Vegetation gaps in the propagation area allow swamp glimpses, with mist sometimes lifting from the water. Despite the forest fullness at the sides of the trail, the overhead cathedral remains open. At 0.7 mile, reach the open grassy meadow sprawling north to Pond 1, its open water often busy with geese. Low rounded ridges shape the backdrop; snags claim one end of the pond. Encounter the first of a handful of interpretive signs, this one on waterfowl migration. Scopes and binoculars enrich travel.

The singletrack affords flat, comfortable hiking. Young aspen, maple, and beech edge the route. At 1.2 miles, secure the next open viewing of the ponds and the Buzzard Swamp interior. Nearby, cattails dress a tiny circular pond; beyond sits the more extensive open water of Pond 6. A dozen or more artificial potholes dot the perimeter meadow. The trail alternates between meadow and wooded aisle.

By 1.8 miles, a grassy track leads to the levee, dam, and spillway crossing at Pond 6. View a small grassy island and reflections of snags. The concrete spillway feeds a pretty tree-lined waterway, with aquatic plants mottling the surface. In the expansive meadow straining north, find an open scatter of black cherry trees. Such open travel is unusual in the land of Penn's Woods. Hawkweed, daisy, and myriad other wildflowers decorate the grasses.

At the 2.2-mile junction, proceed forward past the levee cutoff on the left to travel the east perimeter of Pond 4. Look for beaver lodges, scent mounds, nesting boxes, and popular roosts. Swallows dart about, and the heavy scent of moist grass hangs in the air.

Continue the South Loop, bearing left at the junction at 2.5 miles. Proceeding straight here adds a visit to the northern chain of ponds; keep your map handy. Loop travel follows the gravel jeep trail of closed FR 157, passing between Ponds 4 and 5. In the channel's dark, murky water, look for sunfish; butterflies and moths flit about the wildflowers. Pass a large grove of young aspen and, soon after, gain modest shade.

At 2.75 miles, the cutoff trail from the 2.2-mile junction arrives on the left; keep to the gravel road. The route skirts the small auxiliary ponds north of Pond 1. Deer may be spied browsing along the shore in the protected propagation area. After 3 miles, leave the pond/meadow core of Buzzard Swamp, passing through forest-transition habitat. The Songbird Sojourn Interpretive Trail branches to the right just as the hike ends at the east end of the parking lot (near the kiosk, 3.9 miles).

For the **Songbird Sojourn Interpretive Trail,** hike east past the kiosk, turning left at the attractive Songbird Sojourn trail sign to follow the seventeen numbered stations in order. Silver diamonds identify the route, as do some blue cross-country ski markers. Follow the grassy track for 0.1 mile, then turn left onto foot trail. At the stepping-stone crossing of a small drainage, admire the tall interrupted ferns of shore. Visit hardwood forest, planted spruce and pine, and a transition habitat near a tiny wildlife pond, steamy with transpiration and evaporation.

At Post 5 (0.4 mile), bear left, following markers. At 0.5 mile, again bear left; the trail to the right accesses the northern swamp and its chain of ponds. Follow a small drainage uphill to edge a wildflower opening, still remaining in woods. Black cherry, maple, beech, birch, ash, and hornbeam enfold the tour. With a slow descent, begin a mildly rolling, woodland meander. Pass a spring and a salamander pond, and revel in the forest tranquility. Leaves float lazily to the ground.

Cross a small footbridge (1.1 miles), passing through open woods with single and multitrunked trees. Deer may frequent the apple trees in a clearing off to the right. Emerge from the shady woods at the northwest corner of trail parking, 1.5 miles.

17 Cook Forest State Park

Overview

Threaded by the Clarion River, this hallmark 6,668-acre Pennsylvania state park protects one of the largest old-growth white pine–eastern hemlock forests in the eastern United States. The ancient trees clad fully a third of its total acreage, with three large groves: Cathedral, Swamp, and Seneca. Some 30 miles of interlocking trails explore ancient and second-growth forest, the Clarion River, Toms Run, and plateaus of rhododendron and mountain laurel. Top a rocky vantage (Seneca Point) and historic Cook Fire Tower to survey the park's majesty.

General description: The trail system presents a variety of round-trip, loop, and shuttle-hike options; the five selected hikes provide a strong appreciation for the park.

General location: 13 miles northeast of Clarion.

Special attractions: Primeval forest; Clarion River; 1929 fire tower; freshwater and mineral springs; rhododendron, laurel, and dogwood blooms; swinging bridge; wildlife; fall foliage; 1976 tornado legacy.

Length: Nature Trail, 0.25-mile loop; Forest Cathedral Hike (tours Longfellow and Birch Trails), 3 miles round trip; Joyce Kilmer Trail, 3.5 or 4 miles round trip; Fire Tower Loop (linking the Hemlock, Deer Park, Seneca, and Birch Trails), 4.2-mile loop; Rhododendron Trail, 3 miles round trip.

Elevation: Nature Trail, flat; Forest Cathedral Hike, 200-foot elevation change; Joyce Kilmer Trail, 300-foot elevation change; Fire Tower Loop, 400-foot elevation change; Rhododendron Trail, 300-foot elevation change.

Difficulty: Nature Trail, Forest Cathedral Hike, Rhododendron Trail, all easy; Joyce Kilmer Trail and Fire Tower Loop are moderate.

Maps: State park brochure.

Special concerns: Control pets on a leash at all times. Trails in the park are unblazed, but remain easy to follow for the most part. Find trail junctions signed, with the occasional arrow indicating a direction change. No camping is allowed along the trails. Within the park, overnight camping is restricted to the Ridge Camp Family Campground or the organized group tent camping areas.

Season and hours: State park, year-round. Day use, 8:00 A.M. to sunset. Hiking, spring through fall, with winter hiking or cross-country skiing popular.

For information: Cook Forest State Park.

Cook Forest State Park

Key points:

Nature Trail:

    0.0   Trailhead.

    0.2   Complete loop.

Forest Cathedral Hike:

0.0 Longfellow Trailhead.
0.5 Indian Trail junction.
1.2 Reach Toms Run.
1.5 Cross swinging bridge to Birch Trail.
1.8 Cross Toms Run, backtracking first 1.2 miles.

Joyce Kilmer Trail:

0.0 Longfellow Trailhead.
0.5 Indian Trail junction.
1.2 Indian Spring.
1.7 Bridle Trail (alternative turnaround).
2.0 Cemetery Road; backtrack to trailhead.

Fire Tower Loop:

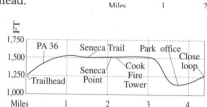

0.0 Vowinckel Road/Hemlock Trailhead.
0.5 Cross Pennsylvania 36.
1.5 Seneca Trail; detour right.
2.1 Seneca Point.
2.3 Cook Fire Tower.
3.0 Resume loop at 1.5-mile junction.
3.7 Park office.
4.2 End at trailhead parking.

Rhododendron Trail:

0.0 Indian Cabins Area trailhead.
1.5 Forest Drive; return as you came.

Finding the trailhead: On PA 36, reach the park 7 miles south of Leeper or 16 miles north of Brookville. Vowinckel Road/State Route 1015 represents the main north–south artery through the park; it heads north off PA 36 north of the Clarion River Bridge and park office at Cooksburg.

The hikes: For the **Nature Trail**, turn east off Vowinckel Road at the sign for Sawmill Area and Pool. Before the Sawmill Area, turn left onto a dirt road signed for the Nature Trail. In 0.25 mile, reach the paved wheelchair-accessible parking lot, with nearby open parking for the general public.

This 0.25-mile paved circuit offers a first-rate window to what makes Cook Forest so special. Leisurely pass through an area of old-growth and second-growth trees, touring a dark eastern hemlock forest with huge beech, oak, and black cherry trees. Listen to the whisper of a breeze in the lofty treetops and succumb to relaxation. Among the impressive big trees, downfalls and stumps hark to bygone days; logging ended in Cook Forest in 1915.

For **Forest Cathedral Hike** and **Joyce Kilmer Trail**, start at the historic Log Cabin Inn Visitor Center, near the intersection of Vowinckel Road (SR 1015) and Toms Run Road. Both hikes begi0 n on the Longfellow Trail, starting uphill to the right of the visitor center.

The Forest Cathedral Hike travels the Forest Cathedral Natural Area. Here, discover old-growth white pine and hemlock trees exceeding 300 years in age, 200 feet in height, and 3 feet in diameter. These trees date to the time of William Penn, Pennsylvania's first governor. On the Longfellow Trail, skirt a picnic area and "Tree of Peace" planted by the Mohawk Nation Council of Chiefs. Beautiful big hemlock, birch, and white pine engage from the start. The wide, well-traveled Longfellow Trail is the most popular gateway to the park's old growth.

At 0.1 mile, visit Memorial Fountain; mosses and lichens adorn its attractive stonework. Only the occasional road noise intrudes on the forest solemnity. Rustic log benches invite a slow-paced appreciation. Towering snags as well as live trees tickle the sky; tilt your head back to gain a full measure of the forest. Alphabet-labeled trails (A through G), as well as other named trails, branch from or cross over the path; keep to the Longfellow Trail.

Next, visit the "windthrow" area of 1956, where a storm of cyclonic intensity leveled many of the evergreen giants within a four-acre site. Downfalls have since been removed, but the openness of the forest now stands testament to the event. A pileated woodpecker may emerge from a snag.

At 0.5 mile, the Indian Trail heads left; along it a plaque shows the national natural landmark status of these woods. The Longfellow Trail continues forward, rolling along the forested slope. In hollows, find massive beech trees in addition to the evergreens. Mossy rock slabs and the rare appearance of a rhododendron can vary viewing.

Angle downhill to a footbridge spanning Toms Run (1.2 miles), but forgo crossing. Instead, follow the east shore of Toms Run downstream to the park's swinging bridge (1.5 miles). Cross here and turn right onto the Birch Trail for the loop's upstream return. This trail overlooks Toms Run, passing below Vowinckel Road. Explore an area of big hemlock and ancient birch, enjoying accents of hay-scented fern and rhododendron. The birch trees attain sizes seldom witnessed.

Where the trail approaches the road, pass through the small parking area that serves the Hemlock Trail, and descend a set of earthen steps. Reach the west bank of Toms Run and cross the bridge (1.8 miles). The 15-foot-wide tannin-colored water captivates onlookers. Retrace the Longfellow Trail to the trailhead, 3 miles. Or explore the alphabet spurs.

To hike the Joyce Kilmer Trail, retrace the first 0.5 mile of the Longfellow Trail, turning left onto the Indian Trail for 50 feet. Then turn right to begin the actual Joyce Kilmer Trail, which travels a higher contour through the Forest Cathedral Natural Area. Study junction signs to keep to the path. More of the spectacular big trees, snags, and snaking roots keep eyes darting. The leaves of beech and black cherry trees complement the evergreen boughs. Look for mosses and conches on stumps; some ghost trees show a twisted, silvered wood grain.

Find an easy-to-moderate ascent or rolling tour, with the trailbed gradually narrowing. As the trail explores the forest of upper Henry Run, briefly stroll a dense pine plantation (0.9 mile). At 1.1 miles, bear right for a slow descent to Indian Spring—a 6-inch gurgling spout housed in a boulder cleft (1.25 miles).

With a slight descent, meet the Bridle Trail at 1.75 miles. Given that the Joyce Kilmer Trail now leaves the old growth, many hikers choose to turn around here. Hikers who remain on the trail pass into second-growth hemlock forest, with many trees showing multiple trunks. A grassy floor and oaks complete the character change. Cross under a small power line to end at Cemetery Road (2 miles). Return as you came, or explore an intersecting trail.

For the Fire Tower Loop, start at the small trailhead turnout on the east side of Vowinckel Road/SR 1015, 0.3 mile north of the PA 36–SR 1015 junction. On the Hemlock Trail, ascend the west side of the road, passing through a dark, full forest of big hemlock, birch, and pine—the Seneca old growth. Hay-scented ferns color the slope toward a small drainage. Pursue it upstream, soon being diverted away from a washout.

At 0.5 mile, cross PA 36, to continue now on Deer Park Trail. The tornado of July 11, 1976, swept this area, culling trees, stealing evergreen crowns, and bringing light to the forest floor. The chaos and crash must have been thunderous. A tumbled tree near the trail gives a sense of perspective to the trees' standing height.

Normally the trail is well tracked, but a few places can cause you to stop and study. Clearings of hay-scented fern alternate with younger forest. Find mossy boulder jumbles and guiding orange arrows. At 1.3 miles, cross the Mohawk Trail, again passing stately trees. The trail is more meandering than the park map would indicate.

Rhododendron interweaves the forest, as oaks and maples join the ranks. Here meet the Seneca Trail (1.5 miles). A turn to the right adds a visit to Seneca Point and Cook Fire Tower; a left completes the loop.

Go right to add the vistas and explore the best floral realm in the park. As the Seneca Trail gently rolls along a plateau, view grand displays of rhododendron, later adding mountain laurel and dogwood for three floral seasons. At 1.75 miles, come to a junction: The left path travels a scenic arbor of rhododendron and rock. Where the path straight ahead meets a wide lane, follow it left. Both lead to the picnic area on Fire Tower Road, 2 miles. (Fire Tower Road—a one-way loop—can also be reached off PA 36, for an easier 0.5-mile round-trip hike to Seneca Point and Cook Fire Tower.)

From the upper end of the picnic area parking lot, ascend 200 feet to the plateau, reaching a fork. Hike 0.1 mile to the right to the natural sandstone outcrop of Seneca Point for a vegetation-framed view of the Clarion River. Footbridges span the widened rock fissures. Hike left 0.1 mile to reach the 70-foot fire tower. Views overlook the Clarion River and Toms Run and sweep the Allegheny forest beyond. Mount the tower at your own risk, heeding the posted ten-person limit. As the stairs spiral skyward, piece together a 360-degree view.

After pocketing both vistas, return to the picnic area (2.5 miles) and retrace your steps to the loop junction, 3 miles. Remain on the Seneca Trail, descending steeply away. Revisit the big hemlocks joined by rhododendron, snags, and stumps. At 3.4 miles, overlook the Clarion River, flowing at the

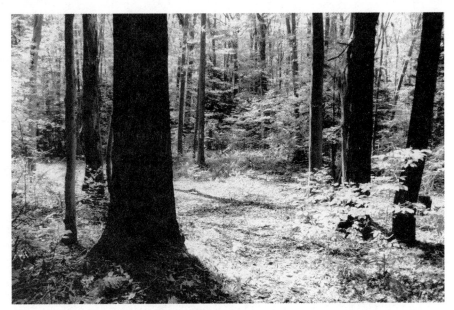
Ancient hemlock–pine forest, Cook Forest State Park.

foot of the slope. The roadway bustle below breaks the woodland spell. Watch your footing where the mineral springs have been captured in small pipes.

At 3.6 miles, the Seneca Trail bears left (upstream); a spur leads downstream 200 feet to a rocky shore and closer look at the popular canoe water. At the foot of the slope, cross the road to Cook Forest Park Office, where rest rooms are available. Round in front of the park office, go past the children's fishing pond, and ascend the loop road back toward PA 36, turning right onto the gated trail before the stop sign (3.8 miles). This is the Birch Trail, which parallels Toms Run upstream to trailhead parking on Vowinckel Road, 4.2 miles. Bluish green lichen tint the bark of the ancient birch trees.

The **Rhododendron Trail** begins off the end of the Indian Cabins Loop. Park near Cook Forest Park Office and hike past the children's fishing pond to reach this area of historic cabins. These cabins, built from salvaged American chestnut by the Civilian Conservation Corps, are on the National Register of Historic Places.

Hike the east shore of Toms Run upstream in a hemlock–birch forest, passing the swinging bridge at 0.1 mile. Mossy boulders dot the forest floor. At 0.25 mile, ascend into the Forest Cathedral Natural Area and the enchantment of the big trees. Showings of any kind of understory greenery, including rhododendron, are rare. Enjoy a straightforward tour, noting junction signs.

With the climb, younger hemlock and beech trees generate a midstory. Rocks and logs invite contemplation. At 0.9 mile, spy impressive twin beech trees, sadly marred by carved initials. The trail halts at dirt Forest Drive (1.5 miles); return as you came.

18 Little Drummer Historical Pathway

General description:	This interpretive trail within the Owl's Nest Ecosystem Management Demonstration Area of Allegheny National Forest allows hikers to choose between a short and a long loop.
General location:	Elk County, 8 miles west of Ridgway.
Special attractions:	Both managed and natural habitats of forest, shrub, wetland, and meadow; Cole Run Pond; historic lumber camp sites, railroads, and skid roads; varied and abundant wildlife; fall foliage.
Length:	1.1-mile loop or 3.1-mile loop.
Elevation:	Find a 50-foot elevation change.
Difficulty:	Easy (easy to moderate when wet).
Maps:	Little Drummer Historical Pathway brochure (secure from ranger district's local office before arriving).
Special concerns:	In late fall and spring, the trail serves hunters. Although it is best to avoid the area during hunting, at least wear fluorescent garments. Rubber-soled boots are recommended for the frequently wet long loop. No-trace, walk-in camping is allowed along the trail.
Season and hours:	Year-round, depending on winter snows.
For information:	Marienville Ranger District, Allegheny National Forest.

Key points:

0.0 Trailhead; hike north.
0.1 Post 2 (initial loop junction); turn left.
0.5 Post 9 (separation of short and long loops); turn left.
1.2 Post 27/pipeline corridor.
2.2 Trace dike along Cole Run Pond.
3.0 Loops end at post 2; hike left to trailhead.

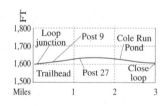

Finding the trailhead: From Ridgway, go 8 miles west on Spring Creek Road/Laurel Mill Road (Township 307). Trailhead parking for up to a dozen vehicles is on the north side of T 307. A toilet is at the trailhead.

The hike: Forty numbered interpretive stations mark this double-loop system exploring the managed ecosystems surrounding man-made Cole Run Pond, constructed for wildlife. The trail owes its name to the breeding grouse or "drummers" in the area and to the historical record of early logging that can still be detected here. Besides the numbered interpretive posts, off-white diamonds and arrows help guide hikers along the loops. The brochure explains the management practice, its intended benefits and beneficiaries, and the area's logging history. The brochure also identifies some of the wildlife at this designated watchable wildlife site.

Little Drummer Historical Pathway

Round the gate and hike north on a gravel path through woods of maple, black cherry, birch, oak, and witch hazel. At 0.1 mile (post 2), reach the initial loop junction and turn left onto a grassy bed to pursue the numbers in order. Areas of hardwood and planted spruce and openings of ferns or wildflowers and herbs shape vital habitats, providing cover and food for various wildlife species. At 0.25 mile, the trail rolls up a slight hill, and at 0.4 mile it crosses a grassy pipeline corridor.

At post 9 (0.5 mile), hikers must choose between the short loop, continuing toward interpretive station 10, and the long loop, proceeding left on a narrower lane toward post 18. If you opt for the short loop alone, you should at least detour to Cole Run Pond at post 10 before completing the tour. For this description, bear left to encircle the area of Cole Run Pond. In autumn, a mat of yellow, orange, and bronze leaves shapes a "yellow brick road." Mature hardwoods frame travel.

By 0.75 mile, a boardwalk advances the tour, traversing a meadow and young forest site. The pond is glimpsed off to the right. Pencil-point stumps near the pond hint at beaver. After the boardwalk curves away from the pond, a grassy bed continues travel. A tamarack stand, another stretch of boardwalk, highbush blueberry, and aspen keep feet moving.

At post 27 (1.2 miles), the trail turns right, following a pipeline corridor for a mild, direct-line ascent. At 1.3 miles, markers point hikers left into a hardwood realm. Club moss and ferns pierce the leaf mat. Keen-eyed hikers may detect the dark ball of a porcupine huddled close to a tamarack trunk; songbirds can also divert attention. The hike again slips through the pipeline corridor before turning right at post 29 (1.7 miles).

In openings, cotton grass is common and easily identified by the white balls it sports in fall. Whereas spruce alternated with the hardwoods at the start of the hike, tamarack is the interloper now. The woods take on a different look with their tall grass–bracken fern understory. Although Cole Run Pond is generally kept a mystery, when the trees lose their leaves hikers do gain glimpses.

Encounter benches and some bridging sections of boardwalk. At the bench at 2.2 miles, the trail drifts toward the pond to travel a man-made dike along its shore for unobstructed views. Cole Run Pond has a meadow shore and finger islands of grass, birdhouses, and ringing gray stumps and snags. Beaver ponds span left of the dike, their origin betrayed by lodges, muddy dams, and girdled trees. The beaver ponds have greater character than artificial Cole Run Pond, but each tosses back a pleasing reflection. Upon leaving the dike, cross a gravel spill to reach interpretive post 10 at 2.5 miles and turn left to complete the loop, following description numbers 10 through 17.

Cole Run Pond, Allegheny National Forest.

The trail passes at the edge of two habitats, hardwood forest and transitioning meadow, with pockets of aspen. Beyond, it returns to the spruce seen at the start of the hike. Travel is along the historic Tionesta Valley Railroad grade from the logging era. Muddy spots can record the tracks of deer. Complete the loop at 3 miles (post 2), and turn left to backtrack to the trailhead (3.1 miles).

19 Pine Tree Trail

General description:	This interpretive trail explores the 276-acre Pine Tree Trail Natural Area, with its old field-growth white pines.
General location:	Elk State Forest, 20 miles northeast of Weedville.
Special attractions:	Old field-growth white pines and rich and varied second-growth forest, the scenic forks of Hicks Run, wildlife, a bear-clawed tree, fall foliage, Hicks Run Camping Area.
Length:	2.7 miles round trip.
Elevation:	Find a 500-foot elevation change.
Difficulty:	Easy.
Maps:	Pine Tree Trail brochure (request from state forest office in Emporium before visiting).
Special concerns:	In late fall and spring, hunters may be in the area. A camping permit is required for overnight use of Hicks Run Camping Area (request an overnight permit from state forest office in Emporium before visiting).
Season and hours:	Spring through fall.
For information:	Elk State Forest.

Key points:

- 0.0   Western trailhead.
- 0.8   Loop junction; turn left.
- 1.5   Spur right to homestead ruins.
- 1.9   Close loop; descend to western trailhead.

Finding the trailhead: From the junction of Pennsylvania 255 and PA 555 in Weedville, head east on PA 555 for 17.8 miles, turning left onto gravel Hicks Run Road after crossing over Hicks Run east of the village of Dents Run. In 0.7 mile, pass a small ranger station on the left and continue another 1.5 miles to the junction of East and West Hicks Run Roads. Turn left onto West Hicks Run Road, crossing Hicks Run to reach the camping area and western trailhead in 0.1 mile. From the junction of East and West Hicks Run Roads, find the other marked trailheads left off East Hicks Run Road near the lower and upper bridges in 1.2 miles and 1.9 miles, respectively.

Pine Tree Trail

The hike: The Pine Tree Trail System consists of the access spurs arriving off East and West Hicks Run Roads and the loop atop the divide plateau that is isolated by the Hicks Run forks. Although not virgin pines, the site's old white pines date to the late 1800s, when the field and pasture were abandoned. The trail brochure is a good forest primer, pointing out dozens of species and explaining the various uses for each. Arrows and orange blazes guide hikers along the trail; the white numbers on red correspond to the brochure. This hike description starts off on West Hicks Run Road opposite the camping area.

From West Hicks Run Road, ascend the marked woods road, angling up-slope, overlooking West Fork Hicks Run and its parallel forest road. The trail traces the old wagon road used by the settler to access his summit homestead; evidence of the cabin can be seen along the loop. The angle of the grade allows for a comfortable ascent of the steep, treed slope. Squirrel, grouse, owl, and deer might be among the wildlife encounters. The tall high-canopy forest affords full shade. Woody grapevines twine up some tree trunks.

By 0.7 mile, hikers claim the upper slope, which is less steep. A hummocky moss dresses the trail's shoulders. Ahead, come to the blazed loop junction and turn left for a clockwise tour. Insects enliven a forest that is otherwise still. On the loop footpath, hikers must rely more on the blazes.

At 0.9 mile, reach the Juneberry, or shadbush (number 20 in the brochure), that reveals the claw marks from a bear that climbed after the tree's red berries. The scarring can be seen on several places on the trunk. After the trail dips through a spring-fed drainage that flows seasonally, top the plateau, passing signature tall, straight white pines. The aptly named hay-scented ferns cap the plateau.

Reach a T-junction at 1.3 miles. Here, the loop turns right; the path to the left leads to East Hicks Run Road and its namesake water in 1.5 miles, emerging near the south end of the upper bridge on East Hicks Road. For this hike, stay on the loop, coming to an arrow at 1.5 miles. This 150-foot spur heads right, leading to the homestead flat, its cabin ruins, and a root cellar depression, all being reclaimed by nature.

Resuming the loop, at 1.6 miles, reach a blazed junction where the interpretive numbers follow the access spur heading left. It descends 0.5 mile to East Hicks Run Road, emerging at the curve above the lower bridge. For hikers choosing to follow it, a 1.2-mile hike right on East Hicks Run Road then returns them to the camping area for a 3.3-mile loop.

For this hike, though, turn right to complete the loop and retrace the west access spur to the camping area, avoiding any road travel. Alert hikers may spy other signs of bear and can test their knowledge about trees. Close the loop at 1.9 miles and backtrack the grade downhill to the trailhead (2.7 miles).

20 Fred Woods Trail

General description:	This comfortable family trail swings a lasso across the summit plateau of Mason Hill. Pass through woods, fern meadow, and laurel-and-berry fields; explore rocky realms; and visit natural overlooks.
General location:	30 miles west of Renovo.
Special attractions:	Vistas; rocky slots, hollows, and overhangs; mountain laurel; wildlife sightings (seek elk in the old clear-cut at the center of the loop); fall foliage.
Length:	5 miles round trip.
Elevation:	Find minimal elevation change traveling the summit plateau, elevation 1,900 feet.
Difficulty:	Easy, with 0.5 mile of moderately difficult rocky footing.
Maps:	Fred Woods Trail map.
Special concerns:	In spring and late fall, hunting occurs. When climbing through the rocks, be alert for rattlesnakes.
Season and hours:	Spring through fall.
For information:	Elk State Forest.

Key points:

0.0   Mason Hill trailhead.
0.8   Loop junction; keep right.
1.7   Fork (hike option).
2.0   First vista; trail forks merge.
2.9   Final vista spur.
4.2   Close loop; backtrack
        to trailhead.

Finding the trailhead: From the junction of Pennsylvania 120 and PA 555 in Driftwood (28 miles west of Renovo; 18 miles south of Emporium), go west on PA 555 for 0.9 mile and turn right onto dirt Mason Hill Road. Although this road is passable for most conventional vehicles, expect some rough patches with rocks wearing through the road surface. Follow Mason Hill Road for 3.7 miles to find the marked trailhead on the left; there is parking for a handful of vehicles on the right. When wet, investigate the parking before pulling off the road.

The hike: This wide trail, which honors a forest foreman, starts in a stand of hemlock. Orange blazes mark the way, few at first, then becoming more regularly spaced. Maple, oak, and striped maple later contribute to the bordering woods. Cross a grassy swath of a logging road and, at 0.4 mile, traverse a fern field dotted by birch, maple, and hemlock. As the trail curves out of the meadow, spy a stone wall off to the left.

A scenic open forest of hardwoods with a grass–fern floor now hosts travel; low berry bushes flank the trail. The openness of the woods and gentle terrain allow hikers to scan a broad area for deer and other wildlife. A

Fred Woods Trail

spring can muddy the trail. At 0.8 mile, reach the loop junction. Keep right, remaining on the wide hiker lane for a counterclockwise tour. Soon after, the trail angles across an even wider grassy logging road. A congested younger woods follows.

At 1 mile, pass the first hemlock-shaded array of rocks as a footpath now advances the loop. Rock slabs and boxy outcrops become common forest additions. Ahead, bear left, passing through a broadened rock fissure. Some of the sandstone shows weathered, raised veins and peculiar ruffles, resembling features in a cave.

At 1.4 miles, enter an area of mountain laurel, finding dogwood and cucumber (a magnolia), which also blooms. Beyond lies a realm of rocks 12 to 20 feet high, with intriguing hollows, nooks, squeezes, and overhangs—a natural funhouse for children and the childlike. At 1.7 miles, hikers have the option of journeying among the rocks or skirting the perimeter for a more straightforward tour; the blazed paths again meet near the first vista, 2 miles.

Opting for the rocky spur, hikers explore a split-level narrow passage. There,

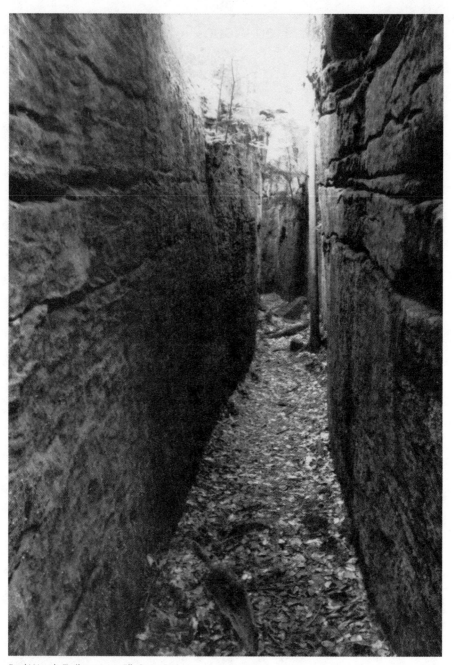

Fred Woods Trail outcrop, Elk State Forest.

view an intersecting fissure, venture beneath an overhang, and round a fallen rock, shaping a tight hiker stile. Hemlocks grow from the sheer wall, but a few carved initials mar the sandstone. Follow blazes.

After emerging from the next slot, bear left and descend cautiously into another assembly of rocks. A small hollow, 15 feet deep with a 3-foot-high ceiling, may invite the smallest party members to snoop inside. At the fork at 1.9 miles, go right to find the vista and the perimeter spur; a left continues the loop.

Turn right, soon reaching a flat outcrop for a natural overlook of the forested watershed of Bennett Branch Sinnemahoning Creek, the rural valley floor, and Miller Run across the way. From this vantage, hikers who took the rocky spur must backtrack; perimeter-spur hikers proceed straight. At 2.1 miles, all hikers bear right to complete the counterclockwise loop.

An open maple–oak woods next hosts travel. Enjoy berry bushes and dogwood before passing through a slot between 8-foot-tall outcrops and rounding right. At 2.4 miles, come upon an easy-to-miss fork. Snuggled in the rocks 100 feet to the right is a scenic framed view overlooking a curvature of Bennett Branch Sinnemahoning Creek. In early to mid-June, mountain laurel blooms enhance the image.

Resume the loop on a neatly narrow path traversing a field of berry and mountain laurel before graduating to woods. At 2.9 miles, a 30-foot spur to the right leads to the final vista in a small clearing with low berry bushes. Views encompass the ridges shaping Bennett Branch Sinnemahoning Creek. A silvered snag and weathered pines may add to the presentation. Round the nose of the ridge, keeping toward the edge of the plateau, and then at 3.5 miles drift away to close the loop.

For the next 0.5 mile, encounter fewer of the big rocks but more rocks underfoot; be careful when the rocks are wet or leaf-covered. Red efts may wiggle past your boots. The multitrunked maples above a sea of ferns provide a soothing backdrop as the loop draws to a close at 4.2 miles. Retrace the first 0.8 mile to the trailhead.

21 S. B. Elliott State Park

Overview

Similar to much of Pennsylvania, climax pine and hemlock once clad this quiet 318-acre state park cradled in Moshannon State Forest. Today, find upland hardwoods and mature planted pines. At the end of the logging era in the 1920s, this site held a tree nursery promoted by the conservationist legislator Simon B. Elliott. To this day, locals refer to the site as "the nursery." A system of lightly traveled hiking trails wanders the park's shady woods, picturesque meadows, and riparian environments.

General description:	A relaxing, most-of-the-day circuitous hike strings together several of the park's named trails, exploring the best the park has to offer.
General location:	9 miles north of Clearfield.
Special attractions:	Artificial pond, sparkling runs hosting native brook trout, mixed forest, mountain laurel, diverse ferns, blueberry fields, wildlife sightings, solitude.
Length:	Old Horse–Doctor's Fork–Rattlesnake Trail Circuit, 7.5 miles round trip, with opportunities to lengthen or vary.
Elevation:	Find a 420-foot elevation change.
Difficulty:	Moderate.
Maps:	Park map and S. B. Elliott State Park Hiking Trails brochure.
Special concerns:	Encounter soggy sites and areas of brushing vegetation. Expect brief trail segments to go unmarked. During hunting seasons, wear bright colors. Although seldom seen, timber rattlesnakes do find habitat here.
Season and hours:	Spring through fall for hiking.
For information:	S. B. Elliott State Park.

Key points:

0.0   Start near campsite 22; descend Old Horse Trail.
0.4   Pond.
1.6   Loop junction; go right.
2.0   North Fork Trail.
2.8   Doctor's Fork Trail.
4.7   Rattlesnake Trail.
6.3   Old Horse Trail.
7.0   Complete loop; return via cabin area.
7.5   End at campground.

S. B. Elliott State Park

Finding the trailhead: From Interstate 80, take exit 18 and go north on Pennsylvania 153 for 1.1 miles. At the sign for the park and Moshannon State Forest District Office, turn east (right) onto Fourmile Road, and quickly bear right onto Old Route 153. Reach the park in 0.8 mile.

The hike: Start the Old Horse–Doctor's Fork–Rattlesnake Trail Circuit next to site 22 in the state park campground. A sign and blue diamond signal the way. On the Old Horse Trail, slowly descend in a tall maple–oak woods richly interwoven with mountain laurel—an enchanting setting during the mid- to late-June bloom. Birdsongs ride the breeze, pushing aside the hum from I–80. After you cross a faint road grade, impressive stumps recall the bygone forest.

At 0.3 mile, bear left for the marked tour; a well-tracked path journeys right. In another 100 feet, again bear left to skirt a pine plantation on a wide grassy lane. Next, watch for trail markers showing the way through the laurel–blueberry meadow, and view the park's small levee-rimmed pond and its still-water reflections.

Cross a footbridge over the gurgling inlet brook and bear left near a meadow-isolated boulder. The trail pursues the inlet upstream, meandering through open woodland, mixed-fern meadows, and a stump-dotted berry patch.

Deer, fox, or turkey may divert attention. Continue crisscrossing the inlet, following trail posts through the meadow. Dew-soaked vegetation can dampen pants, and the midday sun can make things steamy. Stones help elevate feet in soggy sites. A pallet boardwalk delivers hikers from the meadow.

Here, light penetrates the forest, feeding waist-high fern and adding dogwood to the mix. After the inlet crossing at 0.9 mile, bear right upstream and, at 1.1 miles, bear left onto a grassy lane, reaching a dead-end dirt road and trail post. Hike left on the road to cross over paved, lightly used Kennedy Road (1.2 miles). A wide grassy lane then continues the tour; proceed forward, where a secondary lane curves uphill to the right. The trail goes unmarked until the four-way intersection at 1.6 miles; just keep to the lane.

At 1.6 miles is the loop junction: Go right on the Old Sinnemahoning Trail for a counterclockwise tour. Orange circle paint blazes mark this trail. Ascend a soft grassy lane draped by maple and oak, coming to a junction and hiker's choice at 2 miles. To the right, the Old Sinnemahoning Trail leads to the South Fork Trail for a longer loop, passing through a regenerating burn. For this tour, go left onto the North Fork Trail, noted for its mountain laurel displays. The tour remains similarly blazed with orange circles.

The footpath descends and rolls in more of the beautiful woods and captivating laurel. Nearby, the North Fork, a disorganized stream, largely goes unrecognized. At 2.8 miles, a 6-foot-tall wooden post marks the next junction. Here, the South Fork Trail arrives on the right; follow the Doctor's Fork Trail straight ahead. Crows may chastise an owl from its roost; woodpeckers tap out telegrams. Still the mountain laurel, blueberries, and varied ferns contribute to travel.

At 3 miles, bear right, briefly traversing a disturbed area of old logging grades. The scenic water of Doctor's Fork soon restores the wilderness spell, shaded by birch, beech, and witch hazel. Tulip poplar and black cherry grow farther back from the stream. The trail seldom strays more than 100 feet from the fork; logs and rocks create scenic cascades.

After passing through a meadow opening, cross a small side water, reaching a junction on the shore of Lick Run (4.3 miles) just upstream from its confluence with Doctor's Fork. The loop now pursues this attractive run upstream on the Lick Run Trail before drifting away at 4.6 miles.

At 4.75 miles, follow the Rattlesnake Trail left. For the adventuresome, Lick Run Trail continues upstream, traveling a rockier trailbed and passing tempting berry patches before reaching the headwater springs in another 1.25 miles.

The Rattlesnake Trail serves up a steady, moderate climb angling uphill. Initially, some large boulders punctuate the drainage-influenced forest. By 5 miles, find only oak, maple, tulip poplar, dogwood, and chestnut oak, with a mountain laurel midstory.

At the top of the slope, emerge at a small clearing and bear right onto a grassy gas well road. The aisle, at first open, later affords partial to full shade. Sassafras and cucumber magnolia join the ranks, but the laurel departs. Meet the Old Horse Trail at 6.3 miles and turn left. To the right, the Central Pennsylvania Lumber Company Trail heads north 7 miles to Parker Dam State Park.

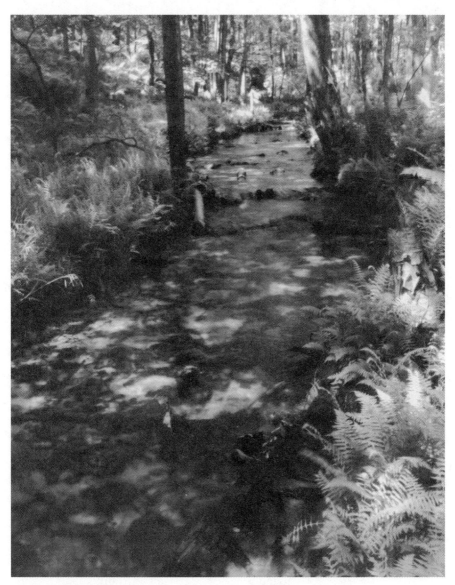

Doctor's Fork, S. B. Elliott State Park.

The Old Horse Trail extends a narrower grassy lane through similar woods, but goes unmarked. Avoid a second forest lane to the right; it returns to the day-use area at an open field. Continue straight past the park cabins to close the loop back at the 1.6-mile junction (7 miles).

From here, hikers may retrace the first 1.6 miles to the campground. Or turn right onto the Old Sinnemahoning Trail, cross over Cabin Loop Road, and bear right upon meeting this road a second time at 7.2 miles. Follow the road 0.1 mile to the gate, ignoring a cabin spur to the right. Bear left for the park road or cross through the day-use area to end the hike at 7.5 miles.

Pocono Mountains Region

This northeast region spans between the Alleghenies and the Delaware River and features a broad, flat, mountainous plateau sliced by deep-cut stream and river valleys. The Pocono landscape is one of flat horizons, its scenery one of beauty. Enjoy some of the state's finest waterfalls, large lakes and reservoirs, wetlands, and more of the state's signature woods. Despite the Poconos being a longtime favorite playground for residents of the Mid-Atlantic states, hikers can still stroll to quiet corners and bask in the area's treasures.

22 Worlds End State Park

Overview
In the plateau country of Sullivan Highlands in Wyoming State Forest, this 780-acre state park enfolds an S-bend on Loyalsock Creek. The park's name can be traced to the area's earliest road, which ran parallel to the creek, hugging the steep canyon slope. At the point where the creek hooks sharply back on itself, roadway travelers thought it spelled the "end of the world" for them.

Today, hikers find splendid discovery with ledge vistas, mazes of boxy boulders, sparkling runs, picturesque Loyalsock Creek, waterfalls, and tranquil woods. The long-distance Loyalsock Trail passes through the park, calling the more adventurous to don their backpacks.

General description:	The two selected day hikes travel to falls and vistas, incorporating some of the park's fine short trails and offering a peek at the 59-mile Loyalsock Trail.
General location:	7 miles northwest of Laporte; 2 miles south of the village of Forksville.
Special attractions:	Vistas, scenic waterways, waterfalls and cascades, rock features, wildlife sightings, fall foliage.
Length:	Double Run Nature Trail–Link Trail Hike, 4.1 miles round trip; Loyalsock Trail to Alpine Falls, 9.1 miles round trip.
Elevation:	Double Run Nature Trail–Link Trail Hike shows a 600-foot elevation change; the Loyalsock Trail to Alpine Falls has an 800-foot elevation change.
Difficulty:	Both are moderate.
Maps:	State park brochure.
Special concerns:	Expect some rocky, uneven footing along Double Run. Camping permits are required for the Loyalsock Trail; contact Wyoming State Forest. Overnight backpackers wishing to leave their vehicles at the state park must first register with the park office and then park near the office.
Season and hours:	Spring through fall for hiking.
For information:	Worlds End State Park.

Worlds End State Park

Key points:

Double Run Nature Trail–Link Trail Hike:

0.0 Double Run Trailhead.
0.7 Cottonwood Falls.
1.8 Mineral Springs Road.
2.4 Canyon Vista.
2.5 Rock Garden; descend to trailhead (4.1 miles).

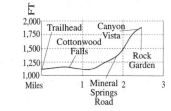

Loyalsock Trail to Alpine Falls:

0.0 High Rock–Butternut Trailhead.
0.7 High Rock Vista.
1.6 Angle across Loyalsock Road.
3.0 Cross back over Loyalsock Road.
4.1 Ken's Window.
4.5 Alpine Falls; backtrack to trailhead.

Finding the trailhead: From the intersection of U.S. Highway 220 and Pennsylvania 154 (just north of Laporte, 8.5 miles south of Dushore), travel north on PA 154, reaching the turnoff for the campground in 6.2 miles, Double Run Nature Trail in 6.7 miles, and the turnoff for the park office and High Rock/Loyalsock Trailhead in 7.1 miles.

The hikes: The **Double Run Nature Trail** offers a fun streamside tour and serves as a springboard to three park destinations: Cottonwood Falls, Canyon Vista, and the Rock Garden. Visit any one or choose all three.

From the trailhead parking area off PA 154, hike south (upstream) on the green-on-white-blazed trail, touring a wooded flat removed from Double Run. Where the trail pinches to the east bank of Double Run, find a charming cascade spilling through a broken bedrock ledge. Continue along the stair-stepped stream.

At the bridge at 0.25 mile, reach the Link Trail (red cross on yellow disk) and a decision point. For Canyon Vista and the Rock Garden, hike the Link Trail left. To visit Cottonwood Falls, proceed across the bridge.

For the falls tour, cross this bridge and quickly after cross a bridge over West Branch Double Run. Now proceed upstream, tracking the green blazes of the nature trail, as the Link Trail turns downstream. Pass a pretty chute and Water Beech Pool, where a 6-foot cascade spills into a tannin-steeped natural pool ringed by low ledges.

The trail continues to hug the creek. Where it forks, find both a poolside and an overlook view of Cottonwood Falls (0.7 mile). This lacy, tiered veil graces a half-moon broken ledge; to its left, view a tearful falls in a mossy hollow. Return as you came for a 1.4-mile round trip, or backtrack (0.45 mile) to the Double Run bridge, crossing to ascend the Link Trail to the vista and rocks.

For the full 4.1-mile hike, follow the Link Trail upstream from the bridge, passing the Loyalsock Trail (red dash on yellow). The hike's trailbed appears to have been an old cart path. A blazed cross-country trek then takes the baton. Where the trail travels at water level, be careful on the wet rock. The stream's rippled sandstone and broken ledges shape a pretty flow. Jack-in-the-pulpit and fern-capped rocks accent the way. With one last look at a cascade, hikers switchback uphill to cross gravel Mineral Springs Road (1.8 miles).

Rocky footing follows, as the trail weaves above the road. A natural cliff overhang foreshadows the rock garden yet to come. Maple, black cherry, and ash replace the hemlock and birch of Double Run drainage. At 2 miles, the blue-blazed Canyon Vista Trail arrives on the left to share the remaining climb. Hemlock and beech dress the upper slope, as the trail angles to the ridgetop vista at 2.4 miles.

From this railed viewing site, peer across a steep shrub slope to the folding even-height ridges shaping the Loyalsock drainage. Turn right, ascending away from Canyon Vista and its small picnic area to enter the Rock Garden in 0.1 mile. Here, find a gallery of boxy 10-foot-tall outcrops, where the broadened frost-formed fissures shape natural passages. When ready, retrace the Link Trail and the east-shore part of the Double Run Nature Trail, returning to the trailhead at 4.1 miles.

For the sampling of the acclaimed **Loyalsock Trail,** start at the High Rock–Butternut Trailhead (on the left after crossing the park's cabin bridge over Loyalsock Creek, 0.2 mile east of the park office). With limited day-use parking at the trailhead and at the west end of the bridge, hikers may need to park near the park office and hike to this trailhead, following the signature Loyalsock Trail blaze: red dash on yellow. All overnight parking is next to the park office.

Take the Loyalsock/High Rock Trail left. To its right is the start of the Butternut Trail (brick-colored blaze). Ascend from Loyalsock Creek, passing beneath a leafy umbrella pierced by hemlock boughs. Beech, black cherry, maple, ash, and hornbeam contribute to the deciduous array. Besides the Loyalsock Trail blazes, the yellow disks of the park's High Rock Trail point the way.

Where the trail dips to cross High Rock Run, rough secondary paths descend 100 feet along either shore for a view of a downstream falls; the west shore holds the better vantage. The 30-foot falls spills from an overhang and washes over a canted outcrop slope. It is a genuine falls during times of high water. In low water, its watery glaze brings out the color of the rock.

Upon crossing the run, the blazed trail enters a more intense climb, stair-stepping and switchbacking up the rugged natural rock slope. A few flowering cucumber magnolia add to the forest. Atop a ledge shoulder, the blazed route switchbacks right before rolling to High Rock Vista at 0.7 mile. A wooden rail signals the viewpoint.

Here, overlook a chestnut-oak-clad slope to the bending Loyalsock Creek drainage and park below. Autumn colors particularly recommend the destination. A few mountain laurel decorate the vantage in mid-June. Vultures sometimes soar the thermals; deer may pause for a curious look.

From the vista, continue on the Loyalsock Trail, which heads right on a scenic, faint road grade; the High Rock Trail proceeds straight, eventually coming out on PA 154. Along the lower ledge of a boulder jumble, spy fern and rock tripe lichen. Oaks dominate the upper canopy; where hemlocks cluster, find richer shade. Nettle, violet, jewelweed, and berry bushes favor the marshy side drainages, as do maple, beech, and striped maple. After 1.3 miles, overlook High Rock Run.

At 1.6 miles, angle across Loyalsock Road to tour east along the ridge; a large wooden sign indicates a partnership of landholders. Stay on the well-blazed route, passing High Rock Spur, a gated jeep trail heading left. Enjoy a relaxing stretch through mixed, sometimes open woods. Gray squirrel, woodpecker, and porcupine may add to travel. At 2.1 miles, reach a T-junction at a woods road; turn right, following the blazes to cross back over Loyalsock Road, 3 miles.

Descend via foot trail through open, fern-dressed woods, soon skirting a snag-riddled, shrub-reclaimed beaver pond. Meander from hemlock stand to deciduous woods. At 3.3 miles, cross Big Run via stones. An abandoned timber railroad grade next advances the trail; a thin traveled footpath parts the lush knee-high greenery. At 4.1 miles, reach the "50-mile" marker for the Loyalsock Trail and Ken's Window, a clean aisle look out the Big Run drainage.

The blazed route then descends through choked forest to follow another railroad grade upstream along Tom's Run. At 4.5 miles, meet the falls spur marked by a red cross on yellow disk. Here, forsake the Loyalsock Trail to

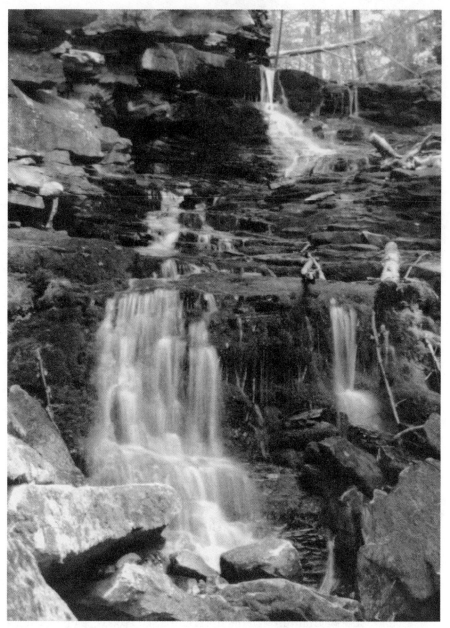

Alpine Falls, Wyoming State Forest.

follow the spur, crossing Tom's Run and hiking upstream 250 feet to view Alpine Falls. The generally whispering falls courses over platy sandstone ledges, spilling in tiers. A fractured cliff shapes its west wall, a steep forested slope the east wall. A clearwater pool catches its splash. Return as you came or explore more of the saga of the Loyalsock Trail.

23 Shuman Point Natural Area Hiking Trail

General description:	Exploring a Pennsylvania Power and Light (PP&L) natural area, this circuit travels a wooded peninsula on Lake Wallenpaupack, periodically reaching shore for lake views and relaxation.
General location:	3 miles southwest of Hawley.
Special attractions:	Lake access, fishing, mixed forest, colorful mushrooms, wildlife sightings, fall foliage.
Length:	3.5-mile loop.
Elevation:	Find a 100-foot elevation change.
Difficulty:	Easy.
Maps:	Shuman Point Natural Area and Beech House Creek Wildlife Refuge trail map (available at PP&L Visitor Center and at the trailhead).
Special concerns:	No camping, campfires, or picnicking. Hunting occurs in spring and late fall.
Season and hours:	Spring through fall for hiking, dawn to dusk. No parking after 9:00 P.M.
For information:	Lake Wallenpaupack, Pennsylvania Power and Light Company.

Key points:

- 0.0 Pennsylvania 590 trailhead; hike counterclockwise.
- 0.2 Top of a rise.
- 1.1 First Lake Wallenpaupack access.
- 2.0 Avoid cut-across trail.
- 3.5 End loop at parking.

Finding the trailhead: From Interstate 84, take exit 7 and go north on PA 390 and PA 507, following signs for Lake Wallenpaupack. In 6.7 miles, continue north, now on U.S. Highway 6 West. In another 1.1 mile, find the visitor center on the left. Go 0.3 mile more and turn left (west) onto PA 590 to reach the marked trailhead and parking area in 2.1 miles.

The hike: This trail explores an undeveloped 250-acre wooded natural area on the northern shore of Lake Wallenpaupack. Stone walls on Shuman Point hint at the land's onetime use as farmland. The lake site holds historical interest—it was once owned by William Penn and later the property of James Wilson, a signer of the Declaration of Independence.

Built in 1926, the 5,700-acre man-made lake has 52 miles of shoreline. It captures the waters of Wallenpaupack Creek; *Wallenpaupack* is the Leni-Lenape (Delaware) Indian word for "stream of swift and slow water."

From the kiosk at the west end of the parking area, round the boulder barricade and quickly veer left uphill on a blue-blazed foot trail for a counterclockwise peninsula tour. Find a steady, moderate gradient and a rock-studded

Shuman Point Natural Area Hiking Trail

but good trail. Maple, black cherry, and oak clad the lower slope, with huckleberry, sarsaparilla, chestnut, oak shoots, and witch hazel filling out the woods.

At 0.25 mile, top the rise in a stand of white pine. Mats of moss and reindeer lichen add interest to the forest. The trail then descends through a low-canopy oak woods. Deer, turkey, bear, and eft may number among the wildlife sightings. Colorful mushrooms or the colorless Indian pipe may dot the forest floor. Winds enliven the canopy.

At 0.8 mile, avoid a spur heading right. As the trail flattens, glimpse the lake glare beyond the young woods. At 1.1 miles, find the first 70-foot spur to shore, as the loop arcs left. This spur leads to a gravelly beach overlooking a large cove on Lake Wallenpaupack. Willow and birch frame the shore, while a large treed island and ring of even-height Pocono Mountain ridges contribute to the lake view.

Resume the counterclockwise hike, staying with the blazes. At 1.25 miles, access a half-circle beach with washed reddish gravels and flat-topped outcrops. The smooth seating invites sunning or lake admiration. The lake view here looks out at the wooded points that pinch together, shaping a gateway to the distant lake waters. Kingfisher and heron are common sightings. A few dogwoods decorate shore. The loop then continues just removed from

Rock wall, Shuman Point Natural Area.

the lake edge, rolling up and away at 1.7 miles. Young maples alter the forest character.

Encounter fragments of stone wall, some more defined than others, coming to a blazed fork (2 miles). Bear right for the full loop; the path straight ahead is a cut-across for shortening the hike. At an intersection of the stone walls, take a moment to study the careful balance of the flat plates and round boulders. White pines again join the forest ranks.

The trail next approaches rim ledges but swings away, descending back to the lake at 2.4 miles. Here, a 40-foot spur accesses a lake view that spans the blue waters to the dam. Continue the loop, passing trees of greater diameter, with the cut-across returning on the left. Rocky patches briefly mark travel. Where the loop arcs left at 2.75 miles, avoid a spur to a tiny private dock.

At the junctions at 3.1 and 3.3 miles, continue to bear left for the loop, strolling a scenic lane. Pass two especially noteworthy white pines (one with a triple trunk) before emerging on the east side of the parking area (3.5 miles).

24 Ricketts Glen State Park

Overview

This 13,050-acre state park is a shining prize of national merit, drawing visitors with its natural beauty and premier outdoor recreation. Although approved for national park status in the 1930s, the advent of World War II shelved its opening. The park joined the Pennsylvania state park system in 1942.

The Glens Natural Area—the park's sterling heart—won national natural landmark distinction in 1969. In the shady glens of the Kitchen Creek drainage, discover twenty-two named waterfalls, old-growth trees exceeding 500 years in age and displaying diameters of 5 feet, shale cliffs, a boulder tunnel, chance wildlife encounters, and a superb network of trails by which to admire it all.

General description: A lollipop-shaped tour explores The Glens Natural Area, joining several named trails along Kitchen Creek drainage. The hike offers close-up views of the named and unnamed waterfall features. A short hike at the southern extreme of the natural area rounds up the final named falls.

General location: 25 miles west of Wilkes-Barre.

Special attractions: A bombardment of exciting waterfall images, captivating forest, wildflowers, fall foliage.

Length: The Glens Natural Area Hike, 7.4 miles round trip; Adams Falls Hike, 0.2 mile round trip.

Elevation: For The Glens Natural Area Hike, find a 1,250-foot elevation change. For Adams Falls Hike, the elevation change is minimal.

Difficulty: The Glens Natural Area Hike, moderate; Adams Falls Hike, easy.

Maps: State park brochure.

Special concerns: Expect muddy and rock-studded stretches, rock stairs, and some awkward stepping along the shale canyonsides at the falls; boots are strongly recommended. Due to the popularity of the trail, midweek and off-season visits allow for more leisurely hikes and a full appreciation of the falls and their setting. Hikers planning to walk the upper falls loop alone should know that the upper trailhead parking lot fills rapidly in summer, requiring hikers to park near the park office and walk the dirt roadway to the trail's start.

Season and hours: Spring through fall, daylight hours.

For information: Ricketts Glen State Park.

Ricketts Glen State Park

To Dushore

Park road

0   0.5   1

Miles

Park office

Midway Crevasse

Onondaga Falls

F. L. Ricketts Falls

Mohawk Falls

Oneida Falls

Cayuga Falls

Ganoga Falls

Seneca Falls

Shawnee Falls

Huron Falls

Glen Leigh

Ozone Falls

R. B. Ricketts Falls

Delaware Falls

Ganoga Glen

B. Reynolds Falls

Mohican Falls

Wyandot Falls

Conestoga Falls

Waters Meet

Erie Falls

Tuscarora Falls

Harrison Wright Falls

Sheldon Reynolds Falls

Murray Reynolds Falls

487

N

Kitchen Creek

Ricketts Glen

To Dallas

118

To Hughesville

To Dallas

Adams Falls

Red Rock

Key points:

The Glens Natural Area Hike:
- 0.0 Lower trailhead (north side of highway).
- 1.4 Murray Reynolds Falls.
- 1.8 Waters Meet (loop junction); cross bridge.
- 2.8 Highland Trail.
- 3.5 Midway Crevasse.
- 4.1 Ganoga Glen Trail.
- 5.0 Ganoga Falls.
- 5.6 Close loop at Waters Meet; backtrack to trailhead.

Adams Falls Hike:
- 0.0 Lower trailhead (south side of highway).
- 0.1 Adams Falls overlook; backtrack.

Finding the trailhead:

From the junction of Pennsylvania 309 and PA 415 in Dallas, go north on PA 415 for 2.2 miles and turn west onto PA 118. Remain on PA 118 for 16.5 miles, reaching THE GLEN ENTRANCE (lower trailhead), with trail parking on both sides of the highway.

For the upper trailhead, from the junction of PA 118 and PA 487 in Red Rock (1.5 miles west of the PA 118 trailhead), go north on PA 487 for 3.5 miles and turn right for the Lake Jean Area. Go 0.3 mile, turn right onto the dirt access road just past the Lake Rose Park Office, and follow the dirt road for 0.6 mile to the marked falls trailhead.

The hikes: The Glens Natural Area Hike strings together the Kitchen Creek, Glen Leigh, Highland, and Ganoga Glen Trails. From the PA 118 trailhead, follow the Kitchen Creek Trail north (upstream) along the west bank of Kitchen Creek. A crosswalk accesses the trail from the southern parking lot; a bridge accesses the trail from the northern lot.

The wide, well-traveled trail travels the broad canyon bottom, overlooking the tea-colored clearwater and its rocky bed. Overhead tower big hemlock, birch, and ancient snags, with an interweaving of maple and ash. Nettle look-alikes, ferns, and sarsaparillas brush green to the floodplain.

Footbridges span Kitchen Creek at 0.2 and 0.9 mile, with a third bridge spanning a side water at 0.6 mile. Upon return to the west shore at 0.9 mile, look for the trail to drift apart from the creek as the canyon gains definition. At 1.4 miles, arrive near the top of 16-foot Murray Reynolds Falls, where it spills through a rocky cleft. The rounded rock at the head of the falls forces the water to spout. The whorled bedrock likewise adds visual interest.

Just upstream beckons two-tiered Sheldon Reynolds Falls; enjoy views from base, side, and top. Next comes the graceful shower of 27-foot Harrison Wright Falls spanning the breadth of the creek ledge, but Kitchen Creek deserves acclaim even in its gentler moments. Stairs now ascend to the loop junction at Waters Meet (1.8 miles).

Cross the West Branch bridge for a counterclockwise tour of the upper canyon, now on the Glen Leigh Trail. Natural rock steps lead past engaging Wyandot Falls, tucked in its dark hollow. The trail then crosses East Branch Kitchen Creek between Wyandot Falls and the 40-foot B. Reynolds Falls, which shows a rubble base and west-shore overhang. Big birch trees rise among the hemlocks, with jewelweed and witch hazel gracing the creek-hugging trail.

At 2 miles, cross the footbridge below R. B. Ricketts Falls. Complemented by a cascading and weeping side drainage, this falls serves up a lovely union of water, rock, and greenery. More deciduous trees shade the trail as hikers pursue the artful, twisting East Branch upstream. Next, find Ozone Falls in its corner.

Footbridges continue to crisscross the East Branch, presenting the waterfall gallery. Platy cliffs contribute to viewing. Ahead, the spiral-and-tiered waters of 41-foot Huron Falls mark off distance. Upstream, view a cliff grotto as stairs ascend toward Shawnee, F. L. Ricketts, and Onondaga Falls. Later, old-growth trees and impressive snags command attention.

At the trail junction at 2.8 miles, go left onto the Highland Trail to continue the falls loop. The trail upstream leads to the cabins area.

The Highland Trail journeys west to meet West Branch Kitchen Creek. Stroll a relaxing woodland of beech, birch, black cherry, and striped maple, finding a mild uphill grade. In places, flat stones ease the crossing of muddy spots; elsewhere, hikers must slog through. Despite the busy hiker thoroughfare, bears have been sighted prowling in the ferns.

Pass a split-rock ledge, coming to a narrow passage (Midway Crevasse) leading through the jumbled sandstone blocks. The Highland Trail then remains flat and shady. Where it meets Ganoga Glen Trail at 4.1 miles, bear left. To the right lies the upper trailhead (0.1 mile).

With the descent, the sound of the West Branch urges hikers to pick up their stride for the next parade of falls. Short, steep grades punctuate travel. At 4.2 miles, bear right per a sign and, soon after, cross a footbridge. At the next junction, a left continues the Ganoga Glen Trail and natural area tour; to the right is the Old Beaver Dam Road Trail.

Downstream from the junction, find the first West Branch cascade/waterfall series—the 37-foot Mohawk Falls. A steep set of rock steps descend alongside its lacy veil, ledge cascade, and skirt of skipping water. A classic beauty, Oneida Falls continues the watery story.

The side-by-side streamers of Cayuga Falls precede the glen's tallest falls, the 94-foot Ganoga Falls, which reveals a different persona, depending on angle. Look for a spur to the left leading to the base of the falls for a full-length view. This stately waterfalls generates its own breeze and nurtures a wall of greenery with its spray.

The countdown continues with Seneca, Delaware, and Mohican Falls. With the beautiful zigzagging waters, it is difficult to tell where one falls ends and

Mohawk Falls, Ricketts Glen State Park.

the next begins. Side streams likewise arrive in cascades. The 17-foot Conestoga Falls, the billowing lace of 47-foot Tuscarora Falls, and elegant Erie Falls end the exciting tale before the loop closes at Waters Meet, 5.6 miles.

From here, backtrack downstream along the Kitchen Creek Trail, renewing acquaintance with the first three waterfalls and the beauty of Kitchen Creek. End at 7.4 miles.

For the **Adams Falls Hike,** descend on the path at the north end of the southern trailhead parking area off PA 118, hiking toward Kitchen Creek. In 0.1 mile, overlook 36-foot Adams Falls, spilling snowy white through a recessed drop where the cliffs fold together. The keyhole look engages. By traveling atop the rocky vantage, view the swirling chute that escapes the upper plunge pool as well as potholes fed by the chute. The chasm sets this falls apart from the upstream ones.

25 Bruce Lake Loop

General description: This hike follows a maintenance road and a foot trail, touring 2,845-acre Bruce Lake Natural Area, crossing the isthmus of Egypt Meadow Lake and encircling Bruce Lake.

General location: 25 miles east of Scranton.

Special attractions: Bruce and Egypt Meadow Lakes; swamps; flowering rhododendron, mountain laurel, and sheep laurel; blueberries; wildlife sightings; fall foliage.

Length: 6.8 miles round trip.

Elevation: The trail has less than a 100-foot elevation change, traveling between 1,700 and 1,800 feet in elevation.

Difficulty: Easy.

Maps: Delaware State Forest; Promised Land State Park.

Special concerns: There is no camping, but visitors may hunt or fish in season, with valid licenses. Hikers, take precautions during hunting seasons. Carry insect repellent and expect areas of brushing vegetation. Pass softly and practice no-trace wilderness ethics.

Season and hours: Spring through fall for hiking, daylight hours.

For information: Delaware State Forest.

Key points:

0.0 Bruce Lake Trailhead.
0.9 Egypt Meadow Lake.
2.1 Loop junction; keep to road.
2.5 Turn right onto Bruce Lake Trail.
3.7 Cross outlet bridge to West Branch Trail.
4.7 Close loop; backtrack west to trailhead.

Finding the trailhead: From Interstate 84, take exit 7 for Promised Land State Park and go south on Pennsylvania 390. In 1.5 miles, find marked trailhead parking on the left.

The hike: Round the stone pillar and entry gate, traveling closed, mildly rolling **Bruce Lake Road** (a woods road trail) east into Bruce Lake Natural Area. An occasional blue blaze marks the way.

Logged of its towering pine and hemlock in the late nineteenth century, then ravaged by fire, the natural area now sports a low-canopy hardwood cloak. Pass amid maple, oak, and hickory, with a complement of hemlock, laurel, a handful of rhododendron, fern, sassafras, and sarsaparilla. A few spruce appear where the trail approaches the southern edge of snag-riddled, shrubby Panther Swamp. Despite the wooded fullness at the trail's shoulder, the overhead cathedral remains open.

At 0.4 mile, stay on Bruce Lake Road; to the right is the Brown Trail, a footpath allowing a longer loop option. Before long, cross the bridge over

Bruce Lake Loop

the outlet of Panther Swamp to find the next trail junction. Here, the Panther Swamp Trail heads north to Egypt Meadow Road (another hiker avenue into the natural area). Again stay on Bruce Lake Road. By 0.75 mile, the woods to your right take on a wetland character.

At 0.9 mile, reach the picturesque mirror-dark waters of Egypt Meadow Lake; a secondary path travels north along its west shore. Built by the Civilian Conservation Corps in 1935, Egypt Meadow Lake measures forty-eight acres, with open waters spanning north of the isthmus, vegetated waters grading south to hundred-acre Balsam Swamp. A narrow neck and bridge shape the lake isthmus. Water lilies and reflection rocks add to northern lake views; ducks, frogs, and herons animate the southern lake.

As Bruce Lake Road gradually ascends away from Egypt Meadow Lake, find the trees more draping and occasionally spy rock outcrops and glacial rock deposits. At 2.1 miles, keep to Bruce Lake Road, hiking past the West Branch Trail (the loop's close) on the right.

Unmarked spurs now lead to the Bruce Lake shore. Spring-fed, fifty-six-acre Bruce Lake occupies a glacier-melt depression or kettle. More of the white-blooming lilies adorn this broad natural lake, with highbush blueberry and mountain laurel adding flourish to its rim. The flat Pocono Plateau sculpts a level skyline of trees. Additional spurs to the lakeshore arrive at attractive grassy flats.

At 2.5 miles, the roadway narrows and bends right, signaling the start of the Bruce Lake Trail, although no sign indicates it as such. Turn right for a clockwise perimeter tour of Bruce Lake, passing through an oak–blueberry complex. More secondary trails branch away to the lake glare, with the last one occurring at 2.7 miles, near an old pump.

Mountain and sheep laurel now intermingle with the low- and highbush blueberry, squeezing the trail to boot width. Despite the woods stealing lake views, the berry walk engages, especially when the bushes hang heavy with fruit. Glimpse the marsh and open water at the southern extent of Bruce Lake; here, snags rise among the oaks. Now cross the outlet bridge and in a couple of strides turn right onto the **West Branch Trail** to close the loop.

This trail offers a similar narrow footpath stroll through brushing vegetation, with the laurel more dominant and the forest fuller. Initially enjoy looks toward the marsh and red maples. A slight elevation gain allows for such views before the wooded lake buffer again builds. No spurs access the west shore. At 4.7 miles, return to Bruce Lake Road and turn left to end at the trailhead, 6.8 miles.

26 Pinchot Trail, Northern Loop

General description:	A northern loop of the 23-mile Pinchot Trail System explores the Pocono Plateau, visiting an observation tower and an intriguing spring. Rejoice in pink-and-white splendor when the mountain laurel attains peak bloom in mid- to late June, indulge in the tasty bounty of the area's highbush blueberries in mid-July to August, or enjoy the fire-blaze of autumn-colored leaves in October.
General location:	12 miles east of Wilkes-Barre.
Special attractions:	Observation tower for a Pocono panorama; flowering laurels and grasses; blueberries; mixed-hardwood forest for vibrant autumn color; swamp, meadow, and springs; solitude; wildlife.
Length:	11.2 miles round trip.
Elevation:	Find a 450-foot elevation change, with the high point atop Big Pine Hill (2,250 feet) and the low point at Painter Creek crossing (1,800 feet).
Difficulty:	Moderate.
Maps:	Pinchot Trail System; Lackawanna State Forest.
Special concerns:	Find the trail system blazed at 100-foot intervals. Orange blazes (formerly blue) mark the Pinchot Trail, red the connecting trails. Overnight travelers must secure a camping permit from Lackawanna State Forest District Headquarters or Thornhurst Forest Foreman's Office (1.5 miles east of the trailhead). The maximum stay at any single site is two nights; limit your hiking party to four people. No swimming or wading; check posted rules for campfires. Because rattlesnakes find habitat here, watch hand and foot placements, and look before you sit. Seasonally, springs overflow parts of the trail.
Season and hours:	Spring through fall.
For information:	Lackawanna State Forest.

Pinchot Trail, Northern Loop

Key points:

Finding the trailhead: From Interstate 80, take exit 43 and go north on Pennsylvania 115 for 5.7 miles, passing through Blakeslee. Then turn right onto State Route 2040/River Road to Thornhurst, 4.5 miles. Go 0.3 mile past Thornhurst, and turn left onto SR 2016/Bear Lake Road to reach the trailhead on the right in 4 miles.

The trail may also be accessed via I–380: Take exit 6, go north on PA 435, go west on River Road (here, SR 2013) to Bear Lake Road, and turn right.

The hike: Named for Gifford Pinchot, the first chief of the U.S. Forest Service, the Pinchot Trail, together with its associated trails, offers tranquil passage through the varied habitats of the Pocono Plateau, with numerous hike options.

For the selected northern loop, ascend north via the Powder Magazine Trail, part of the Pinchot Trail. Pass through a semiopen forest of maple, oak, birch, and sassafras, with both mountain and sheep laurel, bracken fern, highbush blueberry, and low berry shrubs. Stepping stones ease travel across a soggy site. Ahead, reach a trail register, where maps are often available.

At 0.5 mile, come upon the loop junction. Here, turn left onto the red-blazed Pine Hill Trail for a clockwise tour of the state forest, returning via the Powder Magazine Trail straight ahead. The foot trails are well cut and maintained, with some protruding roots and rocks, but generally they allow for carefree strolling. Deer, woodpecker, cedar waxwing, and songbirds offer brief interludes. As June wanes, both kinds of laurel and a beautiful flowering grass add to travel.

Past a planted stand of spruce, reach the next signed junction. Here, the Frank Gantz Trail (also blazed red) heads left, offering alternative loop travel. Proceed forward on the Pine Hill Trail. Tackle the brief challenge of a rock field, tour amid hip-high ferns and shrubs, and skirt a rocky ledge and knoll before meeting a forest road at 1.5 miles. Detour left on the road to visit Pine Hill Observation Tower atop Big Pine Hill; the loop continues directly across the road.

At 1.6 miles, reach the two-story tower for a 360-degree panorama of the flattened, tree-clad Pocono Plateau, with just a few higher hilltops punctuating the terrain. Overlook the Delaware and Susquehanna River drainages, with the shining sliver and dark basin of Bear Lake to the south. In fall, the mosaic of changing leaves brings a sense of texture to the leafy stage. Day hikers find the tower a satisfying 3.2-mile round-trip destination.

For the full loop, return to the point where the Pine Hill Trail crosses the forest road and resume north (a left at 1.7 miles). The trail gradually ascends near some whitish gray rocks, touring similar forest. In many areas, the low-canopy, snag-riddled woods owes its stature and character to the plateau's depleted minerals—the aftermath of a series of fires in the postlogging era. The trail then tops out and descends, meeting a closed road grade. Turn left, rounding the gate at 2.1 miles.

The branches of black cherry, maple, and oak lace over the grassy lane, with tall laurel and some American chestnut adding to the trail's border. At 2.75 miles, proceed forward to meet the orange blazes of the Scrub Oak Trail (2.8 miles), which now continues the loop to the right.

While easily passable, this foot trail at times cries out for a manicure. Pass from low-stature forest to tall oaks and maples. A couple of rocky sites mark travel. With a mild rolling ascent, cross Pittston Road (another forest road, at 4 miles); keep to the orange blazes. Here, the Painter Creek Trail takes the relay pass.

Glimpse a marshy area beyond the woods to the left, and encounter a few spruce amid the woodland. At 4.25 miles, hikers have an option: Either keep to the orange-blazed Pinchot Trail, traversing a wooded plateau before making a plummeting descent to Painter Creek, or take the red trail for a direct descent along the creek. To prevent further erosion of the steep drainage slope, take the red creekside spur.

At 4.75 miles, the hike rejoins the orange-blazed route near the forest boundary. Bear right, crossing the log footbridge over Painter Creek in a picturesque dark hemlock cove. Next, look for orange blazes, pointing out the ascent. With a rolling journey find a rocky spring, introducing the signature bloom and leaf of the tulip poplar. The trail remains near the forest boundary.

At 5.4 miles, swing right, still tracking orange blazes. A downed post likely signals another trail-name change, but all hikers really need to remember here is to stay with the orange blazes. Sheep laurel abounds, lending its own seasonal flourish when the mountain laurel parades out pink-hued blooms. Alternately travel open woods and shady pockets. Hayes Run Swamp is below to the left but remains a mystery. Birch, shad, and pitch pine dot the woodland.

At a junction post in a grassy opening (6.4 miles), turn left onto a grassy lane, staying with the orange blazes. A foot trail then advances the loop as the trail arcs right at 6.5 miles. Expect some rocky footing, climbing to a low rocky hilltop; a sheep laurel and berry flat lie below to the right.

Pass a second rocky cap, touring a fern-filled woods. At 7.2 miles, turn right for a straight-line tour, still vacillating between sun and shade. At 7.5 miles, looks left find a small wetland. The trail then descends a canted outcrop and divides a clover–grass meadow, meeting Sassafras Road.

Cross this forest road for a dazzling hike in mountain laurel. Scenic stands of sassafras and white birch likewise contribute to the overall image. The easy trail allows eyes to roam. As the trail dips and the woods fill out, the laurel disperses. A couple of rocky fields require attention to footing. At 9.75 miles, reach a spring, gurgling beneath and up through the rocks. From it emerges Spring Run, a full-fledged creek. A towering white pine and its braided root contribute to the mystical scene. Day hikers who travel the loop in reverse will find the spring a satisfying destination.

Again meet Pittston Road and follow it left for 0.1 mile to pick up the orange-blazed Powder Magazine Trail on the right. Initially walk a rocky trailbed, with framing laurel, birch, and meadow habitat. Pockets of shade offer reprieve from the open-woods travel. Cross a small, rocky spring and close the loop at the red-blazed Pine Hill Trail (10.7 miles). Proceed on the orange-blazed Powder Magazine Trail, retracing the first 0.5 mile to the trailhead, 11.2 miles.

27 Painter Swamp–Stillwater Natural Area Hike

General description: This barbell-shaped tour swings a circuit around Painter and Big Bear Swamps, with the latter located in Stillwater Natural Area. This 1,931-acre native area has been set aside to prosper relatively undisturbed. During the Civil War, deserters and draft dodgers hid out in the swamps. Shack remnants still remain in the dense growth.

General location: 12 miles southwest of Milford.

Special attractions: Swamps; hardwood and conifer forest; flowering azalea, rhododendron, mountain laurel, and sheep laurel; a beaver dam; wildlife sightings; fall foliage.

Length: 8.6 miles round trip.

Elevation: Find a mildly rolling trail, traveling between 1,300 and 1,400 feet in elevation.

Difficulty: Moderate, due to rocky footing.

Maps: Thunder Swamp Trail System (generally stocked at the trailhead map box during hiking season); Delaware State Forest.

Special concerns: This hike is part of the 45-mile Thunder Swamp Trail System. Identify the main trails by orange (formerly blue) blazes, connector trails by red blazes. Hikers may backpack-camp; secure a free permit from Delaware State Forest. When applying by mail, submit the request ten days before a visit. Carry a backpacker stove, drinking water, and insect repellent.

Season and hours: Spring through fall for hiking.

For information: Delaware State Forest.

Key points:
- 0.0 Flat Ridge Road trailhead; hike east.
- 0.1 Painter Swamp loop junction; turn right.
- 0.7 Swamp outlet.
- 2.0 Little Bushkill Creek bridge.
- 2.7 Big Bear Swamp loop junction; go left.
- 6.0 Close the loop; backtrack to Painter Swamp.
- 7.8 Painter Swamp loop; turn right.
- 8.6 End at trailhead.

Finding the trailhead: From the junction of U.S. Highways 6 and 209 in

Painter Swamp–Stillwater Natural Area Hike

Milford, go south on US 209 for 7.9 miles and turn right onto Pennsylvania 739 North. Go 1.1 miles and turn left onto Silver Lake Road, heading toward Porters Lake. Go 7.4 miles, turning left onto dirt Flat Ridge Road (0.7 mile past the Edgemere Ranger Station). Find the marked trailhead on the left in another 1.9 miles.

Alternatively, take exit 8 off Interstate 84, going south on PA 402 for 8.8 miles. There, turn left (east) onto Silver Lake Road, go 3.9 miles, and turn right onto Flat Ridge Road to reach the trailhead in another 1.9 miles.

The hike: Follow the red-blazed path, heading east in a multistory forest of

red maple and white, black, and chestnut oak. Sarsaparilla invades the grasses, while low, angled rocks penetrate the trailbed, straining ankles. At 0.1 mile is the Painter Swamp loop junction; turn right to follow the west shore. During high water, hikers should forgo this loop, keeping to the east shore to avoid the beaver-dam crossing at the outlet. Both shores hold similar merit.

To the right, the trail hugs the west shore, passing within 50 feet of the snag-pierced, shimmering open water of this large swamp. Vegetated islands; pockets of aquatic grass, rush, and cattail; and mats of lily pad complete the impression. Herons, frogs, turtles, splashing fish, and swallows call for the raising of binoculars. When painted with autumn color, the fully wooded perimeter ups the ante. Highbush blueberry and sheep laurel favor the shoreline.

At 0.4 mile, a rock slab offers swampside seating and an invitation to relax (when insects cooperate). At the 0.6-mile junction, turn left for Stillwater Natural Area; the path ahead leads to Lake Minisink. The shoreline opens up, adding azalea to the mix of shrubs.

Next, cross Painter Swamp Creek (the swamp outlet) via a makeshift bridge and the sticks and mud of a beaver dam. A few sloshing steps seem unavoidable. Just beyond is a junction. Turn right, tracing a jeep trail for twenty strides to pick up the semimasked foot trail on the right. Although it is blazed, stay alert.

At 1 mile, bear left for the natural area as a second path to Lake Minisink branches right. Orange blazes now guide the way. Encounter a couple of quick turns: Go right at the T-junction and left at the fork. At 1.6 miles, pass a register box, coming out at Coon Swamp Road. Keep to the orange blazes, angling across this restricted-access road.

Enjoy a pleasant woods meander on foot trail, encountering a few

Painter Swamp, Stillwater Natural Area, Delaware State Forest.

spring-soaked bottom areas. Birdsongs, a breeze, and lighting changes add to the relaxation. On higher plateaus, bracken fern reigns; in moist depressions, blueberry and huckleberry. Past Coon Swamp Road, lose much of the rockiness.

At 1.8 miles, turn right for the Big Bear Swamp tour of Stillwater Natural Area; to the left, a red-blazed loop explores the area's northern block. Stay with the orange blazes, descending to a footbridge crossing of Little Bushkill Creek (2 miles). Dotted by islands of greenery, the shallow waterway flows smooth and dark. Geranium and violet adorn its banks. As the trail draws away from the creek, mountain laurels dress the woods. View low rock ledges where a carriageway advances travel.

At 2.4 miles, turn left, following blazes upstream along a creek to the point of crossing. At 2.7 miles, reach the loop junction for Big Bear Swamp. Go left (clockwise), once again traveling a grassy woods lane, but stay alert for the foot trail on the right that continues the tour, at 3 miles.

Travel a woods lacking in swamp views, coming to a 10-foot-high rock ledge. Where it ends, mount the low plateau. Snags now open the skyline. Pass between woodsy flats and low rock tiers. By 3.8 miles, spruce, birch, rhododendron, and highbush blueberry signal that the swamp is near. In places spy the wetland floor, green with sphagnum moss, fern, and bog grass.

The circuit continues, mildly rolling. Where oaks reclaim the tour, again spy pockets of mountain laurel. At 5.5 miles, meet a woods lane and follow it right, passing through posted private property to close the Big Bear Swamp loop (6 miles). Turn left, backtracking to Painter Swamp (7.8 miles). There, turn right to complete the Painter Swamp circuit along the east shore, enjoying new perspectives. End at the trailhead, 8.6 miles.

28 Delaware Water Gap National Recreation Area: Dingmans Creek Area

Overview

This 70,000-acre national recreation area (NRA) spans the Pennsylvania and New Jersey shores of a 40-mile stretch of the Delaware Wild and Scenic River. At the southern end of the park, view Delaware Water Gap, where the Delaware cuts an S-shaped chasm through 1,400-foot Kittatinny Ridge. Throughout the corridor, find exceptional river recreation. Within the river's vital watershed, hikers explore wooded slopes, the Pocono Plateau, and picturesque ravines. Sparkling waterfalls, mature eastern hemlocks, and rhododendron dress the side-creek canyons. Trails of varying length and difficulty serve NRA visitors.

General description:	Two popular short trails visit the waterfall galleries along Dingmans Creek. One is at Dingmans Falls Visitor Center; the other, Fulmer Falls, is at George W. Childs Picnic Area.
General location:	8 miles south of Milford off U.S. Highway 209.
Special attractions:	Five dramatic waterfalls, scenic Dingmans Creek, dark hemlock forests, early-July rhododendron blooms, chance wildlife sightings.
Length:	Dingmans Falls Nature Trail, 0.8 mile round trip (fully accessible); Fulmer Falls Loop, 1.2-mile loop.
Elevation:	Dingmans Falls Nature Trail shows 150 feet of elevation change; Fulmer Falls Loop has some 200 feet of elevation change.
Difficulty:	Dingmans Falls Nature Trail, easy; Fulmer Falls Loop, easy to moderate.
Maps:	Dingmans Falls Nature Trail; *Delaware Water Gap: Selected Hiking Trails* brochure.
Special concerns:	Keep to the trail, do not disturb natural objects, and no swimming. During peak travel season, the visitor center parking lot frequently fills.
Season and hours:	Spring through fall, daylight hours. For Dingmans Falls Visitor Center, phone ahead to make sure it's open and check on times.
For information:	Delaware Water Gap NRA.

Key points:

Dingmans Falls Nature Trail:
- 0.0 Trailhead; head upstream.
- 0.1 Silver Thread Falls.
- 0.2 Lower Dingmans Falls viewing.
- 0.4 Upper Dingmans Falls; return to trailhead.

Delaware Water Gap National Recreation Area:
Dingmans Creek Area

To Porters Lake

To 84

0   0.5   1
Miles

N

Mill ruins

Park Road

Silver Lake Road

Factory Falls

Fulmer Falls

Dingmans Creek

Silver Thread Falls

Dingmans Falls

Deer Leap Falls

Visitor center

To 209

Fulmer Falls Loop:

0.0	Easternmost trailhead.
0.1	Fulmer Falls.
0.2	Factory Falls and mill ruins.
0.8	Lower canyon bridge/Deer Leap Falls.
1.2	End loop at trailhead.

FT

1,000 Factory Falls
750   Close
500   Fulmer loop
250   Falls   Trailhead   Deer Leap Falls
Miles   1

Finding the trailhead: From the junction of US 6 and US 209 in Milford, go south on US 209 for 7.9 miles, reaching the intersection with Pennsylvania 739 North.

For Dingmans Falls Visitor Center and trailhead, remain on US 209, continuing south another 0.2 mile. There, turn right (west) onto Dingmans Falls Road and proceed 0.8 mile to the visitor center/trail parking.

For George W. Childs Picnic Area, turn right onto PA 739 North. Go 1.1 miles and turn left onto Silver Lake Road, heading toward Porters Lake. Find the first Childs Park access in 1.7 miles, the second 0.1 mile farther west, and the third by turning left onto Park Road in still another 0.1 mile.

The hikes: The popular **Dingmans Falls Nature** Trail heads upstream from the visitor center parking area. Footbridges twice span Dingmans Creek, allowing for travel between the 80-foot Silver Thread Falls on a side tributary and the 130-foot Dingmans Falls on Dingmans Creek.

Travel the cool, dark mystery of the hemlock-clad ravine, crossing the first bridge to visit Silver Thread Falls. This elegant, shimmery ribbon spills through an eroded shale crevasse. Hemlock, birch, and beech contribute to its tranquil, shady bower.

Next, proceed upstream to the second bridge, admiring the waters and bedrock of Dingmans Creek. Upon crossing, turn upstream to a trail fork—the gateway to the pair of Dingmans Falls vistas. Bear right to reach the lower viewpoint—a boardwalk platform offering a full-face view of this exciting multidirectional, multitier, forceful white surge. When the falls attains full glory, billows of mist shroud the canyon. Dry-season visits present a much altered face. Crowning hemlocks, fanning deciduous trees, and delightful rhododendrons complement the union of water and shale. Below the falls, Dingmans Creek quickly gentles the churned water.

As you ascend the stairway to the upper viewing site, discover changing views of Dingmans Falls. Also, admire the mossy bedded outcrop shaping the trail. A bilevel viewing deck presents the top of the falls and a grotto along the opposite wall. Return to creek level and backtrack to the visitor center at 0.8 mile.

On the **Fulmer Falls Loop**, five footbridges span Dingmans Creek, facilitating loop travel and presenting new perspectives on the area's three falls: Fulmer, Factory, and Deer Leap.

Starting from the first (easternmost) parking lot for George W. Childs Picnic Area, descend the slope to the creek's north shore and bear right (upstream), reaching a fenced viewing area. Here, obtain a side perspective overlooking two-thirds of the 70- to 80-foot drop of Fulmer Falls. After periods of rain, admire a thundering plummet and the pounding of rock.

Continue upstream, passing through the picnic area of the north shore to admire the 30- to 40-foot shimmery pyramid of Factory Falls. Below the second Childs' parking area, discover the ruins of an old mill (0.2 mile). The

Rhododendron, Delaware Water Gap National Recreation Area.

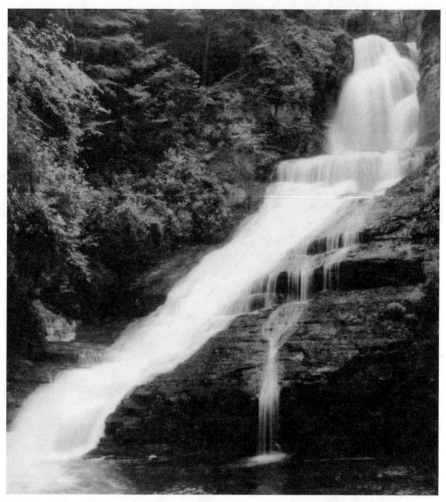

Dingmans Falls, Delaware Water Gap National Recreation Area.

plunging waters on Dingmans Creek powered early-day industry in the Delaware River Valley. Here, view stone walls 10 feet high.

Continue upstream to the uppermost bridge (0.3 mile) for the full loop. Spruce, hemlock, pine, hickory, maple, and oak weave shade. On the south shore, the trail drifts apart from the creek. Find more ground cover and some mountain laurel. Eventually, log-braced earthen steps return hikers to Dingmans Creek, for just a glimpse at the head of Fulmer Falls. Due to canyon angles, the appreciation is primarily by ear.

Avoid bridge crossings, proceeding downstream to Deer Leap Falls. A detour onto the footbridge at the head of this falls, however, provides a stirring perspective on the steep canyon drop and the gash carved into the stream shelf. For the close of the loop, delay crossing until the lower-canyon bridge (0.8 mile). From its span, view 15- to 18-foot Deer Leap Falls. Then ascend on wooden stairs and round the slope. Cascades add to this upstream return. Close the loop at Fulmer Falls and end back at the parking area, 1.2 miles.

29 Delaware Water Gap National Recreation Area: Pocono Environmental Education Center

Overview

Straddling the Pennsylvania–New Jersey shore of the Delaware Wild and Scenic River, this popular 70,000-acre national recreation area (NRA) extends exceptional scenery, first-rate river recreation, hiking trails, and an acclaimed residential environmental education center. In what was a former honeymoon resort in the quiet beauty of the Pocono Plateau, Pocono Environmental Education Center (PEEC) holds classes and offers walks and talks designed to increase environmental awareness. For these, visitors must register and pay a fee, but the PEEC also has a fine series of short, interlocking trails open free to the public.

General description: Three hikes incorporate several of the site's six color-coded named trails, visiting ponds, waterfalls, a vista, a fossil bed, mixed woods, streams, and rocky ledges.

General location: Off U.S. Highway 209, 12 miles south of Milford, 15 miles north of East Stroudsburg.

Special attractions: Delaware River Valley–Kittatinny Ridge view, waterfalls, wildlife ponds, wetlands, flowering shrubs, wildflowers, marine fossils, rock ledges, fall foliage.

Length: Two Ponds–Tumbling Waters Trail, 3 miles round trip; Fossil Trail, 1.3-mile loop; Sunrise–Scenic Gorge Trail, 4 miles round trip.

Elevation: Two Ponds–Tumbling Waters Trail, 200-foot elevation change; Fossil Trail, 300-foot elevation change; Sunrise–Scenic Gorge Trail, 150-foot elevation change.

Difficulty: All moderate.

Maps: PEEC trail map and interpretive brochures (there is a modest charge for some printed materials).

Special concerns: Come prepared for ticks and poison ivy. Find trails well blazed with generally good beds. Use care on one precarious ledge descent/ascent along the Sunrise–Scenic Gorge Trail; a guide rope aids travelers over the challenge. Keep to the trails; no collecting is allowed in the park. Hikers may seek out fossils but may not remove any of them.

Season and hours: Spring through fall for hiking, daylight hours.

For information: Pocono Environmental Education Center.

Delaware Water Gap National Recreation Area:
Pocono Environmental Education Center

Key points:

Two Ponds–Tumbling Waters Trail:
- 0.0   Two Ponds Trailhead/Front Pond.
- 0.3   Pickerel Pond.
- 0.6   Tumbling Waters Trail.
- 1.2   "Killer Hill."
- 1.5   Falls.
- 1.7   Hermits Hill.
- 3.0   End at main building.

Fossil Trail:
- 0.0   Cabin 10 trailhead.
- 0.8   Fossil outcrop.
- 1.1   Campfire talk/amphitheater site; bear left.
- 1.3   Close loop.

Sunrise–Scenic Gorge Trail:
- 0.0   Sunrise Trailhead.
- 1.0   Cross ravine.
- 2.5   Small wetland.
- 3.2   Gorge cascade.
- 3.6   Campus Road; bear right.
- 4.0   End at main building.

Finding the trailhead: From the junction of US 6 and US 209 in Milford, go south on US 209 for 12.6 miles and turn right (west) onto Briscoe Mountain Road at the PEEC sign. In 0.8 mile, bear right onto Emery Road to reach the main building, parking lot, and trails in 0.1 mile.

The hikes: Start the **Two Ponds–Tumbling Waters Trail** on the boardwalk across Emery Road from the main building. An interpretive brochure pairs up with the white-blazed Two Ponds Trail; orange blazes mark the Tumbling Waters Trail.

Travel a shrub-enclosed boardwalk for 50 feet to a wildlife blind. There, wooden panels open to the shrubby environment and inhabiting bird life of Front Pond. Pass an artificial bat roost and edge a field, spying a decomposition graveyard—an educational message on litter and waste. At 0.25 mile, angle right across Briscoe Mountain Road.

Travel from locust woods to pine–spruce plantations, descending to Pickerel Pond. Stone walls crisscross the trail system. Elongated, even-width Pickerel Pond shows an edge of submerged grasses and a rim of planted conifers with hardwoods. Follow the blazes, rounding the pond's right shore. A few beaver gnawings or the noisy pass of a kingfisher may draw attention.

Veer away from the pond, coming to a junction (0.6 mile). Here, the white Two Ponds Trail swings left, returning to the center for a 1.5-mile round trip. Proceed forward, tracking the orange blazes of the Tumbling Waters Trail. Travel an oak–maple woods, encountering the occasional large hemlock or forgotten white pine. As the trail rolls and contours, hear the whisper of a stream in the ravine below. Hemlocks become more prevalent as the trail tops "Killer Hill," 1.2 miles. Descend and round to the falls spur.

The loop bears left, while the falls spur switchbacks downhill to the right. Two falls actually grace the ravine at 1.5 miles. Glimpse the upper portion of the first falls before reaching the bottom of the ravine, attaining a full-face view of the second falls. This divided and tiered 50-foot veil enchants with fanned ferns and rhododendron. Do not go cross-country trying to better the first falls view.

Resume the loop, making a fairly steep ascent through low-stature oaks to arrive atop the open sandstone outcrop of Hermits Hill (1.7 miles). Overlook Delaware Gap, the long, wooded rise of New Jersey's Kittatinny Ridge, and a series of distant blue shadows. Occasionally, a hawk circles overhead. During fall migration, kettles of hawks spiral skyward.

Continue across the top of Hermits Hill, turning left at an old stone foundation and fireplace. Descend and later bear right, touring a woods road through a choked pine–deciduous woods; again bear right at the fork. Scenic old maples entwined by Virginia creeper now frame travel. Tiger lilies grow where the trail again crosses Briscoe Mountain Road.

Travel a narrow footpath in an open shrub–wildflower habitat. On ascent, red cedars appear. At 2.8 miles, bear right, descending to the next pine plantation; be alert for this easily missed turn. The blue-blazed Fossil Trail then arrives on the right, sharing the closing distance. Emerge on the cabin campus road opposite Cabin 10. Hike left on the road to return to the main building (3 miles).

For the **Fossil Trail,** start opposite Cabin 10 (0.1 mile east of the main building). A sign and blue blazes point the way; an interpretive brochure identifies features keyed to the numbered blocks. Hike the shared distance with the orange Tumbling Waters Trail through mixed forest before bearing left and ascending and rounding a rocky knoll. Deer may pause for a curious look. Next, skirt a small wetland, where frog or muskrat may be spied. Ahead, keep close tabs on the blue blazes, because there is a maze of tracked paths.

With a fairly steep descent, pass through a taller forest and cross a small drainage and then a ravine to reach the base of the fossil-bearing outcrop cliff. An interpretive board identifies each of the marine fossils found here. Crinoids, fingertip-size circular depressions, seem particularly numerous. Also discover brachiopods and trilobites. Generally, a previous traveler will have left some fossils near the sign, cluing you as to what to look for; remember that no collecting is permitted.

Ascend steeply, paralleling the ravine upstream to emerge at the campfire talk/amphitheater site, near the end of the cabin campus loop. Bear left, following the road past the dining hall. Keep left to close the loop at 1.3 miles; return to the main building and parking at 1.4 miles.

For the **Sunrise–Scenic Gorge Trail,** start at the bridge north of the main building, near Cabin 1, ascending through a red pine plantation. Dogwood and young maple grow among the pines. Yellow blazes indicate the Sunrise Trail; red, the Scenic Gorge Trail.

Where the trail tops out, bear right, skirting a small outbuilding. On this rolling tour, oak–huckleberry woodlands claim the plateaus; taller forests of white pine and mixed hardwoods, the dips. Birds pair melodic notes to the

Red eft, Delaware Water Gap National Recreation Area.

shuffle of the boot. As the trail bottoms out at 0.4 mile, stay on the yellow-blazed trail, bearing left. In another 0.1 mile, watch for the trail to turn right.

The trail twice passes through a flattened stone wall before the red trail returns at 0.9 mile. At the upcoming ravine, stay with the yellow trail, making a stone-hop crossing; here, the red trail turns right, following the ravine. Cross a slow drainage and stroll along the foot of a low slope with a scalloped-ledge crest. The trail again climbs and dips.

At 1.5 miles, come to a steep descent at a pair of ledge overhangs. A guide rope aids hikers down the upper half; a sure boot helps on the skidding gravels of the lower slope. Upon reaching the base, turn around to admire the jutting ledges. A hemlock woods next hosts travel. Mayapple and jack-in-the-pulpit lend spring accents.

Again the trail rolls before entering a straight-arrow course, passing a 15-foot-tall rock chimney and dipping to skirt a meadow and skunk cabbage bog. At 2.5 miles, edge a small wetland and round a hemlock slope to follow a small brook downstream. Cross it, and ascend along a second drainage. Cross this drainage above a picturesque corner falls to again meet the red trail.

Now pursue the dual blazes, following the joined creek waters downstream. Small tiered cascades and low rock banks shape a mini gorge. At 3.25 miles, a larger cascade and the 10-foot-high mossy rock walls forge a final gorge impression. The trail then ascends away, reaching an oak–pine habitat for a comfortable stroll back to the PEEC.

Reach the campus loop below Cabin 49 and bear right. Upon meeting the next paved road, again bear right. Hike past Cabin 10 (the Fossil Trail's start), and the historic stone-ring pledge site to return to the main building, 4 miles.

30 Susquehanna Riverlands

Overview

At this Susquehanna River education and recreation site, jointly operated by Pennsylvania Power and Light (PP&L) and the Allegheny Electric Cooperative, three of the four land parcels extend hiking: Council Cup above the east shore and, on the west shore, the Wetlands Nature Area and Riverlands Recreation Area. Each has its signature offering.

General description: Hikes at Council Cup offer Susquehanna River overlooks and an upland woods stroll. The superb Wetlands Nature Trail System travels along river, marsh, swamp, and the North Branch Canal. The Riverlands Recreation Area completes the offering with a pair of hikes: One explores an artificial pond and the historic canal; the other, the river.

General location: 5 miles northeast of Berwick.

Special attractions: Susquehanna River; the historic North Branch Canal (1831–1900); wetlands, swamps, and marsh; riparian and upland woods; wildflowers; wildlife; fall color.

Length: Council Cup hikes: South Loop, 0.25 mile; North Loop, 0.8 mile; Wetlands Nature Trail System, 1-mile loop; Towpath Trail, 1.7-mile loop; Riverside Trail, 1-mile loop.

Elevation: Find a modest roll to the Council Cup hikes, touring at 1,100 feet in elevation. The river floodplain trails are all flat, at 500 feet in elevation.

Difficulty: All easy.

Maps: Susquehanna Riverlands and Wetlands Nature Area brochures.

Special concerns: Seasonally, carry insect repellent and netting. Beware of poison ivy. No pets or fishing in the Wetlands Nature Area, and no swimming or wading at any area. Register upon entering the wetlands.

Season and hours: Generally, spring through fall for hiking, 8:00 A.M. to dusk.

For information: Susquehanna Riverlands.

Key points:

Council Cup, South Loop:
- 0.0 Council Cup Trailhead.
- 0.1 Bluff escarpment; bear left.
- 0.3 End at south end of parking.

Council Cup, North Loop:

- 0.0 Council Cup Trailhead.
- 0.1 Bluff escarpment; bear right.
- 0.3 Loop junction; go left.
- 0.6 Close loop; hike forward and then left.
- 0.8 End at northeast corner of parking.

Susquehanna Riverlands

Wetlands Nature Trail System:

0.0   Wood Duck Trailhead.
0.5   Beaver Trail.
0.8   Waterfowl Pond overlook.
1.0   End loop at kiosk.

Towpath Trail:
- 0.0 Towpath Trailhead.
- 0.8 Cross third bridge and turn north.
- 1.2 Boat launch/canal interpretive sign.
- 1.7 End at trail parking.

Riverside Trail:
- 0.0 Riverside Trailhead; hike clockwise.
- 0.5 River vista.
- 1.0 End on east shore of North Branch Canal.

Finding the trailhead: At the junction of U.S. Highway 11 and Pennsylvania 239 South in Shickshinny, go south on PA 239 for Council Cup. In 5.9 miles, turn left onto Hobbie Road at Wapwallopen. Following signs, go 1.9 miles and turn left onto Maple Lane. Go 0.6 mile on Maple Lane and again turn left. Drive 0.5 mile more, and turn left. Then go 0.3 mile and turn right onto the gravel road indicated for Council Cup Scenic Area to reach parking in 0.4 mile.

For the west-shore offering, proceed south on US 11 from Shickshinny. In about 4 miles, turn left for the Energy Information Center/Riverlands Recreation Area. Find Susquehanna Wetlands on the left, 1.4 miles farther south.

The hikes: For the **Council Cup hikes,** walk west into a mixed upland woods from the northwest corner of trail parking. The wide grass and then gravel path ascends modestly. Reach a chain-link fence and bench overlooking the bluff escarpment of Council Cup (0.1 mile). To the right is the North Loop; to the left, the South Loop. From the bench, view the Susquehanna River Valley, its rural floodplain, small communities, and a tower of steam above the nuclear power plant.

The **South Loop** holds additional views. Come to a second bench in another 0.1 mile. It lends new perspective on the river valley and extends looks north at the cliff profile. The view opens up when the trees lose their leaves. From here, the trail swings back into woods. Ascend in the shadow of oak, maple, tulip, hickory, sassafras, hop hornbeam, and pitch pine. Close the loop, emerging near a utility tower at the south end of the parking area, 0.25 mile.

The **North Loop** initially remains along the bluff rim, but the forest blocks any views. In another 0.1 mile, traverse a utility corridor where lines extend an open-aisle look toward the river. Afterward, faded blue blazes mark the woods-shaded trail. Proceed forward where a trail branches right at 0.25 mile. Soon after, reach a blazed junction. Go left; the main woods road ahead marks the return of the loop.

Make a slow descent, passing through areas of white pine and birch, coming to a four-way intersection (0.5 mile). The path ahead and the one to the left both dead-end; go right, still following faint blazes. At 0.6 mile, complete the loop. Proceed forward a couple of hundred feet and turn left to end at the northeast corner of trail parking.

Reach the **Wetlands Nature Trail System**, 0.6 mile east off U.S. 11, via Hicks Ferry Road. Three trails tour the natural area: the Wood Duck Trail,

Spice Bush Shortcut, and Beaver Trail. Interpretive panels introduce natural and cultural history. Start at the northeast corner of the parking area, returning near the kiosk.

The Wood Duck Trail tours the field–forest habitat of the west bank Susquehanna River, passing ruins from an old coal dredge. When water levels are low, look for eel walls along the riverbed. In the early 1900s, these V-shaped 2-foot-high stone weirs funneled eels together for easy harvest. Beautiful old-growth ash, maple, and oak shade the way. Long ago, the Iroquois Indians walked this path en route to council meetings.

At 0.2 mile, the Spice Bush Shortcut heads left. Continue forward for the full 1-mile loop. Follow the broad, smooth-coursing Susquehanna River north (upstream). In another 0.1 mile, turn away from the river, merging with a service road to edge a marsh. Cattails, snags, and a surface of duckweed contribute to the rich wetland, while frogs, turtles, muskrats, and dragonflies lend animation.

Variously framing the trail's shoulder, find honeysuckle, highbush blueberry, azalea, and sensitive fern. Next, reach the North Branch Canal and turn left, following the towpath along its east bank. Duckweed, overhanging trees, sunning turtles, and snags have replaced the bustle of this once vital transportation corridor. Gone are the days when mules plodded the towpath, pulling cargo boats of coal to fuel early Philadelphia industry.

Birch, hickory, tulip, and locust add to the treed edge as the towpath passes between canal and marsh. Sedge, rush, arrowhead, and loosestrife vary the wetland tapestry. Haughty geese may voice prior claim to the trail. At 0.5 mile, the Spice Bush Shortcut arrives on the left. Continue forward on the towpath; culverts link the marsh waters.

Next, view a sleepy bend on the retired canal. In 200 feet, the Wood Duck Trail turns left, returning to the parking lot for a 0.7-mile tour. Proceed forward on the towpath (now the Beaver Trail) for the full 1-mile loop. Enormous trees, tangled woods, and wetlands continue to dazzle. Ahead, reach a bench near an intersection; views span east to the cliffs of Council Cup. Keep to the towpath.

At a four-way junction (0.7 mile), turn left, leaving the towpath. Pass a skunk cabbage bog and again turn left for the closing leg of the loop. Here, a 50-foot detour straight ahead adds a look at Waterfowl Pond—an open water with small shrub islands and cross-pond views toward Council Cup. Now pass a beaver-cut stump, interpretive sign, and birch swamp before turning right to end at the trailhead kiosk.

Several parking areas within Riverlands Recreation Area access the **Towpath Trail.** Start this hike from the trail parking lot just east of the Energy Information Center. A trail kiosk marks the site. Hike south along the west bank of the historic canal. A fine cinder surface makes the flat 8-foot-wide towpath ideal for exercise walkers. Silver maple, black locust, oak, and dogwood edge the trail, screening looks at the murky canal water. Noise from US 11 rivals the chorus of birds and croaking frogs.

Cross a breach between the canal and artificial Lake Took-a-while. Now look for the first of three bridges to cross the canal at 0.2 mile. Keep to the western towpath. Looks west find a billow of white steam from the power station. Alder, willow, and ash join the tangle of trees. View Canada geese, swallows, kingfishers, turtles, and fish. An angler may cast a line for bass. At 0.8 mile, cross the southernmost bridge over the canal and trace the east bank north to close the loop.

While the canal impressions remain similar, field, woods, and a developed recreation area abut the east-shore path. Birders find ample reason to raise their binoculars. At 1.25 miles, pass a boat launch and interpretive sign on North Branch Canal. Beyond are rest rooms and tables of the developed park. Keep to the towpath, coming out at the park road. Turn left to close the loop at trail parking, 1.7 miles.

From the same parking area (east of the Energy Information Center), look on the north side of the road for the signed **Riverside Trail.** For a clockwise tour, hike north along the west bank of the nearly dry canal. Travel a scenic grassy lane shaded by silver maple, dogwood, black cherry, elm, and ash; the floodplain boasts some noteworthy big trees. Virginia creeper, sassafras, poison ivy, and waist- to chest-high jewelweed color the plain. Beware of roots.

The trail bends riverward (0.4 mile), reaching the blinding light of a pipeline corridor. Turn right, following this grassy riverside aisle; shrub thickets rise at its border. From a riverside bench, admire the smooth, brownish green Susquehanna River and enjoy the shade trees on shore. The fairly fast but steady current transports bubbles downstream.

Strawberries, wildflowers, ducks, herons, and tiny toads may add to discovery. Keep to the mowed path to avoid poison ivy. At 0.75 mile and again at 0.8 mile, side trails branch right; follow either of these to close the loop. Where the paths merge in 200 feet, continue west, edging a field to come out on the east shore of the North Branch Canal, 1 mile.

North Branch Canal, Susquehanna Riverlands.

31 Lehigh Gorge Trail

General description: Part of Lehigh Gorge State Park, this abandoned stretch of the Jersey Central Railroad welcomes multiple-use recreation along the Lehigh River. Interpretive kiosks spaced along the route explain features of the Delaware–Lehigh Canal National Heritage Corridor, of which the railroad is a part.

General location: West of Interstate 476, between White Haven and Jim Thorpe.

Special attractions: Overlooks and access to a changeable, class III whitewater river; exciting gorge; sheer cliffs; a spectacular rhododendron showcase; fishing; side-creek waterfalls; wildflowers; wildlife; fall foliage.

Length: 21.5 miles one-way from White Haven to Glen Onoko.

Elevation: Find an easy, comfortable grade, descending from 1,200 feet to 600 feet in elevation.

Difficulty: Easy to strenuous, depending on length.

Maps: State park brochure.

Special concerns: No overnight camping or swimming. Mileage markers and benches ease travel, with compost or chemical toilets at White Haven, Rockport, and Glen Onoko. Park officials regularly patrol the trail; locate the park office at Rockport. Midweek visits are quieter. Be aware that timber rattlesnakes can be spied.

Season and hours: Year-round, 8:00 A.M. to sunset. Snow may linger in the gorge until early May.

For information: Lehigh Gorge State Park.

Key points:

- 0.0 White Haven trailhead.
- 1.1 Cross Tannery Road.
- 3.0 Sandy Run.
- 5.1 Leslie Run.
- 9.0 Rockport and falls.
- 11.4 Drakes Creek and river spur.
- 15.2 Outcrop overlook.
- 15.5 Penn Haven.
- 19.0 Pass beneath old river suspension bridge.
- 21.5 Glen Onoko.

Lehigh Gorge Trail

Finding the trailhead: From Pennsylvania 940 in White Haven, turn south onto Main Street before the White Haven Shopping Center. At the end of Main Street, turn left, and then bear right on an improved-surface road heading south. Reach trailhead parking at 0.5 mile.

For the Rockport Access, follow PA 940 south from White Haven, turning left onto Lehigh Gorge Drive/State Route 4010. Follow SR 4010 to SR 4014 and turn left, passing through the village of Rockport to the park office and trail access.

For the Glen Onoko Access Area, from the junction of U.S. Highway 209 and PA 903 in Jim Thorpe, go 0.4 mile north on PA 903, turning left onto Front Street, which becomes Coalport Road. In 0.3 mile, turn left onto the gravel access road; reach parking in another 1.7 miles.

The hike: For a north–south downstream journey, begin at White Haven. Round the gate and hike south, traveling the west bank of the Lehigh River. Swallows dart from nests in the trestle crosswork. Crushed stone surfaces the wide railbed. Despite a varied woods of aspen, maple, sumac, oak, cherry, and birch, find an open cathedral, with canyon shadows for shade.

From here to Sandy Run, the park service encourages fishing; farther downstream, rafting numbers may cause conflict. Hear the rush of the Lehigh River, but gather only token views. To the right, sandstone and siltstone cliffs rise above the corridor. Enjoy showers of rhododendron blooms in early July; at other times, admire the large radial leaves.

The trail travels some 50 feet above the river, often with a steep bank slope. A handful of secondary trails branch to the waterway—some border on the insane. Bikes are not allowed off the main trail. Pine and hemlock join the leafy gallery.

At 1.1 miles, cross Tannery Road, pass through a small parking area, and proceed downstream. At 1.5 miles, a foot trail crosses the rail-trail, descending 200 feet and branching to a shoreline outcrop or sandy beach. The song and face of the river may change from calm to agitated. Side creeks cascade to the river, marking off distance. Cross-canyon views present the opposite treed rim, an active railroad, and features of shore.

Despite the trail's popularity with cyclists, hikers gather ample solitude. Also, their slower mode of travel allows for wildlife viewing and a better appreciation of the gorge and river. Deer, porcupine, snake, scarlet tanager, frog, and hawk may each break the hypnotic spell of this gently bending river tour. A few mountain laurels appear but cannot rival the rhododendron display—one of the best in the state.

Now and then, uncover clues to the abandoned railroad or another transportation milestone—the Lehigh Canal, which had twenty-nine locks between White Haven and Jim Thorpe. Before Sandy Run (3 miles), travel a sunken grade and pass a small landslide. Mid-March through June, river runners may negotiate the rapids created at the mouth of this run.

Past Leslie Run (5.1 miles), a 40-foot-wide meadow isolates the trail from the canyon cliff. The river flows calm and brown between sets of riffles. At the Mud Run distance marker, a wide side trail descends to the shrubby floodplain and thin dirt shore. From shore, view the lively confluence and framing arch of Mud Run Bridge across the way.

On rare occasions, an impressive cicada hatch enlivens the tour with clicking excitement. Honeysuckle, highbush blueberry, and brier may win notice. Look for the trail to grade closer to the river approaching Rockport (9 miles), where three boat launches descend to shore. Admire a zigzagging falls and cascading Indian Run upon arrival and an open river overlook on departure.

View another falls sheeting over a cliff at 9.2 miles, with a round stone tower set back in the hemlock darkness. Vegetated islands and the occasional boulder alter the river's image or flow. At 11.4 miles, reach the Drakes Creek distance marker, a bench, and another hiker path to the river. Drakes Creek arrives on the east shore.

In another mile, it is Stony Creek parting the east shore. Downstream views afford a better sense of the gorge. Once again find a 50-foot slope to the river, as the aisle becomes more open. Tour beneath exposed cliff, with sumacs, young trees, and wildflowers. As a trade-off for the increased sun and heat, find unobstructed river views.

Past a pretty side creek pouring through a cove of laid stone (15.2 miles), find a natural outcrop that overlooks the river. Be sure of the ground beneath your boots here, because erosion is trying to make this pinnacle an island. Admire an upstream bend, the rocky east shore, and a dizzying look down to the water. No diving.

At 15.5 miles, reach Penn Haven. To the right above Black Creek, look for stone ruins that hint at an old incline plane. The active Conrail line crosses the river to travel the west shore at Penn Haven, and the trail in turn crosses the railroad tracks. Be careful at this juncture.

The tour downstream from Penn Haven is then sandwiched between river and railroad. The river helps you forget the downward-beating sun. But eventually the trees of the floodplain steal all river images. Downstream, the rocky bank of the railroad track graduates in height, rising some 10 feet above the trail. Past Bear Creek (18 miles), hikers again find paths to shore.

In about a mile, pass beneath an old river suspension bridge. The railroad then grades lower, approaching Glen Onoko. Round the gate to enter this popular access, 21.5 miles. The gorge tour continues through the parking area, along a gravel road, and on paved surface streets to reach the Jim Thorpe terminus, but this addition has little merit for foot travelers.

Lehigh River, Lehigh Gorge State Park.

Valleys of the Susquehanna Region

This vital piece of the Pennsylvania puzzle features the state's north-central Black Forest Region and the Susquehanna River drainage. Trails travel the perimeter of the Allegheny Mountains and explore the bold ridge arcs of the central state. Pass through rich forests and old-growth groves, tag natural vista outcrops and manicured vista sites, and explore flagstone outcrops and mountain laurel realms. Here, too, discover the lowland domain at Montour Preserve with Lake Chillisquaque.

32 Naval Run–Black Forest Trail Loop

General description:	This rolling loop excursion accesses a central portion of the extensive 42-mile Black Forest Trail (BFT), passing back and forth between scenic drainages and wooded ridges and visiting numerous manicured vistas. Start on Naval Run Trail for clockwise travel, concluding above Slate Run. The final 2 miles occur on road but overlook Pine Creek.
General location:	25 miles northwest of Jersey Shore.
Special attractions:	Rich and varied forest, vistas, cascading runs and hollows, mountain laurel, wildlife sightings, fall foliage, a genuine sense of Pennsylvania "wilderness."
Length:	17-mile loop.
Elevation:	Travel between 800 feet near Pine Creek to more than 2,100 feet atop the ridges.
Difficulty:	Moderate backpack, strenuous day hike.
Maps:	Black Forest Trail map and guide (by the Tiadaghton Forest Fire Fighters Association; the forest district office will explain how to order); Tiadaghton State Forest.
Special concerns:	Hikers should sign the area trail registers. Fires are prohibited at mountain vistas. Refrain from all fire building by carrying a backpacker stove. Slate Run is open for fly fishing only. The BFT is blazed at regular intervals with orange circles, its associated trails with blue circles.
Season and hours:	Spring through fall for hiking.
For information:	Tiadaghton State Forest.

Naval Run–Black Forest Trail Loop

Key points:

0.0	Naval Run Trailhead.
1.0	Meet BFT; go right.
3.1	Ledge Lookout spur.
5.9	Bicentennial Trail spur.
7.2	Slide Hollow–Little Slate Run confluence.
11.5	Foster Pond.
13.6	Cross Slate Run Road.
15.1	Turn left onto Slate Run Road.
17.0	End at Naval Run Trailhead.

Finding the trailhead: From the junction of U.S. Highway 220 and Pennsylvania 44, west of Jersey Shore, go north on PA 44 for 11.9 miles, turning east onto PA 414 for another 13.8 miles. At the village of Slate Run, turn west to cross a Pine Creek bridge, coming to a marked T-junction. Turn left to reach the Naval Run Trail at a barricade in 1.2 miles. Find parking for a handful of vehicles. Additional parking may be reached by going right at the T-junction on Slate Run Road.

The hike: For Naval Run Trail, step over the barricade and follow a closed dirt road to cross skipping Naval Run via stones or a plank (0.1 mile). Meet a second woods road on the opposite shore and follow it upstream. A steep fern–hardwood slope sweeps uphill to the left. The drainage cool supports conifers.

At 0.3 mile, spy a tiered 12- to 15-foot cascade slipping over bedrock in a ledge amphitheater. Avoid the precarious trail that descends to it. Downstream from the cascade, the run engages with broad pools linked by pinched waters. Hemlocks weave a dark hollow character.

At 1 mile, find the Black Forest Trail and follow the orange blazes right for Gas Line Trail; the left leads to Hemlock Mountain. Descend the slope and cross Naval Run via stones or wading to ascend and pursue the opposite slope downstream for a new perspective on Naval Run. Rains bring forth red efts and toads. After again overlooking the falls, follow the BFT as it turns uphill for a well-designed switchbacking ascent.

At 2.2 miles, a trailside ledge may suggest a breather. Dogwoods interweave the woods of oak, maple, and beech. Ahead, top and follow a side ridge before resuming the ascent. At 2.75 miles, a berry-clad slope presents the first view of the tour. Overlook Pine Creek, with Half Dome rising above it, for a 1,360-foot vertical relief.

Top the main ridge and trace its spine left. At 3 miles, a 50-foot spur on the left reaches flat rocks and an opening to Hemlock Mountain. The pines of the vantage slope complement the view on clear days, compose the view on misty ones. Days of low humidity find this vista-packed tour at its finest.

Resume the tour along the ridge. Here, small-diameter oaks, berry bushes, and a few scorched mountain laurels fashion a low cover. Reach the Ledge Lookout spur, which serves up a view on the opposite side of the ridge. The site's rocky point and clearing present a landscape of rounded leafy crowns. Back on the BFT, ascend to the next ridge level, now on shady woods lane. On the left at 3.3 miles, add a Naval Run vista. At 3.5 miles, the BFT turns left on foot trail.

Find a trail register, where the BFT serves up a Pine Creek Gorge view (3.9 miles). As the BFT continues, several secondary trails wiggle away; follow the blazes. At 4.25 miles, hike left on a sun-exposed two-track lined by chestnut oaks and tall laurel. Here, the blaze interval lengthens, so stay alert. At 4.7 and 4.8 miles, find back-to-back vistas on opposite sides of the ridge: Moss Hollow Lookout and White Birch View.

At 5 miles, reach Slide Hollow and turn right; the blue Gas Line Trail continues forward. Descend steadily in fuller forest, finding a campsite at the head of Slide Hollow. The BFT now follows the hollow downstream, weaving back and forth across the rocky drainage; watch your footing. At 5.6 miles, a sign points hikers left out of the drainage.

Switchback to a ridge, coming to the junction with the Bicentennial Trail (5.9 miles). Here, the BFT hooks right, touring atop the ridge. But first, detour 800 feet on the Bicentennial Trail for an audience with an impressive virgin hemlock, measuring 4 feet in diameter. A few other big trees grow in its shadow.

Resume the BFT, soon descending along a ridge with attractive white birch in the forest mix. Glimpse neighboring ridges as the descent steepens. By 7.2 miles, briefly tour alongside the cool richness of lower Slide Hollow. Above its confluence with refreshing Little Slate Run, the BFT swings left briefly, sharing a portion of the Little Slate Run Trail. Pursue a former road grade upstream. At 7.75 miles, ascend a side hollow, admiring its mossy bed, high-canopy forest, and a few rhododendron.

At 8 miles, cross over the hollow to hike downstream and out of the drainage. Old corduroys and roots help hikers keep their feet dry. Again birch complement the forest. At 8.75 miles, meet lightly used Manor Fork Road (a forest road) and follow it right, resuming on footpath where Manor Fork Road intersects Pine Hollow Road (9 miles). Travel through pine plantation, emerging in a laurel-laden open forest. With a mild descent, cross a secondary forest road in another mile.

Keep to the BFT, heading toward Foster Hollow on a meandering forest trail. At 10.4 miles, descend along another small, rocky hollow until an arrow points right. This leads to the upper reaches of Foster Hollow. Hike upstream, enjoying pine–hemlock shade and a few tiny pools. Then skirt stark Foster Pond and the private hunting camp (11.5 miles).

Stay with the orange blazes, traveling an aesthetically pleasing woods with multitrunked trees and a sea of bracken fern. At 12 miles, the BFT heads right as the Fill Trestle Trail heads straight. At 12.1 miles, a reroute advances the BFT through similar open woods. Reach a northern rim for the first of a series of views as the trail descends the nose of the ridge. Flagstone outcrops bring added interest; views now sweep the Slate Run drainage. Poison ivy dots rocky nooks.

At 13.4 miles, follow a hollow out to Slate Run Road and turn right to pick up the BFT where it descends to follow Slate Run downstream. Enjoy varied woods of hemlock, birch, beech, maple, oak, and tulip poplar, touring a wide woods lane midway between Slate Run and Slate Run Road. While sounds of the run contribute to the relaxation, it remains a mystery.

At 15.1 miles, orange blazes ascend the slope to road shoulder parking; turn left onto Slate Run Road, following it and Naval Run Road back to the starting trailhead (17 miles). Pine Creek hosts the road tour. During hot weather, look for trout to collect at the mouth of Little Slate Run.

33 Golden Eagle Trail

General description:	This rolling woods circuit tours the drainages of Bonnell and Wolf Runs, topping the dividing ridge for a couple of superb natural vistas, looking out over the Pine Creek drainage and Wolf Run.
General location:	20 miles northwest of Jersey Shore.
Special attractions:	Vistas, scenic drainages, flagstone outcrops, hints at an old quarry and logging camp, mountain laurel, wildlife, fall foliage.
Length:	9 miles round trip.
Elevation:	Travel between 800 feet at the trailhead and nearly 2,200 feet on the ridge between Bonnell and Wolf Runs.
Difficulty:	Strenuous.
Maps:	Golden Eagle Trail; Tiadaghton State Forest.
Special concerns:	Overnight camping is prohibited. Expect some rugged sections of travel. Due to multiple crossings of the two runs, avoid hiking during times of high water.
Season and hours:	Spring through fall, daylight hours.
For information:	Tiadaghton State Forest.

Key points:

0.0 Bonnell Run trailhead.
0.3 Cascade/loop junction; go right.
1.6 Ravens Horn.
2.2 Wolf Run.
5.0 Beulahland Vista.
8.7 Close loop; backtrack to trailhead.

Finding the trailhead: From the U.S. Highway 220–Pennsylvania 44 junction west of Jersey Shore, go north on PA 44 for 11.9 miles, turning east onto PA 414 for another 11.3 miles. Locate the trail heading east at Bonnell Run, with trail parking on the west side of PA 414 at Clark Recreation Access (midway between the villages of Cammal and Slate Run).

The hike: On the south shore of Bonnell Run, step over the turnout barrier and hike the unmarked foot trail heading upstream. As the trail angles upslope, find a posted notice: NO HORSES. An old road grade now leads the way. Large-diameter trees contribute to the varied hemlock–deciduous complex, while mosses paint the forest floor green. Enjoy Bonnell Run overlooks and its refreshing song.

Golden Eagle Trail

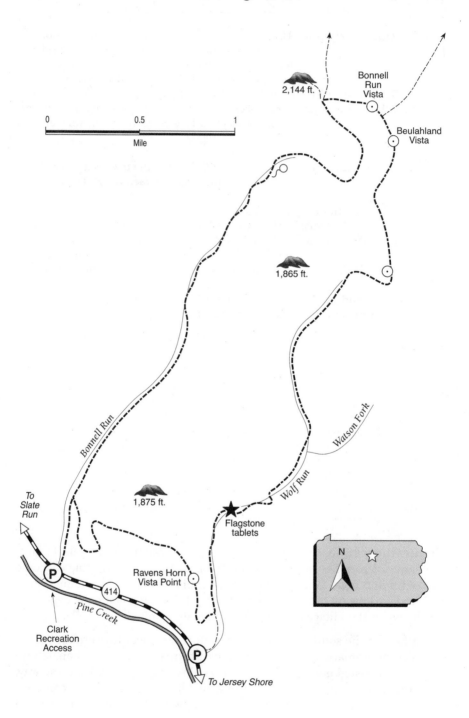

0 0.5 1
Mile

2,144 ft.

Bonnell
Run
Vista

Beulahland
Vista

1,865 ft.

Watson Fork

Bonnell Run

Wolf Run

1,875 ft.

Flagstone
tablets

To
Slate
Run

Ravens Horn
Vista Point

P

414

Pine Creek

Clark
Recreation
Access

P

To Jersey Shore

N

Keep alert for a junction at 0.3 mile. The path to the left descends to a chute and cascades in a small gorge on Bonnell Run. The paths straight ahead and to the right form the loop of Golden Eagle Trail. Turn right, ascending first toward the vista ridge, now following orange circle blazes.

Berry bushes replace the showy drainage moss as the trail tours an oak–hickory–maple woodland. At 0.6 mile, edge a grassy meadow frequented by white-tailed deer. The trail then switchbacks left on a grassy jeep trail for a snaking ascent. The fuller forest offers more complete shade.

By 0.8 mile, a footpath continues the tour, angling and contouring upslope. Where the trail tops out at 1.3 miles, arrows point the way right for a steep descent along the dividing ridge between Bonnell and Wolf Runs. Outcrops shape a ragged crest.

At 1.5 miles, a spur to the right leads to an outcrop jut and the first vista. Be careful when descending the rock; there is little room for false steps. Enjoy a grand view of the Wolf Run drainage with Watson Fork and the beautifully folded, treed ridges—green in summer, a kaleidoscope in fall.

Resume the descent, tagging Ravens Horn (1.6 miles), a vantage named for the jet-black birds that commonly roost here. A scenic flagstone block affords seating, with looks up Wolf Run, down Pine Creek, and across at an attractive long saddle to a conical peak. Watch your footing on this flaking rock.

More of the eroded flagstone pedestals mark the ridge as the trail approaches the third vista (1.75 miles). Neighboring growth censures this view, but the first two excel. Follow orange blazes along the left side of the outcrop, admiring the crossbeds, hollows, and fissures. Striped maples grow amid the rock.

Ravens Horn, Golden Eagle Trail, Wolf Run Wild Area, Tiadaghton State Forest.

At 2 miles, the trail plunges steeply from the ridge, entering switchbacks. As it settles into a steady contouring descent, hear Wolf Run at the foot of the slope. At 2.2 miles, a second PA 414 access spur arrives on the right. Proceed forward. Within the drainage, encounter fern, hog peanut, nettle, sarsaparilla, and mayapple. Serial cascades, chutes, and deep pools accent the sandstone bedding of Wolf Run.

At 2.5 miles, the trail begins crisscrossing the run, but beware—the sidewalklike sandstone can be slippery when wet. The bedrock records ripples from an ancient sea. Hemlock and birch hug the run. At 2.6 miles, look left to view a domino scatter of rectangular flagstone tablets, recalling an old quarry. On this zigzagging upstream tour, water level dictates the number of crossings. Amid big pine and hemlock (3.8 miles), discover an old stove left from a logging camp.

Where the path grows undefined, stay alert for blazes. Then, at 4.1 miles, ascend away from the drainage. As the trail steepens, a spur to the left leads to a mountain-laurel- and berry-clad vista slope. Soon after, top the broad ridge.

Turn right at 4.9 miles to follow a wide, grassy swath maintained by the game commission. Reach Beulahland Vista, elevation 2,180 feet. A vulture may grace the northeast panorama. At 5.25 miles, turn left onto an intersecting grassy lane to reach the next view—Bonnell Run Vista. Here, peer out Bonnell Run to Pine Creek and its west ridge.

At 5.5 miles, again turn left, following a saddle to Bonnell Run and returning to footpath. To the right, the secondary-looking Hilborn Trail leads to Pine Creek. With a steep, loose rock descent, enter an oak–mixed woods with laurel and berry bushes. By 6 miles, descend the dry headwater hollow of Bonnell Run, weaving back and forth across the drainage. Springs dampen the sides. Slowly gain a trickling flow, and later a reliable stream. Downfalls can complicate travel. Although blazed, the trail now has a cross-country character.

At 8.2 miles, reach the woods road on the left (south) side of the creek for a straightforward journey out the canyon. Close the loop at 8.7 miles, and end the hike at PA 414, 9 miles.

34 Cherry Ridge Trail

General description: This split-character woods loop travels aptly named Cherry Ridge. Maintaining an untamed charm throughout, it begins easy but degrades to a rigorous log scramble before drawing to a close.

General location: 20 miles north of Williamsport.

Special attractions: Attractive woods of black cherry and beech; solitude; wildlife sightings of deer, bear, turkey, and porcupine; wildflowers.

Length: 5.7-mile loop.

Elevation: The rolling trail passes between 2,100 and 2,200 feet in elevation.

Difficulty: The first half and closing distance are easy, with a strenuous middle distance.

Maps: Tiadaghton State Forest; Tiadaghton State Forest Old Loggers Path and Hawkeye Cross Country Ski Trails.

Special concerns: Secure a permit from the district office for primitive backpack-camping. On the latter half of the hike, a broader blaze interval and taxing downfalls complicate travel; newcomers to hiking should avoid this leg, because it will only frustrate. Seasonally, expect some soggy trail segments.

Season and hours: Spring through fall for hiking.

For information: Tiadaghton State Forest.

Key points:

0.0 Krimm Road trailhead; hike counterclockwise.

2.7 Area of rock slabs and ledges.

5.4 Old Loggers Path.

5.7 Close loop.

Finding the trailhead: From the village of Shunk (12 miles south of Canton), head west on State Route 4002 where Pennsylvania 154 enters a curve. At Tompkins Corners in 2.5 miles, the road name changes to SR 4003/1015. Continue for another mile and turn left for Masten on improved-dirt SR 1013. At the Y-junction in 1.1 miles, bear right to find gated Krimm Road (the trailhead) on the left in 0.6 mile. Park to the sides of the gated road; do not block gate.

The hike: Hike south on Krimm Road, rounding the gate. On the right, find the blue-blazed Cherry Ridge Trail. The orange blazes straight ahead mark the Old Loggers Path (a 27-mile circuit through the eastern block of Tiadaghton State Forest), the closing leg for this loop. Go right, touring counterclockwise.

Cherry Ridge Trail

Travel a vegetation-narrowed woods road with a gentle gradient for a relaxing tour. Large black cherry trees exceeding 2 feet in diameter dominate the woodland. Beech, striped maple, and sugar maple weave among the dark, scaly-trunked giants. Tall, wispy ferns grow at their feet. The occasional low-swinging branch or small log to step over contributes to the trail's raw charm. The forest sameness brings about a hypnotic quality. Subtle discoveries are hallmarks of this ramble.

At 1.3 miles, pass through a small meadow clearing where hemlock and birch join the forest ranks and the black cherry loses its dominance. Sphagnum moss betrays seasonal wet spots. As the corridor broadens, the blazes are farther apart but remain sufficient to reassure and guide hikers.

Travel a brief area of cobbles before the trail curves left at 1.6 miles. At 1.8 miles, pass below a scenic multitrunked black cherry sporting both living and dead trunks. Starflower, mayflower, and other delicate spring blooms dress the trail's shoulders. A few unmarked side trails branch away; watch for the guiding blue blaze at or near each junction.

Black cherry trunk, Tiadaghton State Forest.

At 2.75 miles, the terrain reveals rock slabs and ledges above the trail, with a gentle wooded slope below. Striped maples favor the area of rocks. Blazes point hikers across a couple of springs, before returning them to woods road travel. At the fork at 3.75 miles, blazes mark the upper fork, but the prongs merge in another 0.2 mile.

Larger fallen trees obstruct and confuse the line of travel. Stay alert, noting the last spied marker in case you need to backtrack in search of the trail. The hike still conveys woodland serenity and solitude, but with added challenge and exercise. At 4.1 miles, cross a couple of seasonal rocky drainages, returning to a better stretch of woods road showing a two-track. Enjoy a reemergence of ferns along the path's shoulders and beneath the trees.

In 0.5 mile, as the two-track curves left uphill, go right, touring a fainter, longer-retired woods road. Then, at 4.75 miles, turn left onto another two-track, briefly hiking alongside an electric fence. Continue straight on this two-track.

At 5.4 miles, the orange-blazed Old Loggers Path arrives on the right from the ghost town of Masten (a former logging town, now marked only by a sign); find a register near the trail junction. Resume forward now on the joint Old Loggers Path/Cherry Ridge Trail to conclude the loop at the gate, 5.7 miles.

35 Little Pine State Park

Overview

At this 2,158-acre park along Little Pine Creek, trails explore the shore of the free-flowing creek and the reservoir floodplain, mount the steep forested flanks of the enfolding Appalachians, and meander along the broad summit plateau. Discover routes that both challenge and entertain, and others that invite Sunday strolling for nature study. In the logging era, springtime floods on Little Pine Creek transported rafts of logs to downstream mills. During Hurricane Agnes in 1972, the waters overflowed the dam, modifying the landscape.

General description:	The selected four hikes explore much of the park: Buttonball Nature Trail, Carsontown Trail, Lakeshore Trail, and Panther Run Trail.
General location:	12 miles north of Jersey Shore.
Special attractions:	Creek and reservoir access, flagstone outcrops, vistas, mountain laurel and wildflowers, diverse wildlife sightings, colorful fall foliage.
Length:	Buttonball Nature Trail, 0.5 mile round trip; Carsontown Trail, 0.85-mile loop or 1 mile round trip (depending on trail conditions); Lakeshore Trail, 3.6 miles round trip; Panther Run Trail, 5.5-mile loop.
Elevation:	Buttonball and Carsontown Trails, minimal elevation change; Lakeshore Trail, 100-foot elevation change; Panther Run Trail, 1,150-foot elevation change (high point, 1,900 feet; low point, 750 feet).
Difficulty:	Buttonball, Carsontown, and Lakeshore Trails, easy; Panther Run Trail is strenuous.
Maps:	State park brochure.
Special concerns:	Trailside camping in the state park is prohibited; camp only at designated sites within the family campground. Floods can alter the floodplain trails. Expect rigorous, steep pitches and inclines along Panther Run Trail. Color-coded blazes distinguish the trails.
Season and hours:	Year-round.
For information:	Little Pine State Park.

Key points:

Buttonball Nature Trail:

  0.0   Buttonball Trailhead.
  0.2   Grassy turnaround point.

Carsontown Trail:

  0.0   Carsontown Trailhead; head left.
  0.5   Midpoint; either traverse floodplain or backtrack.
  1.0   End at Carsontown Trailhead.

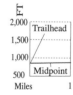

Little Pine State Park

To English Center

Panther Run

Panther Run Trail

Love Run

SR 4001

Little Pine Creek

Carsontown Trail

N

Naval Run

Little Pine Lake

Lakeshore Trail

0   0.5   1

Miles

To Jersey Shore

Buttonball Nature Trail

Lakeshore Trail:
- 0.0   Dam trailhead.
- 0.9   Pass beneath flagstone outcrop.
- 1.2   Cross lower Naval Run.
- 1.8   Turn around near "trashboom."

FT		
2,000	Trailhead	Naval Run
1,500		
1,000	Flagstone outcrop	
500		
Miles	1	

Panther Run Trail:

- 0.0 Love Run/Panther Run Trailhead.
- 1.2 Old quarry site/Y-junction; go right.
- 1.6 Top ridge.
- 2.5 Leave Mid State Trail.
- 4.5 State Route 4001.
- 5.5 End loop at trailhead.

Finding the trailhead: From the junction of U.S. Highway 220 and Pennsylvania 44, west of Jersey Shore, go north on PA 44 for 10.4 miles, turning right onto SR 4001. Go 3.2 miles to reach the campground entrance (and Buttonball Nature Trail), 3.5 miles to reach the dam (and Lakeshore Trail), 4.3 miles to reach Love Run/Panther Run Trailhead, 5.6 miles to reach the northern Panther Run Trailhead, and 6.4 miles to reach Carsontown Trailhead.

The hikes: At the bridge to the campground, the **Buttonball Nature Trail** heads downstream between the campground and Little Pine Creek. It offers a fine riparian walk with ample opportunity to get close to the water. By 0.1 mile, sycamores dominate the flat, joined by pine, hornbeam, and ash. The creek flows broad, flat, clear, and tea-colored, drawing trout anglers. The shore becomes more cobbled, approaching the attractive grassy point that isolates the free-flowing stream from a stagnant backwater. Reeds push up through the cobble, and beautiful grassy mounds adorn the point and far shore. Spy kingfisher, heron, and swallow. Return as you came, 0.5 mile.

The **Carsontown Trail** travels along a snaking section of Little Pine Creek upstream from Little Pine Lake (the reservoir). Its floodplain documents the power of water and the resilience of nature. From the trail sign, hike a mowed swath across the grassy canyon bottom. Wallflower, sweet clover, and other wildflowers decorate the knee-high grasses. Lone-standing pine, willow, and hornbeam dot the meadow. Often, a marvelous chorus of birdsongs rides the breeze. At the loop junction in 50 feet, bear left for a clockwise tour.

Travel the upper edge of the floodplain, touring meadow or meadow-dressed woods, crossing a footbridge over Schoolhouse Run. Markers count off 0.1-mile increments. Along the woods lane, discover deer tracks. At the 0.4-mile post, the trail swings toward Little Pine Creek. Hike the outskirts of a sycamore stand to reach this scenic braided water. Some sycamores reach 3 to 4 feet in diameter.

Because floods can steal the trail past the 0.5-mile post, hikers may either backtrack or pick their own downstream return, which may require a rock-hopping or wading of Schoolhouse Run. Note how the racing floodwaters straightened the upstream bend to overflow the plain, tumbling trees, distributing uprooted debris, and shifting cobbles and rock.

For the **Lakeshore Trail,** start at the parking area near the dam (avoid blocking the gate when parking). Traverse the dam for a length-of-the-lake view and then turn left, hiking north along the east shore of artificial Little Pine Lake. Descend to a grassy flat, passing an angler's path that branches left. Views upstream feature the enfolding wooded ridges. In the field, swallows dart after insects.

By 0.4 mile, enter woods, finding the first red blaze. The 5-foot-wide, mildly rolling trail has a carriageway character and ease. Enjoy a leafy cathedral of maple, oak, hickory, and beech, with complements of white pine. Although the lake is visible, the steep forested slope denies access. A cross-bedded flagstone outcrop partially overhangs the trail at 0.9 mile. Springs can muddy the way.

Before reaching often dry Naval Run, the blazed trail turns left and descends to floodplain level. Here, overlook the marshy upper end of the lake and spy frog, goose, mallard, or kingfisher. The trail then crosses lower Naval Run and grades back uphill into a transition forest. Find an open spacing of pine and hickory above a grassy floor. Watery channels web the floodplain.

With a switchback at 1.6 miles, return to the floodplain, touring a cropped-grass path between waist- to chest-deep grasses. Cross a culvert over a muddy side channel and edge a sycamore stand. Near the metal "trashboom," which keeps debris out of the reservoir (1.8 miles), nettles win a stronghold and the trail loses definition. Turn around, returning to the dam.

For a clockwise loop on the Panther Run Trail, start at the Love Run/Panther Run Trailhead, hiking west on closed Love Run Road for 50 feet to find the Panther Run Trail on the right. Pursue its yellow blazes through a forest of oak, hickory, and maple. Woody vines string between the trees, and aspen dot the canopy.

Enter a steady climb, with a few sharp, angled bursts. By 0.2 mile, reach the mountain laurel belt of the slope for a showy July display. Mosses pierce the decaying leaf mat, while small pines rise amid the laurels. Next, stroll a ridge spine marked by ragged flagstones. With the climb, the oaks and pines lose stature. Among the outcrops, discover startling profiles, anvil overhangs, windows, and gravity-defying balancing acts.

Where the trail crosses a flat of broken rocks between the outcrops (an old quarry site at 1.2 miles), detour left to top a rocky point for a view overlooking the treed watershed of Little Pine Creek. An oriole may adorn a nearby branch. After snaring the vista, follow the fragment of woods road from the quarry to the marked Y-junction, 1.25 miles.

A left leads to Love Run Road for an alternative loop back to the same trailhead. For this hike, turn right, following the dual blazes of the orange Mid State Trail and yellow Panther Run Trail. Continue the ascent in a tight aisle of pine, hickory, and oak, with mountain laurel and berry bushes.

At 1.6 miles, top the ridge and pursue the blazes north along it. At first narrow, the ridge presents downward looks over both its steep sides. The ridge itself extends a relaxing stroll. Small toads, drumming grouse, and scratching birds may draw attention. As the ridge broadens, travel a dense field of mountain laurel.

Depart the Mid State Trail at 2.5 miles, turning right and remaining on the yellow Panther Run Trail for a treacherous descent. Despite switchbacks, attend to your footing. Ferns replace the laurel, and maples abound, shading

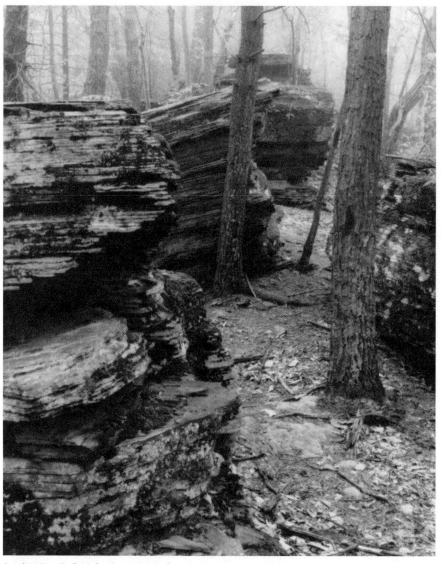

Panther Run Trail, Little Pine State Park.

the Panther Run drainage. At 3 miles, the trail contours the steep run slope downstream. A cut trailbed provides surer footing.

A washout at 3.5 miles then puts hikers on a bypass route that travels through stinging nettles. Its price may be higher than that of hiking downstream via the rocky streambed. The blazed trail continues crisscrossing the stream before assuming a higher line of travel above the run. Come out at a steep eroded descent to SR 4001 (4.2 miles); be careful. Upon reaching the road, turn right to close the loop back at Love Run/Panther Run Trailhead, 5.5 miles. From the roadway, overlook Little Pine Creek and Little Pine Creek Lake.

36 Loyalsock Trail to Smiths Knob

General description: This short but fairly challenging sampling of the 59.3-mile Loyalsock Trail (LT) travels steep flank and summit plateau, snaring both cleared and natural vistas. Wander amid mountain laurel and mayapple, and visit the impressive sandstone outcrop and cliff of Smiths Knob.

General location: 10 miles northeast of Montoursville.

Special attractions: Smiths Knob, Loyalsock Creek panorama, mountain laurel and forest wildflowers, wildlife sightings, fall foliage.

Length: 3.6 miles round trip, or 4.7 miles adding an end loop.

Elevation: Find a 1,150-foot elevation change between the trailhead (770 feet) and Smiths Knob (1,920 feet).

Difficulty: Moderate to strenuous.

Maps: Tiadaghton State Forest; the Alpine Club of Williamsport map and trail guide to the Loyalsock Trail.

Special concerns: Obtain a camp permit at district headquarters. Loyalsock Trail has a signature red dash on yellow blaze or LT disk markings; its alternate routes or bypasses show a red X on a yellow disk. You will also encounter blue access trails and white unmaintained trails. Expect steep inclines and pitches, and be especially attentive when rounding Smiths Knob.

Season and hours: Spring through fall for hiking.

For information: Tiadaghton State Forest.

Key points:

- 0.0 Little Bear Creek Road trailhead.
- 0.7 Helen's Window.
- 1.4 Loop junction; go left.
- 1.8 Smiths Knob; backtrack or add loop return.

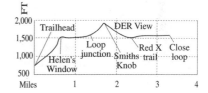

Loop Return:

- 2.1 DER View.
- 2.4 Follow red X trail right.
- 3.3 Close loop; backtrack to trailhead.

Finding the trailhead: From Interstate 180/U.S. Highway 220 at Montoursville, go north on Pennsylvania 87 about 10 miles, and turn east onto improved-dirt Little Bear Creek Road. Go 0.8 mile to find road-shoulder parking for the trail near the bridge to Little Bear forest headquarters.

The hike: From the headquarters entrance, hike 200 feet west along Little Bear Creek Road to follow the Loyalsock Trail (LT) north up the hill. A sign

Loyalsock Trail to Smiths Knob

for Smiths Knob marks the start. White pine, mixed oak, aspen, hemlock, and maple rise above the hiker-only trail. Cross the road to the ranger's residence and find a trail register.

The assault on the wooded slope steepens, quickly drawing out of the conifers and into the mountain laurel belt. Hear Little Bear Creek below and the wind rustling through the canopy. Find the foot trail in good condition and well used. Woodpeckers, songbirds, and soaring vultures enliven the air. A flattening of the trail allows hikers to catch their breath before the next charge. In places, striped maples win root.

Where the trail flattens out and follows the rim of the slope (0.7 mile), find Helen's Window and a white trail descending to PA 87. Overlook a clearing to a long straightaway of Loyalsock Creek and the framing even-height ridges. A jagged wildlife snag pierces the clearing. Flat rocks provide gallery seating, while hemlocks offer shade. A second clearing at 0.8 mile overlooks the wooded flanks of the neighboring ridges for a fine autumn mosaic.

Atop this shoulder of Laurel Ridge, find the trail rocky and ample laurel to give credence to the ridge's name. Where the trail drifts away from the rim, the rocks disappear and large chestnut oaks and low berry bushes frame a gentle walk. At 1.3 miles, meet a blue-blazed horse trail (a woods road arriving from PA 87) and follow it right for 0.1 mile to pick up the foot trail of the LT on the left. Note the red X disks on the woods road ahead; these mark the optional loop return.

The LT presents a sharp climb to the summit spine of Laurel Ridge. Birches briefly add to the forest. Hornbeam and mayapple favor the lofty flat. A clearing at 1.6 miles offers a view south–southeast toward Allegheny, Red, and Tar Kiln Ridges, parted by the drainages of Little Bear Creek and Painter Run.

Tag the ridge high point and descend, coming upon the blue circular sign for Smiths Knob (1.8 miles). The cliff creates a natural gap for admiring the wooded countryside, rural Loyalsock Valley, and the lichen-whitewashed cliff itself, plunging 30 to 50 feet. Keep back from the edge, and no horseplay. Vultures soar at hikers' feet.

From Smiths Knob, hikers have the option of returning as they came for a 3.6-mile round trip, or proceeding on the LT to meet the red X trail, adding a loop to the return. For the loop, continue the ridge descent, hugging the cliff and easing over and between rocks. Use care on this brief treacherous stretch.

An easy foot trail then travels along the north rim of the slope. Enjoy an attractive forest cathedral with old-growth maple and oak, tulip, and hemlock. At 2.1 miles, pass the marker for DER VIEW; this stolen peek between the tree trunks may easily go unnoticed but for the sign.

Drift from the rim, finding the red X trail at 2.4 miles. Follow it right, departing the LT, which curves left. Laurels again set the stage, and a deer's curiosity may cause it to linger. Round a vernal pond and turn right onto the woods road of the blue horse trail. At 2.8 miles, red X disks point hikers off the horse trail onto a lower parallel route, only to return to the woods road at 3 miles. Close the loop at 3.3 miles, and retrace the LT to the trailhead at 4.7 miles.

37 Chuck Keiper Trail, East Loop

General description:	This hike explores the offering of the eastern component of the 50-mile, double-looped Chuck Keiper Trail System (CKT). Travel mixed woodlands, picturesque hollows, meadow, and burn habitat. The CKT follows old logging grades and named foot trails, bridged by some road travel.
General location:	35 miles west of Williamsport, 30 miles north of State College.
Special attractions:	Solitude; rhododendron, laurel, and dogwood blooms; vistas; wildlife sightings; fall foliage.
Length:	25.6-mile loop, with the Big Rocks Vista detour.
Elevation:	This rolling trail shows a 1,200-foot elevation change, with a low point of 1,100 feet at Hall Run and a high point of 2,300 feet atop Barneys Ridge.
Difficulty:	Strenuous.
Maps:	Chuck Keiper Trail; Sproul State Forest.
Special concerns:	During high water, hikers may need to wade larger runs. Forest roads regularly intersect or advance the CKT, allowing hikers to partition the loop; consult the Sproul State Forest public-use map. The trail is orange-blazed.
Season and hours:	Spring through fall for hiking.
For information:	Sproul State Forest.

Chuck Keiper Trail, East Loop

Key points:

19.0 Cross Clendenin Branch.
19.8 Cross Shoemaker Ridge Road.
22.1 Junction with CKT, West Loop; turn right.
25.0 PA 144 at "State Camp."
25.6 End loop at trailhead.

Finding the trailhead: From the junction of PA 120 and PA 144 South in Renovo, go south on PA 144 for 9.8 miles and turn right (west) onto a dirt road opposite Swamp Branch Road for the trail. At the fork, go left 0.1 mile to find parking atop a vista plateau; access the Chuck Keiper Trail off the right fork for a clockwise tour.

The hike: From the parking area, survey the Fish Dam Run Wild Area, and then head northward, following the two-track bearing right up the slope away from the trail kiosk. Where the jeep trail curves, take a quick left past a stand of pines to follow the orange blazes of the CKT along an open meadow swath. Wildflowers sprinkle the grasses of Barneys Ridge. Young maples grow to the side. Although hikers lose views of Fish Dam Run Wild Area, eastern glances find Coffin Rock Fire Tower.

The CKT then gently descends from Barneys Ridge, passing through an area of bigger trees and shade. Reach Barneys Ridge Road (0.8 mile), and follow this dirt forest road left for a sunny walk, despite the framing trees. At 1.2 miles, reach a sign for Big Rocks Vista.

This 0.4-mile, round-trip detour to the right travels woods road and foot trail beyond a rock barricade to an area of large outcrops. A slot allows fairly easy access to the top, although views are limited. Laurel adorns the site, but graffiti and broken glass prove strong detractors. Resume the main hike at 1.6 miles, bearing right.

At 2 miles, bear right onto Dry Run Road, passing amid hardwoods and berry bushes. Then, at 2.2 miles, turn right, following a grassy lane uphill for an easy stretch on both eyes and feet. Sassafras, laurel, and witch hazel shape the gateway. Where the jeep trail arcs right, proceed forward on footpath; watch for blazes on trailbed rocks and trees.

The CKT now dips into the cool, full-canopy forest of Drake Hollow for a steady, sometimes steep descent on Drake Hollow Trail. Ferns abound. Where the trail crosses to the right bank, an old road bench offers easier footing, with the occasional obstacle of nettles or springs. At 3.7 miles, a side drainage reveals a seasonal waterfall or weeping wall. Downstream, the hollow shows more reliable water, with cascades. Hemlock, birch, tulip poplar, and rhododendron accent shore. At 4.8 miles, cross back to the left bank to exit onto PA 144 (5.1 miles).

Cross Drake Hollow bridge, ascending along PA 144 south for 0.9 mile. Generally the sun's angle affords some shade, and the bending route keeps traffic light and slow. At 6 miles, turn left, following the CKT blazes, now on Diamond Rock Hollow Trail. Descend and cross the gravelly stream of Hall Run to follow the north shore of Diamond Rock Run upstream. Cross this run at 6.2 miles; the lower drainage shows varied woods. The stepped run is a pleasing host.

At 6.5 miles, encounter sections of improved trail as the CKT pursues the headwater fork to the right. Crisscross the fork and eventually walk the rocky drainage itself. Be alert here, or the rocks and masking leaves could cause a twisted ankle. With a steep burst of climbing, reach a jeep road (7.5 miles) and ascend it left. Turkeys may startle hikers. Striped maple, sassafras, and berry frame the way. Meet Petes Run Road, another dirt forest road, at 7.75 miles.

Turn left onto Petes Run Road to resume the CKT on the right in 200 feet, quickly crossing a utility-line corridor. Return to fern-floored forest for a moderate descent, crossing the upper drainage of Boggs Hollow at 8.2 miles. A worn cart path advances the trail. Next, enter a bowl where several headwater streams meet. Twice cross the run to continue downstream along the left bank. As the slope steepens, the trail draws above the run. Rhododendrons accent the tour.

Cross springs and side tributaries, dropping down to cross Boggs Hollow and follow its right bank downstream (10.5 miles). Jewelweed, violet, nettle, and mayapple grow along the drainage. The rolling trail traces a contour well above the run, offering glimpses. At 11.8 miles, enter the recess of a large side drainage and follow this tributary upstream.

At 12.5 miles, cross the right headwater fork to follow the left fork upstream. The trail then charges out of the drainage, passing through a drier forest intermixed with laurel. Cross Mill Run Road (13.3 miles), finding the blazed path (a grassy secondary jeep trail) just to the right of a gated jeep road. The grassy path descends fairly sharply en route to Sled Road Hollow. The blazes may be farther spread, with laurel and berry bushes sometimes hiding them until the last minute.

At 13.8 miles, the jeep trail fades, entering a meadow; look for a blaze at the far end. A foot trail then descends to the rocky head of Sled Road Hollow, where a soothing hemlock darkness cloaks travel. The CKT hopscotches between banks of this bending hollow before settling on the west bank for an easy stroll. Laurel and mushrooms lend seasonal accents as the trail nudges the pine–oak forest. Pieces of old lane and foot trail advance the CKT on its downstream sojourn. Tour meadowy shore and pine stand, crossing the foot of a descending logging road (14.8 miles).

Keep to the meadow and mixed woods of shore, cross a muddy side spring, and pass a piped spring. At 15.1 miles, follow the orange blazes along a two-track, hiking past a small white building; keep out, no camping. Cross the road bridge over Benjamin Run to meet a dirt forest road, Sled Road Trail, and turn right.

Briefly follow Benjamin Run upstream, staying on the road where it curves left past the mesh fence at a gas pipeline. Again, blazes occur farther apart. Ascend past some buildings (state forest camps), proceeding straight on a wide grassy swath where the road hooks right.

Another ascent follows, gradually growing steeper. Cross a power-line corridor (15.7 miles), returning to woods. Laurels join and later replace the trail's edge of small pines. Top the ridge at 16.4 miles and cross a dirt forest road. Soon after, the trail again dips, passing a wealth of laurel and berries. At 17.3 miles, cross a footbridge over Cranberry Run and head left downstream. Upstream to the right is Cranberry Swamp Natural Area, but currently no marked trail accesses it. Seasonally, insects bother both hikers and deer.

Be sure to carry plenty of drinking water for the hot stretch ahead. With the next ascent, enjoy another profusion of laurel. This is now Four Ridge Trail. Where it tops out in burn habitat (17.8 miles), find hundreds of silver snags, thick berry bushes, and laurel, along with young sassafras, maple, and pine. Stakes help guide hikers. Songbirds favor the site, and views stretch across the neighborhood of flat-topped ridges.

Fire zone, Chuck Keiper Trail, Sproul State Forest.

At 18.3 miles, cross a jeep trail/firebreak, entering semiopen forest for a slow descent to the Clendenin Branch (19 miles). Cross via stones, passing a campsite. After a brief burst of climbing, the grade eases. Cross a small drainage near another state forest camp, and then ascend foot trail and jeep road to cross Shoemaker Ridge Road (19.8 miles).

In a select cut, knee-high fern, laurel, and berry bushes brush passersby. Descend to cross Rock Run, coming out near a building. Follow the closed jeep road through an opening to the right. In this clear-cut maintained for wildlife, the vegetation grows waist-deep. At 21.1 miles, bear left. The trail reenters forest at 21.6 miles. Where it nears another state forest camp structure, meet a jeep track and follow it out to Beech Creek Road (21.75 miles).

Now hike a grassy lane into open forest, descending to a gentle drainage. At 22.1 miles, reach a marked junction with CKT, West Loop. Turn right, hiking upstream along a typically dry drainage to cross attractive East Branch Big Run. Walk up the East Branch, crossing it twice more.

The gentle terrain shapes an easy walk away from the run. Discover a few larch and white pine as low quartzite boulders litter the forest floor. Leave the boulder field, arriving at Coon Run Road (23.7 miles).

Turn right to pick up the CKT on the left in 0.1 mile, now traveling the East Branch Trail. Return to woods, skirting the headwater marsh of East Branch Big Run, a large shrubby flat with a few cattails. Old yellow blazes may linger. Travel a disturbed zone where a tornado thrashed about trees, and cross a deep, thin headwater. More tornado-disturbed forest follows, and then open grasses.

Navigate blaze to blaze, crossing a wide grassy swath at 24.9 miles to reach PA 144 at an old foundation—"State Camp" on maps (25 miles). Turn left on PA 144, hike 0.6 mile, and turn right onto a dirt road, returning to the trailhead. The West Loop proceeds south along PA 144.

38 Montour Preserve

Overview

Cradled in the broad Appalachian Valley between Montour Ridge and Muncy Hills, this 966-acre Pennsylvania Power and Light (PP&L) preserve invites outdoor recreation and nature study. At the heart of the preserve sits 165-acre Lake Chillisquaque, an important waterfowl stopover on the Atlantic Flyway. Historically, the Muncy–Mahoning Indian Path passed through what is now the preserve. Today, a fine series of interlocking hiking trails welcome contemporary boots.

General description: Five hikes incorporate many of the trails and spotlight the preserve's cultural and natural history. Interpretive panels and brochures help unfold the story.

General location: 10 miles north of Danville.

Special attractions: Visitor center with habitat dioramas; lake and wildlife ponds; meadow and riparian–valley woods; Devonian fossil pit; maple sugar shack; flowering shrubs, wildflowers, and pond lilies; wildlife sightings, with peak waterfowl migration in late March; colorful fall leaves.

Length: Chilisuagi Trail, 4.25-mile loop or 6.2-mile loop with side trips to Ridgefield Point and the restricted-access blinds (secure permits before starting out); Goose Woods/Braille Trail, 0.9 mile round trip (0.5 mile for Braille Trail alone); Wildlife Management Trail, 0.75 mile round trip; Laura Smith Trail of History, 0.25-mile loop; Fossil Pit Trail, 0.2 mile round trip.

Elevation: Find a minimal elevation change along the trails; preserve lands range between 550 and 650 feet in elevation.

Difficulty: Chilisuagi Trail, moderate; all others are easy.

Maps: Montour Preserve brochure; individual trail booklets (generally available at each trailhead).

Special concerns: Entry permits are required to cross the designated wildlife refuge to the preserve's two wildlife blinds; inquire at the office for a permit and keys to the structures. No pets, no bikes, no swimming, no collecting (except at the fossil pit), and no overnight camping. Keep to designated trails and heed area and state boating and fishing rules.

Season and hours: Year-round, sunrise to sunset. Office and visitor center, 9:00 A.M. to 4:00 P.M., weekdays; weekend hours 9:00 A.M. to 4:00 P.M., May through September only.

For information: Montour Preserve.

Montour Preserve

To Turbotville

To Whitehall

44

Middle Branch Chillisquaque Creek

To Whitehall

McCormick Road

Alder Swamp Trail

Smokehouse Blind

Goose Cove

Muskrat Cove

Chilisuagi Trail

Jellyfish Cove

Heron Cove

Oak Woods Trail

Ridgefield Point Trail

Fossil Pit

To SR 1006

Goose Cove Picnic Area

Lake Chillisquaque

Heron Cove Picnic Area

T423

Wildlife Management Trail

Goose Cove Overlook

Laura Smith Trail of History

To Washingtonville

SR 1006

To Millville

N

Braille Trail

Environmental Study Pond

Chillisquaque Creek

Goose Woods Trail

Maple Sugar Shack

0   0.25   0.5

Miles

Key points:

Chilisuagi Trail:

0.0	Goose Cove Overlook trailhead; cross dam.
1.0	Heron Cove recreation site.
1.8	Ridgefield Point Trail.
3.2	Middle Fork Chillisquaque Creek.
4.1	Detour left to Smokehouse Blind. (Permit needed.)
5.2	Detour left to Muskrat Blind. (Permit needed.)
6.2	End loop at overlook parking.

168

Goose Woods/Braille Trail:

0.0   Braille Trailhead.
0.2   Goose Woods Trail.
0.3   Sugar Shack.
0.6   Lily pond; return to
       Braille Trail.
0.9   End at trailhead.

Wildlife Management Trail:

0.0   Wildlife Management Trailhead.
0.1   Loop junction at wildlife pond;
       go left.
0.7   End at trailhead.

Laura Smith Trail of History:

0.0   Laura Smith Trail of
       History Trailhead.
0.2   End at trailhead.

Fossil Pit Trail:

0.0   Township
       423 trailhead.
0.1   Fossil Pit;
       backtrack.

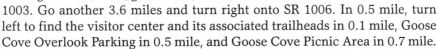

Finding the trailhead: From Interstate 80 west of Bloomsburg, take exit 33 and travel north on Pennsylvania 54 West toward Washingtonville. Following signs for the preserve, in 4.6 miles turn right onto PA 254, go 0.5 mile, and turn left onto State Route 1003. Go another 3.6 miles and turn right onto SR 1006. In 0.5 mile, turn left to find the visitor center and its associated trailheads in 0.1 mile, Goose Cove Overlook Parking in 0.5 mile, and Goose Cove Picnic Area in 0.7 mile.

For the Fossil Pit, stay on SR 1006, driving past the visitor center turnoff. In 0.5 mile, bear left onto Township 423 toward Heron Cove Boat Launch and Picnic Area. Park on the right opposite the Bluebird Trail in another mile.

The hikes: Hikers may access the **Chilisuagi Trail** at the Goose Cove and Heron Cove recreation areas or from Goose Cove Overlook Parking. Starting from the latter, round the gate to cross the dam for a counterclockwise tour. Enjoy cross-lake views at the surrounding low wooded rises, the tongue dividing the Lake Chillisquaque coves, and the preserve mosaic. Loons, swallows, and geese are common sightings. *Chillisquaque* means "song of the wild goose."

In 0.5 mile, bear left onto a gravel lane, continuing to round the lake. Myriad thistle, pea, daisy, clover, chicory, and milkweed color the grassland. At 1 mile, pass through groomed Heron Cove recreation site, finding rest rooms, water, tables, a fishing dock, and boat launch. Hikers may spy a turtle's head piercing the lake surface.

The tour resumes amid maple, elm, and hawthorn, with hedgerows of flowering shrubs and poison ivy separating the trail from the open field. Later, a marsh habitat with cattails and the lively notes of red-winged blackbirds and frogs extends right. Still enjoy filtered looks left at the lake.

At 1.3 miles, reach an interpretive panel and the 0.75-mile Bluebird Trail, which heads right. Continue the lake tour, counting down the numbered interpretive panels. The aisle grows more shaded with scenic old maples. Lake views now sweep the cattail extent of Heron Cove. Cross an inlet bridge and continue passing interpretive stations and bench seats. Keen-eyed hikers may spy the toothy evidence of beaver.

View Jellyfish Cove and hike in a woodland of tall hickory and oak to meet the Ridgefield Point Trail (1.8 miles). Turn left to add this stroll, exploring the dividing lake tongue, touring field and forest. Follow the mowed and raked track for a clockwise tour. Side mowings facilitate wildlife by creating a braided habitat, but can add confusion. Discoveries may include a beaver lodge of mud and sticks, the noisy passage of a turkey, or deer tracks in the soft sand of shore. Conclude this side trip at 2.6 miles, turning left onto the Chilisuagi Trail.

The lake trail now shows a mild roll, passing amid mixed woods and skirting wild and groomed fields, removed from Lake Chillisquaque. At 3.25 miles, cross the bridge over Middle Fork Chillisquaque Creek. Where the mowed track of the 1.5-mile West Branch Trail heads right (3.5 miles), stay on the gravel lane ahead. Young transition woods and open meadow prescribe a sunny stroll. Hawks and cardinals add to the bird-watcher's roster.

Near McCormick Road (4.1 miles), find a gated entry to the restricted wildlife refuge and Alder Swamp Trail (Trail 10 on the preserve map) to Smokehouse Blind. Hikers must possess a permit to add this 0.7-mile round trip. Travel a transition-woods aisle to the enclosed blind, with camouflaged windows and viewing cutouts for scopes and camera lenses. Overlook the head of Goose Cove.

Resume the lake trail at 4.8 miles, crossing the inlet creek to Muskrat Cove. At 5.25 miles, the mowed swath of the Oak Woods Trail (Trail 9; entry permit required) passes through field and oak–hickory woods, meeting a service road near Muskrat Blind (5.5 miles). This larger blind looks out at Muskrat Cove and a shrubby island, offering views on three sides.

Back at the Chilisuagi Trail (5.75 miles), turn left to come out at the developed Goose Cove recreation area. Proceed south through this area or along its entrance road to conclude the loop at Goose Cove Overlook Parking, 6.2 miles.

Three hikes start next to the visitor center: the **Goose Woods/Braille Trail, Wildlife Management Trail,** and **Laura Smith Trail of History.**

Start the Goose Woods/Braille Trail at the Braille Trail sign in the parking lot. Quickly cross SR 1006, traveling a wood-shavings path framed by young forest of elm, ash, and dogwood, with showings of honeysuckle, Virginia creeper, jewelweed, and rhododendron. Cross a footbridge and begin a clockwise hike, passing alongside Middle Branch Chillisquaque Creek. A guide rope leads the way; wooden beads along the rope signal interpretive signs in both Braille and large print.

The framing woods and trailside vegetation show great variety. Jet-black and neon-colored damselflies hover over the stream. At 0.2 mile, the Braille Trail swings right to complete its loop along a lily pond. Proceed forward for an upland woods hike on Goose Woods Trail (no guide rope). This trail, too, concludes along the pond.

Cross the creek bridge to reach the Sugar Shack, where visitors learn about the making of maple syrup in late February and early March. At other times, just enjoy the big maples. Continue along the creek bank, learning about the natural and cultural history of the area. Then cross back over the creek, viewing billows of vapor from the site's steam electric plant.

At 0.6 mile, reach the lily pond to complete the tour, following the Braille Trail along the east shore. Pink and white pond lilies, cattails, bulrushes, and soothing reflections of clouds add to the pond's charm. A muskrat may part the still water. Reenter woods, close the loop, and return to the visitor center, 0.9 mile.

Start the marked Wildlife Management Trail on the west side of the preserve road, opposite the entry to the visitor center. Croaking frogs announce their presence in a small cattail pond to the right. In less than 0.1 mile, reach another wildlife pond and the loop junction; go left for a clockwise tour. Travel the mowed track, passing amid field, meadow, transitioning shrubs, pine plantation, and elm–oak–maple woodlands. Find the trail mostly sunny. Deer, dragonfly, red-winged blackbird, and songbirds may provide companionship. Pass a butterfly garden, then turn left upon closing the loop to return to the center.

For the 0.25-mile Laura Smith Trail of History, follow the point-to-point description in the trail brochure, hiking past the Victorian farmhouse, now the PP&L Preserve office. The circuit visits an herb garden and rusting farm equipment and overlooks Chillisquaque Creek before returning to the center. The pamphlet ties images from the present to the past. Even on this short hike, hikers may spy deer, woodchuck, and songbirds.

For the **Fossil Pit Trail**, hike east off T 423 for 0.1 mile, reaching the quarry slope. The shale holds evidence of an ancient sea dating to the Devonian period 395 million years ago. An interpretive board and brochure identify the fossils by shape and name. Collect corals, lamp shells, cephalopods, and crinoids (plantlike animals). Search the freshly exposed shales. The more serious seeker should come with a clay knife or hammer and a paintbrush to clean the fossils. At this shadeless site, bring plenty of drinking water and wear a hat. Be careful of the sharp-edged shale.

39 Mid State Trail

General description: This long-distance, north-to-south-trending hiking trail lays a loose sash across the middle of Pennsylvania. The Mid State Trail (MST) travels up Pine Creek Valley and rolls against the grain, passing up and over the serial arced ridges of the central state. While the MST is incomplete, this hike features some 168 adjoining miles.

General location: This hike runs north–south between Blackwell on Pennsylvania 414 and the village of Water Street on U.S. Highway 22.

Special attractions: Fire towers and natural vistas, a section of the Great Island Indian Path, an abandoned railroad tunnel, mixed forest, mountain laurel, solitude, fall foliage.

Length: 168 miles one-way.

Elevation: The rolling trail has a total elevation change of 25,000 feet, passing from ridgetops in excess of 2,400 feet to valley bottoms less than 550 feet in elevation.

Difficulty: Easy to strenuous, depending on length and selected section.

Maps: Mid State Trail Association maps; *Guide to the Mid State Trail in Pennsylvania.*

Special concerns: Find overnight camping within the developed campgrounds of the state parks (at usual fees) or on state forest lands outside the natural areas and away from Penns Creek where it passes between Cherry Run and Poe Paddy. Secure a free overnight permit from the appropriate state forest district headquarters. Because water is not dependable along the full length of the trail, carry adequate amounts between known water sources; purify all trail sources.

Thru-trail hikers will need to plan for resupplying, know what to do in case of an emergency, and arrange for pickup at the end of the trail; the *Guide to the Mid State Trail in Pennsylvania* offers hints. The MST is orange-blazed with official distances expressed in metric units; side trails have blue blazings. Pass respectfully on private lands.

Hikers should be aware that the MST portion that follows PA 414 may be rerouted into forest (the final decision is still pending from Tiadaghton State Forest). In the future, carefully watch blazes here to take advantage of this trail improvement.

Season and hours: Spring through fall for hiking.

For information: Tioga, Tiadaghton, Bald Eagle, Rothrock, and Buchanan State Forests; Mid State Trail Association.

Mid State Trail

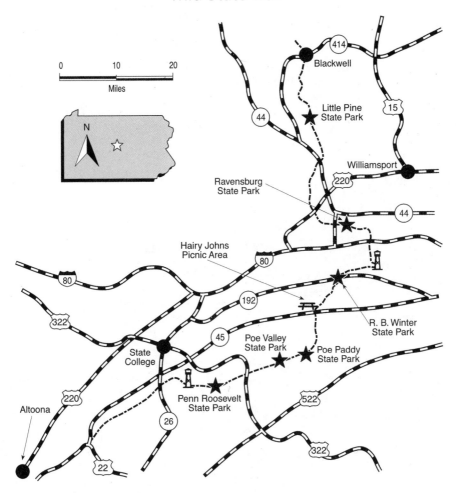

Key points:

0.0	Canoe access at Blackwell.
11.0	Oregon Hill.
25.2	PA 414 at Little Pine State Park.
35.0	Houselander Mountain.
38.0	PA 44/low-water fording or Conrail bridge detour.
49.0	Woolrich.
50.8	Cross PA 150.
57.0	Scree slopes of Round Top.
64.3	Ravensburg State Park.
76.0	Span over Interstate 80.
81.0	Sand Mountain Fire Tower.
84.2	PA 192/R. B. Winter State Park.
95.5	Hairy Johns Picnic Area/PA 45.
107.3	Tunnel through Paddy Mountain.

122.7	Culvert under US 322.
128.8	Penn Roosevelt State Park.
133.2	Pass Greenwood Spur.
136.5	Indian Wells Overlook.
141.0	Tussey Mountain.
148.0	Jo Hays Vista/PA 26.
163.0	Leave Tussey Mountain.
168.0	End at US 22–State Route 4014.

Finding the trailhead: Access the northern end of the MST at Blackwell off PA 414; the current southern terminus is at the corner of US 22 and SR 4014 east of Water Street. Find midway accesses at state parks and highway crossings.

174

The hike: Mostly utilizing footpaths and old roads, the Mid State Trail travels mainly on public lands, with a few private properties bridging trail fragments. Pass through five state forests, half a dozen state parks, state forest picnic areas, a state game land, and a handful of natural areas, enjoying a mostly forested tour with occasional views and stretches along waterways. Volunteers do a fine job maintaining the trail.

The MST crosses creeks, forest roads, highways, and an interstate as it cuts across Pennsylvania. Roadways allow hikers to partition the tour into manageable segments. The lightly used MST has won the nickname "Wildest Trail in Pennsylvania."

On this rigorous journey, name-dropping Pennsylvania ridges becomes routine. The MST passes through hemlock and mixed-hardwood forests and sites of plantation pine. Atop the flat-topped ridges, find low-stature oaks, laurel, and berry bushes.

On a north–south trek, the Grand Canyon of Pennsylvania launches the hike. Begin from the community of Blackwell at the canoe launch, following the blazed route east into town and across Babb Creek before turning south. (Or add two days to the trek by starting at Ansonia and following the West Rim Trail to Bohen Run.) Perhaps one of the bald eagles nesting in the canyon will salute your journey. At 1.3 miles, the MST tops Gillespie Point for an early view. It then rolls from hollow to run, with a stretch along Brown Fork.

State Game Lands 75, Wolf Run Wild Area, and Bark Cabin Natural Area (old-growth hemlock) advance the MST from mile 5 to mile 18, still in the Pine Creek countryside. Enjoy a view from Oregon Hill (11 miles). If you pitch a camp along this stretch, be sure it lies outside the state game land and natural areas.

By 20 miles, the MST passes through Little Pine State Park, meeting and sharing a leg of the yellow-blazed Panther Run Trail for a ridgetop journey where laurel abounds. A detour left where the Panther Run Trail departs the MST leads to an old flagstone quarry flat (in a matter of strides) and an outcrop overlooking Little Pine Creek Valley. The MST follows closed, dirt Love Run Road, crosses Love Run, and shares the trailbed with two additional park trails before crossing Little Pine Creek at the park campground off SR 4001 (25.3 miles).

Southbound, the MST parallels Little Pine Creek away from the park before making a rolling ascent. Rugged Houselander Mountain, with its vista opportunities, then takes the baton at 35 miles. Upon descent, cross PA 44 and ford Pine Creek at Camp Kline (38 miles); this crossing requires low water. In the future, the old Conrail bridge at Ramsey will allow an easier crossing. MST blazes already lead to this bridge, but keep to the fording until the bridge is made trail-safe.

The trail again rolls, pursuing runs up- and downstream, snaring views along Nepley Ridge, and crossing Big Springs Road (45 miles). The MST then descends, passing through the first stretches of private land at about 47 miles. On this leg, the MST passes through Woolrich near the factory outlet store and traverses lands owned by Woolrich Woolen Mills and others.

Cross PA 150 at 50.8 miles and travel roads to the West Branch Susquehanna River bridge. Cross, hike east along River Road East, and then continue weaving via roads through West Branch Valley. Sights along this stretch include a roadside marker for a Delaware Indian Village, a side-road marker for Fort Horn (1777), and remnants of old canal. As the MST ascends out of private land (56 miles), find foot trail. At 57 miles, traverse the scree slopes of Round Top to win rewarding views of the West Branch, Allegheny Front, and Gates of Pine Creek.

Continue tracking the weaving route, hiking along Ramm Road for a spell. Where the MST next descends, walk the Great Island Indian Path. Today, an old road replaces the original footpath, but it is one of the few areas where history has not been paved over. Reach PA 880 and follow the blazes to enter Ravensburg State Park (64.3 miles). From the park, the MST ascends Big Mountain, entering the ridge-hopping phase of travel. Where it levels out, tally more views.

The trail then dips to cross White Deer Creek (about 71 miles), followed by a more modestly rolling stretch. At 76 miles, a span over I–80 advances the MST. At 81 miles, visit Sand Mountain Fire Tower. Hikers may ascend the twelve-story tower, but beware: The landings lack protective cages. Use railings, heed posted numbers, and no horseplay. A 360-degree view awaits, combining farmland, rural towns, the folded ridges traveled by the MST, and the beauty of Penn's Woods. The MST then eases downhill and trends southwest, traversing Bake Oven Mountain.

Where the trail meets PA 192 (84.2 miles), travel pine plantation and deciduous woods, overlook dammed Halfway Lake, and admire the scenic outlet of Rapid Run in R. B. Winter State Park. Next, ring up travel on Brush, Shriner, Sharpback, Buffalo, and Winkelblech Mountains, interrupted by a dip to cross Pine Creek (Centre County's, not Lycoming's). Views are denied until Winkelblech Mountain (94 miles).

Where the MST passes through Hairy Johns Picnic Area and crosses PA 45 (95.5 miles), find the trail well blazed but sometimes lacking a tracked path. Snare views atop Thick Mountain before descending via Cherry Run to the attractive Penn Central Railroad grade along Penns Creek. At 107.3 miles, pass through Paddy Mountain via the abandoned tunnel. Only an arc of light at the far end breaks the darkness. At the culvertlike opening, hikers may need to stoop.

From the tunnel, travel a private drive and forest road, pursuing MST blazes to Poe Paddy State Park. Find amenities at the park before making a rocky climb to travel Long Mountain. Here, vistas present Penns Creek. At mile 112, a trail leads to Poe Valley State Park.

Between the Millheim–Siglerville Pike and Stillhouse Hollow, the MST thrice crosses Greens Valley, a pretty, tree-draped, gurgling stream. A rocky ascent follows. Once again atop Long Mountain, gather southern views from Chickadee Rocks and Big Valley Vista. Then dip to pass under US 322 in a culvert (122.7 miles).

Now the MST follows the grain of the long, flat ridges, smoothing out the tour. At 128.8 miles, reach Penn Roosevelt State Park, with its small pond.

Mid State Trail railroad tunnel, Bald Eagle State Forest.

Next, follow Detweiler Run downstream before climbing to the top of Thick-head Mountain. Along this mountain find Indian Wells Overlook, lauded as one of the best vistas in the state (136.5 miles). Here and beyond, gather views of Bear Meadow Natural Area before reaching Little Flat Lookout Tower.

Extensive flat-topped Tussey Mountain, with only a brief cut down to Shaver Creek for water, next advances the southbound MST from mile 141 to mile 163. At the Shaver Creek cut, hikers have the option of keeping to the mountaintop.

Despite its rugged, often rocky footing, Tussey Mountain serves up a feast for the eyes, with frequent vantages overlooking the natural scree and talus slopes. Chestnut oak and striped maple dress the ridge, interwoven with berry bushes and laurel. At 148 miles, find Jo Hays Vista parking north of the MST's crossing of PA 26. Here, overlook State College, the valley flat, and multi-hued green and gold fields.

The next 15 miles on Tussey Mountain roll out perhaps the finest vista stretch of the hike, but the descent to the Little Juniata River holds little to recommend it. The descent travels areas disturbed by quarrying and cutting. The selected hike ends at the corner of US 22 and SR 4014. Plans, though, call for completing the trail south to the Maryland border; large blocks are already in place, especially in Buchanan State Forest.

Thru-trail hikers should purchase a guide and maps from the Mid State Trail Association for point-to-point directions. To obtain alerts to the latest reroutes and extensions, consult the *Keystone Trails Association Newsletter* or visit its Web site at www.pennaweb.com/kta/.

40 Tunnel and Iron Horse Trails

General description: These adjoining trails explore second-growth forest and meadow habitats, tracing a remnant of railroad history (late 1800s to early 1900s).

General location: 40 miles west of Harrisburg.

Special attractions: Diverse second-growth forest, clues to the railroading past, wildflowers, wildlife sightings, fall foliage.

Length: 10.4-mile loop; 1-mile loop for Tunnel Trail only.

Elevation: Travel between 850 and 1,700 feet in elevation.

Difficulty: Moderate.

Maps: Iron Horse Trail brochure; Tuscarora State Forest.

Special concerns: Red blazings indicate the Iron Horse Trail; blue, the Tunnel Trail. Hikers may camp overnight along the Iron Horse Trail, but not within Big Spring State Park or on private lands along or near the trail. Contact the district headquarters about permits. Because the Iron Horse Trail often abuts and for 1 mile traverses private land, keep to the trail, pass respectfully, and obey posted restrictions. Flooding necessitated a reroute on the southern Iron Horse Trail; watch for blazes.

Season and hours: Spring through fall for hiking.

For information: Tuscarora State Forest.

Key points:

Iron Horse Trail:

- 0.0   Hemlock Road trailhead; hike south.
- 0.3   Abandoned tunnel.
- 0.7   Tunnel Trail–Iron Horse Trail junction.
- 2.6   Cross Hemlock Run bridge.
- 4.7   Cross Sherman Creek footbridge.
- 5.1   Eby Cemetery.
- 6.6   Top Eby Ridge.
- 10.3   Cross Pennsylvania 274 at Big Spring State Park.
- 10.4   End loop at Hemlock Road trailhead.

Finding the trailhead: From the Pennsylvania Turnpike, Interstate 76, take exit 14 and follow PA 75 north for 11 miles, turning east onto PA 274. In 4.7 miles, turn right onto dirt Hemlock Road to reach the marked trailhead and upper parking area for Big Spring State Park. For the park's main entrance and picnic area, go 0.1 mile farther east on PA 274. Find a second trailhead on PA 274, 3.8 miles east of Big Spring State Park, 2 miles west of New Germantown.

Tunnel and Iron Horse Trails

The hike: On the south side of PA 274, the Iron Horse Trail incorporates grades from the Perry Lumber Company Railroad (1901 to 1905). On the north side of PA 274, travel fragments of the Path Valley Railroad—a failed venture, halted by the geology of Conococheague Mountain. The Tunnel Trail visits the site that spelled the end for Path Valley Railroad. Intended to extend 0.5 mile through the mountain, the tunnel penetrates just 100 feet. The site's metamorphosed rock (flint) resisted blasting, and when the pay stopped coming, the workers walked.

From the Hemlock Road trailhead, hike south across the road, following the Tunnel Trail for a counterclockwise circuit. Pass amid oak, birch, hemlock, and laurel, paralleling Hemlock Road east. Fragments of the historic railroad grade advance the rolling tour. Where the trail curves left to descend (0.3 mile), proceed forward to view the abandoned tunnel in the hemlock darkness. A fence denies a close inspection of the skyward-angled void.

Resume the Tunnel Trail by crossing Hemlock Road. Meander in a tight young forest of birch and gum to reach the Iron Horse Trail/Perry Lumber Company Railroad (0.75 mile). Turn left to complete the Tunnel Trail at Big Spring State Park (1 mile). Turn right for the 10.4-mile loop. Red is now the guiding color. The grade begins with areas of loose rock alternating with wet-meadow stretches. Ripples beneath the boot hint at the former railroad ties. Ferns favor moist sites.

Before long, follow gurgling Big Spring Run downstream, crossing the stream four times via simple footbridges, some in disrepair. Encounter bigger oak, tulip, and maple trees, with islands of hemlock interrupting the hardwoods. Deer and small trout may be seen.

With the fourth crossing, ascend to skirt a private parcel. Where the trail tops out (2.3 miles), turn left per markers, hiking in a selectively cut forest. After a level passage, descend to cross a bridge over Hemlock Run at 2.6 miles. Ahead, patches of bramble and brier snatch at hikers. Keep to the trail, still edging private land.

At 3.1 miles, bear right at Sherman Creek, following the waterway downstream. Born at the confluence of Hemlock and Big Spring Runs, Sherman Creek hosts a more mature forest of maple, oak, hickory, tulip, ash, hemlock, and beech. At 3.6 miles, follow a jeep trail past a private cabin, cross a dirt forest road, and resume travel on a footpath marred by illegal motorcycle use.

Stay alert upon crossing a footbridge over an unnamed run. The actual trail proceeds forward, while a more worn path swings right. Cross a pair of pipeline corridors, keeping an eye out for blazes and ribbons, and then cross the Sherman Creek footbridge (4.7 miles). Admire the wide, clear, rocky waterway. Cross a secondary flow and bear right where the trail forks.

At 4.9 miles, hike left on a narrow forest road. Where the blazed trail turns right to parallel PA 274 northeast, hikers may opt instead to hike along the highway to avoid the shrubs and poison ivy that overwhelm the trail. Look

Iron Horse Trail, Tuscarora State Forest.

for the Iron Horse Trail to resume on the north side of PA 274 at the eastern edge of Eby Cemetery. This tiny, rustic cemetery houses tasteful markers dating to the mid-1800s.

Continue northeast just removed from PA 274, coming to a marked junction opposite the lower trailhead (5.4 miles); bear left onto Path Valley Grade. With a gentle ascent, the trail meanders among planted pine and spruce. Rains can create a gummy mud. Soon a raised grade hosts travel.

At 6.3 miles, bear right to travel Eby Ridge. Atop the ridge, stroll a classic oak–wild berry forest. Western glimpses present impressive Conococheague Mountain. At 7.1 miles, descend to follow a pipeline corridor left, wading through deep grass.

Turn right at 7.3 miles, hiking on an elevated railroad grade. Then descend sharply, cross a side drainage, and pass through another pipeline corridor before returning to the grade. At 7.8 miles, proceed forward through a cut log. The grade, breached in places, still advances the trail.

Along the lower reaches of Conococheague Mountain, traverse posted private land (8.4 to 9.4 miles); no hunting, driving game, camping, or fires. Despite the young trees, enjoy a mostly shaded hike. Reentering public land, find mature forest.

The trail again rolls to skirt a private parcel before it contours southwest along the wooded slope above lightly traveled PA 274. The trail then descends to cross PA 274 southwest of the main entrance to Big Spring State Park. Follow the blazed trail back to Hemlock Road (10.4 miles).

41 Hemlocks Natural Area

Overview

This 120-acre site, recognized as a national natural landmark, preserves an uncut drainage of original white pine–eastern hemlock forest—a habitat that once dominated much of the state of Pennsylvania. In this old-growth domain, hemlocks boast the greatest count. Here, the state tree reaches heights in excess of 100 feet and diameters greater than 2 feet. The average age for the trees is between 300 and 500 years old. Because the Patterson Run canyon spans only 0.25 to 0.5 mile across, it allows for an intimate acquaintance with the regal gallery.

General description:	This lasso-shaped hike explores upstream along the drainage bottom and eastern hillside of Patterson Run before making a loop joining the Rim and Hemlock Trails.
General location:	40 miles west of Harrisburg.
Special attractions:	Old-growth hemlock and hardwoods; clear, cascading Patterson Run; mountain laurel; fall foliage.
Length:	3 miles round trip.
Elevation:	Find a 500-foot elevation change.
Difficulty:	Moderate.
Maps:	Hemlocks Natural Area brochure; Tuscarora State Forest.
Special concerns:	No camping or fires in the natural area, along the bordering roadway, or at trailheads. Entry is by foot only; boots are recommended. Because the area is allowed to prosper undisturbed, hikers may expect downfalls, brushing passages, and minimal trail markings. Flooding can necessitate reroutes; be alert.
Season and hours:	Spring through fall, daylight hours.
For information:	Tuscarora State Forest.

Key points:

0.0   Lower trailhead; hike upstream.
0.5   Rim Trail.
1.0   Loop junction; proceed forward.
1.5   Hemlock Trail.
2.0   Close loop; backtrack to lower trailhead.

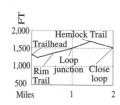

Finding the trailhead: From the Pennsylvania Turnpike, Interstate 76, take exit 14 and follow Pennsylvania 75 north for 11 miles, turning east onto PA 274. In 4.7 miles, turn right onto dirt Hemlock Road to reach the Hemlocks Natural Area. Find the lower trailhead in 2.2 miles, the largest trailhead in 3.8 miles. Small accesses lie in between.

Hemlocks Natural Area

To Big Spring State Park and (274)

0   0.25   0.5
Miles

N

The hike: Maps are often available at the trailhead. Follow the orange-blazed Patterson Run Trail southeast into forest above the trail parking lot. After a gradual descent, it traces a contour south along the deciduous-clad western slope. In autumn, the dispersed evergreens provide a splendid contrast to the flame-colored foliage of birch, tulip, oak, and maple.

Soon, find a picnic table and Patterson Run bridge, cross, and swing an arc upstream along the east slope. Patterson Run is narrow and whispering. The striking feature of the virgin forest is the tall straight trees, not just the hemlocks but also the towering hardwoods, especially here. Piercing the duff are wintergreens. Encounter intriguing forest monarchs—cucumber magnolia, oak, and hemlock—as the trail grades higher.

At 0.5 mile, meet and follow the Rim Trail, heading upstream into the core of the natural area. The Patterson Run Trail heads left uphill. Elude muddy spots and downed trees. Colorful mushrooms, balls of moss, and lichen-mottled stones add to the forest tapestry, as do small laurels. The snap of a branch might betray the flight of a deer, while birdsongs compete with the song of the run. Cross-canyon views offer a different perspective on the forest.

By 0.7 mile, ascend to the laurel belt of the canyon slope. Chestnut oak, birch, and gum contribute to the scene. After nearly tagging the rim top, the trail works its way downhill, again finding the bigger hemlocks that favor the drainage bottom. At 0.9 mile, the trail passes at the base of one that dares you to ignore its size. Although small, Patterson Run is loaded with character, punctuated by small pools and cascades.

At 1 mile, reach the loop junction and proceed straight on the Rim Trail. The return is to the right. Hemlock needles and cones soften the narrow footpath as the trail rolls upstream, staying about midway between run and rim. The trail passes from smaller hemlocks back into an area of big trees; a sentinel pair of hemlocks marks the change. Where the cant of the slope reveals the run, admire more of its stepping, sparkling character. The huge hemlocks have become almost commonplace but still cause heads to tilt and fingers to point.

After the trail again nears Patterson Run, find the next trail junction (1.5 miles). For the loop, hook right onto the Hemlock Trail, descending stone steps to cross the run on the lower footbridge; the Rim Trail continues upstream. The longer bridge span straight ahead leads to the 3.8-mile trailhead; avoid taking it.

Head downstream on the Hemlock Trail. Rustic benches welcome hikers to pause and admire a grand union of images: the statuesque forest, crystalline Patterson Run, and the mossy rocks and logs. The deeper pools seclude tiny trout. Another spur climbs to Hemlock Road. Because masking ferns and shifting mossy rocks fashion the drainage bottom trail, be careful not to turn an ankle. Sphagnum moss claims wet spots.

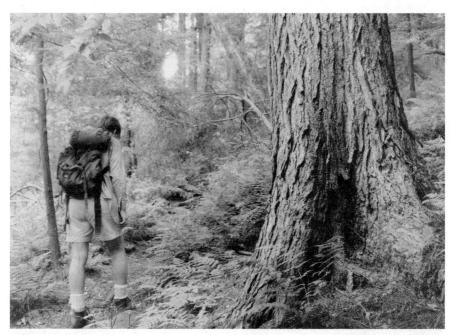
Ancient hemlock, Hemlocks Natural Area, Tuscarora State Forest.

Pass within feet of the run, but the towering hemlock, large birch, and snags draw eyes skyward. In this narrow canyon, witness the ongoing process of nature, with tumbled and snapped-top trees, snags and rotting logs, and renewing young forest.

Ahead, cross the footbridge back over Patterson Run to return to the Rim Trail (2 miles), closing the loop. At the bridge, another spur ascends to Hemlock Road. Head downstream, retracing the Rim and Patterson Run Trails to the lower trailhead (3 miles).

Pittsburgh Region

In the rolling countryside near Pittsburgh, hikers can explore an exciting boulder-riddled creek gorge, a remnant prairie ecosystem, a wildflower reserve, wetlands, mixed woods, waterfalls, lakes, and reservoirs. Echoes to the past mark travel: a gristmill, a mineral springs spa dating to the early 1800s, a covered bridge, a farm, and a limekiln. Along roadways, furnaces hark to the era of iron. Long-distance trails traverse the region, but with much of their distance crossing private land and subject to change, we have chosen not to include them.

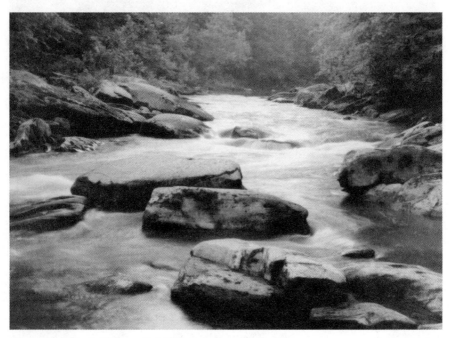

Slippery Rock Creek, McConnell's Mill State Park.

42 McConnell's Mill State Park

Overview

A national natural landmark, this 2,529-acre park serves up the beauty and excitement of Slippery Rock Creek Gorge and the shady charm of Hell Run. Worn 400 feet deep into the landscape, the gorge features enormous boulders both on shore and within the creek, altering its flow. Trails parallel the distinctive waterways. Overlook the alternating whitewater and eddy-swirled calms of Slippery Rock Creek and the crystalline flow of Hell Run. A pair of bridges span Slippery Rock Creek, allowing hikers either to partition the hike or walk a loop. The trails also visit a restored rolling mill—one of the first in the nation—a covered bridge built in 1874, and a limekiln.

General description:	The park's creek and run trail system welcomes round-trip, loop, or shuttle hikes.
General location:	40 miles north of Pittsburgh.
Special attractions:	Exciting, picturesque waterways, house- and elephant-size boulders, waterfalls, fishing, historic sites, spring wildflowers, fall foliage.
Length:	Alpha Pass Trail, 0.5 mile one-way; Kildoo Trail, 2-mile loop; Slippery Rock Gorge Trail, 6 miles one-way; Hell's Hollow Trail, 0.8 mile round trip; Alpha Pass to Upper Hell's Hollow, 7.6 miles one-way, combining trails.
Elevation:	Find a 400-foot elevation change between Alpha Pass and the confluence of Hell Run and Slippery Rock Creek.
Difficulty:	Moderate to strenuous, depending on length.
Maps:	State park brochure.
Special concerns:	Within the park, there is no overnight camping and no swimming. Pets must be leashed and controlled. In this steep-sided gorge, expect areas of rugged, difficult footing, slippery wet rock, and side-drainage crossings. During hunting seasons, wear fluorescent colors. Blue blazes mark park trails.
Season and hours:	Spring through fall for hiking, daylight hours. Mill hours, 10:15 A.M. to 5:45 P.M., Memorial Day through Labor Day.
For information:	McConnell's Mill State Park.

Key points:

Alpha Pass to Upper Hell's Hollow Hike:
- 0.0   Alpha Pass Trailhead.
- 0.5   McConnell's Mill.
- 1.5   Eckert Bridge.
- 3.7   Walnut Flats.
- 7.5   Hell's Hollow Trail junction.
- 7.6   End at Hell Run Trailhead.

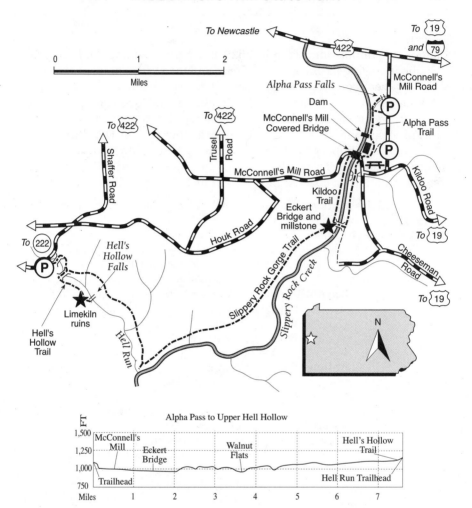

McConnell's Mill State Park

To Newcastle

To 19 and 79

Alpha Pass Falls

McConnell's Mill Road

Dam

P

McConnell's Mill Covered Bridge

Alpha Pass Trail

P

To 422

Trusel Road

McConnell's Mill Road

Kildoo Trail

Kildoo Road

Shaffer Road

Eckert Bridge and millstone

To 19

To 222

P

Houk Road

Slippery Rock Gorge Trail

Cheeseman Road

To 19

Hell's Hollow Falls

Slippery Rock Creek

Limekiln ruins

Hell's Hollow Trail

Hell Run

N

0 1 2
Miles

Alpha Pass to Upper Hell Hollow

FT

1,500 — McConnell's Mill

1,250 — Eckert Bridge — Walnut Flats — Hell's Hollow Trail

1,000

750 — Trailhead — Hell Run Trailhead

Miles   1   2   3   4   5   6   7

Hell's Hollow Trail:

- 0.0   Hell Run Trailhead.
- 0.1   Cross bridge.
- 0.4   Falls and limekiln; return to trailhead.

FT

1,500 — Falls/limekiln

1,250

1,000 — Bridge

750 — Trailhead

Miles   1

Finding the trailhead: From Interstate 79, take exit 29 for Moraine and McConnell's Mill State Parks, and go west on U.S. Highway 422. In 1.7 miles, turn left (south) onto McConnell's Mill Road, reaching the park office in less than 0.1 mile, Alpha Pass Trailhead parking in 0.6 mile, and the Kildoo Picnic Area/Old Mill Access in 1.1 miles. For Hell Run, follow McConnell's Mill Road through the covered bridge, negotiating Lawrence County roads to the trailhead; consult the state park map/brochure (available at park office).

The hikes: For the full **Alpha Pass to Upper Hell's Hollow Hike**, start at the Alpha Pass parking area. Hike the steep Alpha Pass Trail downhill; rustic pole railings help hikers keep their balance. Black cherry, maple, birch, hemlock, tulip, and beech shade the gorge.

At the fork at 0.1 mile, the main gorge trail swings left, heading downstream to the mill. A 0.3-mile, round-trip detour along the second blazed route leads to Alpha Pass Falls. It descends to an impressive bouldery shore and noisy rapid along Slippery Rock Creek. From there, look for the path to cross and ascend along a side drainage, traveling root and rock steps to Alpha Pass Falls. This 30- to 40-foot falls consists of sparkling droplet chains spilling over a cliff.

Opting to forgo the falls detour, keep to the gorge path, passing amid hemlock, birch, and mossy rocks. The boulders of the slope intrigue as they fold together, shaping dark hollows, passages, and dens. Despite the rugged trailbed, many boots pass this way.

A stiff current remains, even where the 25-foot-wide Slippery Rock Creek quiets. Rafters and kayakers share the corridor; lifesaving rings placed along the trail allow hikers to assist creek runners in trouble. The trail rolls, nearing and then drifting away from the waterway. Benches welcome lengthier creek views.

At 0.5 mile (0.8 mile with the Alpha Pass Falls spur), reach the mill area with its viewing decks. Overlook the dam, raceway, and spillway falls, with the historic covered bridge downstream. Find amenities and a natural spring. Here, too, hikers may spy river travelers portaging around the dam.

The 2-mile loop of the Kildoo Trail, an interpretive trail (brochure available at park office), next hosts gorge travel. Hikers may opt to keep to the east shore or pass through the covered bridge and follow the west shore downstream. For this description, keep to the east shore. Although initially paved, wet mosses can still make for slippery footing. Enjoy the rich forest of the gorge and frequent creek views. Pocket sandy beaches contribute to shore; their size and location can vary, depending on seasonal flooding.

A footbridge at 0.75 mile offers views at a bouldery side drainage with cascading chutes. Where the trail forks, keep toward the creek. Another turbulent, squeezed rapid amplifies excitement. Before long, steps descend to a boaters' take-out below Eckert Bridge.

Cross Eckert Bridge, closed to traffic. On the opposite shore (1.5 miles), turn left near a millstone to continue the hike to Hell Run Parking, now on Slippery Rock Gorge Trail—part of the North Country National Scenic Trail. A right turn completes Kildoo Trail with new perspectives.

The rugged Slippery Rock Gorge Trail promises a workout, traversing the western gorge slope. A mix of elm, locust, tulip poplar, and oak enfolds the way, with sycamore along the creek. Baneberry, fern, jewelweed, and witch hazel weave the understory. Find poison ivy where more light penetrates.

The trail rolls to and from the creek, crossing side drainages and springs. An even band of Slippery Rock Run parts the flats. By 2.1 miles, the trail climbs to contour some 100 feet above the creek. Although the steep wooded slope censors views, the creek's song goes unrestrained. Be alert for switchbacks as the trail marches up a side ridge, passing among tilted layered sandstones and small ledges. By the time the trail tops out, hikers have easily doubled the distance between trail and creek.

Along the upper slope, find a fairly easy woods stroll. Where the trail dips through an upper drainage, admire big-diameter trees. Clearings result in brushy passages but allow gorge overlooks. Wildflowers sprinkle the forest floor. Work the toes of your boots as the trail switchbacks downhill to again contour some 100 feet above the creek. "Beech lovers" find ample numbers of the prized tree; do not deface trunks. With steep pitches, reach Walnut Flats (3.7 miles) and a trail distance sign.

Basswood, tulip poplar, and cucumber magnolia now interweave the forest. Proceed downstream, again contouring the slope, now above a quieter creek persona. Darker hemlocks contain the trail. At 4.8 and 5.6 miles, find filtered looks at whitewater rapids. At muddy trail sites, improvise crossings. At 5.7 miles, come upon another distance sign. Here, a downhill detour (0.2 mile round trip) on unmarked trail delivers a confluence view of Slippery Rock Creek and Hell Run. Proceed forward for Hell Run Parking.

The hike now follows Hell Run upstream, contouring its north slope some 80 feet above the waterway. Cross an unmarked trail, staying with the blazes, to descend to a rocky shore for a better view of pretty, babbling Hell Run. Blazes then return hikers to the rim.

View an attractive, dark, corner hollow with mossy rocks and a spring before drifting away to travel a black cherry flat and later an oak–hickory woods interspersed with flowering shrubs. On the rolling descent, footbridges and boardwalks span side drainages. Reach the junction with Hell's Hollow Trail (7.5 miles). Go left across the footbridge to visit Hell's Hollow Falls (see following description); proceed forward to end at Hell Run Parking (7.6 miles).

For **Hell's Hollow Trail,** hike 0.1 mile downstream from Hell Run Parking or reach it from the west end of Slippery Rock Gorge Trail. Cross the footbridge over Hell Run to follow the south shore downstream. Jewelweed, cardinal flowers, and nettles dress the stream; maple and elm overhang the banks.

Cross a bridge over a side tributary. The trail remains wide, with green shoulders, shaded by high-canopy forest. Enjoy fine old maple, hickory, black cherry, and basswood. Midway, a bench seat overlooks a miniature gorge on Hell Run. Downstream, view a bedrock slide to a deep pool.

Where the trail forks, stay along the run, descending to the head of Hell's Hollow Falls and an arched opening to an old limekiln built in the natural rock. A peek inside the kiln reveals a circle cut to the sky and 10-foot-tall walls. Stairs now descend to the base of the waterfall. The main watery drop spans 15 feet and measures 10 feet high; its white streamers dance over a rounded ledge. By negotiating streambed rocks, secure looks at the upper 3-foot cascade.

On the upstream return, a detour along the untraveled fork leads to the fenced top of the kiln. Hepatica and trillium seasonally adorn the site. Return to Hell Run Parking (0.8 mile).

43 Jennings Environmental Education Center

Overview

At this 320-acre environmental education center, visitors can tour and study a relict (prehistoric) prairie, similar to the classic prairies of the Midwest. About 2000 B.C., the prairie ecosystem spanned between the Rockies and the Appalachians, but climatic changes opened the door to forest succession. In the East, all but a handful of these prairies were claimed by leafy woods.

The specialness of this site prompted the establishment of the first reserve in Pennsylvania for the protection of an individual plant species—the blazing star. This prairie dweller captured the attention of botanist Otto Emery Jennings and lends its name to the site's prairie ecosystem. In early August, be dazzled by the rose-purple radial blooms of the 4- to 6-foot-tall wildflower.

General description:	Interlocking nature trails explore the center's lowland and plateau woods, wetlands, and prairie ecosystem. The selected four hikes encapsulate the offering.
General location:	40 miles north of Pittsburgh.
Special attractions:	Relict prairie; one of the state's best wildflower shows; man-made wetland; bird-watching; a swamp habitat suitable for a reclusive, endangered rattlesnake—the Massasauga; fall foliage.
Length:	Woodwhisper Trail, 0.25-mile loop; Black Cherry–Ridge Loop, 1.4 miles round trip; Blazing Star–Prairie Loop Hike, 0.5 mile round trip; Massasauga–Deer–Oakwoods Loop, 2.1 miles round trip.
Elevation:	Woodwhisper Trail and the Blazing Star–Prairie Loop Hike, both flat; Black Cherry–Ridge Loop and Massasauga–Deer–Oakwoods Loop, both less than 100 feet of elevation change.
Difficulty:	Black Cherry–Ridge Loop, moderate. All others are easy.
Maps:	Environmental education center brochure.
Special concerns:	Keep to the trails, and leave pets at home or control them on a tight leash. Watch where you step or place hands, because the Massasauga rattlesnake dwells here. If a snake is spied, keep a 6-foot safety margin. The snake is reclusive by nature and just as eager to avoid an encounter as the hiker is. Although the trails go unblazed, the junctions are signed.
Season and hours:	Spring through fall for hiking, 8:00 A.M. to sunset; office, 8:00 A.M. to 4:00 P.M., weekdays.
For information:	Jennings Environmental Education Center.

Jennings Environmental Education Center

To Slippery Rock

To Harrisville

173

8

Deer Trail

Prairie Loop Trail

Oakwoods Trail

Blazing Star Trail

Woodwhisper Trail

Massasauga Trail

Visitor center

P

P

To Butler

Big Run

N

Old Mill Trail

Mill ruins

528

Black Cherry Trail

To Prospect

0   500   1000

Feet

Ridge Trail

Key points:

Woodwhisper Trail:
- 0.0   Education Center trailhead; follow boardwalk.
- 0.2   End loop at center.

FT

1,400

1,300   Close loop

1,200

1,100   Trailhead

Miles   1

Black Cherry–Ridge Loop:

0.0 Education Center trailhead; bear right.
0.1 Big Run bridge and loop junction; go left.
0.3 Ridge Trail.
1.3 Complete loop; return to center.

Blazing Star–Prairie Loop Hike:

0.0 Prairie Trailhead; head right.
0.2 End Blazing Star Trail; add Prairie Loop to right.
0.4 Close Prairie Loop.
0.5 End at trailhead.

Massasauga–Deer–Oakwoods Loop:

0.0 Prairie Trailhead; head left.
0.3 Loop junction; bear right.
0.5 Meet Deer Trail loop.
1.8 Close loop; backtrack to trailhead.

Finding the trailhead: From Interstate 79, take exit 29 and go east on U.S. Highway 422 for 5.6 miles. Turn north onto Pennsylvania 528 and go 7.5 miles more to find the entrance to the prairie trails on the left. Less than 0.1 mile to the north, reach the center and woodland trails on the right.

The hikes: The **Woodwhisper Trail** and **Black Cherry–Ridge Loop** start out the back door of the Environmental Education Center.

For the wheelchair-accessible Woodwhisper Trail, begin on the boardwalk of the Old Mill Trail. A beautiful old oak presides over the neighborhood of oak, maple, birch, and black cherry. Rhododendron splash seasonal color through the midstory. Proceed from the end of the boardwalk on paved trail for 200 feet. There, a gravel spur leads to a hexagonal gazebo that overlooks a small wetland consisting of an open pond, cattail marsh, and wetland meadow. While providing habitat for wildlife, this man-made wetland is also helping cleanse Big Run of contaminating acids—the result of a burst seal on an upstream abandoned coal mine.

The tour then continues through similar woods, with mayapple and club moss among the ground flora. PA 8 overwhelms the whisper of the trees. The pavement ends at 0.2 mile, with a gravel spur returning to the center (0.25 mile). Wheelchair users may wish to forgo this difficult gravel passage, returning instead as they came.

For the Black Cherry–Ridge Loop, bear right upon exiting the center, descend steps, and travel a gravel path through similar lowland woods, with witch hazel, a few elms, jewelweed, and ferns. Look for the Old Elm Trail to branch right as you approach the footbridge over Big Run (0.1 mile). Across the bridge, find the loop junction. Go left for a clockwise tour.

Hike upstream, overlooking muddy-flowing Big Run. Green banks and areas of skunk cabbage and cardinal flower grace its course. At 0.2 mile,

Forest boardwalk, Jennings Environmental Education Center.

detour left 100 feet onto the bridge of the Old Mill Trail for a view of the old mill site. The remaining stone foundation blends into the woodland–run setting. From here, hikers may opt to return to the center via Old Mill Trail for a 0.4-mile loop.

To complete the Black Cherry–Ridge Loop, follow the steps up the rise at 0.2 mile to travel an earthen trail away from Big Run. Hickory and oak share ranks with the big black cherry. Before long, the North Country Trail arrives on the left; keep to the loop. At the next junction, a right turn completes a 0.75-mile loop by following the Black Cherry Trail alone. For the selected hike, bear left on the Ridge Trail to extend the tour.

On the Ridge Trail, enter the wildflower–shrub habitat of a utility corridor, quickly returning to a full multistory forest, vibrant with greenery. Songbirds, squirrels, and perhaps a skittish deer may provide a passing acquaintance. Keep right for the Ridge Trail. A few rocks embed the path; the ascent is mild. Cucumber magnolia and tulip poplar join the woodland, with grapevines snaking to the sunlight.

At 0.5 mile, the trail tops out and rolls, passing a spring adorned by jewelweed and skunk cabbage. Half a dozen fern varieties contribute to the understory mantle. On the loop's descent, watch for the North Country Trail to depart on the left. A pileated woodpecker may startle hikers out of their woodland reverie.

Black cherry trees precede a footbridge leading to a T-junction with the Black Cherry Trail; turn left. Complete the loop (1.3 miles), and again turn left to cross Big Run and return to the center (1.4 miles).

Start the **Blazing Star–Prairie Loop Hike** and **Massasauga–Deer–**

Oakwoods Loop from the prairie trails parking lot on the west side of PA 528. Hike through the stone gateway.

In 100 feet, the trails separate, with the Blazing Star Trail heading right, the Massasauga Trail heading left, and the picnic shelter straight ahead. Go right for the Blazing Star Trail. Prairie habitat sweeps away in both directions from the mowed path. View a dense growth of knee- to waist-high vegetation, with a parade of white, pink, purple, yellow, and red wildflowers announcing the passage of the seasons.

Young aspen and maple shoots pierce the blanket of yellow primrose, yarrow, blazing star, and lily. Beware of poison ivy. Depleted glacial soils and a regimen of burning keep the forest in check. Interpretive signs introduce the area.

Cross a footbridge over a Big Run tributary. The flowing water gives rise to skunk cabbage, cattail, and cardinal flower. Past the bridge, reach the first Prairie Loop junction and proceed forward for clockwise travel, still on the Blazing Star Trail. At 0.2 mile, turn right for the loop; the Blazing Star Trail ends at the Deer Trail, 150 feet ahead.

Enjoy a slow tour of the Prairie Loop. A hawkmoth, which hovers like a hummingbird, may draw study. Where the trail nears PA 173, a tree–shrub buffer holds back the visual distraction but not the noise. The intrusion only reinforces the foresight of the state in protecting this prairie island. Small burrows riddle the edge of the prairie. Close the loop (0.4 mile) and turn left to retrace the first 0.1 mile to the parking area.

A left at the 100-foot junction starts the Massasauga–Deer–Oakwoods Loop via the Massasauga Trail. Hike a trimmed grass-and-gravel path between herbaceous meadow and the framing shingle oaks and maples. Proceed forward at the four-way junction near an old oak. In a few strides, the Glacier Ridge Trail branches left. Hike in a mixed lowland woods with hawthorn and dogwood, spying a small wetland pond to the right. With a rolling descent, reach the signed loop junction (0.3 mile). Stay on the Massasauga Trail, bearing right; the Oakwoods Trail holds the return.

Counterclockwise, the trail overlooks a skunk cabbage drainage and bog. A footbridge spans the thin flow. At 0.5 mile, the Massasauga Trail ends at the Deer Trail loop; choose either fork to continue. Beyond the trees to the right is Blazing Star Prairie. Keep to the Deer Trail to meet and follow the Oakwoods Trail (0.6 mile).

In the gentle woodland terrain housing this trail, ditches and depressions hint at old ore pits reclaimed by nature. The meandering trail strains to the property boundary. Surrender to the woodland's relaxing spell. Descend at 1.2 miles, and cross a drainage footbridge. At 1.5 miles, the Old Field Trail arrives on the left; proceed forward.

Descend again to tour a low wooded flat, with hornbeam, hawthorn, and hazelnut. The collage of leaf shapes engages eyes. Glimpse Big Run before reaching the 1.7-mile junction. Here, the Hepatica Trail heads right, crossing Big Run on a footbridge. Continue forward, passing between Big Run and a skunk-cabbage-lined side water. Soon, cross a footbridge over the latter. Bog and run habitats continue to frame travel. Close the loop (1.8 miles) and turn right, backtracking the first 0.3 mile to trail parking.

44 Raccoon Creek State Park

Overview

At this 7,323-acre state park, hikers can tour the interlocking nature trails of an exceptional wildflower reserve, strolling both floodplain and bluff. Elsewhere, paths visit a historic mineral spring and explore mature hardwood forest, overlooking Traverse Creek and man-made Raccoon Lake.

General description: Four hikes present the area offering.

General location: 25 miles west of Pittsburgh.

Special attractions: 314-acre wildflower reserve, with more than 500 species of blooming plants (April through October); Traverse and Raccoon Creeks; Raccoon Lake; platy cliffs, mature trees, mineral springs, wildlife, fall foliage.

Length: Max Henrici–Old Field Loop, 1.5-mile loop; Jennings–Audubon Loop, 2.1-mile loop; Frankfort Mineral Springs Loop, 0.4-mile loop; Valley Trail, 2.5 miles round trip.

Elevation: Trails all show less than 100 feet of elevation change.

Difficulty: Max Henrici–Old Field Loop, Jennings–Audubon Loop, and Valley Trail, all moderate; Frankfort Mineral Springs Loop is easy.

Maps: State park brochure; Wildflower Reserve map/flyer.

Special concerns: Within the wildflower reserve, there is no collecting, no smoking, no pets, no picnicking, and no bicycles. Beware of poison ivy. Mosquitoes seasonally annoy. Watch footing on the descents; pathways can be muddy.

Season and hours: Year-round, spring through fall for hiking. Wildflower Reserve, 8:00 A.M. to sunset.

For information: Raccoon Creek State Park.

Key points:

Max Henrici–Old Field Loop:

0.0 Wildflower Reserve Nature Center trailhead.
0.2 Loop junction; stay on Max Henrici Trail.
0.6 Multiple junction below bluff; hike left.
1.2 Travis Trail junction.
1.3 Close loop; return to center.

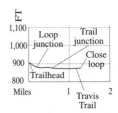

Jennings–Audubon Loop:

0.0 Wildflower Reserve Nature Center trailhead.
0.1 Cy Hungerford Cabin.
0.7 Old Oak snag.
1.6 Multiple junction; angle left uphill.
2.1 End loop at center.

Raccoon Creek State Park

Frankfort Mineral Springs Loop:

0.0	Pennsylvania 18 trailhead; hike west.
0.2	Falls and mineral springs.
0.4	End loop at parking.

Valley Trail:

0.0	Western (upper) trailhead.
1.3	End at beach; backtrack.

Finding the trailhead: From Pittsburgh, go west on U.S. Highway 30 for 9.1 miles to reach Raccoon Creek State Park Wildflower Reserve on the right. Go 0.2 mile more and turn left, now following the park road west. Pass the beach turnoff in 1.7 miles, the picnic area in 2.8 miles, the campground in 5 miles, and meet PA 18 in 5.7 miles. Locate the park office less than 0.1 mile north on PA 18. Locate parking for Frankfort Mineral Springs on the west side of PA 18, 0.3 miles south of the junction (0.4 mile south of the park office).

The hikes: Two loops introduce the Wildflower Reserve and access the site's other named trails for additional exploration: the **Max Henrici–Old Field Loop** and the **Jennings–Audubon Loop.** A month-by-month bloom schedule (available at the nature center) speeds rifling through wildflower field guides. Wooden trail signs at the parking area and near the nature center identify starts for hikes.

Look for the Max Henrici Trail as you approach the nature center. Bear left as the Audubon Trail heads right. Travel a wide mowed lane between field and woods, hike past a park residence, and descend along a thin jewelweed

197

drainage to reach the Raccoon Creek floodplain. Hickory, elm, black cherry, maple, and walnut contribute to the woods. A rich, moist understory spills at their feet, with skunk cabbage, mayapple, trillium, and jack-in-the-pulpit seasonally gracing travel.

Enjoy myriad leaf shapes, layers, and textures. Keep right, hiking past a trio of link trails to the Old Field Trail. At the foot of a bluff, come to a multiple junction at 0.6 mile: Uphill to the right lies the Audubon Trail; straight ahead is the Jennings Trail; and, to the left, the Old Field Trail continues the selected loop.

Go left, passing between an old field and Raccoon Creek. The creek flows broad and cloudy, with alternating muddy and green banks. Big sycamores overlook the proceedings. Morning sunlight floods the forest with beams and starbursts. Intricate spiderwebs capture both light and dew. The tall meadow understory holds a host of blooms, appearing in sprays, multifloral crowns, and single flowers—yellow, white, pink, red, purple, and orange.

Keep to the Old Field Trail, ignoring the link trails back to the Max Henrici Trail. Spurs to the right present creek overlooks. Muddy beaches may hold the tracks of deer or raccoon. Complaining crows and damselflies add to travel.

At 1.2 miles, the Old Field Trail bears left; the Travis Trail heads right. Because these paths merge before reaching the center, hikers have an option. Go right to enjoy more creek overlooks, including a deck view at the confluence of Traverse and Raccoon Creeks. At 1.3 miles, meet the Old Field Trail where it arcs, and turn right to close the loop in 250 feet. Retrace the hike's start to the center, 1.5 miles.

The Jennings–Audubon Loop pays tribute to two renowned naturalists: botanist Otto Emery Jennings and ornithologist John James Audubon. Find the start of the Jennings Trail behind the flagpole, and hike toward Hungerford Cabin. Ascend steadily in a setting of planted pine and spruce. On the right in 200 feet, an impressive spreading oak stands in marked contrast to the tall, straight plantation trees. At 0.1 mile, reach the Cy Hungerford Cabin, cross its porch, and continue the same line of travel to enter deciduous forest.

At the upcoming descent, shun the steep path that heads straight downhill; instead, use the switchbacks. At 0.2 mile and 0.25 mile respectively, the Deer and Big Maple Trails branch left. Noise from PA 30 and a flyway for the Pittsburgh airport makes conversation difficult.

As the Jennings Trail travels the edge of a bluff, come upon the Ridge Trail. Hikers may opt to descend via the Ridge Trail to tour along a wetland pond, passing below the platy cliff. Or they can keep to the Jennings Trail for rim overlooks of the pond. The paths merge before coming upon Old Oak—now a snag, broken and bare of its bark (0.7 mile). Past the snag, travel floodplain woods via the Jennings Trail.

Beyond a skunk cabbage bog, the Big Maple Trail tags up on the left. Shortly after, stay left as the Old Wagon Road heads right. At 1 mile, a spur heads left to the parking area; again keep to the Jennings Trail. Even a slight elevation change can alter the vegetation mix. Muddy sites can complicate travel, but the cliff ledges, hollows, and protrusions engage.

In another 0.25 mile, the Meadow Trail/Old Wagon Road returns on the right. As the trail proceeds downstream, Raccoon Creek invites looks right. Big oaks grow at the foot of the cliffs, sycamores along the creek. Only a few roots drape the bare rock.

At 1.5 miles comes the next choice. Here, the Beaver Trail travels alongside Raccoon Creek (note that wet weather can make this trail impassable). The Jennings Trail keeps to the base of the cliff. At 1.6 miles, the trails again merge. With a farewell look at Raccoon Creek, the Jennings Trail halts at a multiple junction with the Max Henrici, Old Field, and Audubon Trails. Turn left, angling upslope on the Audubon Trail to complete the selected loop.

Atop the bluff plateau, the trail is removed from the rim. Ahead, the ridge narrows. Discover relaxing woods and upland flora. At 1.8 miles, a spur descends right. At the cordoned junction at 2 miles, hikers may take either fork. Meet the Max Henrici Trail at the side of the visitor center, completing the hike at 2.1 miles.

For **Frankfort Mineral Springs Loop,** start at the historical marker and parking area west off PA 18. The mineral springs contain fifteen different minerals, purported to have healing qualities. From the early 1800s through early 1900s, a resort and health spa served summer guests.

Cross the closed road bridge over a tributary of Traverse Creek and, in a few feet, turn left onto a gravel trail. Wild grape flourishes along the tributary, songbirds harmonize in the treetops, and a moist woods flora grows at the foot of the trees. Hike upstream, crisscrossing the tributary waterway via culvert crossings. In places, floods have stolen the trailbed and accompanying rockwork.

At 0.2 mile, a footbridge crosses the creek for a frontal view of an 8- to 10-foot falls, veiling from a broken ledge and cupped in a rocky grotto. Hemlocks fan the sides of the grotto, while deciduous trees dress the rim. Ascend to view the mineral springs streaking the cliff orange. The natural rocks beneath the dripping springs reveal worn catch basins.

Next, ascend to view a restored stone building from the nineteenth-century health spa. Lilies grow at its side; a big oak wrapped in poison ivy stands sentinel. Buried in the tall uphill grasses are other clues to the spa. Turn right onto the old road for a loop return to the parking area (0.4 mile). Ancient oaks line the way.

For the **Valley Trail**, start at the west end of beach parking or from a marked trailhead on the north side of the park road, 0.2 mile east of PA 18, 0.5 mile west of the campground. When choosing the latter, find parking 0.1 mile west of the trailhead.

The more tranquil hike starts at the western trailhead off the park road and ends at the beach. Pass through an egress in the guardrail, descending into woods on a narrow earthen path. Enjoy a full, mixed woods as the rolling trail contours the slope above Traverse Creek, following it downstream. Sugar maple, birch, beech, ash, elm, cherry, and basswood contribute to the shady realm. Sharp pitches may steal footing.

Cross side waters and muddy spots via footbridges, devised means, or wading. Beautiful, big, mature trees are the trail's hallmark. Woodland wildflowers,

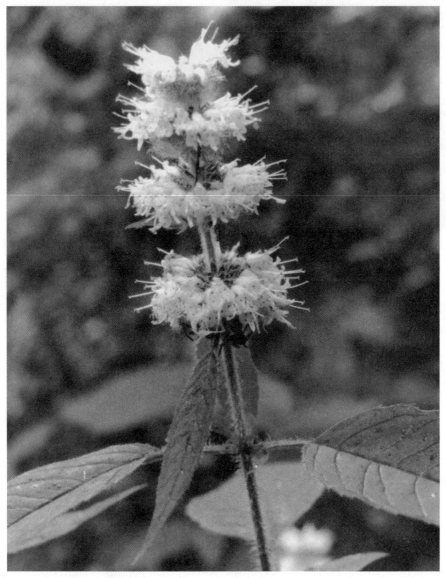

Raccoon Creek State Park Wildflower Reserve.

dogwood, and drainage cardinal flower, bee balm, and skunk cabbage lend accent. Collapsed shacks sit below the trail.

At 0.8 mile, a spur descends left to Traverse Creek and a "low road" to the beach. Keep to the Valley Trail, rounding between 60 and 150 feet above the creek, still enjoying the glorious gathering of big trees. Soon the glare of Raccoon Lake replaces Traverse Creek, and sounds of the lake bustle drift to the trail. At 1.2 miles, bear left, descending along the wide trail linking the campground and beach. Cross a footbridge and enter beach parking (1.25 miles).

45 Beechwood Farms Nature Reserve

Overview

In the low, rolling hills at the northern outskirts of Pittsburgh, the Audubon Society of Western Pennsylvania leases a portion of land from the Western Pennsylvania Conservancy. This leased site allows visitors to discover the region's traditional landscape, including abandoned fields, thickets, and forest. Within each microcosm, discover the native plants and wildlife that make it special. Five miles of interlocking trail allow visitors to explore the reserve at their own pace. In spring and fall, the valley flyway hosts migrating birds.

General description: Two loops help introduce the 134-acre reserve and provide access to the site's other trails for outward exploration.

General location: In Fox Chapel, 8 miles northeast of downtown Pittsburgh.

Special attractions: Wildlife pond, forty-acre Native Plant Sanctuary, wolf trees (candelabra-branched trees), a small waterfall, bird-watching, spring and fall wildflowers and shrubs, educational programs, nature center/nature store.

Length: Spring Hollow Walk, 0.6-mile loop, with spurs to pond and Treetop; Upper Fields–Meadowview–Pine Hollow Loop, 1.6 miles round trip.

Elevation: Spring Hollow Walk has a 100-foot elevation change. The rolling Upper Fields–Meadowview–Pine Hollow Loop has a 150-foot elevation change and rings up 550 feet of cumulative elevation.

Difficulty: Spring Hollow Walk, easy; Upper Fields–Meadowview–Pine Hollow Loop, moderate.

Maps: Reserve map.

Special concerns: At this extremely popular site, the parking lot fills on summer weekends. No bikes, no dogs, no picnicking allowed. For each trail, the initial junction is well signed, but the return may go unmarked. Keep to the path to avoid poison ivy. When wet, the clay soils on Pine Hollow Trail prove slippery.

Season and hours: Grounds, daily, dawn to dusk. Center, 9:00 A.M. to 5:00 P.M., Tuesday through Saturday; 1:00 P.M. to 5:00 P.M., Sunday; closed some holidays.

For information: Beechwood Farms Nature Reserve.

Key points:

Spring Hollow Walk:
0.0 Nature center trailhead; bear right.
0.1 Spur to pond.
0.2 Cross Hart's Run.
0.6 Close loop at center.

Beechwood Farms Nature Reserve

Upper Fields–Meadowview–Pine Hollow Loop:

- 0.0   Nature center trailhead; head left.
- 0.1   Loop junction; proceed forward.
- 0.7   Cross Pine Hollow Run.
- 1.5   Complete loop; backtrack to trailhead.

Finding the trailhead: From the Pennsylvania Turnpike, Interstate 76, take the Butler Valley exit (exit 4) and go south on Pennsylvania 8 for 3.1 miles. There (north of Allison Park), turn left (east) onto Harts Run Road (State Route 1010/1006), the Green Belt. Go another 3.5 miles, and turn right onto Dorseyville Road to reach the reserve on the right in 0.2 mile.

Alternatively, from PA 28 take exit 5B, go north on PA 8 for 0.4 mile, and turn right onto Kittanning Street in Etna. Proceed another 4.3 miles to find the reserve on the left. Leaving Etna, Kittanning Street becomes Dorseyville Road.

The hikes: For both hikes, round the front of the adjoining farmhouse and barn of Evans Nature Center, passing through a breezeway to reach the back.

While in the breezeway, take a moment to admire the richly carved and hand-painted reserve signs. Carvings around the map depict the four seasons. Ahead, reach the trail-map kiosk and junction post.

For the **Spring Hollow Walk,** bear right, traveling a wide maintained path through a clearing of Canada thistle, milkweed, Queen Anne's lace, and goldenrod. Monarch butterflies and hovering hawkmoths frequent the blooms. Ahead, a few birch- and silver maple edge the field of elbow- to shoulder-high vegetation. Keep to Spring Hollow Walk.

Soon view the cattail outskirts of the reserve's small pond, a nesting post, and backset area of full, rounded deciduous trees. Opposite Toddler's Trail, take a spur to the pond boardwalk and bench. Red and silver maple, along with spruce, edge the site; a few lilacs hark to the days of the farm. Hear croaking frogs and the vibrating wings of dragonflies. Watch for turtles, fish, kingfishers, herons, and spotted sandpipers. Patches of duckweed, cattails, and a birch and willow-vegetated island contribute to the acre pond's charm.

Back on Spring Hollow Walk, maples lace over the trail, later joined by oak, black cherry, and tulip poplar. Benches welcome visitors to sit and let the bird life come to them. The reserve trails welcome slow, reflective travel. At 0.2 mile, bear left, easing downhill to the Hart's Run crossing. Plaques identify tree and plant species.

Keep to the Spring Hollow Walk, still passing named trails, including the lightly traveled Woodland Footpath with its stand of 250-year-old oaks and unusual wolf trees that show evidence of lightning strikes. On the hollow walk, wild grape entangles the upper tree branches; gray-stemmed dogwood appears in the midstory. Past the midway point, an elevated boardwalk leads visitors to the octagonal observation platform dubbed "Treetop." From here, admire the crowns of the surrounding oak, cherry, maple, and sassafras for a squirrel's-eye view of the forest.

As you resume counterclockwise travel on Spring Hollow Walk, ascend back into meadow, proceeding forward at the four-way junction with the Meadowview and Upper Fields Trails. Fruit trees provide clues to a farming past. Wildflowers abound. On wide mowed lane, hike below the education center and past the Native Plant Sanctuary to close the loop at 0.6 mile.

For the **Upper Fields–Meadowview–Pine Hollow Loop,** head left on the Upper Fields Trail from the trailhead mapboard. Ascend through open field of Canada thistle, goldenrod, daisy, and grass. Cardinals may adorn the branches of nearby aspen. Later, shrubs rise in the field. Keep left, hiking past the Goldenrod Trail. At 0.1 mile, come upon the unmarked loop junction. Proceed straight on the Upper Fields Trail for a counterclockwise tour. Soon after, a spur heads right, leading to benches for group talks or wildlife viewing.

Cross Spring Hollow Walk, continuing the loop via the Meadowview Trail. Quickly pass the Woodland Trail and cross a paved, private drive to travel between meadow and meadow-transitioning woods. In some meadows, stringy orange dodder webs the vegetation. Elsewhere, showy orange butterfly weed attracts attention. Fruit trees grow in the young woods of maple, sassafras, dogwood, ash, and hawthorn.

Wildlife pond boardwalk, Beechwood Farms Nature Reserve.

At 0.4 mile is an abandoned pumphouse. Approach quietly, because wildlife may take sanctuary there. Beyond the pumphouse, bid farewell to the Meadowview Trail and hello to the Pine Hollow Trail. Hikers may shorten the trip by staying on Meadowview Trail.

The Pine Hollow Trail takes a couple of marked bends, passing from woods to goldenrod–shrub meadows. Descend and cross Pine Hollow Run to find a seasonal 15-foot waterfall gracing a natural ledge on the right. With the following ascent, pass from leafy woods to red pine plantation (0.8 mile). A chaotic shrub midstory contrasts with the order of the pines, while the whir from a windmill conjures images of giant insects.

Continue the steady ascent, grading into a woods of mixed conifers and black cherry. The trail then rolls, leaving behind the plantation trees. Cross a bridle path and descend to return to the Meadowview Trail. Bear right for an ascent.

Before the private drive, a vista spur heads left 100 feet. Overlook a meadow slope to spy flattened hilltops beyond the rimming trees, with the Allegheny and Ohio River Valleys barely visible in the distance. Return to Meadowview Trail, cross the private drive, and descend to meet the Upper Fields Trail (1.5 miles). Bear right, retracing the initial 0.1 mile to the center.

Laurel Highlands Region

In the southwest corner of the state, hikers will find great diversity. They can trace the region's ridges, walking the superb Laurel Highlands Hiking Trail and the often rugged Tuscarora Trail. Or stroll an exceptional rail-trail paired with the whitewater excitement of the Youghiogheny (pronounced *yock-ah-gain-ee*) River. A temperate-forest jungle of old growth and rhododendron at Alan Seeger Natural Area and the history of Friendship Hill also call to hikers. Find hideouts for solitude and lively, multiple-use recreation trails. Mountain laurel—the state flower—dresses nearly every site, giving credence to the region's moniker.

Toad, Stone Valley Recreation Area.

46 Stone Valley Recreation Area

Overview

At this 700-acre recreation area of the Pennsylvania State University, hikers find 25 miles of blazed trail open to the public. Paths explore forest, abandoned fields, thicket, lakeshore, and marsh. Within the outdoor and rustic cabin setting, the facility also offers a full lineup of fee recreational and educational pursuits. At Shaver's Creek Environmental Center, the mission is "to interpret Penn's Woods to all visitors"; live exhibits promote that end.

General description:	Four hiking circuits explore much of the recreation area, touring a variety of habitats.
General location:	10 miles south of State College.
Special attractions:	Seventy-two-acre Lake Perez, marsh boardwalk, fishing, a vista, environmental center, wildlife viewing, fall foliage.
Length:	Lake Trail, 2.5-mile loop (2.7 miles with the Grapevine boardwalk detour); Old Faithful–Mountain View Loop, 2-mile loop; Shaver's Creek–Wood's Route Loop, 3.9-mile loop; Woodcock Trail, 1-mile loop.
Elevation:	Lake Trail, 200-foot elevation change; Old Faithful–Mountain View Loop, 350-foot elevation change; Shaver's Creek–Wood's Route Loop, 250-foot elevation change; Woodcock Trail, less than a 100-foot elevation change.
Difficulty:	Lake and Woodcock Trails, both easy; Old Faithful–Mountain View Loop and Shaver's Creek–Wood's Route Loop are both moderate.
Maps:	Recreation area map; purchase at park office or equipment rental.
Special concerns:	The following are prohibited within the recreation area: pets, alcoholic beverages, swimming, fishing from docks, and overnight camping along trails or in parking areas. Find the trails color-coded, with numbered junctions corresponding to the map. Beware of poison ivy.
Season and hours:	Year-round, spring through fall for hiking, 8:00 A.M. to sunset.
For information:	Stone Valley Recreation Area.

Key points:

Lake Trail:

0.0 Start at Mineral Industries (MI) parking; hike the lakeshore southwest.

0.5 Cross dam.

2.1 Shaver's Creek Environmental Center.

2.4 Grapevine Trail boardwalk.

2.7 End loop at MI parking.

Stone Valley Recreation Area

To State College and (26)

Woodcock Trail

N

Shaver's Creek Environmental Center

Lake Trail

Mountain View Trail

Charter Oak Road

Lake Perez

Old Faithful Trail

Greenwall Road

To (305)

Shaver's Creek Trail

Wood's Route

Shaver's Creek

Park Headquarters and Mineral Industries Day Use Area

0   0.5   1

Miles

Old Faithful–Mountain View Loop:

0.0 Start opposite entry to MI parking.
0.5 Mountain View Trail.
1.5 Sawmill Trail.
2.0 End loop at MI parking.

Shaver's Creek–Wood's Route Loop:

0.0 Start at MI parking; hike the lakeshore to Shaver's Creek Trail.
1.5 Wood's Route.
3.0 Cross Greenwall Road to viewpoint.
3.4 Descend Old Faithful Trail.
3.9 End loop at MI parking.

Woodcock Trail:

0.0 Woodcock Trailhead; hike east.
0.1 Loop junction; bear right.
0.9 Complete loop; return to trailhead.

Finding the trailhead: From U.S. Highway 322 in State College, take exit 1 and go south on Pennsylvania 26 for 11.2 miles. Turn right (west) onto State Route 1029/Charter Oak Road, heading toward Mooresville. In another 1.6 miles, turn left onto the east entrance road for the recreation area, environmental center, and trailheads. Park at Mineral Industries (MI) Day Use Area for all but the Woodcock Trail, which has a separate trailhead near the turnoff to the environmental center.

The hikes: For a clockwise tour of the **Lake Trail** from MI parking, hike southwest along Lake Perez, traversing the lower end of the pine-shaded picnic area; orange blazes point the way. Enjoy glimpses of the attractive manmade lake with Tussey Mountain in the backdrop. Although shrubs build toward shore, anglers still find lake access.

Descend along the spillway, cross the outlet footbridge, and ascend a grassy slope to traverse the dam at 0.5 mile. Bear left upon leaving the dam to follow a grassy jeep track for a contouring hillside tour; avoid the well-tracked secondary path closer to shore. Pass amid hawthorn, black walnut, hickory, tamarack, and pitch pine, with an entangling array of honeysuckle, wild grape, and poison ivy.

After tagging a high point (0.75 mile), descend to round a gate and cross the paved west entrance road. On the rolling trail, small meadow clearings interrupt the pine–deciduous woods, and shade can be precious. Pass through a utility corridor to share the way with the Ironstone Trail (dark blue blazes). Beyond the next power-line corridor, pass a grouping of large sugar maples.

Return to the lake at 1.6 miles and bear left to round an inlet cove. Here, hike past the red-blazed Bluebird Trail. Wildflowers sprinkle the forest's meadow floor. Farther along, the woods' fullness again steals lake views. Keep to the orange/dark blue blaze scheme until 2 miles, where the orange (lake) trail bears right, only to be joined by a yellow-blazed trail before continuing solo.

Buildings precede arrival at Shaver's Creek Environmental Center (2.1 miles). Detour right to tour the center; a modest admission fee is charged. Find a museum, outdoor garden, live wildlife exhibits, and amenities.

Resume the Lake Trail, now wide, groomed, and accompanied by interpretive panels; ignore the other color-coded trails. Songbirds and woodpeckers divert attention, while girdled trees and raised waters hint at beaver.

At 2.4 miles (at the second meeting with the red-blazed Grapevine Trail), detour right onto the 300-foot boardwalk to overlook the marshy end of the lake. Alder, dogwood, cattail, sensitive fern, gurgling water, frog, and fish all contribute to the tale. Beyond the army of cattails stretches the open lake water. Resume the clockwise hike, and where the Lake Trail forks, take either branch to end at MI parking (2.7 miles).

For **Old Faithful–Mountain View Loop,** look for junction post 18 opposite the entry to the MI Day Use Area and follow the indigo (actually more like lavender here) blazes of the Old Faithful Trail into a deep woods of hemlock, white pine, and oak. A spring on the left hosts mayapple, skunk cabbage, and fern; some trees reach 2 feet in diameter. Ahead, take either blazed fork to ascend to the Mountain View Trail (0.5 mile).

Upon meeting the rose-blazed Mountain View Trail, turn left for the loop. To the right, the rose blazes lead to Tussey Mountain View at Greenwall Road (about an 0.8-mile round-trip detour). On the loop, pass an electric fence that keeps deer out of a regenerating select cut. The ridge ascent features younger woods, snags, and only partial shade. Later, when oak, hickory, maple, and shad fill out the forest, hikers can just glimpse the shadowy profile of the outlying ridges.

Eventually, a steep descent returns hikers to the hemlock-darkened lower slope. Cross the east entrance road at 1.5 miles, coming to the light blue blazes of the Sawmill Trail. Turn left, quickly meeting the orange-blazed Lake Trail, and again bear left to return to MI parking (2 miles). Conclude the hike in floodplain woods.

For the **Shaver's Creek–Wood's Route Loop,** follow the orange blazes of the Lake Trail southwest through the picnic area to find the aqua-blazed Shaver's Creek Trail. Bluebird, duck, and goose animate the shore, while sailboats and rowboats weave across Lake Perez. At junction 24, veer left, angling past the picnic pavilion to enter the woods. Travel a scenic woods road, where tulip poplar and cucumber magnolia shower their blooms in late spring and early summer.

From 30 feet above the lakeshore, gain just a hint of blue beyond the trees. Along Shaver's Creek outlet, the woods road grades lower; still track the aqua blazes. Shaver's Creek flows sleepy and wide. The trail then traverses a wild meadow dotted with walnut trees to resume along the shady floodplain distanced from the creek.

At 1.5 miles, cross a footbridge over a side tributary to meet junction 11. Go left onto Wood's Route for the selected loop. By bearing right, a roadway return presents itself at junction 12. On the seldom-tracked footpath of

Wood's Route, follow the tributary upstream. At 1.8 miles, a steep outcrop slope looms over the voiceless stream. Cross a footbridge and contour the hillside.

Where a younger deciduous woods claims travel, bear right, crossing a tiny headwater. Hemlocks wane from the forest, and a couple more footbridges advance travel. Next, parallel the roadway return of Shaver's Creek Trail, traveling an aisle through a red pine plantation.

At 3 miles, angle right across Greenwall Road to a vista bench (Tussey Mountain View) on the rose-blazed Mountain View Trail. Across the valley, Tussey Mountain draws a striking wooded line across the sky. Differing hues of green hint at past forestry practices.

To return to the trailhead, follow the rose blazes, contouring and descending to junction 15/17 (3.4 miles). From there, descend on the hemlock-shaded Old Faithful Trail (indigo blazes) to reach the park road and MI Day Use at 3.9 miles.

For the **Woodcock Trail,** hike east from the marked trailhead on the east entrance road. Blue and orange blazes initially mark the way; where they separate, keep to the orange blazes. Generally, find brochures at the start and/or interpretive plaques at each of the nine stations.

This site features abandoned farmland, critical for the woodcock to breed and nest. Elsewhere, development and encroaching woods have deprived the bird of such habitat. Along Shaver's Creek, explore meadow, wetland, shrub thickets, and young woods, with arrows guiding hikers through the shrub–meadow sites. Much of the tour is shadeless, and the vegetation can create a sauna effect. Deer, turkey, squirrel, and even a bear may be spied.

47 Alan Seeger Natural Area to Greenwood Lookout Tower

General description:	This hike combines both the 0.6-mile Alan Seeger Trail, touring spectacular old-growth forest and a rhododendron jungle, and the 2-mile Johnson Trail segment of the Greenwood Spur that leads to Greenwood Lookout Tower atop Broad Mountain for a 360-degree central-state panorama.
General location:	8 miles southeast of State College.
Special attractions:	Some of the oldest trees in Pennsylvania, natural arbors and tunnels of rhododendron (peak bloom early July), mountain laurel, accessible lookout tower, sweeping views, wildlife sightings, rustic picnic area.
Length:	5.2 miles round trip.
Elevation:	Pass from 1,000 feet in elevation at Alan Seeger Natural Area to 2,400 feet at Greenwood Lookout Tower.
Difficulty:	Moderate.
Maps:	Rothrock State Forest; the Mid State Trail Association's Mid State Trail System Map (map 203.1).
Special concerns:	No overnight camping. Blue blazes mark the Greenwood Spur and Johnson Trail.
Season and hours:	Spring through fall for hiking, sunrise to sunset.
For information:	Rothrock State Forest.

Key points:

- 0.0 Stone Creek Road trailhead.
- 0.6 Cross Seeger Road to the Johnson Trail segment.
- 1.5 Cross upper Seeger Road.
- 2.6 Greenwood Lookout Tower; backtrack to trailhead.

Finding the trailhead: From U.S. Highway 322 East at Laurel Creek Reservoir, turn west onto Stone Creek Road and continue 7.3 miles to the Alan Seeger Natural Area. Find the road mostly paved. To access Stone Creek Road from US 322 West, travelers must make a U-turn at the next crossover point, some 2 miles west of Laurel Creek Reservoir.

Alternatively, from Pennsylvania 26 at McAlveys Fort, take Stone Creek Road/State Route 1023 east for 6.4 miles, traveling paved road.

The hike: Find the marked start for the Alan Seeger Trail south off Stone Creek Road near its intersection with dirt Seeger Road. To the left of the map-board, a footpath enters the exciting, dark old-growth realm. Pass among massive hemlock and white pine, with some hemlock exceeding 500 years in

Alan Seeger Natural Area to Greenwood Lookout Tower

age. The broad wooded flat invites carefree strolling, allowing eyes to roam and trace the trunks skyward. Plaques identify the interweaving tree species.

As the hike transitions into younger forest, arrive at the signed junction for the Mid State Trail, Greenwood Spur. To the left, it offers northbound exploration. For the chosen tour, proceed forward on the Alan Seeger Trail and southbound leg of the Greenwood Spur. Virgin forest again enfolds travel, giving way to a chaos of rhododendron at a small drainage. Here, admire the radial leaves, 10- to 20-foot heights, and seasonal pom-pom blooms of the rhododendron bushes.

Next, cross a trio of footbridges over the braided water of Standing Stone Creek. Small trout dart through the clear water, and rhododendron still engage. Cross Seeger Road at 0.6 mile and take the marked Johnson Trail of the Greenwood Spur to continue to the lookout. For the Alan Seeger Trail alone, bear right on the road, returning to the trailhead (0.75 mile), or retrace your steps for an encore tour of the natural area.

Greenwood Lookout Tower, Rothrock State Forest.

En route to the lookout, proceed through tall forest of hemlock, pine, and oak, twice crossing a gurgling spring-fed stream. Squirrel and woodpecker enliven the treetops. Bigger trees in the forest impose a natural circle around themselves, perfect for paying homage. By 1 mile, pursue a ravine upstream.

At the fork at 1.2 miles, the left spur leads to a spring in about 100 feet; the main trail bears right. Striped maples become a familiar sight as snags open the cathedral. Here, the climb intensifies, with rocky sites. At 1.5 miles, cross upper Seeger Road.

Switchbacks follow, leading past rhododendron, laurel, mature birch, and leaning hemlock. Broad Mountain wildlife encounters may include deer, fox, and black rat snake. At the fourth switchback, spy a white birch with eight major trunks. Rocks displace beneath the boot.

As switchbacks end at 2.1 miles, laurel and blueberry bushes go on parade in the semiopen, oak–hickory woods. On arrival at Greenwood Lookout Tower (2.6 miles), the blue-blazed trail heading south is the Telephone Trail to Greenwood Furnace State Park. The destination tower rises nine flights; the crow's nest is closed to the public.

Scale the tower at your own risk, heeding posted numbers. From the upper landings, attain a full 360-degree view, overlooking the signature long arc ridges of Pennsylvania; rural flats sprawl east. Fall brings a kaleidoscope of blazing color. Return as you came, retracing the Alan Seeger Trail for a grand old-growth finale (5.2 miles). Or backtrack the Johnson Trail alone and turn left at 4.6 miles onto Seeger Road to end at 4.75 miles.

For an altogether different and longer return, seek out the Ross Trail. It descends from the northeast corner of Greenwood Lookout Tower. Where it emerges at Stone Creek Road, turn left and hike the road back to the trailhead.

48 The Lower Trail

General description: The Lower Trail (pronounced like *power*) is a relaxing, multiple-use rail-trail that hugs a river and passes through wooded canyon and rural countryside. Along it, discover remnants of the Pennsylvania Canal (1830s to 1850s) and Petersburg Branch of the Pennsylvania Railroad (1879 to 1979).

General location: Along Frankstown Branch Juniata River between Alexandria and Williamsburg.

Special attractions: Rail, canal, and quarry ruins; varied woods; periodic river access; fishing; wildflowers; bird- and wildlife-watching; fall foliage.

Length: 11 miles one-way.

Elevation: Pass from 700 feet in elevation at Alexandria to 900 feet at Williamsburg.

Difficulty: Easy to moderate, depending on the length of the hike.

Maps: Rails-to-Trails, *The Lower Trail* brochure (generally available at the trailhead).

Special concerns: On spring and fall weekends, parking lots commonly fill. No overnight camping is allowed; beware of poison ivy when venturing off the trail. Between 4.75 miles and 5.1 miles, travel private property; pass respectfully, keeping to the trail. Mileposts count off distance. Find chemical toilets at the northern and southern termini; bring water for the hike.

Season and hours: Year-round, spring through fall for hiking, daylight hours only.

For information: Rails-to-Trails of Central Pennsylvania.

Key points:

0.0 Alfarata Trailhead; hike south.

2.5 Goodman Quarry.

4.7 Cross first trestle bridge.

5.2 State Route 2017 trailhead.

7.7 Cove Dale trailhead.

9.4 Cross river bridge to east shore.

11.0 End at Williamsburg trailhead.

Finding the trailhead: For the northern terminus (Alfarata Trailhead), from U.S. Highway 22 east of the village of Water Street, turn north onto SR 4014 at the west end of the Frankstown Branch Juniata River bridge. Go 0.3 mile to find a large gravel parking lot on the right. Find the southern terminus off Pennsylvania 866 at the corner of Liberty and First in Williamsburg.

The Lower Trail

The hike: For a north–south, upstream tour of this family-oriented trail, begin at the Alfarata Trailhead. Hike the 8-foot-wide crushed-limestone path, gaining early overlooks of the sleepy Frankstown Branch Juniata River. The overlacing trees show great variety, with silver maple, elm, black walnut, ash, box elder, and sycamore. Virginia creeper and poison ivy scale the trunks.

Pass under the US 22 river bridge, where a mural decorates the concrete support and pigeons roost overhead. A large talus slope now marks the opposite wooded rim. While this early pairing with US 22 intrudes, the river wins out.

Heron, swallow, goose, cardinal, bluebird, and woodpecker are on the roster of bird sightings. A local Audubon chapter made an official count for the corridor, identifying some 250 bird species. Benches dot the route, while joe-pye weed, lily, yarrow, daisy, black-eyed Susan, and honeysuckle lend splashes of color to the bordering grasses. Steep angler paths descend to shore, but at 0.7 mile an easier path presents itself. A treed slope then builds to the right, vanquishing US 22.

Along the corridor, modest signs identify the historic sites. View channels, foundations, walls, white obelisks, and whistle-stop posts. At 1 mile, the river narrows, showing greater energy. Small vegetated islands interrupt its flow. Tulip poplar, basswood, and cucumber magnolia add their signature leaves. With bicyclists but fleeting companions, hikers find ample blocks of solitude for reflection and wildlife-watching.

At 2.5 miles, spy the parallel 20-foot-high concrete walls recalling the Goodman Quarry. At 3.5 miles, a cornfield isolates the trail from the river, and a rolling field and a barn contribute to glances right. Later, a shrubby floodplain steals the river view. Approaching a bench at 4 miles, admire a long straightaway of the scenic rail-trail. At Fox Run, the lichen-etched stones of the arched bridge invite a look over the railing.

At 4.75 miles and 4.9 miles, cross back-to-back trestle bridges over a tight bend in the river. The first allows both up- and downstream viewing; the second, only a downstream view. Travel posted private land, coming to a small covered bridge that overlooks a tiny waterway where turtles commonly sun. Beyond the covered bridge is a midway access off SR 2017, with tables, benches, and parking.

The harmony of wind, river, bird, and insect dominates. At a pair of benches past the 7-mile post, look for a footpath heading left into the floodplain. It leads to the nearly hidden two-story concrete shell of the Juniata Limestone Company, but be alert as you approach. Sometimes fortunate hikers spy an agile black rat snake probing the concrete crannies for prey. At 7.7 miles, pass the trailhead parking at Cove Dale. Large sycamores captivate travelers.

Gain rock ledges to the right of the trail. Reeds grow riverside. A scenic old stone house and outbuildings lie beyond the fence at 9.3 miles. Again cross the river, passing between crops or fields and river floodplain. The trail itself becomes more exposed. Discover the foundation of an old lock house and pause at a couple more river overlooks before ending at Williamsburg (11 miles).

49 Terrace Mountain Trail

General description: This linear trail traverses the flank of Terrace Mountain, exploring the eastern slope and shore of Raystown Lake. Pass through the Trough Creek Wild Area of Rothrock State Forest, Trough Creek State Park, and lands owned by the U.S. Army Corps of Engineers. The southern third of the trail lends itself to easy strolling, touring a closed management road for much of the way; on the northern two-thirds, find a prescribed, well-blazed route, but one that is often of cross-country rigor.

General location: About 20 miles southeast of Altoona.

Special attractions: Challenge and solitude, mixed forest, occasional lakeshore access and vistas, wildlife sightings, an ice mine, flowering shrubs, fall foliage, swimming at Tatman Run Recreation Area, fishing.

Length: 18.6 miles one-way, with logical break points at Trough Creek State Park and Tatman Run Recreation Area.

Elevation: Travel between 800 and 1,700 feet in elevation.

Difficulty: Strenuous.

Maps: Rothrock State Forest; U.S. Army Corps of Engineers Raystown Lake map/brochure; Trough Creek State Park brochure.

Special concerns: Backpackers may camp at the designated campground in Trough Creek State Park or at Paradise Point/Peninsula Camp, a boat-in/hike-in campground on the southern leg of the journey. For the latter, first prepay at Lake Raystown Resort (on the east shore, off Pennsylvania 994). Putts Camp (also on the southern leg) is a Boy Scouts–only camp. Find the trail blazed, with mileage markers and Terrace Mountain Trail (TMT) signings. Expect patches of poison ivy.

Season and hours: Spring through fall for hiking.

For information: Raystown Lake, U.S. Army Corps of Engineers.

Key points:

0.0 Northern (Fink Road) trailhead; hike south.
6.3 Cross Trough Creek.
10.3 Overlook.

Terrace Mountain Trail

11.3   Tatman Run Recreation Area.
12.0   Cross PA 994.
13.4   Spur to Lake Raystown Resort.
14.1   Paradise Point/Peninsula Camp turnoff.
18.6   End at southern (Weaver Bridge) trailhead.

Finding the trailhead: From the junction of U.S. Highway 22 and PA 26 in Huntingdon, go south on PA 26 for 14.1 miles, and turn left (east) onto PA 994, crossing Raystown Lake. Go 4.5 miles to reach Tatman Run Recreation Area. Go 0.5 mile more and turn left on State Route 3031 for Trough Creek State Park and the northern terminus. Reach the park in 1.7 miles. Continue northeast through the park via gravel Paradise Road, reaching the northern trailhead at the junction of Paradise, Fink, and John Bum Roads, 4.7 miles past Trough Creek Lodge. Locate parking north of gated Fink Road (the trail).

For the southern trailhead, continue south on PA 26 all the way to PA 913; there, turn east toward Saxton. From the center of Saxton, continue east on PA 913 for 0.7 mile. There, turn left onto SR 3003 for Weaver Falls and

Raystown Lake and stay on it. Locate the trail, a gated service road on the right in 1.5 miles, just before the bridge. A few cars can park without blocking the gate. Find additional parking and amenities at Weaver Falls Access Area, across the bridge in another mile.

The hike: For a north–south tour of the TMT (counting down the mileposts), round the gate on dirt Fink Road to descend west toward Raystown Lake. Initially, no blazes mark the route. Maple, oak, birch, and locust frame the road, while laurel, jewelweed, and fern crowd the shoulders. At a second gate (0.3 mile), the blazes begin; keep to the road for a moderate descent. At a double blaze and mile marker 17 (1.25 miles), turn left (south) off old Fink Road. Be alert, because older blazes can blend with the shadows.

Basswood, tulip poplar, and ash join the maple along the lower slope. Spy squirrel, deer, turkey, songbirds, and perhaps even a wood turtle. A secondary jeep trail continues the contouring descent to 1.75 miles, where a TMT emblem and arrow point hikers left. The old jeep trail itself curves right, reaching shore and a small bay in 0.4 mile, suggesting an early lake detour. Ignoring the temptation, proceed south.

At 1.9 miles, bear right and then left following TMT markers to cross a rocky run via footbridges. Next, angle left up the slope, negotiating a log-strewn oak rise before finding the next faint jeep trail advancing the rolling TMT. The woods alternately show dominant oak or varied hardwoods. Only the bright westward lighting hints at the lake.

Find a rustic log bench at 2.6 miles. In another 0.5 mile, the jeep trail bends lakeward, descending parallel to a drainage. At the bottom of the grade, cross

Wood turtle, Terrace Mountain Trail.

the drainage. Although the trail fails to reach the lake, it puts hikers within striking distance.

At a T-junction (3.6 miles), turn left, following an overgrown grade atop a low bluff for the first open view of long, sculpted Raystown Lake. Across the lake, a wooded peninsula grades to Allegrippis Ridge and a backdrop of folded ridges. In exchange for such views, endure hip-brushing grasses, sunny travel, and the occasional stumble on unseen broken shale. The bluff grades from 50 feet to a mere 5 feet above the lake, but poison ivy invades near lake level.

By 4.5 miles, the trail turns away from the lake, passing some glorious big trees. Encounter thin drainages and rock piles from old before passing through an egress in a stone wall. Ascend along the wall, bearing right per blazes and arrows. Black cherries rank among the bigger trees.

At the end of a more defined stone wall, resume contouring and descending south. The TMT now descends left off a side ridge, passes mile marker 13 (5.3 miles), and crosses into Trough Creek State Park. Round the rocky forest slope, coming to a steep bank descent (5.6 miles).

The TMT now travels an abandoned, tree-shaded, paved lane just above elongated Trough Creek Cove. A steep slope plummets to the water. Emerge at the developed park, rounding a gate and proceeding forward past the roof-covered ice mine (6.3 miles). From the railed sides, peer down at the folded rock of the mine, spying an adit from which cold air rushes. Stairs descend for a closer look. Past the Ice Mine Trail, bear right on the closed gravel road, descending to cross Trough Creek on a footbridge above the dam.

From the bridge, ascend steeply to the gravel road of the TMT and bear right. Shrubs along the lower slope distance hikers from the shade-throwing trees. Overlook the spillway at 6.5 miles. Continue forward on the TMT as the orange-blazed Brumbaugh Trail heads left. Round a barricade and proceed on a contouring footpath. Here, erosion suggests a potential reroute.

Resume traveling an overgrown lane above the lake. Then, at 7.5 miles, ascend left to contour along the upper slope, only to descend along a steep drainage slope, returning within 100 feet of shore. Pass an old shack and, at 8.6 miles, find a steep climb, complicated at times by downfalls and slippery canted rocks covered by leaves.

Dip back toward the lake (9.6 miles) before again rolling uphill and descending along a steep, narrow side ridge (10.3 miles). A detour here onto a point presents an overlook of the lake, its ridges, red shores, and Tatman Run Recreation Area. Descend, rounding south to the recreation area, again encountering a poison ivy stronghold.

At 11.1 miles, the TMT actually angles left into woods before coming out on the recreation area road, but sometimes unruly vegetation makes the trail difficult to find. Instead, follow the pipeline corridor, rounding to the swimming area and rest rooms; find a water pump near the boat launch. When ready, hike up the road to the marked trailhead (11.5 miles) and resume southbound to Weaver Bridge.

Pass through full deep woods, crossing scenic tree-draped Tatman Run via footbridge. At 12 miles, cross PA 994, hike a few strides south on a grassy jeep trail, and cut left into the forest of oak, maple, beech, tulip poplar, and dogwood. The sound of the occasional boat reminds hikers they are still along the lake. Again, snatches of old grade advance travel.

Continue the TMT countdown, passing milepost 6. At 13.3 miles, cross a trimmed grass road, and at 13.4 miles bear left onto the single-lane dirt management road; to the right is Lake Raystown Resort. The TMT now offers lake glimpses, but no access. Chestnut oak, locust, and hickory join the maple along the roadway. Poison ivy and Virginia creeper sometimes hide the blazes, but just stay on the road.

At 14.1 miles, a detour right leads to Paradise Point/Peninsula Camp in 0.2 mile. There, find a tree-shaded, grassy peninsula curving into the lake, bold lake views, and basic amenities. Resume the TMT south at 14.5 miles for a rolling ascent. The woods show greater variety.

A dripping spring lies opposite milepost 4 (14.7 miles). Snags open the cathedral where the trail tops out, and a slow descent follows. At 15.8 miles, bypass Putts Scout Camp. By 16.5 miles, travel at lake level with waters lapping at the road bank.

The TMT again rolls, contouring some 100 feet from shore. With a moderate climb, find more beech and rhododendron along the service road. Upon return to lake level, a heron or family of wood ducks may suggest a pause. Round the gate at 18.6 miles, exiting at the Weaver Bridge trailhead on SR 3003.

50 Laurel Highlands Hiking Trail

General description: Spanning five counties, this premier long-distance trail rolls across Laurel Ridge. It ranks as one of the best in the state—and the nation—for its natural offering, its accessibility, and its amenities. The Laurel Highlands Hiking Trail (LHHT) has won national recreation trail distinction and is part of the Potomac Heritage Trail.

General location: On Laurel Mountain between the Youghiogheny River at Ohiopyle and Conemaugh Gorge near Johnstown.

Special attractions: Mixed woodland, picturesque sandstone and limestone outcroppings, vistas, plant fossils, Adirondack-style overnight shelters, mountain laurel and rhododendron, meadow wildflowers, sparkling runs, wildlife, fall foliage.

Length: 70.1 miles one-way.

Elevation: Travel between a low of 1,300 feet at both end points and a high of 2,950 feet at Seven Springs.

Difficulty: Easy to strenuous, depending on the length and section of the hike.

Maps: Recreational guide for Laurel Ridge State Park and the Laurel Highlands Hiking Trail brochure; the Sierra Club, Pennsylvania Chapter, and Western Pennsylvania Conservancy's *A Hiker's Guide to the Laurel Highlands* (available for purchase from the Pennsylvania Chapter of the Sierra Club, www.alleghenysc.org).

Special concerns: Camping and fires are restricted to designated areas; an overnight camping reservation and fee are required. Contact Laurel Ridge State Park by phone or mail thirty days in advance, with the date and location of entry; the leader's name, address, and phone number; and number in the party. Find a shelter/tent area every 8 to 10 miles along the trail. Yellow blazes mark the LHHT; blue, the side trails. Mileage monuments aid in charting progress and finding trail features. Poisonous snakes dwell here but are rarely seen. Park personnel recommend hikers avoid the LHHT during the two and a half weeks of rifle deer hunting season. No bikes, no horses.

Season and hours: Year-round, spring through fall for hiking.

For information: Laurel Ridge State Park.

Laurel Highlands Hiking Trail

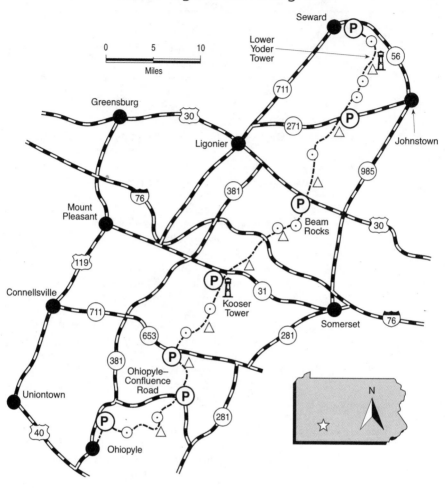

Key points:

0.0	Southern trailhead; follow blue access spur.
1.0	LHHT; turn left.
6.3	Pass first shelter/tent area spur.
11.2	Cross Ohiopyle–Confluence Road at Maple Summit.
18.8	Cross Pennsylvania 653.
30.8	Cross PA 31 at Laurel Summit.
41.0	Beam Rocks.

45.8	Cross U.S. Highway 30.
56.8	Cross PA 271.
66.0	Lower Yoder Fire Tower.
70.1	End at northern (Conemaugh River) trailhead.

Finding the trailhead: Six thirty-car parking areas (most with water) serve LHHT hikers, allowing for piecemeal travel.

At major highway crossings, large wooden signs identify the LHHT.

For the southern terminus, go 0.25 mile north from the PA 381 bridge in Ohiopyle and turn east at a sign for Laurel Highlands Trail Parking. Go 0.7 mile on paved and gravel King Road to reach parking on the right.

Along the south shore of the Conemaugh River, find the northern terminus off PA 56, 7 miles north of Johnstown, 1.5 miles south of the borough of Seward. Signs indicate the turn.

The hike: For a south–north tour from the designated parking lot north of Ohiopyle, follow the blue-blazed access spur to join the LHHT near milepost 1 and turn left. To the righ, the LHHT enters Ohiopyle at Garrett Street. Past the 1-mile mark, look for the trail to enter a rugged climb. Find the path regularly blazed and well groomed.

Mixed hardwoods cloak the hillside, dotted by pockets of laurel. With a 750-foot elevation gain, acquire a Youghiogheny River overlook, with the bend at Victoria Flats and Sugarloaf Knob. The knob becomes a familiar face.

As the trail rolls northeast along the ridge, find more carefree strolling, with additional views when the trees drop their leaves. Rock Spring and Lick Runs sound off distance. Besides woods, discover an old orchard and wildflower meadow. At 6.3 miles, locate the spur to the first shelter/tent area.

From the shelter junction, enter the most demanding climb of the hike, returning to the ridgetop (elevation 2,600 feet). At 8.5 miles, a series of rocks extend vantages, broadening the view. Gentle rolls, outcrops, and rivulet-size streams characterize travel. At 10.3 miles, Little Glade Run engages with its deep hemlock shade, mountain laurel, weeping overhangs, and a small waterfall.

At 11.2 miles, cross Ohiopyle–Confluence Road at Maple Summit, with nearby parking for State Game Lands 111 (no water). Ahead, enjoy a gentle, relaxing stroll in a varied woods of oak, maple, hickory, cucumber magnolia, sassafras, and birch. The understory alternately shows meadow and woods flora. A series of clean-flowing streams recommend the leg.

A wind-disturbed area precedes the trail's arrival at a small lake (13.4 miles). Traverse the dam and follow the east shore before crossing a dirt road. Larger trees now frame travel. Cross Harbaugh Run (15 miles), ascend past outcrops, and twice cross a closed logging road before finding the next set of streams, each about a mile apart. While the rolling LHHT lacks great elevation changes, it can still present some brief steep pitches and rises.

A full forest with patchy laurel, hobblebush, ferns, azalea, and sites of bramble precedes the 18.5-mile spur to the next shelter community. Weathered outcrop jumbles and ledges both accent and prescribe travel. Distanced from the main traffic flow, the trail's attractive shelters are the "Hiltons" of the outdoors and well worth the fee.

At PA 653 (18.8 miles), a short detour east on the road leads to the Laurel Ridge State Park office. Across the highway, find an old cemetery, pass more rock outcrops, and edge an open field with a microwave transmitter. At 21.3 miles, overlook the Middle Fork Laurel Run watershed. Continue north along the ridge and then descend to cross log bridges over the four feeder streams to Fall Creek and, later, Grays Run.

Atop the ridge at 24.2 miles, a 0.3-mile spur leads to the Grindle Ridge Shelters. On the LHHT, a switchback descent leads to the cool drainage of Blue Hole Creek; the following ascent brings a valley overlook. Tag the highest point on the tour, traveling the bumpy ridge through private Seven Springs Resort; pass respectfully. West of the LHHT at 26.6 miles, an observation tower built by the resort presents a 360-degree panorama. The trail then crosses ski slopes before rolling to cross a paved road.

At a wildlife pond, skirt the east shore, and at the saddle at 28.7 miles gain views both west and south. Ahead, travel a state forest beltway through Roaring Run Natural Area. Encounter clearings with brushing vegetation and cross little-used gravel forest roads. Where the LHHT approaches Kooser Lookout, travel in planted spruce and pine; lush ferns color the plantation floor. At 30.8 miles, reach the spur to PA 31 parking.

Pass from scrubby area to young woods, crossing PA 31 at the sign for Laurel Summit (elevation 2,728 feet). Soon after, cross quiet Old Route 31. Nearby stands the 1923 Somerset–Westmoreland County Line Monument. Continue north, finding one of several nice areas of beech. At 32.5 miles, reach the next shelter spur and begin climbing in spurts.

Roll through more stream valleys before reaching the fenced bridge over the Pennsylvania Turnpike, Interstate 76 (about midway). Upon crossing, look for the LHHT to take a switchback, dropping below a snowmobile trail. Bald Knob adds to views.

Before crossing dirt Hickory Flat Road (37.6 miles), pass through a gorgeous stand of tall ferns and snag-riddled forest. Insects claimed these trees. At milepost 38, snare a rare view for this leg, and soon after pass the spur to the next set of shelters. A casual, fairly level woods stroll leads to Rector Edie Road.

From the base of Beam Rocks (41 miles), view the exciting collection of cliffs, crevices, ledges, and isolated boulders. Tracked side paths ascend the adjacent hillside to top the rocks, but rhododendron and laurel may obscure the way. Atop the jumble, gain dizzying looks over the edge, admire the woods below, and scan the terrain straining east. Beam Rocks often bustles with visitors, since a short access trail leads to it from Laurel Summit Road.

Just shy of 43 miles, find a trio of stream crossings at Spruce Run; be alert at the first of these, because an unmarked side trail can mislead. Rocky passages characterize the next saddle. Cross US 30 (45.8 miles).

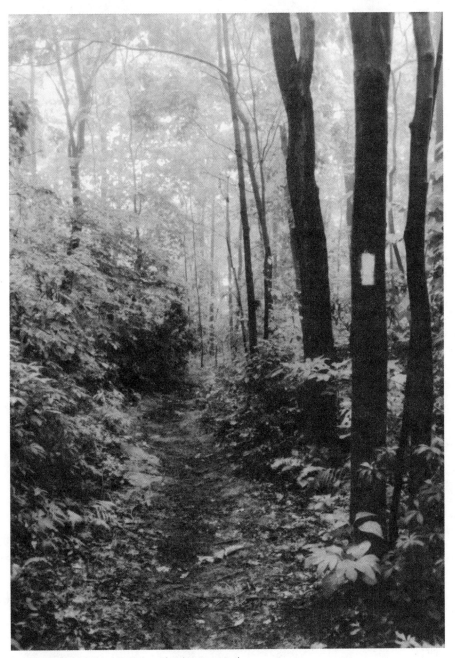

Laurel Highlands Hiking Trail, Laurel Ridge State Park.

The trail rolls over small hills, meeting jeep trails and small streams. At 47.6 miles, cross the historic Forbes Trail (today a jeep trail). In 1758, during the French and Indian War, a colonial military procession of 6,000 men trod this path. The ensuing campaign helped decide control of the Ohio River forks.

South Branch Card Machine Run and Mystery Hill next mark off distance. When the trees lack leaves, find sporadic views. Enjoy another laurel-colored stretch and more rock passages before reaching the 0.7-mile spur to both PA 271 parking and the shelter/tent camping area.

At 56.8 miles, cross PA 271 and hike north, rubbing elbows with cinnamon fern. Side trails break away west, entering State Game Lands 42 or Rachelwood Game Preserve (a research station). Scrubby areas continue to mile 60.

A rare roadway stretch advances the LHHT between miles 61 and 62. The trail then continues passing between woods and clearings. At 64.9 miles, a blue trail heads east to the Decker Avenue (northernmost) shelters. At just under 66 miles, spy radio towers to the east and visit Lower Yoder Fire Tower for a panoramic look at the Johnstown area.

On the final 4-mile descent, overlooks of the Conemaugh River Gorge put a fine cap on the hike. Travel from Lower Yoder Lookout (elevation 2,600 feet) to the trailhead (1,300 feet). Power lines can both open and intrude on views. At 68.4 miles, pass a quarry said to have provided stone for the rail bridge in Johnstown. In the 1889 flood, this bridge held. A full-canopy forest enfolds the trail as the hike draws to an end at Seward Parking (70.1 miles).

51 John P. Saylor Trail, Middle Ridge Loop

General description:	This sampling of the John P. Saylor Trail System in Gallitzin State Forest explores the heart of Clear Shade Wild Area.
General location:	12 miles southeast of Johnstown.
Special attractions:	Hardwoods and hemlock, wetlands and meadow, picturesque springs, wildflowers, wildlife, solitude.
Length:	7 miles round trip.
Elevation:	Find about a 300-foot elevation change, with the low point along Clear Shade Creek (2,300 feet) and the high point partway along the Middle Ridge Loop (2,570 feet).
Difficulty:	Easy to moderate.
Maps:	John P. Saylor and Lost Turkey Trails Map; Gallitzin State Forest.
Special concerns:	Secure an overnight camping permit, limit stays to two consecutive nights, and keep party size small. Locate camps at least 200 yards away from Clear Shade Creek, and 100 yards from any other stream. In places, raised waters can make for sloshing travel. Seasonally, insects can be troublesome; take precautions for ticks. Orange blazes guide hikers on the John P. Saylor Trail. Mileposts apply only to the 6-mile loop, not the access spur (which accounts for the mileage differences).
Season and hours:	Spring through fall for hiking.
For information:	Gallitzin State Forest.

Key points:

0.0 Fisherman's Path trailhead.

0.3 John P. Saylor Trail.

0.5 Cross suspension bridge; keep left for the loop.

1.5 Spring.

4.5 Shelter.

6.5 Complete loop; return to trailhead.

Finding the trailhead: From the junction of Pennsylvania 56 and PA 160 in Windber, go east on PA 56 for 5.7 miles, turning south onto gravel Shade Road (0.3 mile east of the state forest headquarters). Go another 1.6 miles, finding a trailhead turnout on the left for the Fisherman's Path, with parking for five vehicles and additional parking along the road shoulder.

John P. Saylor Trail, Middle Ridge Loop

The hike: Start on the yellow-blazed Fisherman's Path, descending a rock-studded foot trail to the orange-blazed John P. Saylor Trail. Pass through a black cherry–beech woods, with an understory of ferns. An old mossy stump with a burl records the forest of old.

At 0.3 mile, turn right onto the John P. Saylor Trail; here it also shows blue cross-country ski blazings. Just shy of 0.5 mile, arrive at the sign for Middle Ridge Loop, and turn left to cross Clear Shade Creek via a suspension bridge. Given the natural bounce of the bridge, have no more than two people on it at any one time. Hemlocks fan the clear-flowing stream. In 100 feet, reach the loop junction. Find blazes both straight ahead and along the grade to the right; proceed forward for a clockwise tour.

In a couple of strides, bear left on a second raised grade framed by black cherry, birch, maple, and witch hazel. Four varieties of club moss weave a miniature forest at boot level. Wetland depressions support sphagnum moss. The brushing grasses and ferns of the grade are in keeping with the wild area. Birdsongs and the muffled voice of the creek blend for a soothing backdrop.

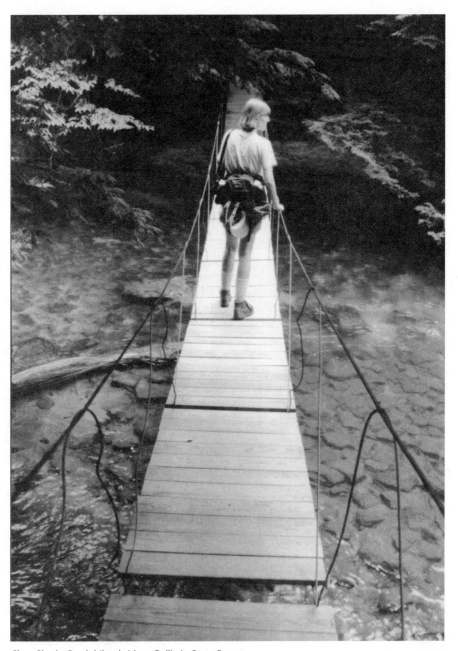

Clear Shade Creek hiker bridge, Gallitzin State Forest.

Cross a side tributary and, near milepost 1 on the loop (1.5 miles into the hike), find a beautiful freshwater spring bubbling up. It immediately launches a 15-foot-wide stream coursing over a mossy bed with grassy banks and islands of aquatic plants. Beyond the spring, travel an eye-pleasing forest consisting of a wispy meadow floor, dark-trunked cherry, and thorny hawthorn.

Self-heal, buttercup, daisy, milkweed, and thistle dot color along the way, while butterflies and damselflies add winged signatures. The meadows variously show grasses, ferns, and a wetland flora with berry bushes. After a few soggy strides, look for the trail to swing right and ascend the slope of Middle Ridge. Black cherry dominates; a woodland flora at times replaces the ferns.

Top the ridge and enjoy a meandering stroll in gentle terrain. Where leaf mat overtakes the trail, be alert for blazes. The trail cuts back on itself before the 3-mile post (3.5 miles). Here, thin-trunked striped maples jail the few big trees, and dark logs overlace the forest floor. The crashing passage of a black bear may emphasize the wilderness.

As the trail slowly descends, find the woods more mixed, with islands of hemlock among the deciduous trees. Again, soggy sites cause you to ponder strategies for keeping dry. Beyond milepost 4, travel a long fern–grass meadow, skirting an open-faced shelter with earthen floor and picnic table. Pockets of blueberry seasonally slow travel; some cattail and rhododendron lend interest and texture. Scan the meadow's length for a blaze on a distant tree and maintain the line of travel.

The trail then turns left for a log crossing of a spring-fed side water flowing to Clear Shade Creek. Follow it downstream and bear right to meet a grassy grade (5.2 miles). Turn right onto the grade to cross back over the side stream.

Ahead stretches a straight-arrow, flat floodplain return just removed from Clear Shade Creek. Pass mainly in the open, touring meadow and dispersed woods of aspen, hawthorn, and black cherry. The rippled trailbed betrays that it was once a railroad grade. Breaches present wet footing.

Close the loop at 6.5 miles and backtrack: recross the suspension bridge, turn right, and then turn left onto the Fisherman's Path. Return to the trailhead at 7 miles.

52 Grove Run–Fish Run Hike

General description: This lopsided, barbell-shaped tour joins Grove Run Trail and Fish Run Trail, exploring the southern hills of Linn Run watershed. Travel lands of Linn Run State Park and Forbes State Forest.

General location: 20 miles southwest of Johnstown, 40 miles southeast of Pittsburgh.

Special attractions: Mature forest, meadows, sparkling cascades, woodland wildflowers, wildlife, fall foliage.

Length: 8 miles round trip.

Elevation: Travel between 1,800 feet at the picnic area trailhead and 2,620 feet at the ridge summit.

Difficulty: Moderate.

Maps: Grove Run and Fish Run Trails map; Forbes State Forest.

Special concerns: Within the state park, no backpack-camping is allowed. Greenbrier grows in strongholds, and rattlesnakes find habitat—but encounters are rare. Blazes and markers indicate the trail, but in places they are faint and few, requiring detective work. No bikes.

Season and hours: Spring through fall for hiking. Linn Run State Park, 8:00 A.M. to sunset.

For information: Forbes State Forest; Linn Run/Laurel Mountain Complex.

Key points:

0.0   Grove Run Trailhead.
0.9   Cross Grove Run.
1.7   Cross Quarry Trail (a service road).
1.8   Grove Run loop; go right, delaying taking the loop.
3.0   Fish Run loop junction; keep to the grade.
3.6   Cross bridge over Linn Run.
4.3   Close Fish Run loop; backtrack to Grove Run loop.
6.8   Cross Quarry Trail.
8.0   End at Grove Run Trailhead.

Finding the trailhead: From Ligonier, go 2 miles east on U.S. Highway 30 and turn south onto Pennsylvania 381. Go 4 miles, reaching the tiny town of Rector. There, turn left onto Linn Run Road for Linn Run State Park. Reach the entrance to Grove Run Picnic Area (the trailhead) on the right in 2.9 miles.

Grove Run–Fish Run Hike

To Ligonier and (381)

Park headquarters

N

Grove Run Trail

Grove Run

Boot Hollow

Linn Run

Linn Run Road

Fish Run Trail

Fish Run

0   0.5   1
Miles

To Laurel Summit Picnic Area

The hike: Start from the picnic area turnaround at the sign for Grove Run Trail. Ascend steadily, pursuing intermittent Grove Run upstream, hiking among tulip poplar, maple, big beech, basswood, and birch. Witch hazel and striped maple fill out the midstory, while large snags open the cathedral. The rich multistory forest erases all memory that these slopes were denuded of trees in 1909.

In places, find trailside vegetation brushing and thorny. At 0.9 mile, cross a canted footbridge over Grove Run and admire a 2-foot cascade upstream. Avoid a secondary path that continues upstream. The primary trail hooks left past the bridge before ascending and contouring away from Grove Run.

Soon, discover a seasonal cascade and 5-foot veiled falls along a feeder hollow to Grove Run. Pursue the hollow upstream before crossing it via stones. Attractive big trees complement travel. For much of the hiking season, some species of woods flora lends bloom.

The upper slope now holds older oak, with young maple and birch and often unrestrained greenbrier. A hummocky moss adorns the path as it switchbacks. At 1.5 miles, sign in at the trail book.

Salvage-logging (for removing insect-infested trees) intrudes on and muddles the trail. Still ascend, bearing right at 1.6 miles. The trail could use a few more blazes, but keep your line of travel to cross Quarry Trail (a dirt service road) at 1.7 miles.

Return to the natural woods of the summit and, at 1.8 miles, reach a signed trail fork. For a 4-mile loop tour of Grove Run Trail alone, bear left. To explore Fish Run Trail, turn right, later returning to this point to complete Grove Run Trail.

This stretch of the Fish Run Trail requires detective work; watch for trail markings both ahead and behind you and look for hints to the path. Clues may include bits of wooden markers bare of color and even the tacks that held them in place. Travel a spatially open woods of mature oak, maple, and black cherry, wading through knee- to waist-high ferns.

By 2.5 miles, travel a more open meadow, dotted by trees or snags, keeping right. In another 0.2 mile, descend to cross a headwater fork of Fish Run. Meet and descend an old grade (2.9 miles), likely associated with a logging/passenger rail line that once traversed the area.

At 3 miles, reach a blazed loop junction for the Fish Run Trail; keep to the grade for a counterclockwise tour. Once again, lower-elevation hardwoods shade travel. For the most part, better blazes guide hikers. Descend past a cut-across (3.2 miles) to cross a bridge over Linn Run at 3.6 miles.

The trail again forks: To the right, Fish Run Trail crosses Linn Run Road. For the chosen loop, go left (downstream), crossing a second bridge. A high-canopy forest laces over rocky Linn Run. Keep an eye out at 3.8 miles for the blaze on the left signaling the loop's footpath return (reach this turn about 150 feet before the third bridge). The serial bridges recall the switchbacking route of the former railroad.

Travel a scenic, rock-studded footpath, passing unspoiled beech trees and overlooking a couple of Fish Run cascades before coming to a T-junction with a lower cut-across grade. Turn right to close the Fish Run loop back at the 3-mile junction (4.3 miles). A birch snag signs off the loop. Retrace the obscure 1.2-mile upper ridge segment to return to the 1.8-mile junction with the Grove Run Trail (5.5 miles). There, bear right to close the second loop on this barbell-shaped tour.

Descend, following a headwater fork of Boot Hollow to begin a rugged, contouring return. The canted trailbed tests ankles, with descents coming in modest measure. Mature forest engages travelers. Woodpecker, turkey, and deer may offer distraction.

Snags disappear from the forest mosaic prior to the second crossing of the Quarry Trail (6.8 miles). Continue contouring. At the marked junction at 7 miles, bear left for Grove Run Picnic Area. To the right lies Linn Run Road. Still the trail rolls and rounds the slope before descending to cross Grove Run via rocks. With an ascent of the drainage slope, emerge at the picnic area between the rest room and turnaround. End at 8 miles.

53 Ryerson Station State Park

Overview

At this 1,164-acre park in southwest Pennsylvania near the West Virginia border, the centerpiece of recreation is man-made R. J. Duke Lake. In addition to fishing and boating, some 10 miles of trail explore the park's hillsides and floodplain. The park takes its name from a 1792 outpost, Fort Ryerson, which was constructed on the orders of Virginia authorities to provide refuge during Indian raids.

General description: Three loops present an overview of the park and its trail offering.

General location: 25 miles west of Waynesburg.

Special attractions: Mixed southern hardwoods, a 300-year-old wolf tree, old cemetery, vistas, floodplain meadow, lake and creek access.

Length: Pine Box Trail, 2-mile loop; Three Mitten Trail, 1.5-mile loop; Lazear Trail, 2.4-mile loop.

Elevation: Pine Box and Three Mitten Trails each have a 300-foot elevation change; Lazear Trail has a 400-foot elevation change.

Difficulty: All are easy to moderate.

Maps: State park brochure.

Special concerns: There is no trail camping; camp only in the park's designated campground. Poison ivy abounds. The trailheads and junctions are marked, but there are no trail blazes.

Season and hours: Spring through fall for hiking.

For information: Ryerson Station State Park.

Key points:

Pine Box Trail:
0.0 Pine Box Trailhead.
0.6 Cross State Route 3022.
1.0 Stahl Cemetery detour.
2.0 Cross SR 3022 to end at trailhead.

Three Mitten Trail:
0.0 Three Mitten Trailhead; go clockwise at loop junction.
0.8 Pass Polly Hollow Trail.
1.5 End at trailhead.

Ryerson Station State Park

To Waynesburg

Three Mitten Trail

Polly Hollow

McNay Ridge Road

R. J. Duke Lake

Bistoria Road

Kent Run

Pine Box Trail

Stahl Cemetery

Wolf Tree

Iron Bridge

Fox Feather Trail

Panther Lick Hollow

Lazear Trail

Munnell Hollow

North Fork of the Dunkard Fork of Wheeling Creek

Riggs Road

0   0.25   0.5

Mile

N

Lazear Trail:

0.0	Lazear Trailhead.
0.3	Wolf tree.
0.8	Hike's high point/overlook.
1.7	Fox Feather Trail.
2.4	End loop at trailhead.

FT

1,500

1,250 — Wolf tree — Overlook — Fox Feather Trail

1,000

750 — Trailhead — Close loop

Miles   1   2

Finding the trailhead: From Graysville (about 15 miles northwest of Waynesburg on Pennsylvania 21), go west on PA 21 for 5.1 miles and turn left (southeast) onto Bistoria Road/SR 3022. Reach the park in another 0.8 mile. To the right, find the south-shore day-use area and trailhead for the Lazear Trail; straight on SR 3022 leads to the park office, campground, and starts for the Pine Box and Three Mitten Trails.

The hikes: For **Pine Box Trail,** start from the parking area at Iron Bridge, opposite the intersection of SR 3022 and McNay Ridge Road (the campground road). Hike south across Iron Bridge, overlooking the North Fork of the Dunkard Fork of Wheeling Creek. Sycamore, locust, and willow shade the banks, with a thick meadow floodplain spanning to the southern hills. Upon crossing, turn left (upstream); to the right is the Iron Bridge Trail.

Travel is shadeless along a broad mowed path. In the bordering tall meadow vegetation, spy lily, fleabane, butter-and-eggs, goldenrod, nettle, and Queen Anne's lace. Jewelweed grows closer to the water. Near the bridge, the creek flows as a broad cloudy band; upstream, it becomes riffling, losing the reservoir's influence. Kingfisher, scarlet tanager, and crow divert eyes.

Where the mowed track forks (0.3 mile), stay right to angle up the wooded slope and overlook the narrowed floodplain to the creek. Via boardwalk, skirt a weeping rock; maple and box elder offer shade. Back on the meadow path, view rustic outbuildings of a neighboring farm and hike past a twin-trunked sycamore before ascending to cross Riggs Road Bridge and then SR 3022.

Now hiking toward Stahl Cemetery, find a steady, moderate switchbacking ascent on an old wagon road shaded by big oaks. In a stand of spruce (1 mile), look for the Pine Box Trail to turn left. Straight ahead, however, a 0.2-mile round-trip detour leads to Stahl Cemetery—an attractive multifamily hillside cemetery in natural woods. Within the rustic rail fence, find stones that date to the mid-1800s.

Resume the Pine Box loop as it contours downhill on a tree-shaded old road, crossing the head and later the foot of a steep ravine draining to Kent Run. Glimpse Kent Run and return to SR 3022. Cross the road, bearing right, to close the loop at trail parking, 2 miles.

Find the marked **Three Mitten Trail** across from Walnut Grove Picnic Area, 0.1 mile west of the park office. Park either in the day-use area or

Stahl Cemetery, Ryerson Station State Park.

at the office. Hike north up a barricaded woods road, drawing away from the reservoir.

In 100 yards, reach the loop junction and proceed forward for a clockwise tour. The vegetation reclaiming the old road is cropped low for easy walking. Elm, oak, and hickory contribute to the woods; honeysuckle and bramble, to the shoulder mesh. With a moderate ascent, the trail wraps around the slope for early overlooks of the reservoir. Sizable oaks cause eyes to linger. Basswood, ash, maple, spruce, and walnut extend the roster.

The intrusive rumbling heard here comes from nearby Holbrook Compressor Station. By 0.5 mile, lose the drone and descend. Tall, straight trunks prove visually appealing. Bear right with the grade at 0.8 mile; to the left is Polly Hollow Trail, which travels past the campground. As the Three Mitten Trail maintains a fairly even contour along the lower slope, younger trees introduce a midstory. Close the loop, bearing left to end at 1.5 miles.

On the east side of the south shore's day-use parking area, above the boat rental and pavilion 3, a sign indicates the path for the Lazear and Fox Feather Trails. Head right from the mapboard, ascending in the maple–tulip poplar woods of the lower slope. At 0.1 mile, reach a four-way junction. An unmarked service road heads left, the Fox Feather Trail takes the center fork, and the Lazear Trail heads right.

On the **Lazear Trail,** tour a spruce–mixed hardwood forest, hiking past a large oak with spreading branches. Then, at 0.3 mile, discover the acclaimed "wolf tree." This 300-year-old oak grew up in a clearing, which accounts for its low-level candelabra branching. The celebrated tree shows a 5- to 6-foot diameter and totally dominates its setting.

Continue the ascent via switchbacking road. Poison ivy scales many of the tree trunks. At a T-junction, stay right; to the left is the Orchard Trail. At a clearing at 0.6 mile, take a moment to admire nature's artwork. Here, wild grape literally cloaks the trees, shaping rounded, curious topiarylike forms. The roadway maintains a pleasant gradient.

At 0.8 mile, reach the high point (elevation 1,389 feet) and an overlook. View the lake some 400 feet below, the rounded crowns of the framing deciduous trees, the opposite wooded ridge, and distant folded ridges. Now descend to an unmarked junction at 1 mile. Go left for the loop, still on a cropped-grass woods road. To the right, the road dead-ends.

Hike past a huge out-of-place sycamore. Uphill, the forest engages with ancient shade trees and twisted, woody grapevines. At 1.3 and 1.7 miles, keep descending right to avoid the Tiffany Ridge Trail. Below lies Munnell Hollow.

At 1.75 miles, tag the Fox Feather Trail, where it loops, and proceed forward on a joint segment of trail. In 200 feet, bypass the Iron Bridge Trail as it heads right. Now above R. J. Duke Lake, view a cattail marsh at the mouth of Munnell Hollow. A heron standing far into the cloudy water may reveal how shallow this part of the reservoir is.

At the next junction, bear right for the unmarked lakeside route and a change of setting. On this easy walk, view the open water as well as fish, heron, kingfisher, and turtle. At the day-use area, follow a service road left to return to the parking area (2.4 miles).

54 Youghiogheny (the Yough) River Rail Trail

General description:	This mostly natural 27-mile rail-trail hugs the exciting Youghiogheny River between Confluence and Connellsville, passing through Ohiopyle. Another 43 miles extend the exploration north, and still it grows. Ultimately the rail-trail system will span 315 miles, linking Pittsburgh and Washington, D.C.
General location:	Between Confluence and Connellsville.
Special attractions:	Open and filtered Youghiogheny River overlooks, tributary waterfalls, picturesque cliffs, rhododendron, fall foliage, fishing, Ohiopyle Falls.
Length:	25.5 miles one-way between Connellsville and Ramcat Put-in (selected section for this description).
Elevation:	Find a 500-foot elevation change.
Difficulty:	Easy to strenuous, depending on length and allotted time.
Maps:	Forbes State Forest; Ohiopyle State Park brochure.
Special concerns:	Find bicycle rentals and amenities at Connellsville, Ohiopyle, and Confluence. Cyclists must yield to pedestrians and stay off all side trails. Mileposts numbered north from Confluence help travelers track progress; trail posts with initials identify river rapids. No swimming.
Season and hours:	Year-round, spring through fall for hiking. Daylight hours.
For information:	Ohiopyle State Park; the Yough River Trail Council.

Key points:
- 0.0   Connellsville trailhead; hike south.
- 11.0   Milepost (MP) 16; cross Bruner Road.
- 16.4   High Bridge.
- 17.0   Ohiopyle.
- 25.5   End at Ramcat Put-in.
- 27.0   Confluence trailhead.

Finding the trailhead: In Connellsville, locate trailhead parking and amenities at Yough River City Park (at the intersection of First and Third Streets). In Ohiopyle, access the trail from Ferncliff Peninsula Parking (at the north end of the Pennsylvania 381 bridge) or at Middle Yough Take-out,

Youghiogheny (the Yough) River Rail Trail

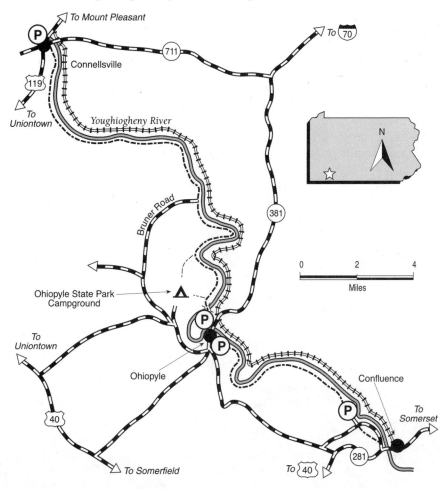

east of the visitor center at the north end of Ohiopyle. From Confluence, the trail heads north off PA 281, following the west bank downstream.

The hike: This rail-trail pairs up with a premier whitewater for Pennsylvania and the eastern United States. Compressed cinders surface the 8-foot-wide trail, which travels between 20 and 100 feet above "the Yough." The river variously presents smooth straightaways, scenic bends, and churned pools with giant boulders. Much of the way, a leafy mosaic laces over the trail. Openings allow for glimpses of the river's 1,700-foot-deep gorge.

On an upstream (north–south) tour, leave Yough River City Park in Connellsville, following the sidewalk or bike lane south along residential Third

Street. The actual rail-trail starts at a kiosk and map box at 0.5 mile. When touring in this direction, the numbered mileposts count down the distance to Confluence. The well-groomed trail invites carefree strolling, with long stretches of solitary travel away from the central bustle of Ohiopyle.

Initially, the overhead cathedral is open, with trees and shrubs screening out views of the industrial river. Upon crossing a pair of railroad bridges, enter an outstanding, uninterrupted natural stretch to Ohiopyle. Fractured, mossy cliffs engage, joined by a leafy umbrella of oak, maple, tulip poplar, sycamore, hickory, ash, box elder, and elm. Benches invite pause, and spur trails branch to the river—a broad, even band along this lower stretch.

Some 2.5 miles into the trip (midway between mileposts 25 and 24), discover a seasonally pretty 15-foot falls, its bold ledge, and rhododendron banks. At 5 miles (milepost 22), pass a river-overlook bench. A wooded flat then spans between river and trail. An active railroad travels the opposite shore.

Slowly, the trail grades higher. At 7.5 miles, pass a private Baptist camp, keeping to the trail. Honeysuckle, trillium, chicory, coneflower, and Queen Anne's lace introduce sprinkles of color, while tulip poplars dominate the pioneering young trees.

For the next 3 miles (between mileposts 19 and 16), open, sunny stretches mark travel, and the trail is 100 feet above the river. Before coming to a landslide, a bench seat presents a fine upstream river snapshot of an S-bend. Postrain trips find side-stream cascades in full glory. At 11 miles (milepost 16), cross lightly traveled Bruner Road, which leads to a river take-out.

Showy rhododendron next frames travel. Ahead, enter "river rapid country," where the Yough drops 200 feet over the next 7.5 miles. A louder river

Youghiogheny River, Ohiopyle State Park.

voice often paired with squeals of river runners accompanies travel. Lettered posts signal a succession of rapids rumbling below the trail; pass Stairstep Rapid at 12 miles (milepost 15).

South of milepost 14, examine the cliff bedding for a coal seam and, shortly after, reach a trail post for the pink-blazed Kentuck Trail, which follows Sugar Run upstream. A 0.2-mile round-trip detour visits a 15-foot cascade on Sugar Run. The rail-trail proceeds upstream, quickly coming to a signed junction for the Jonathan and Kentuck Trails. Here, a similar-length uphill detour finds a serial falls on Jonathan Run.

Pursuing the Yough upstream, pass the Bottle of Wine and the Dimple and Swimmer Rapids. A section of blasted rock follows. South of milepost 11, three trails journey right to explore Ohiopyle State Park. Then, at 16.4 miles, High Bridge presents a grand river perspective, with up- and downstream views. Spectators commonly gather to watch the kayaks and rafts.

The rail-trail then travels past Ferncliff Peninsula Parking to cross the scenic 620-foot railroad bridge that spans the Yough and PA 381 at the borough of Ohiopyle. It arrives at the depot-station-style visitor center, where toilet facilities and information are available. Proceed past the visitor center to Middle Yough Take-out (17 miles/milepost 10) to continue the rail-trail—or detour south into town for food and drink or to visit Ohiopyle Falls, where the river drops 90 feet over a 1-mile distance. In 1754, this wild churn forced George Washington to abandon his plans for using the Yough to move troops and supplies in the capture of Fort Duquesne (Pittsburgh).

As the rail trail resumes, it passes closer to the river and bustles with rent-a-bicycle activity from Ohiopyle. Mowed shoulders open the corridor; better shade follows in another mile. A forested flat sometimes distances the trail from the river, but side paths branch to shore. Midway between mileposts 8 and 7, view another tributary cascade and gain an open river view. As the tree border to the river narrows, hikers are lured aside to watch rafters.

At 21 miles into the trip (milepost 6), find easy river access. Later, islands and bars of sycamore and silver maple punctuate the Youghiogheny River. At 24.8 miles (approaching milepost 2), a river spur leads to a large boulder slab for admiring the waterway. The river shows agitation here; this stretch of the Yough has both class I and II whitewater.

At 25.5 miles, arrive at the Ramcat Put-in, with parking and pit toilets. To avoid road travel, end or turn back here. The bike trail proceeds out the parking access road, crosses a paved road, and passes fields and houses to again cross a road at 26.5 miles. At trail's end (27 miles), a sign points travelers left along a rural road to Confluence. Cross the bridge to enter town at 28 miles.

55 Ohiopyle State Park

Overview

North of the tristate border of Pennsylvania, West Virginia, and Maryland, this 19,046-acre Pennsylvania state park cradles a 14-mile stretch of the impressive Youghiogheny River as it cuts through Laurel Highlands. The spectacular setting boasts both whitewater excitement and a variety of hikes. Besides serving as a gateway to the Laurel Highlands Hiking Trail and a host to the Youghiogheny River Rail Trail, this park offers foot trails that explore a unique natural area, visit river and tributary waterfalls, and top rocky promontories to survey the 1,700-foot-deep gorge.

General description: Four foot trails introduce the park from river to ridge.

General location: At the borough of Ohiopyle.

Special attractions: Youghiogheny River; Ferncliff Peninsula, a national natural landmark; Ohiopyle Falls; tree fossils; old-growth forest; rhododendron, laurel, and azalea blooms; scenic cliffs; fall foliage.

Length: Ferncliff Trail, 2-mile loop; Great Gorge Trail, 4 miles round trip (or 2-mile shuttle); Baughman Trail, 5.5 miles round trip; Meadow Run Trail, 2-mile loop.

Elevation: Ferncliff Trail, 100-foot elevation change; Great Gorge Trail, 200-foot elevation change; Baughman Trail, 1,000-foot elevation change; Meadow Run Trail, 200-foot elevation change.

Difficulty: Ferncliff Trail, easy to moderate; Great Gorge Trail, easy; Baughman Trail, moderate; Meadow Run Trail, easy to moderate.

Maps: State park brochure.

Special concerns: There is no trail camping. Beware of poison ivy, and exercise caution along the river rock. Parking can be chaotic during summer. Color-coded blazes guide hikers.

Season and hours: Year-round, spring through fall for hiking, 8:00 A.M. to sunset.

For information: Ohiopyle State Park.

Key points:

Ferncliff Trail:
0.0   Ferncliff Trailhead.
0.1   Monument and loop junction; stay along river.
0.4   Ohiopyle Falls vantage.
1.9   Close loop at monument; return to trailhead.

Ohiopyle State Park

To Bear Run Nature Reserve

To State Park Campground

Cucumber Falls

Great Gorge Trail

Ferncliff Trail

381

Fossils

Visitor center

Chalk Hill Road

Ohiopyle

Middle Ridge Road

Cucumber Run

Ohiopyle Falls

Baughman Trail

Youghiogheny River

381

SR 2011

Meadow Run Trail

Meadow Run

Falls

Sugarloaf Road

Baughman Rock

To 40

To 40

To Confluence

0   0.5   1
Miles

N

Great Gorge Trail:

0.0	Ferncliff Trailhead; hike the rail-trail north.
0.2	Cross High Bridge to Great Gorge Trail.
1.4	Cucumber Falls detour.
2.0	Cucumber Run Picnic Area; turn around.

Baughman Trail:

0.0	Middle Yough Take-out/Trailhead.
1.9	Top ridge.
2.7	Baughman Rock area; turn around.

Meadow Run Trail:

0.0	Meadow Run Trailhead; head right.
0.8	First spur to Meadow Run cascades.
1.5	Flat Rock spur.
1.6	Loop heads left at Deep Hole spur.
2.0	End at trailhead.

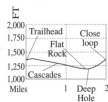

Finding the trailhead: From the junction of U.S. Highways 119 and 40 in Uniontown, go east on US 40 for 10.4 miles. At Chalk Hill, turn left (north) onto State Route 2010/Chalk Hill Road for Ohiopyle State Park. Arrive at a multiple junction in 6.3 miles. Straight leads to the park's Kentuck Campground in 1.5 miles; to the left, Holland Hill Road leads to the Old Mitchell Place; and to the right, Chalk Hill Road leads to Pennsylvania 381, Ohiopyle, and the trailheads. Enter Ohiopyle in 1.5 miles.

The hikes: Start both the **Ferncliff Trail** and the **Great Gorge Trail** from Ferncliff Peninsula Parking: In north Ohiopyle, turn west at the north end of the PA 381 bridge.

For the Ferncliff Trail, take either the closed fire lane that leaves the entrance road or a footpath from the parking area and hike south to a kiosk. From there, pass under the rail-trail bridge to find a plaque for the national natural landmark, which signals the loop.

Proceed forward along the river, passing among tulip poplar, oak, and locust; side paths break away to the roiling river. At 0.2 mile, reach a fossil site. Discover both scaly and stringy tree fossils; an interpretive sign helps with the identification. Look for more examples as you stroll the river bedrock.

The Ferncliff Trail travels the perimeter of Ferncliff Peninsula, housed in a tight horseshoe bend of "the Yough." At 0.4 mile, top a rocky jut that extends into the fury of Ohiopyle Falls for an unmatched front-row seat. Feel the energy, mist, and danger. Opposite the base of the falls, ascend right to enter woods. Here, rhododendrons bombard the senses.

On the peninsula rim, spurs lead to river views but stay well back from the edge. Signed interior trails branch to the right. Old-growth hemlock, white pine, tulip, hickory, oak, and maple generate a soothing backdrop. Where the trail descends at 1.25 miles, spy precarious rock overhangs and boxy boulders. The trail later rolls to traverse a transitioning meadow–woods. Close the loop at the monument (1.9 miles), and turn left to end at 2 miles.

For the Great Gorge Trail, follow the BIKE TRAIL signs north from Ferncliff Peninsula Parking for the Youghiogheny River Rail Trail (see hike 54). Cross the railroad bridge (High Bridge) for an exceptional overlook of the Yough, and then, at 0.25 mile, turn left at the sign TO GREAT GORGE TRAIL. Meet the actual trail in another 200 feet and turn left (upstream). The trail contours the slope some 100 feet above the roaring river, but the thick woodland denies views.

A natural arbor enfolds the 5-foot-wide trail, with rhododendron growing toward the river. Unofficial trails branch in both directions. At 1.2 miles, Meadow Run Trail arrives on the left; a hike along it requires either wading or rock-hopping across Cucumber Run. Stay on Great Gorge Trail.

At 1.4 miles, approach Chalk Hill Road. To add a view of Cucumber Falls, detour left across the old road bridge and descend the stairs for a fine look at this broad, 50- to 70-foot veil. Rhododendrons claim one wall of its rocky bowl.

At 1.5 miles, resume the Great Gorge Trail's pursuit of Cucumber Run upstream. After crossing Chalk Hill Road, admire the clear water of Cucumber

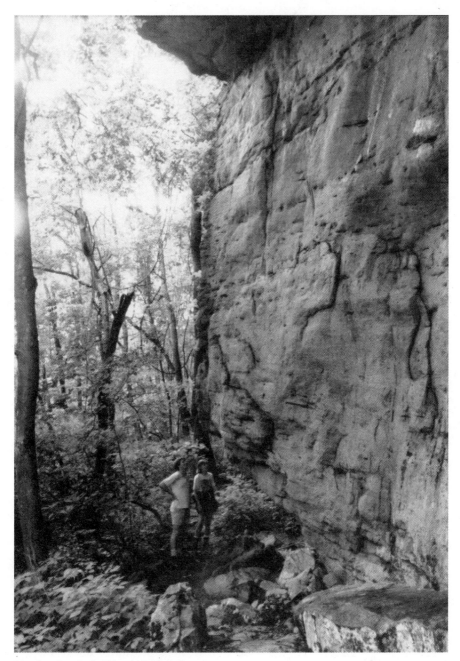

Meadow Run Trail, Ohiopyle State Park.

Run as it sheets over bedrock, spills in cascades, and cuts small chasms. With a footbridge crossing of the run, meet Middle Ridge Road, cross the road bridge, and continue upstream to Cucumber Run Picnic Area (2 miles). On the closing distance, stay toward the center of the mowed path to avoid poison ivy and thorny bramble. Return as you came.

For the **Baughman Trail,** start at Middle Yough Take-out: South of the PA 381 bridge, turn east onto Sheridan Street and drive past the visitor center to take-out parking. A sign marks the Baughman and Sugarloaf Trails.

Head right at the sign and then bear left at the split to contour the slope above the rail-trail. Red blazes soon point out a hard right uphill on rocky footpath. At 0.2 mile, bear left on a woods road for a more moderate ascent. Full forest enfolds travel as sound of the river echoes uphill.

At 0.7 mile, a 100-foot spur to the left leads to a cliff jut and seasonal view. A second woods road now continues the ascent, and boulders add to the forest. The trail advances in pulses, with many of the blazes faded beyond recognition. On the ridge (1.9 miles), ascend along the same track, ignoring side roads that branch away. Where more sunlight penetrates, bramble and brier win footing. Grouse may flush from hiding.

Sounds from Sugarloaf Road signal the trail is closing in on Baughman Rock. At 2.75 miles, arrive between the rock and vista parking. Turn left to mount the natural rock incline for an open overlook of the bending Yough, its wooded canyon, the Flats, and Laurel Highlands. Oaks and maples frame the site; rhododendrons seasonally add to views. When ready, backtrack to trailhead.

To reach the **Meadow Run Trail,** 0.5 mile south of Ohiopyle, bear southeast off PA 381 onto SR 2011 for the park office. In 0.1 mile, find trail parking on the left. Behind a park information sign at the foot of the grassy slope below parking, follow the yellow-blazed trail that enters the woods to the right. Travel a mixed maple–oak woods, with an understory of blueberry, laurel, rhododendron, and azalea—a pretty early-summer showcase. Cross a tall meadow clearing, finding tulip poplar and cucumber magnolia. In places, unruly grape shapes a bizarre menagerie of leafy shapes.

The trail contours and descends to follow a former road grade at 0.5 mile. Leave the grade, finding more laurel and rhododendron beneath a gray cliff with ominous overhangs. At 0.8 mile, the first of several short spurs branch to cascade overlooks. Pursue Meadow Run downstream.

The waterway can present a variety of impressions, depending on rainfall. Its hemlock corridor engages. The trail rolls, coming to the spur for Flat Rock—an aptly named feature—at 1.5 miles, and the loop's return leg at 1.6 miles. The return follows the wide grade left uphill. Detour downstream a few strides to view Deep Hole.

The return trail draws out of the hemlock cool, passing beautiful big tulip poplar, cucumber magnolia, and black cherry trees. Remnant rock walls add to the setting. Emerge at the unmarked path directly behind the park information sign (2 miles). The trail to the right leads to "the slides" for additional discovery.

56 Cowans Gap State Park

Overview
In the shadow of Tuscarora Mountain, this 1,085-acre state park offers lake, creek, and woodland recreation. Within the park's 10-mile trail system, find paths that challenge and relax. View the park from ridgetop and valley floor.

General description: Three hikes present the park offering.
General location: 55 miles southwest of Harrisburg.
Special attractions: Vistas, lake access for fishing and swimming, picturesque Little Aughwick Creek, flowering shrubs, fall foliage.
Length: Knobsville Road Trail, 2 miles round trip; Lakeside Trail, 1.5-mile loop; Plessinger–Tuscarora Loop, 4-mile loop.
Elevation: Knobsville Road Trail, 600-foot elevation change; Lakeside Trail, flat; Plessinger–Tuscarora Loop, 800-foot elevation change.
Difficulty: Knobsville Road Trail, moderate; Lakeside Trail, easy; Plessinger–Tuscarora Loop, strenuous.
Maps: State park brochure; Buchanan State Forest.
Special concerns: No trailside camping within the park. Expect difficult, rocky travel on the Plessinger–Tuscarora Loop; on all trails, beware of poison ivy.
Season and hours: State park, year-round, spring through fall for hiking.
For information: Cowans Gap State Park.

Key points:

Knobsville Road Trail:
0.0 Lot 5 trailhead; hike west.
0.1 Knobsville Road.
1.0 Vista platform; return as you came.

Lakeside Trail:
0.0 Lot 5 trailhead; head counterclockwise.
0.7 Cross dam and spillway bridge.
1.3 Pass boat launch and fishing platform.
1.5 Cross Little Aughwick Creek bridge, closing loop.

Plessinger–Tuscarora Loop:
0.0 Lot 5 trailhead; hike Plessinger Trail upstream.
1.1 Cameron Trail.
1.3 Cross Aughwick Road to Geyer Trail.
1.9 Tuscarora Trail.
2.5 Viewpoint.
3.5 Head left on Lakeside Trail.
4.0 End loop at trailhead.

Cowans Gap State Park

Finding the trailhead: From the junction of U.S. Highways 522 and 30 (1 mile north of McConnellsburg), go east on US 30 for 3.4 miles. At Tuscarora Summit, turn left onto State Route 1005/Aughwick Road. Drive another 5.9 miles to find the park office on the left.

From Fort Loudon, go 4 miles north on Pennsylvania 75 and turn left onto Richmond Road. Go 3 miles more and turn left onto Aughwick Road to reach the park office in 0.2 mile.

The hikes: Start all of these hikes from parking lot 5. Reach it via the park road to camping area B, which passes west behind the park office. Lot 5 is the first parking area.

For the **Knobsville Road Trail,** park at lot 5 and hike west on the park road, crossing the bridge over Little Aughwick Creek. Where the park road curves right for camping area B, proceed forward on gravel Knobsville Road, hiking past the group camping area to round a gate. Oak, maple, birch, gum, pine, and dogwood frame the closed fire lane; greenery hugs its sides. With a steady, even ascent, bypass grassy logging roads and twice cross a landslide that opens a tunnel view to Tuscarora Mountain.

Laurel and berry bushes add to the mix after 0.6 mile. Filtered views through the tree crowns build anticipation for the overlook. At 1 mile, reach the vista platform for an open-aisle view. Spy Cowans Gap Lake, Tuscarora Mountain, the low-swinging U of Cowans Gap, and the farmlands and Kittatinny Mountain beyond. Return as you came.

Ideal for that morning exercise walk or for putting a cap on the day, the easy **Lakeside Trail** has multiple starting points. Locate a signed start west of parking lot 5, 150 feet before the Little Aughwick Creek bridge. Follow the yellow-blazed trail along the east shore of the narrow inlet cove, traveling counterclockwise through the spruce-shaded developed park, with its tables, rustic stone shelters, Brightville Interpretive Center, boat rental, and concession. The trail passes within 20 feet of shore and extends cross-lake views at a wooded ridge. Man-made Cowans Gap Lake is an attractive, dark, shimmery host.

Hardwoods replace the spruce as the trail draws away from the developed park, now joined by the blue-blazed (formerly orange) Tuscarora Trail. At 0.75 mile, traverse the dam and spillway bridge. Admire the intricate stonework of the spillway, pierced by grasses and washed by a shallow stream. Upon crossing, stay left for the Lakeside Trail to round below camping area B. Tulip poplar, pine, and spruce shade travel.

Ample clues betray the presence of beaver: girdled and tumbled trees, pencil-point stumps, and a lodge (1.2 miles). Now cross-lake views present Tuscarora Mountain. Round past a boat launch and handicapped fishing platform before crossing the road bridge over Little Aughwick Creek to close the loop at 1.5 miles.

Tied together by the Cameron, Geyer, and Lakeside Trails, the **Plessinger–Tuscarora Loop** offers a superb, but often rugged hike, exploring much of the eastern half of the park. It travels the shore of Little Aughwick Creek and tops the ridge of Tuscarora Mountain.

Locate the signed and red-blazed Plessinger Trail as it heads upstream from the Little Aughwick Creek bridge west of parking area 5. Bending Little Aughwick Creek is a pretty, tree-draped, shallow water flowing over a rocky bed. The trail for the most part hugs its shore. Fern, azalea, and laurel color the understory; a mature leafy forest shades travel. Puddles may collect, and rocks and roots rise in the trailbed.

By 0.4 mile, the trail passes between camping area A and the creek. Watch blazes closely now, because the meandering path makes quick, subtle direction changes. Weirs and islands alter the creek's flow. Find hemlock, some large black gum, and knee- to waist-high laurel. At 1.1 mile, reach a T-junction in an attractive fern flat: To the right lies the now closed Twin Springs Trail; go left on the unmarked Cameron Trail to continue the loop.

Ferns, Cowans Gap State Park.

This grassy woods road climbs steadily to Aughwick Road (1.3 miles), tracing the boundary between the state park and Buchanan State Forest. Across Aughwick Road, the Geyer Trail advances the loop. Follow the white boundary blazes, avoiding an early turn to the right.

The trail streaks up the flank of Tuscarora Mountain, passing in an oak-dominant mixed forest. As the old road tapers to foot trail, find rockier footing. After the trail has leveled out, meet the blue-blazed Tuscarora Trail and follow its footpath left (north); a woods road hosts the way south. More ankle-twisting travel occurs along the ridgetop. Snags, maples, and birches share ranks with the oaks.

A left spur at 2.2 miles offers a restricted view at the upper reaches of the ridge to the west. At 2.3 miles, a rocky slope to the right opens a window to the east-northeast, overlooking the valley to Kittatinny Mountain. Ahead, travel a picturesque realm of rocks and slabs before reaching the finest view at 2.5 miles for a more open look east.

Clamber over the rocky ridge tip, dipping to Cowans Gap. Curled rock tripe lichen caps the rock, laurel abounds, and steep pitches mark travel. Spy red eft, box turtle, and millipede as you watch your footing.

At 3.3 miles, bear left on a woods road, paralleling Richmond Road into the developed park. Now pursue blue blazes through the park to meet the yellow-blazed Lakeside Trail (3.5 miles). Turn left and follow the shore of Cowans Gap Lake to the Little Aughwick Creek bridge and the loop's close at 4 miles.

57 Tuscarora Trail, Tuscarora Mountain South

General description:	This day-hike sampling of the long-distance Tuscarora Trail System (a bypass to the Appalachian Trail) travels atop the southern extent of Tuscarora Mountain, snaring limited views. The bypass spans from southern Pennsylvania through Maryland to northern Virginia. This leg travels State Game Lands 124.
General location:	60 miles southwest of Harrisburg.
Special attractions:	Limited views, rock overhangs, solitude, wildlife sightings, fall foliage.
Length:	10.2 miles round trip.
Elevation:	Find a 300-foot elevation change.
Difficulty:	Moderate.
Maps:	Buchanan State Forest; Keystone Trails Association's Tuscarora Trail Map, Sections 7 and 8.
Special concerns:	No overnight camping on state game land. Blue (formerly orange) blazes mark the trail. Heed postings for neighboring private land.
Season and hours:	Spring through fall.
For information:	Potomac Appalachian Trail Club.

Key points:

0.0 Trailhead; hike southbound.
3.0 Meet Alice Trail.
4.3 Rock jumbles below crest.
5.1 End at east–west vantage; backtrack.

Finding the trailhead: From the junction of U.S. Highway 522 and Pennsylvania 16 in McConnellsburg, go southeast on PA 16 East for 3.5 miles to find a broad turnout for parking on the right. The Tuscarora Trail crosses PA 16 just 0.1 mile farther south. When arriving from Cove Gap—the site of Buchanan's (President James Buchanan) Birthplace Historical Park—go 2 miles north on PA 16 to find the trail.

The hike: On the west side of PA 16 behind the road distance sign, follow the Tuscarora Trail south toward PA 456. With a quick burst of climbing, the trail wraps uphill at an angle. Travel a low-stature, tangled woods with meadowy floor, tracing a thin boot track. Cross a faint woods road and top the ridge. Here, lichen-mottled rock slabs claim the crest. The rocks show an eastern incline and western ledge, presenting partial views west. The trail then rolls southbound.

While the woods have a tangled character, they are not tangled in the classic sense. The disheveled appearance owes to the many bowed trunks, bent

Tuscarora Trail, Tuscarora Mountain South

limbs, and suspended branches and tumbled trees that have yet to crash to the ground. Winds commonly wash over the summit, invigorating leaves and travelers. Oak is notably absent from the array of hickory, birch, maple, ash, and shade. Poison ivy makes a sporadic appearance.

At 1 mile, recent logging has torn apart the setting but opened views. Later, the summit broadens. Enjoy encounters with deer, turkey, and box turtle. Muffled noise from PA 16 sometimes intrudes, but beyond the logging zone, the tour typically conveys an isolated, wild feeling.

Atop the next bump (1.6 miles), steal western glimpses. On tiptoe, view the far end of the rural valley and the blue ridges disappearing in the distance. More visits to the rocky crest follow. Then, at 2.1 miles, angle across an east-to-west-trending grassy woods road. By detouring right a few strides along this road, add another piece to the vista puzzle.

Pass through patches of bramble and greenbrier. Although off the trail, these plants can grow with abandon. Where the ridge narrows, add limited looks east. Snags contribute to the skyline.

Rock lichen.

At scarcely more than 3 miles, the unmarked Alice Trail arrives on the left, after which the Tuscarora Trail drifts onto the western flank and passes a trail register (3.1 miles). Rocky areas alternate with the earthen trail. At 4.3 miles, pass beneath the jumbles and overhangs of the rocky summit crest and return to the summit.

Between 4.6 and 5.1 miles, the hike affords eastern valley and ridge views, culminating with an east–west view at 5.1 miles to bring the described tour to an end. To extend the hike, Maryland beckons to the south. Alternative ending points to shorten the trip include the woods road at 2.1 miles, the register at 3.1 miles, or the rock crest at 4.3 miles.

58 Friendship Hill National Historic Site

Overview

On a bluff overlooking the Monongahela River sits the country manor of Albert Gallatin, a Swiss immigrant who played a key role in this nation's early adventure into democratic rule. He served as secretary of the treasury under Presidents Jefferson and Madison, and he secured funding for both the Louisiana Purchase in 1803 and the Lewis and Clark expedition, 1804 to 1806. Lewis and Clark honored him in naming the three forks of the Missouri River. They are the Jefferson, Madison, and Gallatin Rivers; all flow through Montana.

When Gallatin built this home at Friendship Hill in 1789, it overlooked the edge of the untried western frontier and what Gallatin hoped would be a corridor to prosperity. The Monongahela drains to the Ohio River—a springboard to points west. The water route, however, proved unfeasible. Instead, the National Road and, later, railroads carried the nation west.

Explore the mansion and grounds, learn about Gallatin, and rediscover the growth of our nation. The Friendship Hill Trail System holds national recreation trail distinction.

General description: An interpretive loop explores the grounds of the country estate. Link and side trails allow for varying or extending the hike.

General location: 12 miles southwest of Uniontown, Pennsylvania; 10 miles north of Morgantown, West Virginia.

Special attractions: Guided or self-guided tours of the multi-era thirty-five-room mansion, a holographic likeness of Albert Gallatin that speaks to visitors, a glen of old-growth trees, historic grave sites, waterfalls, a gazebo overlooking the Monongahela River, rhododendron and laurel.

Length: Main Loop, 4-mile loop.

Elevation: Find a 200-foot elevation change.

Difficulty: Moderate.

Maps: The Friendship Hill National Recreation Trail map.

Special concerns: Carry water; do not drink from natural sources, because surface water is highly acidic. Keep to the trails, stay back from the bluff rim, and be alert on the steep, slippery descent to the river. Do not collect or disturb natural features. Find the trail system color-coded and well signed. Green indicates the Main Loop, red the side trails, and yellow the link trails.

Season and hours: Daily year-round, except Christmas Day, 8:30 A.M. to 5:00 P.M. When the snow is sufficiently deep, cross-country skiing replaces hiking (consult park map).

For information: Friendship Hill National Historic Site.

Friendship Hill National Historic Site

Key points:

0.0	Gallatin House parking trailhead.
0.4	Sophia's Grave.
2.5	Cross Dublin Run footbridge.
2.8	Clare Cemetery.
3.8	Mansion.
4.0	End loop at trailhead.

Finding the trailhead: From the junction of Pennsylvania 21 and PA 166 in north Masontown, go south on PA 166, reaching the park entrance on the right in 7.1 miles.

The hike: For the **Main Loop**, from the Gallatin House parking area, follow the broad, sidewinding concrete walk toward the mansion. Pass a wildflower garden and a sculpture portraying Gallatin, the surveyor. Like many of his day, he played multiple roles in life.

Fashioned of brick, frame, and stone, the restored Gallatin House greets visitors with quiet dignity. A stone well, towering shade trees, broad lawns, and sprawling white barn complete the image. Pass through the breezeway (0.2 mile) to find the entrance to the visitor center, which occupies the old stone kitchen. There, gain information on house and trail.

Now follow signs for Sophia's Grave, proceeding south to the gazebo, which overlooks a bluff to the Monongahela River. Rhododendron and picturesque oak add to the country setting; interpretive panels explain trail features. Turn left at the gazebo and hike along the bluff's rim. Here, an abrupt conifer–deciduous slope plunges to the river. Soon find the first of the green-marked posts and an arrow pointing the way to Sophia's Grave.

Skirt the upper edge of a hay field, seasonally dotted by rolled bales, before entering the old-growth glen of Sophia's Woods. A stone enclosure protects the grave; Sophia was Gallatin's first wife. The cathedral forest harks to the woods of Gallatin's time.

The rush of Rhododendron Run now complements the harmonic notes of birds. At the upcoming clearing, overlook the shrubs to the right to glimpse a 15-foot lacy waterfall as it races over a canted cliff. To the left is a wildlife pond active with turtle, frog, and heron. Cross a footbridge over the outlet to resume on a woods path. Poison ivy grows to the sides.

At each upcoming junction, stay on the green trail. Cross a series of footbridges over the waters draining to Rhododendron Run. Beautiful big beech and scenic snags add to the woods character. The industrial noises rising from the Monongahela River would have delighted Gallatin, the entrepreneur. Pass from old-growth to mature second-growth forest, coming to a steep switchbacked descent to the river floodplain.

After the first switchback, view a falls on South Run. A series of cascades transforms this cataract into a ribbon of white racing water after a rainstorm. At the base of the bluff (1.1 miles), bear right on an old farm road. Silver maple, sycamore, and elm inhabit the floodplain. Cross a footbridge over lower Rhododendron Run and pause to admire its serial falls, cascades, and leafy canyon. A couple of huge boulders that tumbled from the bluff now redirect travel. Gather glimpses of the broad Monongahela River.

Drawing away from the river tanglewood, ascend past the South and North Cutoffs (yellow-blazed, at 1.9 and 2.1 miles respectively); both head right. The farm road extends a pleasant woods stroll, interrupted by a pipeline corridor and the crossing of Ice Pond Run. Beyond the trees to the left stretches the Monongahela Railroad.

Gallatin House, Friendship Hill National Historic Site.

Keep left for the outer loop and, at 2.5 miles, cross a footbridge over Dublin Run. In another 0.1 mile, the Main Loop bears right as a spur heads straight to New Geneva—the community begun by Gallatin. A moderate ascent through a younger, tighter woods follows.

As the trail levels and older trees offer shade, look for Clare Cemetery on the left. A rustic stone wall rims this small cemetery, housing the head- and footstones of Thomas Clare, who died in 1814. Clare owned the tract called "Dublin" that adjoined Gallatin's property and is now part of the park.

Resume along the wooded farm road, crossing the yellow-indicated School Spur (3.1 miles), a second footbridge over Dublin Run, and a pipeline corridor with a red trail. Then continue forward past North Meadow Loop and cross a culvert for Ice Pond Run to reach the next junction. Bear right, still on farm road, for the full loop; the yellow trail to the left leads to a parking area.

At 3.5 miles, turn left off the farm road and follow a mowed swath at the edge of an open field. It recalls the agrarian past at Friendship Hill. Next, cross the park road and pass between stone pillars to travel a gravel service road to the mansion (3.8 miles). Enjoy a second look or perhaps join a mansion tour before ending the hike via the concrete walk (4 miles).

59 Quebec Run Wild Area

Overview

In Fayette County, Pennsylvania, at the Pennsylvania–West Virginia border, this 4,765-acre forested area offers hikers a first-rate wilderness retreat. The wild area spans from the eastern slope of Chestnut Ridge to Big Sandy Creek. It is drained by Quebec, Tebolt, and Mill Runs.

General description: A lasso-shaped hike incorporates several named trails and visits some of the area's finest features.

General location: 12 miles south of Uniontown, Pennsylvania; 18 miles northeast of Morgantown, West Virginia.

Special attractions: Clearwater, trout-supporting streams; abundant rhododendron; areas of mountain laurel; mixed mesophytic forest (predominantly maple and tulip poplar), with oak highlands and hemlock flats; gristmill ruins; solitude.

Length: Wild Area Hiking Tour, 8.7 miles round trip.

Elevation: Travel between 1,550 feet along lower Mill Run and a high point of 2,200 feet at the Brocker–Hess Trail junction.

Difficulty: Moderate.

Maps: Quebec Run Wild Area; Forbes State Forest (maps are sometimes available at the trailhead).

Special concerns: Primitive backpack-camping is allowed by permit only; contact the headquarters for a free permit. Do not disturb or collect natural features. During hunting season, wear bright colors. Blazes mark trails for the most part.

Season and hours: Spring through fall for hiking.

For information: Forbes State Forest.

Key points:

Wild Area Hiking Tour:

0.0 Trailhead; follow Mill Run Trail right.
1.1 Loop junction; bear left.
1.3 Spur to gristmill ruins.
2.6 West Road (trail).
3.8 Cross Quebec Road to Brocker Trail.
4.7 Hess Trail.
6.2 Follow Rankin Trail right.
7.6 Complete loop; return left to trailhead.

Quebec Run Wild Area

Finding the trailhead: From the junction of U.S. Highway 40 and Pennsylvania 381 in Farmington, go south on PA 381 for 4.6 miles. There, in the village of Elliottsville, take a right turn off PA 381, followed by a left onto State Route 2004. At the Y-junction in 1 mile, bear right onto Quebec Road (a paved and gravel road). In another mile, cross Mill Run to find marked trailhead parking on the left.

The hike: For this 8.7-mile Wild Area Hiking Tour, head right on Mill Run Trail. The footpath rolls along the lower slope, tracking Mill Run downstream. Hornbeam, witch hazel, and a few hawthorn fill out the leafy forest; along creek flats, hemlock and rhododendron grow. Deer may cross paths with hikers.

Side tributaries thread to Mill Run; cross most via a simple step-over or atop rocks and limbs. At 0.9 mile, make an abrupt right turn to meet the Miller Trail in 100 feet. Bear left for Mill Run Trail and cross a larger side water that may require wading.

At 1.1 miles, reach the loop junction and bear left for a clockwise tour, still on the Mill Run Trail. The Rankin Trail is on the right. Cross a wooden footbridge over Quebec Run and continue along the hemlock–deciduous flat to a footbridge over Mill Run (1.3 miles).

To add a visit to the gristmill ruins, detour across the bridge, ascend the steep eroded east bank, and hike downstream 0.1 mile to the ruins. View a foundation, a millrace, and woods growing in the middle of what was the mill. Moss, fern, and lichen decorate the stones. Upon return to the bridge, resume the Mill Run Trail (1.5 miles). From the bridge, enjoy an unobstructed look at the scenic waterway—one of the hallmark waters of the wild area.

Now follow the west bank of Mill Run downstream. The trail occasionally rolls up the drainage slope. Along side tributaries, view low-growing laurel, fountains of fern, and skunk cabbage bogs. Bending Mill Run continues to enchant, until the trail climbs away at 2.5 miles. At a dip, the Mill Run Trail ends at West Road (now a hiker trail). Turn right onto West Road for the loop.

Travel the recessed bed of leaves and grass for a steady, moderate ascent. At the junction with Tebolt Trail (2.8 miles), hikers have an option, because these are parallel trails. For this loop (the shorter of the two), stay on West Road, proceeding forward on a nicely wooded passage. The trail goes unblazed but the line of travel is clear, despite vegetation piercing the grade and a scattering of logs.

At 3 miles, bear right onto a more defined grassy lane for easy walking. Colorful mushrooms dot the forest floor. Other discoveries may include a dispersal of curled, leathery eggshells from a successful turtle nest, American chestnuts (once the dominant tree of the eastern forest), or a turkey. Remaining on West Road, top a small rise before reaching Quebec Road at 3.8 miles.

The loop resumes uphill to the left in 50 feet, following the Brocker Trail westbound. To shorten the hike, descend along Quebec Road to the Quebec Run bridge and the Rankin Trail junction, turning right. The Brocker Trail gently rolls. Again, the path is vegetated and strewn with a few logs. Large patches of fern dress the oak forest, only to be replaced by rhododendron and laurel. Enjoy full shade from the leafed-out maple and birch trees. At 4.7 miles, reach an unsigned but blazed T-junction with the Hess Trail and turn right.

Before long, follow a contouring woods road that crosses small headwaters where tulip poplars thrive. By 5.7 miles, descend. A rhododendron thicket announces Quebec Run. At 6.25 miles, wade or rock-hop across the 10-foot-wide run to reach the north bank and Rankin Trail.

For the loop, turn right onto the Rankin Trail to parallel Quebec Run downstream. The trail passes within sound of the run, snaring the occasional glimpse. Mossy boulders, along with a seasonal explosion of rhododendron blooms, add to the trek.

At 7 miles, cross Quebec Road and keep to the north bank. The trail briefly rolls uphill before crossing Quebec Run on a footbridge. Meander downstream to cross back over the run (7.5 miles). At 7.6 miles, close the loop at Mill Run Trail and hike left, retracing the first 1.1 miles to the trailhead.

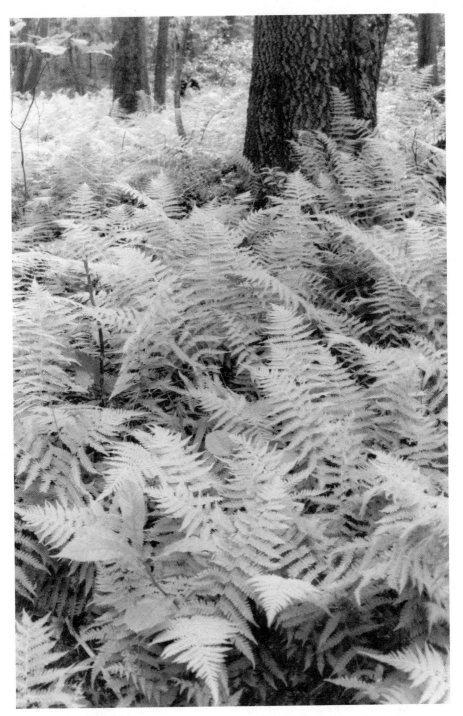

Ferns, Quebec Run Wild Area.

60 Martin Hill Wild Area

Overview

Encompassing Martin Hill and the southern extent of Tussey Mountain, this 11,500-acre wild area beckons hikers with its seldom-walked trails. The featured Tussey Mountain hike travels closed Tussey Mountain/Wigfield Road for a carefree mountaintop stroll. In winter, the route doubles as a cross-country ski trail.

General description:	The selected hike traces the broad plateau of southern Tussey Mountain for a skyline tour—but one lacking views.
General location:	40 miles southeast of Johnstown, Pennsylvania; 15 miles northeast of Cumberland, Maryland.
Special attractions:	An arid, low-stature mixed forest; thickets of laurel and berry bushes; wildlife sightings; quiet; fall foliage.
Length:	10 miles round trip.
Elevation:	Find a 350-foot elevation change between the trailhead and high point south of the Fetters Trail junction.
Difficulty:	Easy to moderate.
Maps:	Buchanon State Forest.
Special concerns:	Carry water. Tent camping is allowed; pitch camps 500 feet off Tussey Mountain/Wigfield Road and 500 feet from any public roadway. Secure permits at the district forest office. Mileage signs allow hikers to track progress. Rattlesnakes dwell here, but ant mounds are more likely to cause trouble. Wear fluorescent orange during hunting seasons.
Season and hours:	Spring through fall for hiking.
For information:	Buchanon State Forest.

Key points:

0.0   Trailhead; hike south.
1.2   Cross Fetters Trail.
2.4   Cross Johnson Trail.
4.5   Tussey Mountain Road becomes Wigfield Road.
5.0   Milepost 5 turnaround.

Finding the trailhead: From Bedford, go 2 miles east on U.S. Highway 30 and turn south onto Pennsylvania 326. At Sweet Root Picnic Area in 14.2 miles, turn right onto Black Valley Road/State Route 3007. In 0.8 mile, turn right onto Beans Cove Road/SR 3005 and proceed another 1.9 miles to find parking for Martin Hill Snowmobile Trail on the right, with closed Tussey Mountain Road on the left.

The hike: Round the gate to hike south on orange-blazed Tussey Mountain Road, which allows for carefree walking. Delicate grasses pierce the gravel, and the incline is comfortable. Oak, sassafras, black gum, pine, maple, locust, and aspen compose the low-stature ridge forest. Laurel, scrub oak, fern, berry

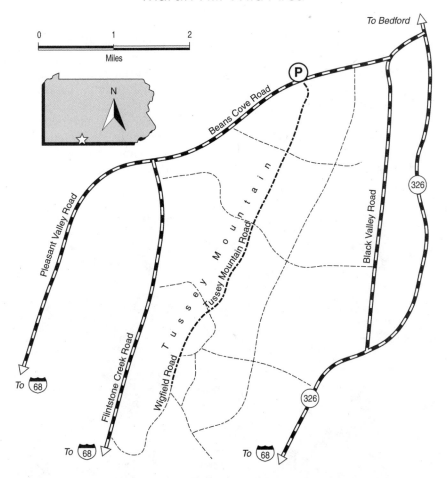

bushes, and honeysuckle weave a tight understory thicket. When ripe, blueberries draw hikers aside. American chestnuts may be spied near the 1-mile sign. At times, itty-bitty, eye-annoying black bugs may accompany travel.

At 1.25 miles, cross Fetters Trail. The broad, mildly undulating ridge denies views. By 1.5 miles, the trail levels off and slowly descends. By 2 miles, thick grasses claim the road and oaks bring fuller shade for a relaxed country-lane appeal. Animals likewise make use of this travel artery. Sightings may include deer, fox, turkey, bobcat, and perhaps a black bear.

At 2.4 miles, cross the Johnson Trail to continue the backbone tour. Then, at 3.75 miles, hike past the Morris Trail on the right and an orange-blazed trail on the left. Tussey Mountain again shows a wilder aspect. More maple and beech and a jungle of small-trunked trees add visual dimension.

Look for Tussey Mountain Road to become Wigfield Road at 4.5 miles. Proceed forward to the 5-mile sign—the chosen turnaround for the day hike. Southbound, the road trail descends to Flintstone Creek Road off the western flank. Return as you came—or go exploring.

Hershey Dutch Region

This region of southeast Pennsylvania unites the Valley and Ridge Province of the Appalachian Mountains and the verdant farm valleys of York, Lancaster, and Cumberland Counties. Traverse the elongated arched ridges and become enmeshed in the Old World charm of Amish country. Discover an intriguing "river of rocks" and the cool-water excitement of Kellys Run. Visit a world-renowned outpost for the fall hawk-watch and revisit the state's industrial past. At and around the Civil War battle site of Gettysburg, discover a rich chapter in American history. Throughout the region, mixed woods, rhododendron and laurel, and treasured valley and ridge vistas enhance travel.

Garter snake, Mill Grove Audubon Sanctuary.

61 Appalachian National Scenic Trail

General description:	This 2,155-mile national scenic trail from Maine to Georgia cuts across southeastern Pennsylvania between New Jersey and the Mason-Dixon Line at Maryland. The Appalachian Trail (AT) traverses ridges and dips through gaps, logging some of its most rugged miles within this state. The Pennsylvania leg takes the better part of a month to complete.
General location:	Between the village of Delaware Water Gap and Pen Mar Park in Maryland.
Special attractions:	Vistas, fall hawk migration, laurel and rhododendron, historic sites, fall foliage.
Length:	232.2 miles one-way.
Elevation:	Travel between a low of 300 feet at the Delaware River and highs in excess of 2,000 feet on South Mountain.
Difficulty:	Strenuous.
Maps:	The official Appalachian Trail guide and maps published by the Keystone Trails Association.
Special concerns:	Hikers need to work out the logistics for carrying and obtaining adequate food and supplies, plan what to do in case of an emergency, and arrange for transportation at trail's end. Expect rocky, difficult conditions. Be careful not to confuse the irregular white blazes that indicate state forest and game land boundaries with the white rectangles of the AT. Blue blazes indicate spurs to lookouts, springs, and high-water bypasses. Always carry a supply of drinking water, because ridgetop sources can be dry. Be alert for snakes.

Normally off limits to all camping, the state game lands along the AT do allow camping for thru-trail hikers. Pitch sites 200 feet from the AT and 500 feet from any water. Stays are limited to one night per site; no open fires are permitted during times of fire hazard. |
| **Season and hours:** | Spring through fall. |
| **For information:** | Appalachian Trail Conference. |

Key points:

0.0	Northern trailhead (Interstate 80 bridge).
15.3	Wind Gap.
35.9	Lehigh Gap (Pennsylvania 873).
50.3	Blue Mountain summit (PA 309).
78.7	Port Clinton, PA 61.
93.7	PA 183.

Appalachian National Scenic Trail

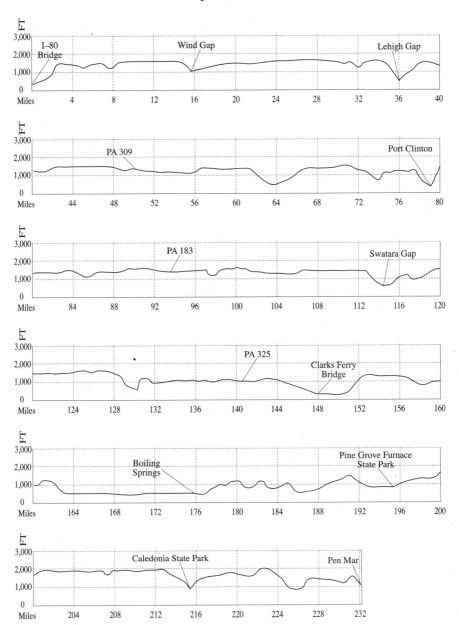

Finding the trailhead: The AT crosses numerous Pennsylvania state routes, traverses Michaux State Forest, and passes through several named parks. Pennsylvania thru-state hikers will find the northernmost access at the I–80 bridge at the village of Delaware Water Gap. Find the southernmost access at Pen Mar Park: At Rouzerville, turn southeast off PA 16 onto Pen Mar Road and follow it to the park at the Maryland state border.

The hike: The first national scenic trail in the United States, the AT salutes the mountain wilds of fourteen eastern states. Conceived in the early 1920s, this hiker filament rolls atop the ancient Appalachian Mountains, dipping to cross the important eastern river valleys. Most of the AT greenway has received permanent public protection; some 4,000 volunteers along with 200 public agencies maintain and oversee the trail.

Open to foot travel only, the AT advances primarily via footpath and woods road, with some sections on developed roads. Because the protected greenway itself can be narrow, keep to the trail to avoid straying onto private land.

While some twenty-eight Pennsylvania shelters sit along or just off the trail, a tent remains standard equipment. Pitch camps in established sites to minimize environmental harm. At Pine Grove Furnace State Park, an American Youth Hostel offers overnight accommodations.

On a north–south journey through Pennsylvania, discover three distinct tour sections: the ridge province, valley flatland, and southeastern forest. The ridge province spans more than 150 miles. Travel is atop the state's signature long, flat ridges with dips through gaps. The valley flatland serves as the bridge; much of the passage here is alongside farms, pastures, hedgerows, and small towns. Forest travel—appropriately enough—signs off the tour of Penn's Woods.

Southbound, the AT climbs from the Delaware River past Winona Cliffs to top Mount Minsi (elevation 1,480 feet). It then follows the ridge of Kittatinny Mountain southwest, gathering occasional views. The most impressive one comes at Wolf Rocks (8.8 miles). Find the trail rolling and rocky. In order to cross Wind Gap at 15.3 miles, the AT dips 300 feet.

Because the Blue Mountain travel ahead can be quite dry, be sure to carry a good supply of water. The ridge holds but modest changes both in grade and forest habitat. Find chestnut oaks common, with gum, sassafras, laurel, and maple. Four named views occur over the next 20 miles. A steep descent to Lehigh River then interrupts the reverie. Cross PA 873 at 35.9 miles.

From Lehigh Gap, climb 1,000 vertical feet to resume Blue Mountain travel, with occasional views. At 45 miles, claim Bake Oven Knob (elevation 1,560 feet) for a 180-degree southern perspective; this site is also famous for its autumn hawk-watches. At 46.8 miles, Bear Rocks extend a full 360-degree valley and ridge panorama. Where the eastern slope steepens, gain dramatic cliffs. At 50.3 miles, cross Blue Mountain summit on PA 309 (elevation 1,360 feet).

Still Blue Mountain hosts the AT. At Tri-county Corner (55.8 miles), gain another sweeping vista. At 60.7 miles, the AT turns east off the ridge. Straight leads to the private Hawk Mountain Sanctuary—the best site in the nation from which to watch the migration of predatory birds. For hikers who take

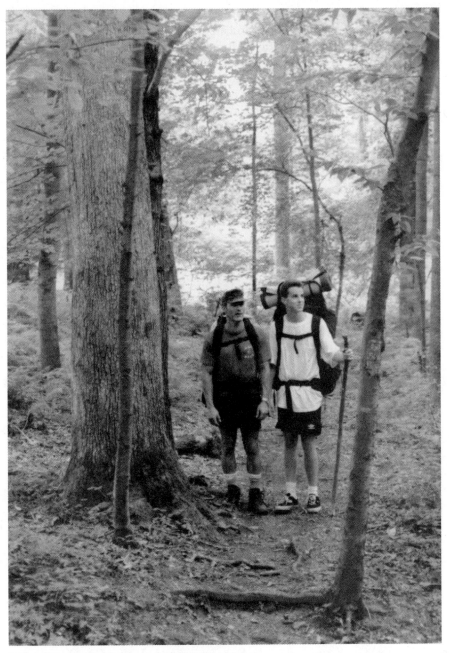

Backpacking the Appalachian Trail, Michaux State Forest.

this worthwhile detour, be sure to pay the entry fee at the museum. The sanctuary's trails visit overlooks and an unusual river of rocks (see hike 62).

Keeping to the AT, follow Blue Mountain as it takes an odd curve. In the woods, keen-eyed travelers may detect barren flats that hint at former charcoal hearths. The AT plunges and climbs 1,000 vertical feet to reach the Pinnacle (elevation 1,635 feet), with its spectacular cliffs and views at 68.4 miles. Pulpit Rock (elevation 1,582 feet) likewise rewards with vistas. Below it, discover a pair of caves and sheer cliffs. More hearths preface the AT's arrival at Windsor Furnace, 72.7 miles. The AT then drops 800 vertical feet for the crossing of PA 61 at Port Clinton (78.7 miles).

Blue Mountain trends southwest—and with it the AT. Find the trail more rocky in places. Auburn Lookout (81.4 miles) offers a natural view. Cross PA 183 at 93.7 miles. At 97.6 miles, a 0.4-mile spur leads to Shikellamy Lookout, and at 99.9 miles find the side-trail loop to Round Head and Showers Steps (500 rough stone steps that complete the loop back to the AT).

PA 501 and PA 645 mark off distance before Swatara Gap signals the next major plunge. It is where the AT crosses under I–81 (at 113.9 miles) and meets and briefly follows PA 443. The trail remains reasonably flat for 4 miles, then climbs to traverse Second Mountain. At Rausch Gap Village, discover a cemetery, foundations, and other clues to the onetime industrial community. An old stage road then advances the hike for 7 miles along Sharp Mountain.

At 124.2 miles, the AT passes through the ruins of Yellow Springs Village, where a blue side trail journeys to the site of a stone tower and old mine adit. Again, travel a stage road. At mile 127, stone-hop across Rattling Run and, soon after, reach Stony Mountain. The next descent leads to the PA 325 crossing in Clarks Valley.

The AT next mounts and travels atop Peters Mountain, until a 1,000-foot vertical descent leads to the Susquehanna River (147.7 miles). Gather views, including a valley overlook from Shikellimy Rocks. Cross the river at Clarks Ferry Bridge for a 3-mile stretch on paved road; watch for blazes.

With a steep ascent, top Cove Mountain and reach Hawk Rock, 151.1 miles. Trailbed rocks nag at the ankles as the AT remains atop the mountain for some 7 miles. Descend to PA 850 and climb up and over Little and Blue Mountains to leave the ridge province at 162.4 miles.

Valley flatland follows, with much of the area along the trail now private. Enjoy rural settings as you cross farm roads. Where the trail passes south through the village of Boiling Springs (175.9 miles), find the Mid-Atlantic Regional Office for the Appalachian Trail Conference. In another 1.5 miles, the AT leaves the Cumberland Valley for a rolling tour across forested mountains and hills to PA 94 (183.4 miles).

Michaux State Forest is now the host. Laurel and blueberry bushes abound as the AT ascends Trents Hill (185.6 miles), only to descend to the PA 34 crossing in another mile. Where the trail descends Piney Mountain, pass a spur to Pole Steeple View.

At Pine Grove Furnace State Park (195.4 miles), hikers find historic buildings, a store, and an overnight hostel. A walking tour introduces the ironworks of Pine Grove Furnace and the village it supported. Cross PA 233 for more forest travel. Along the broad summit of South Mountain, expect to cross a series of state forest roads. Five shelters serve thru-hikers along this AT stretch.

Caledonia State Park greets hikers where the trail next dips. Here, enjoy a wondrous array of rhododendron along the East Branch Conococheague Creek and the old millrace. Cross US 30 at 215.1 miles, and ascend Rocky Mountain.

Still enjoy woods of oak, maple, sassafras, tulip poplar, and black gum. Groves of hemlock vary the trail's look. In 4 miles, the AT turns off Rocky Mountain to climb Snowy Mountain. There, a short side trail leads to a fire tower for views (221.2 miles). Chimney Rocks in another 2 miles again serve up views.

Descend to pass through Old Forge Picnic Area (224.8 miles), where Antietam shelters can be found among the beautiful big trees, laurel, and rhododendron. Rock outcrops, rich forest, and multistory vegetation frame the path. PA 16 marks off travel at 229.3 miles. The trail then rolls up and over Mount Dunlop to the hiker bridge across Falls Creek (231.6 miles). AT hikers bid farewell to Pennsylvania, hello to Maryland at Pen Mar Park, 232.2 miles.

Given that spatial constraints necessarily limit the detail of this description, thru-trail and day hikers should contact the Keystone Trails Association or Appalachian Trail Conference for official maps and detailed guides. Or consult a local library, bookstore, or backpacker/outfitter store.

62 Hawk Mountain Sanctuary

Overview

Astraddle Kittatinny Ridge in eastern Pennsylvania, this 2,380-acre, private nonprofit sanctuary has been proclaimed the best site in the nation for watching the fall migration of predatory birds. Between mid-August and mid-December, an average of 20,000 eagles, ospreys, hawks, and falcons ride the winds south. The spectacle draws visitors from around the world. Superb vistas, seasonal rhododendron and laurel blooms, an unusual periglacial boulder field, and a museum and art gallery further recommend a visit to Hawk Mountain Sanctuary.

General description: A series of short trails explore the sanctuary and offer access to the Appalachian Trail. Two hikes of varying difficulty may be toured separately or joined together to view skyline, woods, and a white flow of rocks.

General location: 20 miles north of Reading.

Special attractions: Ridge and valley vistas, fall migration of raptors, spring migration of warblers, site of a gravity railroad, native wildflower/habitat garden, museum/gallery.

Length: Lookout Trail, 1.75 miles round trip, including spurs; River of Rocks Trail, 3.5-mile trail (4.2 miles round trip from the visitor center); the combined hike, 5.25 miles.

Elevation: Lookout Trail, 200-foot elevation change; River of Rocks Trail, 700-foot elevation change.

Difficulty: Lookout Trail, moderate; River of Rocks Trail, strenuous.

Maps: Trail Guide Hawk Mountain.

Special concerns: An admission fee is charged; pay at the trail gateway or visitor center. No pets, radios, bicycles, horses, smoking, camping, fires, or alcoholic beverages, and no collecting or disturbing natural features. Hike at your own risk; boots are recommended. Visitation peaks in October, with a shuttle operating to ease traffic and parking congestion. Midweek visits offer greater tranquility. Binoculars are available for rent, and trails are color-coded.

Season and hours: Year-round; trails, dawn to dusk; visitor center, 9:00 A.M. to 5:00 P.M. (open 8:00 A.M. during fall migration, September 1 through November 30). Closed Thanksgiving, Christmas, and New Year's Days.

For information: Hawk Mountain Sanctuary Association.

Hawk Mountain Sanctuary

Key points:

Lookout Trail:

0.0 Visitor center trailhead.
0.2 South Lookout.
0.6 Spur to the Slide and Sunset Overlook.
1.0 North Lookout; retrace primary Lookout Trail to center.

River of Rocks Trail:

0.0 Start at northern trailhead (0.5 mile in on Lookout Trail).
1.2 Spring.
2.2 Foot of River of Rocks.
3.5 End at South Lookout.

Finding the trailhead: From Interstate 78/U.S. Highway 22 west of Hamburg, take exit 9, go north on Pennsylvania 61 for 4.4 miles, and turn right (east) onto PA 895 at a sign for Hawk Mountain. In 2.5 miles at Drehersville, go east on State Route 2018/Hawk Mountain Road for 1.9 miles; the park entrance is on the right.

The hikes: Begin hikes at the information pavilion, where daily bird counts are posted. Follow the path indicated TO LOOKOUTS AND SANCTUARY TRAILS. The attractive brick walk travels past the national natural landmark monument and gives way to a woods lane framed by black gum, oak, birch, maple, laurel, and sassafras.

Cross Hawk Mountain Road, pass through the gateway entry station, and ascend. At 0.2 mile, reach South Lookout, where interpretive boards depict the various predatory birds in flight. The natural rock crest presents an open

275

view of the forested ridges, the River of Rocks directly below, and the serene rural valley beyond. To the east, spy three named ridge features: Hemlock Heights, Owl's Head, and the Pinnacle.

From South Lookout, the **Lookout Trail** (orange-blazed) heads left toward North Lookout; the **River of Rocks Trail** (red) heads right. Take the Lookout Trail first, quickly locating Appalachian Overlook—a rocky jumble with comparable views of the area skyline and migration path. Chestnut oaks favor the ridge, as do berry bushes and laurel. Bench seats invite pause. As the Lookout Trail advances, short spurs continue to branch right to unnamed vantages for viewing Hawk Mountain.

At 0.3 mile, the orange-blazed Escarpment Trail heads right for an alternative route to North Lookout or a potential loop return. Continue forward on the Lookout Trail, which narrows and has rocks piercing its bed. At 0.5 mile, pass the northern terminus of the River of Rocks Trail and then the Express Trail, which heads right for yet another approach to North Lookout.

Log-reinforced and natural stone steps take the Lookout Trail to an area of hemlocks and a T-junction (0.6 mile). To the left, discover a forked path that leads to the Slide (straight ahead) and Sunset Overlook (to the left, via a short, difficult rock scramble). To the right, the Lookout Trail travels the Hall of the Mountain King to North Lookout (elevation 1,521 feet). Together, the spurs and Lookout Trail unravel the history of this part of the sanctuary.

Excavated sands from here were used in construction and in the production of glassware. The hiked trail traces the old Drehersville cart road; the Slide records where a gravity-run railroad traveled the steep north flank in the 1890s; and the Hall is where the sand was collected and loaded onto cars.

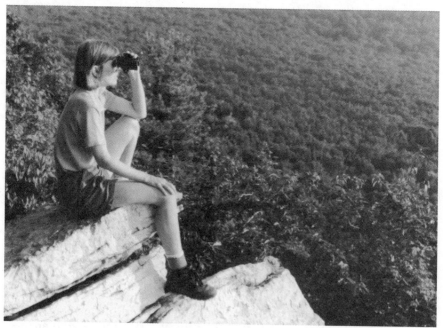

South Lookout, Hawk Mountain Sanctuary.

Ironically, before 1934, hunters would stand at the Slide and shoot migrating raptors.

Reach North Lookout at 1 mile, after taking both round-trip spurs. The site holds a grand 200-degree panoramic view with a fine vantage of Hawk Mountain/Kittatinny Ridge, along which thermals rise to carry the raptors south. View the ridge backbone, valley quilt, and several time-worn plateaus of the Appalachian Mountains.

For hikers interested in extending the hike, the Skyline Trail continues east from North Lookout along Kittatinny Ridge to East Rocks and the Appalachian Trail. Instead, hikers may choose to vary the return to the visitor center by following either the Escarpment or the Express Trail (look for orange blazes veering left as you descend from North Lookout), or to add the River of Rocks Trail. A direct return to the center ends the hike at 1.75 miles.

For a clockwise travel on the 3.5-mile River of Rocks Trail, start at the 0.5-mile junction on the Lookout Trail. The wooded River of Rocks Trail ascends east through a tremendous show of rhododendron and laurel, crosses the Escarpment Trail, and begins its rugged descent. Exercise care among the rocks.

In 0.5 mile, blazes point hikers left to the first of a pair of junctions with the yellow-blazed Golden Eagle Trail, which climbs to Skyline Trail. Stay with the red blazes. Huckleberry joins the laurel, and grouse fright upon approach. Pockets and channels of rock punctuate the meandering descent.

At 1.2 miles, pass an island of rhododendron and a gurgling spring beneath the boulder rubble to travel at the outskirts of River of Rocks. This long, broad stream of glaring white rock against rock and rock upon rock defies plant growth. Continue "downstream" through the rimming woods.

At 1.6 miles, reach the second junction with the Golden Eagle Trail. By turning right on it and passing through a gap in the rocky stream, hikers may shorten the loop. Again, keep to the River of Rocks Trail. The cathedral woods of tulip poplar, maple, birch, and oak hosts easier walking.

At the wide foot of the river, gain intriguing views upstream at the "great white way." Rocks again challenge footing on the uphill return. Be alert for the few sprigs of poison ivy. At 2.4 miles, the trail bears right on an old woods road being joined by the river cut-across of the Golden Eagle Trail. Pursue the red blazes, still ascending.

Rhododendron shapes a pretty passage where the trail crosses a small drainage at 3 miles. On the opposite shore is a junction. Here, an orange spur journeys left to the sanctuary shelters (not for public use); the River of Rocks Trail angles uphill; and a second orange spur descends right to White Oak Swamp (a wetland meadow) in 0.1 mile. Keep to the red-blazed trail for a sometimes steep, switchbacking ascent. Arrive at South Lookout at 3.5 miles. There, turn left to return to parking.

63 Colonel Denning State Park

Overview

This 273-acre wooded park occupies Doubling Gap, created where Blue Mountain makes an S-shaped bend. Doubling Gap Run threads through the park, with man-made 3.5-acre Doubling Gap Lake serving as the recreational centerpiece. Short hiking trails explore the park and link up with the greater area trail system. From the park, access the 105-mile Tuscarora Trail atop Blue Mountain.

General description: Two hikes present the park offering: an easy interpretive trail along the lake/run floodplain (Doubling Gap Nature Trail) and a moderately taxing trail that climbs to a natural ledge atop Blue Mountain for a Cumberland Valley view (Flat Rock Trail).

General location: 30 miles west of Harrisburg.

Special attractions: Cumberland Valley view, swimming and fishing, mountain laurel and spring wildflowers, fall foliage.

Length: Doubling Gap Nature Trail, 1.4 miles round trip; Flat Rock Trail, 4.4 miles round trip.

Elevation: Doubling Gap Nature Trail, 60-foot elevation change; Flat Rock Trail, 1,200-foot elevation change.

Difficulty: Doubling Gap Nature Trail, easy; Flat Rock Trail, moderate to strenuous.

Maps: State park brochure; the flyer titled *Hiking and Nature Trails: Colonel Denning State Park and the Surrounding Tuscarora State Forest;* Keystone Trails Association's Tuscarora Trail Map, Sections 1 through 4.

Special concerns: No trail camping within the state park; camp only within the designated park campground.

Season and hours: Year-round, Nature Trail, 8:00 A.M. to sunset; Flat Rock Trail, 24 hours.

For information: Colonel Denning State Park.

Key points:

Doubling Gap Nature Trail:
- 0.0 Beach trailhead; traverse dam.
- 0.2 Loop junction; bear left.
- 0.7 Cross Doubling Gap Run footbridge.
- 1.0 Cross back over run.
- 1.2 Close loop; backtrack to trailhead.

Flat Rock Trail:
- 0.0 Nature center trailhead; cross Doubling Gap Run.
- 1.0 Wagon Wheel junction.
- 2.2 Flat Rock; backtrack to trailhead.

Colonel Denning State Park

To Landisburg

Doubling Gap Nature Trail

Doubling Gap Lake

Nature center

233

Doubling Gap Run

To Newville

N

Flat Rock Trail

Wildcat Run

Tuscarora Trail

Flat Rock

0   0.5   1
Miles

Finding the trailhead: At the junction of Pennsylvania 850 and PA 233 in Landisburg, go south on PA 233 for 7.5 miles to reach the park entrance on the left. Or go 8 miles north from Newville on PA 233 and turn right.

The hikes: Start the **Doubling Gap Nature Trail** on the west shore of Doubling Gap Lake at the dam. If parked at the beach, traverse the dam and spillway bridge to descend the handicapped-access ramp to a fishing dock and the start of the interpretive trail. (The trail is not wheelchair accessible.) The small open water of Doubling Gap Lake is rimmed half by woods, half by the dam and developed beach. Edge the lake in the shade of maple, oak, birch, hickory, and white pine. Poison ivy grows among the forest wildflowers.

Cross a footbridge over a tiny inlet and avoid the secondary path to shore. At 0.2 mile, reach the loop junction and bear left (clockwise). Hemlocks add to the forest, and interpretive plaques introduce the stream habitat. As the trail ascends the drainage slope, admire big white pines and pass a bench seat from which to glimpse the shimmery thread of Doubling Gap Run.

Proceed forward across the next tributary bridge; a cut-across heads right. Mayapple and hepatica may be spied near the bridge. Travel a spatially open woods with walnut, locust, and ash growing above a meadowy floor.

Back on the floodplain, follow gurgling Doubling Gap Run downstream to a footbridge at 0.75 mile. Cardinal flowers decorate the stream. Mink, deer, and woodpecker may be spied. Cross to hike the east shore downstream. Soon the cut-across trail arrives via a bridge on the right; continue forward. Where the woods grow soggy, jack-in-the-pulpit flourish.

At 1 mile, cross a side-tributary footbridge and travel the hemlock–hardwood flat to cross back over Doubling Gap Run and close the loop (1.2 miles). Turn left and retrace the first 0.2 mile.

At the park nature center near the Nature Program Pavilion and outdoor amphitheater, cross the footbridge over Doubling Gap Run to begin the **Flat Rock Trail.** Ascend wood-braced earthen steps veering away from the campground to travel a hemlock plateau and, later, oak–hardwood forest. Gum, maple, and tulip poplar rise amid the oaks. Witch hazel, striped maple, and berry bushes weave a midstory. Red blazes mark the wide forest path.

At 0.4 mile, follow a narrow woods road uphill to the left for a steep climb to the springhouse ruins. Birch, nettle, and jewelweed grow along the road, hinting at the former purpose of these standing structures.

By 0.7 mile, enter the laurel belt of the slope; a few azalea grow trailside. The trail grows rugged, rocky, and steep before topping Blue Mountain at the Wagon Wheel (1 mile). The journey to Flat Rock resumes via the blue-blazed (formerly orange-blazed) Tuscarora Trail straight ahead.

Radiating outward from the Wagon Wheel, the Tuscarora Trail also branches right, with the yellow-blazed Woodburn Trail soon branching left off it. Angling back to the left at the hub is the Warner Trail, and at diagonal left is the Lehman Trail. Signs help sort out travel options.

Proceed forward on the Tuscarora Trail, wide and earthen, for a slow descent through mixed forest. Muddy pockets precede the grouped-limb crossing of the headwaters of Wildcat Run. The trail then rolls uphill before making

Flat Rock, Tuscarora State Forest.

a mild descent to the vista ledge (2.2 miles); the Tuscarora Trail veers left on narrow footpath just before the ledge.

The natural rock perch presents one of the finest views in the state, looking out over the Cumberland Valley as it sprawls south. Ridges rise up blue in the hazy sunlight. Sparkling communities, silos, and barns and textured fields contribute to the farm–woods tapestry. Enjoy a full 180-degree view, with the ragged limbs of snags adding to looks west. Return as you came.

64 Middle Creek Wildlife Management Area

Overview

In northern Lancaster County, this 6,254-acre wildlife management area (WMA) offers picnicking, fishing, hunting, wildlife-watching, and nature study. Nine miles of trail traverse the site's varied habitats, which include hardwood forest, conifer plantation, cultivated and noncultivated fields, wetland, scrub, and creek and lake impoundment shores. Explore ridgetop and valley floor. Extended by the Coleman Estate/Furnace Hills tract, the WMA contributes to a vast contiguous open space preserving unbroken forest and a vital wildlife corridor between Lancaster and Lebanon Counties.

General description: The selected four short hikes present much of the WMA's varied terrain and wildlife. Altogether eight hikes are possible, including a tour of the Horseshoe Trail, part of a 134-mile hiking trail link between Valley Forge and the Appalachian Trail.

General location: 18 miles southwest of Reading.

Special attractions: 400-acre Middle Creek Impoundment; vistas; birdwatching, with resident Canada geese, eagles seen nearly daily in summer and fall, and migrant snow geese and tundra swans in winter and early spring; laurel and wildflowers.

Length: Conservation Trail, 1.5-mile loop; Willow Point Trail, 0.8 mile round trip; Millstone Trail, 1.1-mile loop; Middle Creek Trail, 2.5 miles round trip.

Elevation: Conservation Trail, 100-foot elevation change; Willow Point Trail, flat; Millstone Trail, 300-foot elevation change; Middle Creek Trail, 50-foot elevation change.

Difficulty: Millstone Trail, moderate; all others are easy.

Maps: State Game Lands 46; Middle Creek Wildlife Management Area map and self-guided tour brochures (available at visitor center).

Special concerns: Become acquainted with the rules governing fishing, hunting, and propagation area closures. Poison ivy grows almost everywhere. No feeding the waterfowl, collecting, or picnicking outside designated areas.

Season and hours: Year-round, daylight hours. Visitor center, Tuesday through Saturday, 8:00 A.M. to 4:00 P.M., March 1 through November 30 only.

For information: Middle Creek Wildlife Management Area.

Middle Creek Wildlife Management Area

Key points:

Conservation Trail:
- 0.0   Visitor center trailhead.
- 1.2   Sunfish Pond.
- 1.5   Close loop.

Willow Point Trail:
- 0.0   Willow Point Trailhead.
- 0.4   Willow Point; backtrack.

Millstone Trail:
- 0.0 Millstone/Braille Trailhead.
- 0.4 Millstone.
- 0.5 Valley View.
- 1.1 End loop at trailhead/White Oak Picnic Area.

Middle Creek Trail:
- 0.0 Middle Creek Trailhead.
- 1.1 Elders Run footbridge.
- 1.2 Elders Run Trail junction; backtrack to trailhead.

Finding the trailhead: From Ephrata, go 4.3 miles west on U.S. Highway 322 to Clay and turn right onto State Route 1035/North Clay Road at a sign for the WMA. In 1.1 miles at Hopeland, turn right onto SR 1026/Hopeland Road, and in another 0.6 mile turn left onto Kleinfeltersville Road. Go 3 miles more and turn left onto Museum Road for the visitor center.

From Pennsylvania 897 in Kleinfeltersville, travel 2.3 miles south on Kleinfeltersville Road to Museum Road.

The hikes: Off the northernmost parking area for the visitor center, start the **Conservation Trail** where a sign indicates HIKER PATH. An interpretive brochure pairs to this trail. Hike the mowed path up the open slope between fields. Geese sound their presence; their harsh notes mingle with the melodies of songbirds. Some 280 bird species have been identified within the WMA. Watch for yellow triangle markers with black tips pointing the direction of travel.

On ascent, admire the vast, shallow lake impoundment, its island, and the framing ridge before entering a woodland of oak and tulip poplar. A chaos of greenery claims the understory. The trail nudges or traverses wildlife management habitats explained by the brochure.

Wildflowers spangle the fields while wild berry, grape, and rose compose the hedgerows. At 0.4 mile, bear left at the fork to follow a footpath and earthen lane and cross a wetland boardwalk. Skunk cabbages seasonally lend a pungent aroma. Summer rains bring mud.

Cross a small drainage to reach the foot of a grassy slope. Bear right and skirt Sunfish Pond with its lei of pond lilies. Sumac and wild rose hinder views. Tag Museum Road at 1.4 miles, turn left, and hike past the visitor center to close the loop at 1.5 miles.

Locate the marked parking and trailhead for the **Willow Point Trail** by driving 0.8 mile north on Kleinfeltersville Road from its intersection with Museum Road. Follow the path that leaves the corner of the parking area to edge a field of clover and Queen Anne's lace; a couple of big chestnut trees preside trailside. Where the path bears right, overlook a cultivated field grazed by geese; yellow songbirds decorate the strangled woods off to the left. Keep an eye skyward to view circling bald eagles or a passing heron.

At Willow Point (0.4 mile) sits a bird-watching bench/table. From it, admire the open shallow lake, the large central island, and folded wooded ridges. Deer may be spied across the way. Return as you came.

For the **Millstone Trail,** take Millstone Road east off Kleinfeltersville Road, 0.8 mile south of the Museum Road intersection. Go 0.7 mile east to the White Oak Picnic Area and the trail's start.

The hike shares its initial 200 feet with the fifteen-station Braille Trail; follow the guide rope uphill. At the double-strike peach blaze, pursue the Millstone Trail up the rock-studded forest path for a moderate ascent. Maple, beech, birch, oak, and tulip poplar weave a full overhead umbrella, with laurel, sassafras, and berry bushes in the understory. The trailbed rock reveals lichen and pebble conglomerates. Atop the slope, a large millstone rests in the rock rubble (0.4 mile). In bygone years, a millstone quarry occupied the crest.

Pass a scenic multitrunked oak to reach Valley View at 0.5 mile, where a hewn-log seat welcomes pause. The view spans a slope of young trees to Middle Creek Impoundment. Beyond the impoundment, discover a small pond, a mosaic of fields and woods, and distant ridges. From the viewpoint, turn left into woods, still pursing the peach blazes for a slow and then moderate descent on wide trailbed. Come out at Millstone Road at 1 mile and turn right to return to White Oak Picnic Area at 1.1 miles.

For **Middle Creek Trail,** park at the Middle Creek Lake dam and walk 0.1 mile south on Kleinfeltersville Road to find this blue-blazed trail as it heads west into forest via boardwalk. The yellow-blazed Horseshoe Trail heads uphill to its right. Tulip poplar and beech are well represented. Mayapple, fern, and hog peanut color the forest floor.

Stroll an abandoned trolley line, paralleling Middle Creek downstream. A few tumbled trees may require either ducking or a step-over. The creek flows smooth and slow but becomes more riffling downstream. A 50- to 100-foot-wide wooded buffer often separates trail from creek. A congestion of young trees, shrubs, and wildflowers claims a utility corridor at 0.4 mile. Shortly after, private property occupies the opposite shore.

Trunks of yellow birch and a lazy creek bend at 0.8 mile add to travel. A low bluff hosts the trail. Where a corduroy spans a drainage, look for

Middle Creek Lake, Middle Creek Wildlife Management Area.

salamanders. At 1.1 miles, cross the Elders Run footbridge; it utilizes masonry from the trolley-line bridge. At the road fork at 1.25 miles, hikers may turn around; hike the Elders Run Trail, which heads right; or take the path straight ahead to dirt Mountain Spring Road (1.4 miles) for a shuttle-hike option.

65 Nolde Forest Environmental Education Center

Overview

At this 665-acre environmental education center (EEC), a series of trails help educators and students learn about natural habitats and develop an environmental ethic. When purchased in the early 1900s by hosiery baron Jacob Nolde, the property consisted of reverting farm fields, meadows, and brush, with a single white pine that inspired Nolde to grow a forest. Under his direction, conifers were planted and the forest reborn. The center office now occupies the Tudor-style Nolde Mansion, and an interpretive trail explores its grounds. Admire the mansion's stonework, slate roof, stained-glass windows, turrets, and balconies.

General description:	Three hikes introduce the EEC offering.
General location:	3 miles south of Reading.
Special attractions:	Mature conifer–hardwood forests, turtle pond, mansion and sawmill, wildlife sightings.
Length:	Chestnut Trail–Middle Road Loop, 1.75-mile loop, including spur to Painted Turtle Pond; Watershed Trail, 2.2 miles round trip; Boulevard Trail, 3 miles round trip.
Elevation:	Chestnut Trail–Middle Road Loop, 200-foot elevation change; Watershed Trail, 400-foot elevation change; Boulevard Trail, 500-foot elevation change.
Difficulty:	All are easy to moderate.
Maps:	State park brochure.
Special concerns:	Keep to the trails and keep pets leashed or leave them at home. Take precautions for ticks. Park only in designated parking areas, not on roadways. No picnicking or overnight use of the park, no swimming, and no disturbing of natural features. Although this is an EEC, trailhead and junction signs generally are few, so carry a park map at all times.
Season and hours:	Year-round. Trails and the Sawmill and North Pond Parking Areas, sunrise to sunset; mansion-area parking, 8:00 A.M. to 4:00 P.M. only.
For information:	Nolde Forest Environmental Education Center.

Nolde Forest Environmental Education Center

Key points:

Chestnut Trail–Middle Road Loop:
- 0.0 Chestnut Trailhead (Mansion Area).
- 0.3 Painted Turtle Pond.
- 0.9 Middle Road.
- 1.7 Close loop.

Watershed Trail:
- 0.0 Sawmill Area trailhead; cross Angelica Creek.
- 0.4 Watershed Trail (footpath).
- 1.1 End at Spruce Trail; backtrack.

Boulevard Trail:

- 0.0 Sawmill Area trailhead; cross Angelica Creek.
- 0.4 Follow Boulevard Trail right.
- 0.7 Loop junction; head left.
- 1.8 Rock outcrop jumble.
- 2.2 Complete loop; backtrack to trailhead.

Finding the trailhead: From Pennsylvania 625/New Holland Road 3 miles north of Knauers, 2 miles south of Kenhorst (a suburb of Reading), turn west onto Main Entrance Road for the mansion and Chestnut Trail–Middle Road Loop. From the main entrance, go 0.8 mile north on PA 625 to Sawmill Parking Area and the start of the other two trails.

The hikes: For the **Chestnut Trail–Middle Road Loop,** look for the sunken grade of the Chestnut Trail heading southwest off the Main Entrance Road opposite a hydrant just before the entrance to Mansion Parking. Plantation forest rises to the right; a mixed conifer–hardwood forest spreads left. Cicadas sometimes lend voice to the woods. Proceed forward past the Oak Trail to enjoy cathedral oaks and tulip poplars and, later, planted spruce.

At an unmarked junction at 0.2 mile, descend left 0.1 mile to visit Painted Turtle Pond. Mats of duckweed top this tiny man-made pond. View turtles on the sunning platforms, newts, and frogs. Although tranquil in appearance, road noise does carry to the site.

Return to the Chestnut Trail (0.4 mile); turn left and bypass Buck Hollow Trail, which heads left, to reach a T-junction with Kissinger Road (a fire road). Turn left for the chosen loop, finding a mild ascent. Spiny conifer snags rise in the forest, while a crash in the treetops and litter of debris may betray a raccoon or red squirrel. Insects can reduce maple leaves to lace.

At 0.8 mile, encounter the first junction marker at a four-way intersection with the Owl Trail; keep to the fire road. In another 0.1 mile, find a picnic area and toilets at a junction of the Owl Trail and Kissinger and Middle Roads. Bear right onto Middle Road, also a fire road, to return to the mansion area. Woody grapevines entangle the woods.

Cross over the hike's high point to pass in and out of conifer plantations. Again hike past the Owl Trail, remaining on two-track Middle Road. An orderly aisle of red pine shapes an eye-pleasing arrow-straight passage; needles soften the lane. Descend past a water tank and massive tulip poplar.

At 1.5 miles, turn left onto Kissinger Road, only to take a quick right off it. In another 0.2 mile, bear left—avoiding the Oak Trail—to cross the Laurel Trail and emerge near Mansion Parking. Turn right to close the loop (1.75 miles).

The **Watershed** and **Boulevard Trails** share a common start at Sawmill Parking. Either cross Angelica Creek on closed Forester Road, or ascend the stairs and cross by way of the sawmill diversion. Hike upstream. Before long, Punches Run, flowing into Angelica Creek, takes the baton as host. Again road noise can intrude. View both natural and man-made cascades. Cross a footbridge over Punches Run and pass a teaching station to arrive at the junction of Mansion and Forester Roads (0.25 mile).

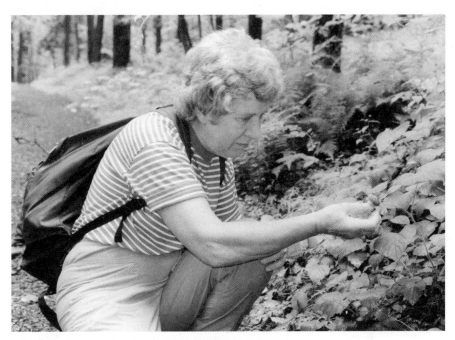

Wild raspberry, Nolde Forest Environmental Education Center.

Bear right onto Mansion Road (now open to hiking only) and hike upstream. Hemlocks, rhododendrons, and a variety of ferns lend to the road's atmosphere. As the road surface changes to pavement, find another teaching station and junction. Leave Mansion Road, coming to the parting of the ways (0.4 mile). Bear left onto a cinder footpath for the Watershed Trail; to the right lies the Boulevard Trail (a gravel fire lane).

The Watershed Trail meanders upstream along Punches Run and its right headwater fork, crisscrossing the waterways several times on footbridges. Large beech trees, small bogs of skunk cabbage, hemlocks, and an array of colorful rainy-year mushrooms contribute to travel. At 0.75 mile, the trail meets Cabin Hollow Road. Bear left to cross the road bridge and resume upstream along the headwater fork. To the right at the junction are Boulevard Trail and rest rooms. Hike past the concrete tank of Upper Reservoir to the Spruce Trail; it marks the end of the Watershed Trail at 1.1 miles. Retrace your steps—or go exploring.

From the 0.4-mile junction, the Boulevard Trail travels a parallel route upstream, overlooking sparkling Punches Run and the Watershed Trail. Find an easy-to-moderate ascent through similar cathedral forest with big beech trees. At 0.7 mile, Cabin Hollow Road arrives on the left; bear right on the Boulevard Trail, quickly coming to the loop junction with tables and toilets nearby. Go left for a clockwise tour.

The fire road again overlooks the waterway and Watershed Trail before switchbacking upslope. At 1.1 miles, bear right as the Spruce Trail arrives on the left. Reach the hike's high point in a mature forest of tulip poplar, oak, walnut, and ash. Beyond a grove of spruce, the descent increases.

At 1.8 miles, the Boulevard Trail curves right past a rock outcrop forty paces off the trail. Despite the absence of views, the jumble of rocks offers a pleasing site to ponder the woods' quiet. Close the loop at 2.25 miles and retrace the first 0.75 mile to the trailhead.

66 Mill Creek Trail

General description:	In the eastern portion of French Creek State Park, this relaxing woodland stroll only briefly meets Mill Creek, but it offers a chance to shake off the cobwebs of society and perhaps discover those in nature. Hikers may extend travel with a visit to the historic iron-making community re-created at Hopewell Furnace National Historic Site (NHS).
General location:	15 miles southeast of Reading.
Special attractions:	Mixed woods, wildlife sightings, charcoal hearths, access to Hopewell Furnace NHS.
Length:	Mill Creek Trail, 6 miles round trip; Lenape Extension, 4.4 miles round trip; Self-guided Historic Site Trail, 0.75 mile round trip. Combined tour, 11.15 miles round trip.
Elevation:	Mill Creek Trail, 500-foot elevation change; Lenape Extension, 300-foot elevation change; Self-guided Historic Site Trail, less than a 100-foot elevation change.
Difficulty:	Mill Creek Trail and Lenape Extension, moderate; Self-guided Historic Site Trail is easy.
Maps:	French Creek State Park map; Hopewell Furnace Official Map and Guide.
Special concerns:	Keep to the marked, color-coded trails; carry a map and water. When adding a visit to Hopewell Furnace National Historic Site, pay an admission fee at the visitor center. No overnight camping, fires, or hunting within the national park; no camping within the state park, except at established campgrounds. Beware of bees.
Season and hours:	Spring through fall for hiking, daylight hours; NHS, 9:00 A.M. to 5:00 P.M. daily, except Thanksgiving, Christmas, and New Year's Days.
For information:	French Creek State Park; Hopewell Furnace National Historic Site.

Key points:

Combined Tour:
- 0.0 Shed Road trailhead; follow Mill Creek Trail.
- 0.3 Lenape Trail junction.
- 0.9 Loop junction; proceed counterclockwise.

Mill Creek Trail

3.3   Cross Mill Creek.
4.4   Millers Point.
5.1   Complete loop; backtrack to add Lenape Trail.
7.3   Baptism–Hopewell Road.
7.9   Hopewell Furnace Visitor Center; take self-guided tour.
8.6   Return to visitor center; backtrack Lenape Trail to trailhead.
11.1 End at Shed Road trailhead.

Finding the trailhead: From the junction of Pennsylvania 10 and PA 23 in Morgantown (reached off Interstate 76), go east on PA 23 for 5.4 miles and turn north onto PA 345. Stay on PA 345 for 4.8 miles to reach Shed Road. The trail heads east off Shed Road near the junction. Gravel roadside parking accommodates up to twenty vehicles.

The hike: Hike east off Shed Road to enter an oak woods intermixed with maple, birch, tulip poplar, and gum. Find a dual blazing: red stripe on white for the Mill Creek Trail; green for the Lenape Trail. A few azalea, fern, and chestnut saplings grow in the understory. Travel a woods road with a dirt-and-cobble bed for a mild ascent. At 0.3 mile, the Lenape Trail splits away to the right leading to the NHS; keep to the Mill Creek Trail.

Bigger trees now punctuate the forest, as the trail edges National Park Service lands. Deer, skunk, and woodpecker may be spied. A power line corridor briefly interrupts the woods at 0.5 mile. In this gentle terrain, the trail shows only a hint of incline before coming to the loop junction (0.9 mile).

Continue straight for a counterclockwise tour. Logs strew the forest floor as a moderate descent follows. Midsummer visitors may hear a parent bird noisily urging its offspring from the nest. At the insistence of squirrels, acorns rain from the oaks.

At 1.5 miles, the red-blazed Raccoon Trail shares the way for about 200 feet, arriving on the right and departing on the left. At 1.75 miles, bear left to avoid a spur to the Buzzards Trail. Ascend among beech trees, some marred by carvings. Because the area was previously harvested to fuel the iron furnace at Hopewell, keen-eyed hikers may detect rounded clearings that betray former charcoal hearths.

The trail rolls to cross a seasonal rocky drainage. On the following ascent, discover mountain laurel. At 2.5 miles, a woods road advances the trail with a descent. At 3.1 miles, be alert: The trail angles back to the left, leaving the road. Cross picturesque Mill Creek via rocks and gravel. The clear-flowing stream engages with humped-back rocks that frame and redirect its flow. Upon crossing, bear right, cross a side drainage, and resume the woods stroll.

At 4 miles, the trail swings right, as a red stripe on blue trail heads straight. Ascend via switchbacks to an unmarked spur that branches right to Millers Point—an outcrop knoll for admiring the forest setting. The blazed Mill Creek Trail then tops a rise to tour the broad oak-clad plateau to close the loop, 5.1 miles. Retrace the first 0.9 mile to end at the trailhead at 6 miles. Or add the Lenape Extension by turning left at 5.7 miles.

The extension offers a similar woods tour on a slowly descending, wide earthen trail. The green blazes occur at a broader interval. Hike past a post indicating a charcoal hearth and gain noise from PA 345. In 0.9 mile (6.6 miles), the trail swings left to descend log-braced earthen steps past a tiny springhouse.

Beyond the spring-fed stream's footbridge, find the Y-junction with the Raccoon Trail. Follow the green and red dual blazes to the right along a wetland drainage that supports tall azalea. Cross a rotting footbridge to reach a woods road at an old picnic shelter (7.2 miles). Continue following the dual blaze, bearing right to round a gate and exit onto Baptism–Hopewell Road.

Hopewell Furnace National Historic Site.

To reach the NHS, turn right, hike along the road for 0.2 mile, cross PA 345, and follow the park entrance road to Hopewell Furnace Visitor Center (7.9 miles). At the center, pay fees to tour the museum and walk the village streets. A 0.75-mile self-guiding tour introduces the village; living-history days bring the picturesque community to life. Discover restored structures and learn about the iron-making era. The history of the furnace dates to 1772. Return via the Lenape Trail to the Shed Road trailhead for an 11.15-mile tour.

67 Kings Gap Environmental Education Center

Overview

This 1,443-acre environmental education center (EEC) on South Mountain in Cumberland County encompasses a variety of habitats through which students and educators learn about nature. The 15 miles of trail that web the park traverse rocky ridgetop, hardwood forest, stream and pond habitats, and conifer plantation. A hilltop mansion houses the center office; its garden and grounds offer yet another microcosm to explore.

General description:	Three areas make up the EEC: the Mansion, Pond, and Plantation Areas. The seven selected hikes introduce each of the three.
General location:	25 miles southwest of Harrisburg.
Special attractions:	Vistas, mixed forests, ant mounds, charcoal hearths, wildlife sightings.
Length:	Rock Scree–Ridge Loop, 2 miles round trip; Woodland Ecology Trail, 0.6 mile round trip; Scenic Vista Trail, 2 miles round trip; White Oak Trail, 0.3-mile loop; Watershed Trail, 2 miles round trip; Whispering Pines Interpretive Trail, 0.25-mile loop; Pine Plantation Trail, 0.6-mile loop.
Elevation:	Rock Scree–Ridge Loop, 150-foot elevation change; Woodland Ecology Trail, 50-foot elevation change; Scenic Vista Trail, 300-foot elevation change; White Oak Trail, minimal elevation change; Watershed Trail, 100-foot elevation change; Whispering Pines Interpretive Trail and Pine Plantation Trail, minimal elevation change.
Difficulty:	Rock Scree–Ridge Loop, Scenic Vista Trail, and Watershed Trail, moderate. All others are easy.
Maps:	EEC brochure (generally available at parking areas and at park office).
Special concerns:	Carry water. Beware of poison ivy and of poisonous snakes, especially along the stonework of the mansion gardens, where snakes seek out rodents. Keep to the trails, keep pets leashed, and no collecting. Color-coded blazes and junction signs aid travelers.
Season and hours:	Year-round, 8:00 A.M. to sunset for trails. Office, 8:00 A.M. to 4:00 P.M., weekdays.
For information:	Kings Gap Environmental Education and Training Center.

Kings Gap Environmental Education Center

Key points:

Rock Scree–Ridge Loop:

0.0   Mansion Area trailhead.
0.4   Loop junction; head left.
1.0   Turn right onto Ridge Trail.
1.4   Overlook.
1.6   Complete loop;
       backtrack to trailhead.

Woodland Ecology Trail:

0.0   Woodland Ecology
       Trailhead.
0.6   Complete loop,
       ending at trailhead.

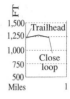

Scenic Vista Trail:

0.0   Pond Area
       trailhead.
1.0   Hilltop vista;
       return as you came.

White Oak Trail:

0.0   Pond Area trailhead;
       bear left at
       loop junction.
0.3   Close loop,
       ending at trailhead.

Watershed Trail:

0.0   Pond Area trailhead.
0.1   Loop junction;
       cross footbridge.
1.5   Stream crossings.
1.8   End loop;
       return to trailhead.

Whispering Pines Interpretive Trail:

0.0   Pine Plantation
       Trailhead.
0.2   End loop at
       trailhead.

Pine Plantation Trail:

0.0   Pine Plantation
       Trailhead.
0.3   Cross Rock
       Scree Trail.
0.6   Close loop at trailhead.

Finding the trailhead: From Interstate 81, take exit 11 and go south on Pennsylvania 233 for 2.4 miles. Turn left onto Pine Road, go 2.2 miles, and turn right to enter the EEC on Kings Gap Road. Find Pine Plantation Area Parking at 0.25 mile, Pond Area Parking at 2 miles, Woodland Ecology Trail Parking at 3.5 miles, and Mansion Area Parking at 3.8 miles.

The hikes: Representing the trails of the Mansion Area are the **Rock Scree–Ridge Loop** and **Woodland Ecology Trail.**

Start the Rock Scree–Ridge Loop at the Mansion Parking Area. From the information kiosk and trail post, proceed downhill. As the trail contours the slope below the mansion, turn left onto the red-blazed Rock Scree Trail, descending log-braced steps to cross the park road at 0.1 mile.

A predominantly chestnut oak forest enfolds the trail. A few mountain laurel dot seasonal color to the scene. Pass a teaching station and twice cross the green-blazed Forest Heritage Trail before reaching the loop junction at 0.4 mile. Head left, still on the Rock Scree Trail. The loop will conclude via the purple-blazed Ridge Trail straight ahead.

Black gum and maple now join the oak. Enjoy tranquil strolling with filtered lighting, insect chirrs, and snaps betraying the movement of wildlife. Alongside the trail, study a logic-defying gum tree with a hollow base and vibrant canopy. Where the trail traverses the foot of a bouldery forest slope, take a pair of switchbacks at 0.7 mile.

White scree patches mark the uphill slope as hikers approach the 1-mile junction. Here, turn right off the Rock Scree Trail onto the Ridge Trail to ascend the ridge backbone. The Rock Scree Trail continues to Pine Plantation. Tree-filtered glimpses foreshadow the scenic view to come. As the ridge gains a bouldery top, the trail briefly dips to the upper reaches of the south flank.

At 1.4 miles is the overlook where a broad gap in the oaks presents a look north at the Cumberland Valley—a patterned quilt of cropland, field, and forest, where vultures ride the thermals. Follow purple blazes away from the post to arc right for an easy descent to close the loop (1.6 miles). Retrace the first 0.4 mile.

The Woodland Ecology Trail (purple-blazed) starts at the parking area below the mansion just before the divided traffic flow. Reach the loop junction in 100 feet; interpretive plaques introduce the natural history. Travel in a woods of chestnut oak, black gum, and pitch pine, with a berry understory.

Kings Gap was repeatedly harvested to produce charcoal to fuel the Cumberland Furnace in Huntsdale (1794 to 1854). Depleted soils account for today's lack of abundant vegetation. The forest's many multiple trunks owe to the trees' starts from stumps. Midway, the ecology trail kisses the yellow-blazed Maple Hollow Trail. Enjoy a pleasant 0.6-mile woods stroll.

Three trails represent the Pond Area offering: the **Scenic Vista Trail, White Oak Trail**, and **Watershed Trail.**

Start the orange-blazed Scenic Vista Trail opposite the kiosk at Pond Area Parking. Ascend through an oak–berry woodland past a group of picnic tables and skirt the paved White Oak Trail for a steady contouring ascent. Gum, tulip poplar, maple, pitch pine, sassafras, and snags fill out the forest. Pass a teaching station and, at 0.2 mile, continue the ascent on a woods road to the right. The climb intensifies at 0.4 mile, but the woods provide a relaxing setting as lone-standing, twisted mountain laurels dot the terrain.

At a junction post at 0.75 mile, bear left to return to foot trail and traverse a barren circular site that has the telltale look of a charcoal hearth. The trail then rolls atop the hill to the vista (1 mile). Here, an arc of three benches extends a northwestern look, with pitch pines partitioning the view. Admire the rural valley, Kings Gap Hollow, and distant Blue Mountain. Through ridge sags, spy more rural landscapes. Return as you came or continue the hike to the Mansion Area.

The paved, all-ability White Oak Trail starts at the paved parking pad reserved for disabled visitors. Bear left at the initial junction for a clockwise tour. Both Braille and large print interpretive panels introduce basic concepts of natural history. Explore a similar oak, gum, maple, and pine forest and pass a hearth site before closing the loop (0.3 mile).

The purple-blazed Watershed Trail starts at the Pond Area kiosk. Follow a pebble-surfaced access trail past a teaching station to a woods road (0.1 mile). Turn left onto the woods road; to the right leads to the pond.

Trees shade the passage. In 200 feet, reach the loop junction and cross a footbridge over Kings Gap Hollow for counterclockwise travel. Kings Gap Hollow is a pretty trickling stream that measures but a couple of feet wide; the summer sun can steal the stream altogether. Pass another teaching station and keep right to avoid a pair of cut-across trails that shorten the loop.

The Watershed Trail then drifts away from the hollow, passing through an oak–pine habitat with high- and lowbush blueberry, elegant fern, and small azalea. Where it travels the valley bottom, find more maple and gum. Colorless Indian pipe pierces the woods floor.

At a wayside at 0.4 mile, learn about the Allegheny mound-building ants that influence the terrain ahead. These red-and-black ants can kill young trees within a 50-foot radius of their mound, but they cannot battle moss. Hike 0.2 mile past the panel to discover an active mound on the right. Most of the ones that follow have been abandoned, reclaimed by moss and pioneer plants. The mounds measure 2 to 4 feet in diameter and stand up to 18 inches high.

Where the purple blazes indicate a swing left at 0.75 mile, the Boundary Trail (green) branches away to the right. The Watershed Trail then rolls up and over a small rise to again turn left at 1.1 miles. A few rocks rise in the foot trail as it follows Kings Gap Hollow downstream. In places, sphagnum moss and skunk cabbage win footholds.

At 1.5 miles, cross a side spring and then the main hollow stream. Keep right as a cut-across merges on the left. At 1.7 miles, proceed forward to avoid the second cut-across and a spur to the right that leads back to the parking lot. Close the loop at 1.8 miles; end the hike just shy of 2 miles.

Two trails travel the Pine Plantation Area: the **Whispering Pines Interpretive Trail** and **Pine Plantation Trail.**

Start the paved Whispering Pines Interpretive Trail off the designated wheelchair-accessible parking site. Bear right at the rest room to reach the loop junction. Interpretive panels in Braille and large print introduce the area; exercise caution where panels instruct you to investigate by feel, because poison ivy has a way of intruding. The plantation's uniform rows address hikers.

Farmland view, Kings Gap Environmental Education Center.

On the loop, hikers learn that the forty-two-acre plantation was once a farm. On the old farmhouse foundation sits a relocated cabin that dates to the 1850s; walnut trees shade the lawn. Conclude in white pines and tamarack.

The **Pine Plantation Trail** (orange-blazed) swings a broader loop, exploring the same plantation; begin at the teaching station. Follow a mowed path to the right, passing among tamarack and pine. The trail alternately shows a cushiony bed of needles or one of vegetation. In the shrub-filled breaks between the plots, find wild rose, grape, brier, poison ivy, and wildflowers. The chaos of shrubs contrasts with the orderly tree rows. An interlude with a doe and fawn may highlight a tour. Midway, cross the red-blazed Rock Scree Trail and tag its end before closing the loop (0.6 mile).

68 Rocky Knob Trail

General description: Reached off the Michaux State Forest Self-guided Automobile Trail, this interpretive loop strings atop and along a mountainside, touring a stunted forest and rocky realm.

General location: Michaux State Forest, 7 miles north of Caledonia State Park.

Special attractions: Intriguing forest, laurel showcase, modest viewpoints, wildlife, fall foliage, solitude.

Length: 4.2 miles round trip.

Elevation: Find a 400-foot elevation change.

Difficulty: Moderate.

Maps: Rocky Knob Trail brochure; Michaux State Forest map.

Special concerns: Use necessary care during rock scrambles, watching footing when conditions are wet. Before starting out, obtain a trail brochure from the forest office for its area map and fine interpretive trail descriptions. The state forest map and the self-guided automobile trail brochure can also help in getting to the trailhead. Carry what water you will need, and wear boots.

Season and hours: Generally spring through fall, depending on road access.

For information: Michaux State Forest.

Key points:

0.0 Ridge Road trailhead; head east.
0.3 Loop junction; turn left.
1.5 Siers Hill.
2.4 Rocky Knob vantage point.
2.6 Old Civilian Conservation Corps (CCC) road.
3.9 Close loop; return to trailhead.

Finding the trailhead: From the junction of U.S. Highway 30 and Pennsylvania 233 at Caledonia State Park (9 miles east of Chambersburg, 15 miles west of Gettysburg), go north on PA 233 for the trailhead. For maps or information, the forest office is 0.25 mile east on US 30.

Proceeding to the trailhead, head north on PA 233 for 1.5 miles and turn left onto gravel Milesburn Road toward Long Pine Dam. This road is passable for conventional vehicles—but go slow, because it is bumpy. Go 2.7 miles and keep right, crossing a bridge to reach a junction in 1.3 miles. Here, turn right onto Ridge Road, reaching the trailhead (stop 10 on the forest drive) on the right in another 1.4 miles. There is head-in parking for up to six vehicles.

The hike: From Ridge Road, round the log gate to follow the orange-blazed trail, a 1937 Civilian Conservation Corps (CCC) road passing through an area

Rocky Knob Trail

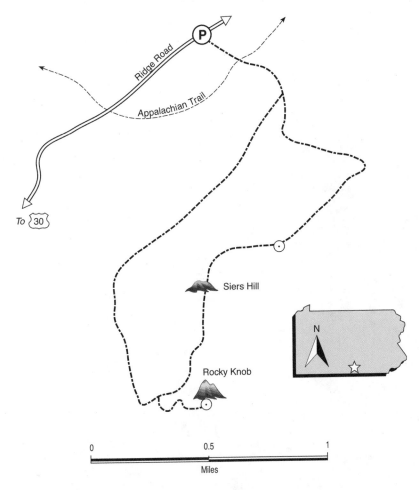

of chestnut oak, maple, and locust. As the trail progresses, black gum and other species fill out the mix. Seasonally, the trail is an attractive gauntlet of mountain laurel. At 0.1 mile, cross over the white-blazed Appalachian Trail. The overhead branches weave shade, and the grade allows carefree strolling.

Thumps, snaps, and cracks reveal that hikers are not alone, but the source is seldom revealed. At 0.3 mile is the loop junction and post 1 for the interpretive tour. Turn left onto the hiker footpath for this clockwise hike, passing along the broad ridgetop. Sassafras and pitch pine vary the look of the woods. The forest's runty quality owes to the thin soil and areas of overbrowsing or fire. Despite their small size, most trees exceed forty years in age.

When the laurel bloom is at its peak, it cannot be adequately praised. By 0.6 mile, gain a glimpse east toward East Big Flat Ridge. Allegheny ant mounds occur in this forest; do not disturb the mounds. The brochure paired with the trail's numbered posts provides important area insights.

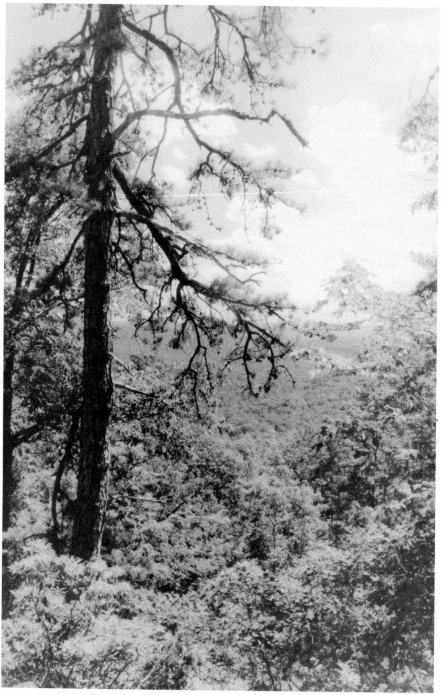

Rocky Knob Trail view, Michaux State Forest.

Before long, the trail drifts south on a rock-studded path along the upper east slope. Views east–southeast improve, adding the south end of East Big Flat Ridge and Long Pine Run Reservoir, along with Rocky Knob, Wolf Hill, and Mitten Hill panning west.

Mountain laurel and blueberry complement travel throughout. After passing over Siers Hill (1.5 miles), the trail descends and gradually grows steeper. At 2.1 miles, arrive at the bouldery quartzite rubble at the north end of Rocky Knob. The rocks are picturesque, fractured and mottled with lichen and moss. Continue to post 11 (2.3 miles) to locate the left spur to the Rocky Knob vantage site; the loop continues right.

This vista spur is only for the boot-clad and surefooted. It travels loose and sometimes wobbly rocks that can steal footing or harm ankles. Keep an eye out for the blazes, passing through rock-studded forest and across a boulder-crowded slope. In 0.1 mile, come to the end of the line at post 12 along the upper reaches of the boulder slope. A short scamper up and to the right gains a better forest window to the outside world, viewing the tip of Long Pine Run Reservoir, the rolling hillsides stretching south, and Michaux State Forest. The view gained earlier in the trek was superior, but spur hikers do get an up-close appreciation for the boulders.

Resume the loop at 2.5 miles, now turning left, still descending. At post 13 (2.6 miles), again meet the old CCC road, which carries the loop northward to return to the trailhead. The grade again allows eyes to travel over the forest. The tan flash of a deer bounding through the woods may cause a double take. A long steady climb recaptures the hike's entire 400-foot elevation loss. Some hemlocks and American chestnuts (a disappearing species) may be sorted from the mix. Close the loop at 3.9 miles and backtrack the first 0.3 mile to the trailhead.

69 Caledonia State Park

Overview

This 1,130-acre South Mountain state park has a 12-mile system of nature, hiking, and history trails. Rediscover the era of charcoal hearths and iron furnaces, and touch a page from Civil War history. Along East Branch Conococheague Creek, explore a wondrous rhododendron realm. The Appalachian Trail (AT) threads through the park on its 2,000-mile odyssey.

General description: Three hikes introduce the park's natural and historical features.

General location: 40 miles southwest of Harrisburg.

Special attractions: A superb rhododendron showcase (one of the best in the state), iron furnace, millraces, Thaddeus Stevens's blacksmith shop, mountain laurel, fall foliage.

Length: Whispering Pine Nature Trail, 0.4-mile loop; Thaddeus Stevens Historical Trail–Charcoal Hearth Trail Loop, 3.1-mile loop; Ramble Trail, 2.6 miles round trip.

Elevation: Whispering Pine Nature Trail, minimal elevation change; Thaddeus Stevens Historical Trail–Charcoal Hearth Trail Loop, 600-foot elevation change; Ramble Trail, 100-foot elevation change.

Difficulty: Whispering Pine Nature Trail, easy; Thaddeus Stevens Historical Trail–Charcoal Hearth Trail Loop, moderate to strenuous; Ramble Trail, moderate.

Maps: State park, Caledonia Trails, and Whispering Pine Nature Trail brochures; Thaddeus Stevens Historical Trail guidebook.

Special concerns: Keep to the trails; no trail camping. In the floodplain, some footbridges may be washed out.

Season and hours: Year-round; daylight hours for hiking.

For information: Caledonia State Park.

Key points:

Whispering Pine Nature Trail:
- 0.0 Whispering Pine Trailhead; follow numbers.
- 0.4 End loop at trailhead.

Thaddeus Stevens Historical Trail–Charcoal Hearth Trail Loop:
- 0.0 Furnace trailhead; ascend left of furnace.
- 0.1 Loop junction; cross millrace footbridge.
- 0.4 Charcoal Hearth Trail.
- 1.6 Top Graeffenburg Hill.
- 3.0 Close loop; backtrack to trailhead.

Caledonia State Park

Ramble Trail:

- 0.0 Furnace trailhead; carefully cross Pennsylvania 233.
- 0.3 Loop junction; head clockwise.
- 1.1 Mill site.
- 2.3 Cross bridge, closing loop; backtrack to trailhead.

Finding the trailhead: The park is at the intersection of U.S. Highway 30 and PA 233. Find Furnace Parking Area off PA 233 at the northeast corner of the intersection. For the park office and Whispering Pine Nature Trail, go 0.1 mile north on PA 233 from US 30 and turn left (west).

The hikes: The **Whispering Pine Nature Trail** begins at the trail shelter west of the park office and east of a large day-use parking area. Pick up an interpretive brochure at the park office and follow the numbered posts and white blazes to tour the braided floodplain of Conococheague Creek. Enjoy an enchanting realm of big white pines, eastern hemlocks, tulip poplars, and rhododendron bushes. The brochure walks visitors through the process of tree identification. Pass a tumbled colossus, and admire the site's rhododendron, which grow 18 feet high. The radial leaves of the rhododendron dazzle year-round. Conclude the loop at 0.4 mile.

Start the other two hikes from Furnace Parking Area. A guidebook (available at the park office) introduces features of Thaddeus Stevens Historical Trail; watch for the furnace symbols.

For the **Thaddeus Stevens Historical Trail–Charcoal Hearth Trail Loop,** hike the paved path that ascends to the left of Caledonia Iron Furnace (site

3 on the tour; discover the first two features across PA 233). Set back in the slope of Graeffenburg Hill, the furnace was built in 1837 by Thaddeus Stevens, a prominent abolitionist. Due to Stevens's political bent, on June 26, 1863, Confederate General Jubal A. Early ordered the destruction of this furnace works community.

At the end of the pavement, bear left for site 4, the former location of a waterwheel. Overlook the attractive rockwork of the millrace stream. At the footbridge is the loop junction; cross to pursue the historical trail upstream along the west levee. Hemlock, pine, oak, and gum offer shade, but the highway drone is inescapable at the start.

At 0.2 mile, cross back over the race to ascend a hemlock-darkened slope for a rolling, contouring hike. At 0.4 mile is a junction. Here the historical trail descends to cross PA 233 to the millrace reservoir (visible from the junction). For the loop, follow yellow-blazed Charcoal Hearth Trail. It remains along the foot of the slope in hemlock forest; avoid a spur to the group camp area.

By 0.9 mile, ascend via wagon road. Where more light penetrates, discover laurel. A countdown of the numbered charcoal hearths starts at site 5—a good introduction for untrained eyes. This cleared and leveled site once held a smoldering woodpile that produced charcoal to fuel the area's iron furnace. Ascend into hardwood forest and bountiful laurel. At 1.4 miles, the trail switchbacks around hearth 1.

Top Graeffenburg Hill (elevation 1,522 feet) and begin a sleepy, meandering descent. Lichens adorn the tree trunks, and hemlocks return to the mix. By 2.3 miles, the descent steepens; beware of roots and loose gravel. Round above the millrace to close the loop at the bridge, 3 miles; descend the fragment of pavement to end in another 200 feet.

For the **Ramble Trail**, hike west across PA 233 from Furnace Parking, cross a footbridge over Rocky Mountain Creek, and traverse lawn to meet a gravel lane. To the left is the Blacksmith Shop, a white-painted brick-and-stone building with a bell tower. Turn right for the Ramble Trail (yellow blazes).

The lane edges an area of lawn and shade trees—the former pastures that served as a field hospital during the battle of Gettysburg. Pass the pool area and Trail Center log cabin. At 0.3 mile (near Pine Shelter), find the loop junction at a bridge over East Branch Conococheague Creek.

Forgo crossing; instead, hike downstream along the south shore. Initially, the white blazes of the Appalachian Trail join the yellow ones of the Ramble. The creek flows swift with small cascades; effusive rhododendron lines its banks. The wide earthen trail, too, is engulfed in a rhododendron jungle with grand old hemlocks. Bear right at the fork at 0.4 mile. Here, too, an island divides Conococheague Creek. US 30 hums above the trail but cannot detract from it.

At 0.6 mile, cross a footbridge over a diversion to hike the levee of Old Rolling Mill race. Then, at 0.7 mile, proceed forward as the AT heads left over a millrace bridge to cross US 30. As the floodplain narrows, overlook both race and creek. At 1.1 miles, cross a stone bridge and view the moss-

Rhododendrons, Lowlands Natural Area, Caledonia State Park.

colored stone walls from the old mill complex. The hike now swings right to traverse the floodplain. Follow blazes to locate footbridge crossings. In places, travel provides an up-close appreciation of the soggy, root-snarled floodplain. The wonderland of hemlock and rhododendron helps you dismiss the occasional misstep. Big oak, tulip poplar, and pine are other trail signatures.

Meander the floodplain to travel a wide gravel lane at 2.1 miles, still crossing side drainages to eventually gain a creek overlook. Hike past Pine Shelter and a bench swing that overlooks Conococheague Creek at 2.3 miles. Then close the loop by crossing the bridge. Retrace the gravel road east across the park, veering off it before the Blacksmith Shop to cross PA 233. End at Furnace Parking, 2.6 miles.

70 Kellys Run Natural Area

Overview

In Lancaster and York Counties, the Pennsylvania Power and Light Company manages 5,000 acres bordering the lower Susquehanna River/Lake Aldred as part of the Holtwood hydroelectric project. Within the vast conservation and recreation area, a 7.5-mile national recreation trail network explores Kellys Run Natural Area on the southeast shore. Discover the scenic glen of Kellys Run with its cliffs, cascades, and rhododendron, and overlook Lake Aldred from 500 feet above at the Pinnacle.

General description:	This hike consists of a loop tour of Kellys Run Trail and a detour along the Conestoga Trail to Pinnacle Overlook.
General location:	15 miles south of Lancaster.
Special attractions:	The scenic glen of Kellys Run, Lake Aldred overlooks, schist cliffs and overhangs, rhododendron and laurel, wildlife sightings, fall foliage.
Length:	Kellys Run Trail, 4-mile loop; Conestoga Trail to Pinnacle Overlook, 2-mile round-trip spur.
Elevation:	Travel between 200 feet near the mouth of Kellys Run to 705 feet at Pinnacle Overlook.
Difficulty:	Strenuous.
Maps:	Kellys Run–Pinnacle Trail System map and *Trails for Hiking or Walking at Lake Aldred* (seasonally available at Holtwood Recreation Area).
Special concerns:	No trail camping. Be careful when fording and scrambling over the slippery rocks of Kellys Run, and avoid during high water. Wear bright colors during hunting season. If time is limited, Pinnacle Overlook is also a drive-to destination.
Season and hours:	Spring through fall, 8:00 A.M. to sunset.
For information:	Pennsylvania Power and Light Company, Holtwood Land Management Office.

Key points:

Kellys Run–Pinnacle Hike:

0.0 Holtwood Recreation Area trailhead.
1.7 Conestoga Trail.
2.7 Pinnacle Overlook; return to Kellys Run Trail.
6.0 End loop at trailhead.

Finding the trailhead: From Interstate 83 at York, take exit 6E and go south on Pennsylvania 74/Queen Street. Proceed 21.1 miles south on PA 74 and turn east onto PA 372/Holtwood Road to cross the Susquehanna River below Holtwood Dam. In 1.8 miles, turn left (north) onto River Road. In another

Kellys Run Natural Area

0.4 mile, turn left onto Old Holtwood Road to find the entrance to Holtwood Recreation Area on the right in 0.3 mile.

The hike: Enter the woods at the foot of the grassy slope below Pavilion 1. Find a dual blaze: Blue indicates Kellys Run Trail; orange, the Conestoga Trail. The shared, wide earthen trail passes through a full woods of tulip poplar, maple, sassafras, and spruce. Woody vines and poison ivy entangle the trees.

In 100 feet, find the first of two junctions with the yellow-blazed Oliver Patton Trail; stay with the dual blue and orange blazes. Twice the trail crosses utility corridors. As it rolls to higher ground, chestnut oaks and laurels make an appearance. When Kellys Run sounds below, find early showings of rhododendron.

After crossing a small tributary, meet the red-blazed Loop Trail (0.8 mile) and descend toward the rush of Kellys Run. Slabs of wavy-patterned schist rise in and along the trail. Approaching the run, find mature forest and an unruly explosion of rhododendron. On a downstream tour, view the alternating riffles, sheets, and cascades as Kellys Run squeezes through pinched rock channels and forms deep pools.

An imposing overhang looms 60 feet above the trail as hikers come upon the first bridgeless crossing. Ford the main run and cross a nearly equal-size side run. Near a couple of larger pools linked by cascades at 1.2 miles, a blazed fork indicates low- and high-water travel options.

Find the trail extremely rugged in the steep-sided canyon. At 1.4 miles, pass the white-blazed Pinnacle Trail that ascends to the right. The Kellys Run Trail then rolls back downhill to a gorgelike setting with overhangs and cliffs

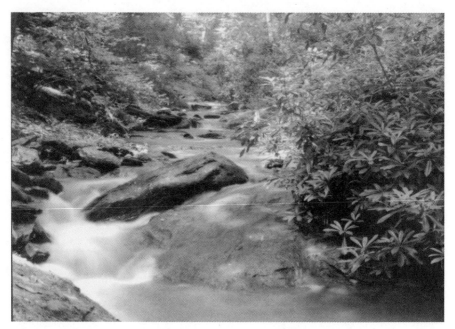

Kellys Run, Kellys Run Trail System.

and exciting pinched waters. Rhododendrons cap the rocks. Hemlock, maple, tulip poplar, and birch bring shade. Be careful of the canted, wet rock surfaces, and loose gravel.

At 1.5 miles and 1.6 miles, blazes on the rock indicate crossings of Kellys Run. The trail then ascends to travel a narrow terrace overlooking the run's cascading plummet to the Susquehanna River. At 1.75 miles, the orange-blazed Conestoga Trail ascends north to Pinnacle Overlook via the rock steps to the right, while the Kellys Run Trail continues forward to an abandoned road in 100 feet (the loop's return).

Turn right to add Lake Aldred overlooks. Ascend and scramble over a rocky point. Cracks in the sharp-edged slabs provide toeholds. At 1.9 miles, ascend via an old woods road. Oak, maple, and gum now compose the ridge woods. In 0.1 mile, veer left on a footpath to emerge at a pipeline clear-cut with views south of Holtwood Power Plant and Norman Wood Bridge.

At a post in the pipeline corridor, again veer left on a woods path. Greenbrier sometimes snatches at passersby. The trail contours to a Virginia pine–dressed rock promontory for an open look across the reservoir. Vultures or a V-formation of passing geese may grace the sky. At the next outcrops, views become more restricted.

At 2.25 miles, the orange-blazed route ascends right to meet and follow a wagon road left. Travel is shared with a yellow-blazed trail. The reservoir is now mostly a glare beyond the trees. At a wagon road junction, follow the route that curves and ascends right; avoid the one on the left.

Cardinals adorn the branches as the trail emerges at a gate at the southwest corner of Pinnacle Overlook, 2.75 miles. Find open and shaded benches, tables, and a board identifying reservoir features. April through October, piped water and rest rooms benefit travelers. Scan the open water of 2,400-acre Lake Aldred, Reed and Duncan Islands (both formerly inhabited by Indians), and the canyon's low, rounded wooded ridges. In the afternoon, vultures pass at eye level as they circle on the thermals. In September and October, watch for migrating birds of prey.

Backtrack along the Conestoga Trail, descending to Kellys Run Trail (3.75 miles), and turn right to complete the counterclockwise loop. Quickly reach the abandoned road and turn left to cross its bridge over Kellys Run for a farewell view. A slow ascent follows. Tour open woods of locust, sumac, and elm. At 4.25 miles, pass under a gate and approach a city street, only to veer away left and round a second gate.

The wide, cropped-grass trail offers carefree strolling, while benches welcome hikers to pause. Wild grape and thorny vegetation thrive. After the trail flattens, look for it to turn left, passing at the edge of a field. While some blazes are masked, the trail offers the only logical course of travel.

Next, turn right onto a sun-drenched mowed path, sometimes enlivened by turkeys. At 5.2 miles, return to the viney forest, proceeding forward past the red Loop Trail. Cross a pair of power-line corridors to enter the far west end of Holtwood Recreation Area. Traverse the park to close the loop near Pavilion 1 at 6 miles.

Philadelphia Region

The southeastern corner of the state, around Philadelphia, holds surprising natural wealth. Even within the metropolitan area itself, discover a prized old-growth canyon realm—Wissahickon Creek Gorge. Totally insulated from the sights and sounds of the city, this gorge would be the pride of any community. Elsewhere in the region, wetlands, fields, and thickets vary travel. While history tracking, you may walk the towpath of the Delaware Canal, revisit Washington's crossing from the days of revolution, and unravel the tale of early industry and commerce.

71 Delaware Canal National Heritage Trail

General description:	The 60-mile Delaware Canal represents the most intact canal of the early and mid-nineteenth century, with many of its operational features still in place. The parallel towpath today is recognized as a national heritage trail.
General location:	Along the Delaware River between Easton and Bristol.
Special attractions:	River and canal views; Washington Crossing; historic locks, aqueducts, and lockkeeper houses; pedestrian bridge to the New Jersey shore and Delaware and Raritan Canal; historic buildings that date to the 1700s.
Length:	41.1 miles one-way, Easton to Washington Crossing.
Elevation:	Find less than 200 feet of elevation change.
Difficulty:	Varies, depending on length and allotted time.
Maps:	Delaware Canal State Park brochure.
Special concerns:	Carry sunscreen and drinking water. Find some amenities at bordering parks. Farm markets, town stores and eateries, country inns, and campgrounds ease thru-trail travel. Washington Crossing State Historic Park (SHP) is a fee site. Respect the private lands that border the route.
Season and hours:	Year-round. Washington Crossing SHP Visitor Center, 9:00 A.M. to 5:00 P.M., Tuesday through Saturday; noon to 5:00 P.M., Sunday.
For information:	Delaware Canal State Park.

Delaware Canal National Heritage Trail

Key points:

0.0 Easton trailhead (Hugh Moore Historical Park); hike south.
2.2 Wy-Hit-Tuk County Park.
5.2 Raubsville.
8.6 Riegelsville.
15.9 Upper Black Eddy.
21.2 Tinicum County Park.
28.0 Lumberville/pedestrian bridge to New Jersey.
34.9 New Hope.
41.1 End at Washington Crossing SHP Visitor Center.

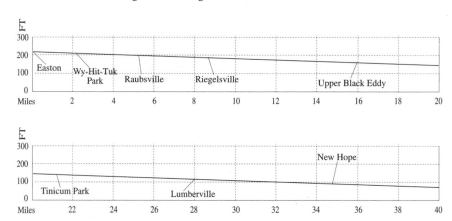

Finding the trailhead: The northern terminus is located in Easton south of the Lehigh River off Pennsylvania 611 at Hugh Moore Historical Park (site of the old Canal Museum). In Bristol, locate the canal towpath between PA 13 and Bristol Pike as it passes through Grundy Municipal Park. Washington Crossing SHP is reached off PA 32 at Taylorsville.

The hike: At Easton, cross the walkway to overlook the thick wooden gates of Lock 24 and hike the east levee south. Stretching north from the park is Lehigh Canal and additional discovery. Towpaths are being switched over from a mowed surface to a crushed-rock surface.

Interpretive panels introduce the Delaware Canal (1831 to 1932) and the lifestyle it supported. The towpath greenway traverses farmland, residential and industrial areas, and charming towns of history. Wetland sometimes claims the canal; elsewhere, the water allows for canoeing. Parallel roadways provide access and some intrusion, but the natural corridor usually wins out. While tracking the canal's history, hikers also discover the beauty of the Delaware River without ever manning an oar.

Night heron and kingfisher lend to waterway views, while sycamore, maple, cottonwood, box elder, ash, elm, and locust bring shade. Poison ivy appears now and then. Gradually, PA 611 drifts away from the canal and towpath. At 2.2 miles, footbridges span the canal to Wy-Hit-Tuk County Park with its tree-shaded lawns, tables, rest rooms, and a five-site canoe camp. When crossing to the county park, heed the no-pets rule.

The canal's cloudy water reflects the leafy shore. Additional panels introduce the role of the canal in the transport of coal to the eastern seaboard. Muskrat, rabbit, and hummingbird increase the list of wildlife sightings. At 4 miles, more bridges span the canal. With no roadside parking along PA 611, these bridges serve local access only.

The towpath continues to offer views of the broad Delaware River. Before long, spy a toothed-gear raised gate and spillway. As the towpath loses its tree border to the west, roads and communities become a part of the tour.

At 5.2 miles, travel through Raubsville, with much of the town situated between the canal and river. Hikers pass at the back doors of private residences; keep to the trail. From the town, pass Locks 22 and 23, a lockkeeper's house, and a west-bank picnic area—part of the Theodore Roosevelt Recreation and Conservation Area.

The canal footbridge at 6.8 miles accesses Fry's Run County Park. It also offers a look at Kleinhan's Aqueduct 10; although rebuilt, it has the original rockwork bottom. The open corridor ahead offers 0.5 mile of unobstructed river views. Farm fields and woodlands obscure PA 611.

At Riegelsville (8.6 miles), discover canal-era inns and eateries still in operation. Where the towpath passes under the Delaware Road bridge, hikers may venture into town. Again, travel parallels PA 611 and river views depart. At Lock 21 (9.7 miles), a sportsman's access and launch offers the next shuttle opportunity.

Farm country follows. While picturesque, the openness of the trail can make for hot travel. Where the towpath next crosses under a road bridge, a farm market invites hikers aside with tastes of the season. Farther south, an attractive stone house and stone-and-frame barn greet travelers. PA 32 now parallels the canalway.

Where the trail journeys past Indian Rock Inn (13.1 miles), study the cliff for the image of an Indian head. South of intermittent Falls Creek, the towpath and PA 32 cross. At Upper Black Eddy (15.9 miles), find the trail distanced from the highway and river. Black Eddy was a popular fishing spot for President Grover Cleveland. Past the state park office, enjoy a more isolated section of travel. At Uhlerstown (19 miles), view an 1832-built covered bridge, Lock 18, and well-kept private structures recalling the era.

At 21.2 miles, take a midway break where the towpath travels the western edge of Tinicum (Bucks County) Park. Find shaded picnic tables, toilets, and a campground just a few strides from the trail. To get water, hike east into the park. The restored Erwin Stover House and a classic bank barn may draw travelers 0.3 mile aside to see them.

Again find the river and canal paired where Marshall Island divides the river flow. During low water, spy stepped rocks that shape the river's Tumble Falls. Enjoy partial shade and discover more remnants from the canal's past. Historic homes at the village of Point Pleasant (26.1 miles) add to the path's charm. Next, pass Lock 13, with its heavy hinged gates, crank box, and stonework.

In Lumberville (28 miles), find access to a general store and a pedestrian bridge over the Delaware River. At Lock 12, depart the canal to travel the

Lock, Delaware Canal State Park.

0.25-mile river span to Bull's Island (New Jersey) State Park, where camping is available. Forgoing the detour, remain on the towpath as it traverses agricultural land.

Communities, most of them scenic and historic, appear with regularity. At New Hope, the canalway and PA 32 again cross, and hikers may encounter mule-pulled barges. The barge concession is at the south end of town.

At 37.1 miles, enter the Bowman's Hill Section of Washington Crossing SHP. By crossing the bridges and hiking west, visit the eighteenth-century Thompson-Neely homesite, where tours are given. View Bowman's Hill rising to the west. From this hill, Washington's men monitored the British troop movements.

As the towpath proceeds south through the park, discover an arc of rocks and a flag toward the river—the nation's first unknown soldiers' plot. It honors the soldiers who died December 25, 1776. Ringing the flag are thirteen polished stones representing the thirteen colonies.

Southbound the route again crosses PA 32 at Jericho Creek, which marks the northeast corner of William Penn's land purchase of July 1682. The national heritage trail then edges the field above the David Library of the American Revolution to emerge at PA 532 at Taylorsville.

Hike the road east to the McConkey's Ferry Area of Washington Crossing SHP (41.1 miles). There, find a visitor center, historical tours and artifacts, and a monument commemorating Washington's crossing of the Delaware River on Christmas night 1776. For thru-trail hikers, this area signals an ideal ending, because the national heritage trail to the south grows increasingly industrial with few amenities.

72 Tohickon Valley Trail

General description:	This hike tours the north canyon wall of Tohickon Creek, passing through Tohickon Valley Park and the High Rocks Area of Ralph Stover State Park. Find overviews and limited access to bending Tohickon Creek, the remote host.
General location:	25 miles northeast of Philadelphia.
Special attractions:	Tohickon Creek overlooks and access, High Rocks cliffs and viewpoints, wildlife sightings, forest wildflowers, fall foliage.
Length:	7.3 miles round trip, with opportunity to shorten.
Elevation:	Find a 200-foot elevation change.
Difficulty:	Moderate.
Maps:	Ralph Stover State Park brochure.
Special concerns:	Keep back from the High Rocks rim. No trail camping.
Season and hours:	Spring through fall; Tohickon Valley Park and High Rocks Area both close at sunset.
For information:	Delaware Canal State Park.

Key points:

0.0 Tohickon Valley Park trailhead.
2.0 Enter High Rocks Area.
2.8 Cross Stover Park Road; keep right at loop junction.
3.8 Tohickon Creek.
4.5 Close loop; backtrack first 2.8 miles.

Finding the trailhead: From Point Pleasant, cross the Tohickon Creek bridge and go north on Pennsylvania 32. In 0.1 mile, bear left onto Cafferty Hill Road and continue 1.1 miles to Tohickon Valley (Bucks County) Park on the left. Go 0.1 mile farther for Deer Wood Campground. Both offer trail access.

The hike: When starting from Tohickon Valley Park, hike the paved road to Doe Run Cabins; find the road to the right of the main parking area. Descend 0.2 mile to where the cabin road bends left and step over a cable barrier on the right to ascend a gravel trail. Dogwood, hickory, maple, tulip, oak, and ash weave the overhead cathedral. Downhill, hear the rush of Tohickon Creek; uphill, view a stone wall.

At 0.3 mile, bear left for this upstream journey, now following a red circle on white blaze. To the right sits Deer Wood Campground. Campers can locate the cable-barred trail off the entrance road as they arrive. The trail skirts the campground plateau. Virginia creeper and poison ivy scale the tree trunks. View the shimmery ribbon of Tohickon Creek and discover challenging side trails that plunge to its shore. After the ascent resumes, look for the blazed

Tohickon Valley Trail

route to angle right at 0.7 mile; a well-traveled but unmarked trail proceeds forward.

Stay on the blazed trail to round the head of a rocky, intermittent drainage, still contouring the upper reaches of the slope. At the next drainage, gain a better perspective on the steep-walled canyon. Dark rocks jut from the lower slope. Their tilt seemingly defies gravity.

Along the rim, pass through a breach in a scenic stone wall. Mayapple, jack-in-the-pulpit, and geranium lend seasonal color. As the blazed trail descends a slight ridge at 1.4 miles, the unmarked trail returns on the left. Proceed forward for more rolling rim travel. Hemlocks enrich shade.

Across the small drainage at 2 miles, enter the High Rocks Area and temporarily lose blazes. Secondary paths descend to the rocks, but avoid the rocks unless you are a credentialed climber. A wire-mesh fence lines the cliff rim. At 2.2 miles, arrive at the first of the named vistas—Doan's Overlook. From here, view a horseshoe bend on Tohickon Creek and win a cliff perspective.

Cedars among the rock herald Cedar Overlook, which is next. At an unnamed vista, feel your heartbeat quicken as you overlook a plummeting red cliff. At 2.3 miles, reach Balcony Overlook for more ledge and overhang views. Deep in the wooded canyon sparkles tea-colored Tohickon Creek. Argillite Overlook (2.4 miles) marks the final named view. It also signals a likely turnaround spot to shorten the hike.

For the full tour, remain along the rim, ignoring the spur at 2.5 miles that branches right to Tory Road Parking—a popular access for climbers and mountain bikers. Maintain the same travel line. A fence still deters hikers from the jutting rock. Before long, white blazes guide the way through mixed woods to paved Stover Park Road (2.8 miles).

Tohickon Creek, Tohickon Valley Park.

Cross the road and reenter woods, coming to a trail fork: The path to the right travels the rim of the north canyon slope, while the path to the left descends to Tohickon Creek. Together they offer loop travel, but neither is blazed.

Travel the tree-shaded rim, avoiding secondary paths that branch away. A steep slope drops to the creek. Off to the right, view a cedar woods. Cross a seasonally dry drainage and the upper end of a rock wall to enter meadow.

Now pass between wooded slope and meadow rise. The chest-deep grasses and wildflowers often host bluebird and seclude deer. The rock wall at 3.5 miles marks a junction. Descend left, crossing the wall, to reach the creek trail (3.7 miles). To the left is the close of the loop, but first, detour right 0.1 mile to a sycamore-shaded gravel bar on the creek. Night creatures harvest shellfish at the bar; by day, insects enliven the canopy.

Resume the loop at 3.9 miles, traveling the wooded creek flat downstream; beware of poison ivy. Beech, ash, and dogwood join maple and oak. Worms churn the soil. The trail narrows as it traverses a small meadow to contour the foot of the wooded slope. Overlook Tohickon Creek—attractive, riffling, and often channeling a welcomed breeze. Pass a fragment of rock wall at a drainage and angle uphill away from the creek. Close the loop at 4.5 miles and retrace the hike's first 2.8 miles.

73 Pennypack Preserve

Overview

Pennypack Preserve is a nonprofit trust project consisting of an expanding natural area for protecting and restoring habitat throughout the central Pennypack Creek watershed. The preserve's fields, forests, and streams represent a vestige of what was. Management's effort to return the land to its native plant species represents what can be. The specialness of the area and its mission to be wild won it recognition as a national urban wildlife sanctuary. A network of short trails explores the 683-acre site.

General description:	The Perimeter Loop introduces the habitats at Pennypack Headquarters and serves as a launch pad to the other named trails. The Hike/Bike Trail travels along Pennypack Creek.
General location:	In Huntingdon Valley, 15 miles northeast of Philadelphia.
Special attractions:	Bird-watching, with 150 bird species identified within the preserve; pretty Pennypack Creek and its historic bridges; wetlands; wildflowers; fall foliage.
Length:	Perimeter Loop, 0.7-mile loop; Hike/Bike Trail, 3.1 miles one-way. (Both consist of several named trails.)
Elevation:	Perimeter Loop, minimal; Hike/Bike Trail, 150-foot elevation change.
Difficulty:	Both are easy.
Maps:	Pennypack Trails Map (available at center).
Special concerns:	Within Pennypack Headquarters Area, no pets or bicycles. They are allowed on the Hike/Bike Trail along the creek; keep pets leashed. Practice wilderness ethics: Keep to the trails, leave no trace, and do not disturb plants or animals. Beware of ticks.
Season and hours:	Year-round, 9:00 A.M. to 5:00 P.M., Monday through Friday; 10:00 A.M. to 2:00 P.M., Saturday; and 2:00 P.M. to 5:00 P.M., Sunday.
For information:	Pennypack Ecological Restoration Trust.

Key points:

Perimeter Loop:

0.0 Woods Edge Trailhead.
0.4 Pond/experimental wetland.
0.7 End loop at parking area.

Hike/Bike Trail:

0.0 Woods Edge/Perimeter Loop Trailhead.
0.3 Left on Meadow Crossing Trail.
0.6 Meet Creek Road near 1817 bridge.
2.2 Cross Mason's Mill Road.
3.1 End at gate; return as you came.

Pennypack Preserve

Finding the trailhead: From Interstate 276 in the north metro area, take exit 27 (Willow Grove) and go south on Pennsylvania 611 for 1.9 miles. Turn east onto PA 63/Moreland Road, go 0.6 mile, and turn left onto Edge Hill Road. Stay on it, crossing Terwood Road, to reach the center in 1.3 miles.

The hikes: The **Perimeter Loop** travels three adjoining trails. Clockwise, they are Woods Edge, Pond, and Crabapple Meadow. From the junction post at the northwest corner of visitor parking, follow the Woods Edge Trail parallel to Edge Hill Road; the Evergreen Trail branches right. Young planted pine and mixed hardwoods frame the cushiony woods lane. Dogwood, sassafras, ash, maple, gum, and oak fashion an intriguing mosaic—but poison ivy abounds.

At the four-way junction in 0.1 mile, cedar-lined Old Lane heads right; the Mitchell Trail heads left across Huntingdon Road to Pennypack Creek and the Hike/Bike Trail; and the Perimeter Loop proceeds forward. Insects enliven the canopy, challenging the occasional plane roar. Beyond the Dogwood Trail, skirt woods that add to a roster of tree species. Where the trail travels along a tangled hedgerow, scan field, woods, and wooded rise.

Reach a bench seat at the Meadow Crossing Trail junction (0.3 mile). This mowed path heads left to meet both the Rosebush and Paper Mill Road Trails that, in turn, access the Hike/Bike Trail. From the bench, view woods, vine thicket, and open fields. Chance sightings include rabbit, fox, butterfly, a Cooper's hawk, and Baltimore oriole.

For this hike, bear right at 0.3 mile to continue the loop via the Pond Trail. Pass the Goldenrod Trail in a matter of strides. The next right leads to the visitor center; keep left for the Perimeter Loop, soon coming to the center's willow-ringed, duckweed-colored pond. The adjacent experimental wetland is designed to cleanse the pond's waters. Skirt a springhouse and pass the Raytharn Trail on the left; it leads to the preserve's Raytharn Farm acquisition, a 160-acre preserve for meadow-nesting songbirds. On the farm trail, discover two spectacular vistas before meeting the south end of the Hike/Bike Trail.

In a setting of conifers, the Pine Straw Trail to the visitor center heads right as the Crabapple Meadow Trail takes charge of the Perimeter Loop. Deer or wild turkey can add an element of surprise as the trail edges shoulder-high vegetation and grape-tangled woods. A few crab apple trees support the trail's name. Close the loop near the entrance gate, 0.7 mile.

With virtually no public parking at the terminus streets to the **Hike/Bike Trail,** access it via the Mitchell or Meadow Crossing Trails from Perimeter Loop or from Mason's Mill Park. (Follow Edge Hill Road north past the entrance to Pennypack Preserve, turn left onto Huntingdon Road, and then turn right onto Mason's Mill Road. Cross the bridge over Pennypack Creek to find this neighborhood park on the left.)

Three trails likewise make up this linear route: Creek Road, Pennypack Creek Trail, and Pennypack Parkway.

For this hike, follow the Perimeter Loop clockwise for 0.3 mile and turn left onto Meadow Crossing Trail—a wide mowed swath that divides two meadows. Pass into Overlook Woods to reach a trail junction: The path to the right leads to Paper Mill Road (our choice); left is the Rosebush Trail. Either path leads to the Hike/Bike Trail. From the junction, view an area of replanted native trees, shrubs, and ferns.

Upon reaching Paper Mill Road (open to foot traffic only), turn left and descend. Hike past the Management Trail, which journeys right exploring an oak–beech woods, and meet the Hike/Bike Trail at abandoned, partially paved Creek Road at 0.6 mile.

Here hikers may opt for a 0.5-mile walk downstream (to the right) or 2.5-mile hike upstream (left). Both extend tranquil, mostly shaded tours, with views of the bending 20-foot-wide Pennypack Creek. They also offer options to vary the return. Cross over the bikeway to view Pennypack Creek and its floodplain from a restored 1817-built stone bridge. A duck or kingfisher may animate the scene. Sycamores dress shore.

On the upstream journey, frogs sound from a wildlife pond and wetland to the hiker's left. Where the Hike/Bike Trail next overlooks the creek, the Rosebush Trail arrives on the left. At 1.1 miles (mileage includes 0.6 mile from trailhead), round a gate to skirt an area of large stone residences; respect private property.

Forest trail, Pennypack Preserve.

Follow the roadway that hugs the creek upstream to reenter the preserve at the next gate (1.25 miles). Tulip poplar, beech, gum, maple, dogwood, and rhododendron clad the abutting slope. The Mitchell Trail arrives on the left at 1.3 miles; keep to the Hike/Bike Trail (Creek Road). Skunk cabbages dot the creekside woods. Spurs to the right access Webb Walk—a short side loop that passes closer to Pennypack Creek. Big sycamores appear near a private church property (1.5 miles).

Next, the footpath of the Pennypack Creek Trail veers left, just before the second historic stone bridge (circa 1840). Hikers may wish to detour onto the bridge for a view, because the trail now pulls away from Pennypack Creek. On the foot trail, tour wild meadow, a vine tangle, and mixed woods to Mason's Mill Road (2.2 miles).

Cross the road and round the gate to resume upstream travel on Pennypack Parkway, a quiet gravel lane. Travel in a cathedral woods of ash, maple, beech, oak, and tulip poplar. After a long absence, Pennypack Creek bends back toward the trail (2.8 miles). Small drainages thread the woods, bringing with them jewelweed and skunk cabbage. Impressive big-diameter trees grace the area, with beech trees preferring shore. At 3.1 miles, a gate signals to stop. Retrace your steps for a 6.2-mile round trip.

74 Wissahickon Creek Gorge, Fairmount Park

Overview

In northwestern Philadelphia, 8,700-acre Fairmount Park enfolds the spectacular setting and outdoor recreation along 7 miles and 1,800 acres of Wissahickon Creek Gorge. Despite its city location, the park is a remarkable island—wild and free from the intrusion of city skylines and traffic sounds. Cathedral forest, broad-flowing Wissahickon Creek, scenic outcrops, historic stone bridges, ruins that date to the 1700s, and a battle site from the American Revolution contribute interest. Hikers, cyclists, joggers, and equestrians explore an exciting network of trails.

General description: Forbidden Drive (closed to vehicles) and an interlocking network of color-coded trails invite a variety of round-trip, shuttle, and loop tours. The featured two loops utilize Forbidden Drive and the Orange Trail, traveling the banks of Wissahickon Creek.

General location: In northwestern Philadelphia amid the neighborhoods of Chestnut Hill, Mount Airy, Germantown, East Falls, Roxborough, Manayunk, and Lafayette Hill.

Special attractions: Ancient hardwood forest, Wissahickon Creek and its side drainages, rhododendron and wildflowers, fall foliage, wilderness solitude.

Length: Southern Loop, 5.7-mile loop, including a round-trip spur to Germantown Battle site; Northern Loop, 5.5-mile loop, including a round-trip spur to the Tree House Visitor Center and Andorra Nature Center.

Elevation: The trails show only a 100-foot elevation change.

Difficulty: Both moderate (Forbidden Drive portions are easy).

Maps: Map of the Wissahickon Valley, for purchase at the Tree House or at book, bike, and outdoor stores in the park vicinity.

Special concerns: No swimming, camping, or alcohol. Keep pets leashed; beware of poison ivy and ticks. Cyclists and joggers must yield to pedestrians; all must yield to horseback riders. (Equestrians and bicyclists over age sixteen must obtain a trail-use permit to ride on any trail other than Forbidden Drive and the park access trails. Permits are available through Fairmount Park.)

Forbidden Drive is regularly patrolled. Mileage posts along it mark off 0.5-mile increments.

Find toilet facilities at Valley Green behind the horse-warming shed and at Andorra Nature Center. Toilets also are available at Pachella Field (Henry

Wissahickon Creek Gorge, Fairmount Park

Northwestern Avenue

Germantown Avenue

Tree House Visitor Center

Bell's Mill Road

Covered bridge

Valley Green Road

Springfield Avenue

Cresheim Creek

Ridge Avenue

Henry Avenue

Wise's Mill Road

Valley Green Inn

Forbidden Road

Shakespeare Rock

Fingerspan

Kitchen's Lane

Wissahickon Avenue

City of Philadelphia

City of Philadelphia

City of Philadelphia

N

0   0.5   1

Miles

Blue Stone Bridge

Wissahickon Creek

Lincoln Drive

Rittenhousetown

Germantown Battle Plaque

and Livezey), Blue Bell Park (Walnut Lane and Park Line Drive), and Northwestern Stable (Northwestern and Germantown Avenues).

Season and hours: Year-round, daylight hours.
For information: Fairmount Park Commission.

Key points:

Southern Loop:

0.0   Valley Green Trailhead; follow Orange Trail south.
0.4   Shakespeare Rock and Devils Pool.
0.9   Fingerspan.
2.1   Forbidden Drive; detour south.
3.0   Germantown Battle site; hike Forbidden Drive north.
5.7   End at Valley Green.

Northern Loop:

0.0   Valley Green Trailhead; hike Forbidden Drive north.
1.3   Restored covered bridge.
2.1   Bell's Mill Road; detour north on crosswalk.
2.7   Andorra Nature Center/Tree House Visitor Center; return to loop.
3.3   Orange Trail.
4.3   Stone archway and bridge.
5.5   End at Valley Green.

Finding the trailhead: Germantown Avenue parallels the park's eastern border; Henry Avenue, the western border. Find primary trail parking at Valley Green: From Germantown Road in Chestnut Hill, go west on Springfield Avenue and Valley Green Road. From Henry Avenue in Roxborough, go east on Wise's Mill Road. Also find sizable parking areas off Bell's Mill Road and Northwestern Avenue, both to the north, and at Kitchen's Lane to the southeast.

The hikes: Start both hikes at the Valley Green Trailhead. For the **Southern Loop**, pick up the Orange Trail at the Valley Green Road bridge and turn south to hike the east bank downstream. Pigeons and ducks animate air and water, while a kingfisher brings a wilder note to the scene. Shading the canyon are maple, locust, box elder, and birch, along with massive beech and tulip poplar, witch hazel, and the occasional rhododendron.

The wide, rolling foot trail contours the lower canyon slope, fluctuating between 15 and 50 feet above Wissahickon Creek. The trail has outstanding natural merit, except for a bit of graffiti at 0.4 mile near Shakespeare Rock. The rock is so named for a plaque bearing a quote from *Two Gentlemen of Verona*. Framed by folded metamorphic rock, neighboring Devils Pool is an engaging dark shimmery basin fed by an attractive cascade.

Pass beneath an abandoned stone arch bridge well overhead and descend to cross Cresheim Creek via rocks. On the opposite shore, bear right, cross back under the stone arch bridge, and resume downstream travel along Wissahickon Creek. Pass the three-story stone house of the Valley Green Canoe Club and a small dam washed by a 3-foot cascade. Cross a dead-end street and ascend steps. Here, spy an old stonework wall that recalls a structure from early-day Philadelphia. Small sandy beaches or rocky overlooks may call hikers to shore.

The "Fingerspan" next marks off travel. Nearly 60 feet long with an arched roof 9 feet high, this metal-grate walkway spans a steep slope and skirts a cliff. Still the mature forest engages. At 1.3 miles, hike past the Green Trail, which crosses a double-arch stone bridge to Forbidden Drive; it allows the loop to be shortened. At the trail junction, Wissahickon Creek measures 100 feet across and is shadowed by big sycamores.

Continue downstream along the east shore. Outcrops can shape the slope and prescribe travel. Along the creek at 2 miles, find a monument denoting a 1723 baptismal site. Cross a picturesque side creek and, at 2.1 miles, cross to the west shore of Wissahickon Creek, reaching Forbidden Drive. The Orange Trail continues south.

Upon crossing, a side trip south (left) on Forbidden Drive leads to 1896-built Blue Stone Bridge in 0.6 mile and the plaque denoting the 1777 Germantown Battle site in 0.9 mile. From the battle site, hikers may extend this side trip into history by taking the path journeying east to Rittenhousetown. Established in 1690, Rittenhousetown was the site of the first paper mill in the United States. The earliest building on the grounds dates to 1707.

Opting for the 1.8-mile round trip to the Germantown Battle plaque, resume the loop at 3.9 miles. The gravel lane of Forbidden Drive travels the west bank for a new perspective on canyon and creek. Forbidden Drive itself dates back to 1823.

Ascend past an old lookout shelter, keeping to Forbidden Drive. Rail fence and attractive stonework add to the area's charm, as do many big trees. Spy another ruins recessed in the hillside. At Valley Green, pass a historic inn that still serves lunch and dinner before closing the loop at 5.7 miles.

For the **Northern Loop** from Valley Green Inn, follow Forbidden Drive north (upstream) along the west bank. Hikers share the way with cyclists and joggers. For a brief stretch, travel the access road to Valley Green's Westside Parking. Carefree travel resumes at 0.2 mile.

Stroll past a creek flat with tables, benches, and a fitness trail. Forest tranquility envelops the hike, while a small dam launches a 5-foot cascade across the breadth of the creek. Wissahickon Creek Gorge boasts some of the finest big tulip poplars in the state. A night heron may preside along shore, or cardinals may adorn a branch. Benches suggest a pause.

At the foot of an eroded rock slope at 0.6 mile, pass a public spring that was dedicated in 1854. After the arrival of a stepped side creek at 0.8 mile, more sunlight rains through the leafy cathedral. Come upon a shelter above the creek and the first bridge link to the Orange Trail for shortening the loop; keep to Forbidden Drive.

At 1.3 miles, view a restored 1737 covered bridge with solid sides and picket-cut entry eaves. Again, keep to the west shore. A parklike greenway separates trail and creek, and enormous sycamores draw attention.

At Bell's Mill Road (2.1 miles), find a corner picnic area and trail option. Hikers may continue north via the crosswalk another 0.6 mile to Andorra Nature Center and the Tree House Visitor Center, where a system of nature trails, trail information, and chemical toilets are available. Or, for the loop alone, turn right and cross the road bridge.

The selected hike includes the 1.2-mile, round-trip spur to Andorra Nature Center. Upon return to Bell's Mill Road, cross the road bridge and follow the east bank downstream at 3.3 miles. Multiple colors blaze the start; follow the Orange Trail blazes.

The wide trail rolls along some 30 feet above shore. At 3.6 miles, sentinel tulip poplars dazzle with diameters in excess of 4 feet. Cross a concrete bridge over a large side creek and bear right. Younger trees briefly clad the slope.

Keep to the east shore, hiking past the covered bridge for a second time. The trail proceeds forward to round an abandoned stone structure and tour a grassy bench. Back in woods, dark rock outcrops bring visual interest. At 4.3 miles, descend the steps through a picturesque stone archway and cross a stone bridge over a cascading side creek to resume southbound travel on the Orange Trail. Hikers wishing to avoid an upcoming rocky area on the Orange Trail should instead cross to Forbidden Drive and backtrack to the hike's start.

Where the Orange Trail again bears right at 4.5 miles, find more rhododendron and the addition of hemlocks. When conditions are wet, be especially cautious scrambling over rock outcrops. Cross a pair of side creeks and bear right to cross Wissahickon Creek on the Valley Green Road bridge. Conclude the hike at 5.5 miles.

75 John Heinz National Wildlife Refuge at Tinicum

Overview

This 1,200-acre national wildlife refuge (NWR) protects the largest remaining freshwater tidal marsh in the state of Pennsylvania. The drone of Interstate 95, the roar from Philadelphia International Airport, and an encroaching industrial skyline all demonstrate how close the state came to losing this vital piece of natural history. Besides the tidal marsh, the refuge encompasses a 145-acre impoundment pond, braided creeks, nontidal marsh, old fields, and woods. Together, they provide critical nesting and resting habitat for birds and other wildlife. A network of trails invites hikers to explore. Tidal-influenced Darby Creek hosts a 4.5-mile canoe trail navigable only between the two hours preceding and the two hours following high tide.

General description: Hikers travel service road, boardwalk, and foot trail, exploring the refuge and visiting observation decks and blinds. Carry binoculars and guidebooks.

General location: 10 miles southwest of the heart of Philadelphia.

Special attractions: Freshwater marsh and estuarine stream habitats, bird and other wildlife sightings, wildflowers and aquatic plants. (Check the refuge calendar of "Phenological Events" to see what wildlife is arriving or nesting and what plants should be in bloom.)

Length: 8.2 miles for a barbell-shaped tour. Shorter hike options exist.

Elevation: Terrain and trails are virtually flat.

Difficulty: Easy to moderate.

Maps: Refuge trail map.

Special concerns: Carry drinking water. Keep to the trails, and keep pets leashed. No swimming, hunting, collecting, or fires. Anglers, please note that the fish in Darby Creek are contaminated.

Season and hours: Year-round, 8:00 A.M. to sunset. Visitor center, 9:00 A.M. to 4:00 P.M.

For information: John Heinz National Wildlife Refuge at Tinicum.

Key points:

0.0 Refuge trailhead; follow gated service road straight.
0.3 Marsh boardwalk viewing platform.
0.8 Observation tower.

John Heinz National Wildlife Refuge at Tinicum

2.2   Western loop junction; turn right.
6.2   Resume impoundment loop.
8.2   Complete impoundment loop at trailhead.

Finding the trailhead: From the junction of Bartram Avenue and 84th Street, north of I–95 and the Philadelphia International Airport, go northwest on 84th Street for 0.7 mile and turn left onto Lindbergh Boulevard. Go 0.2 mile and turn right onto 86th Street to enter the refuge via gravel road.

The hike: From the parking area at the end of the refuge road past the small information station, take the gated service road straight ahead toward the observation tower. The hike's return will be via the service road on the left. To the right, find both a dock and the canoe access to slow-moving Darby Creek.

The hike's service road passes between Darby Creek and the large open marsh of the impoundment pond. Box elder, silver maple, willow, and locust partially frame travel; poison ivy thrives at the shoulders. Benches welcome wildlife-viewing, while a few interpretive signs introduce the refuge inhabitants. At 0.2 mile, stairs descend left to a boardwalk that spans the marsh.

Detour left on the boardwalk to a central viewing platform (0.3 mile) for up-close viewing of the duckweed, yellow pond lily, and arrowhead. Search for turtles, frogs, snakes, and fish. Darting swallows, red-winged blackbirds, wading egrets, and colorful dragonflies may add to a visit. For a 0.5-mile loop, continue across the boardwalk to the east shore of the impoundment, where a foot trail returns north.

For the full refuge tour, turn back at the viewing bench, and resume travel south along the impoundment's west shore. Areas of phragmites (plumed reeds), purple loosestrife, and cattails vary the texture of the refuge landscape. Although the city backdrop is loud, the natural attractions win over travelers, and the service roads allow for carefree strolling.

At 0.8 mile, reach a bilevel observation tower for open-water looks. Keen-eyed travelers may spy turtle snouts barely breaking the water's surface. Small islands dot the south end of the impoundment. At 1.4 miles, follow a spur to the right to a wildlife-viewing blind that overlooks a richly textured open tidal marsh. Observe terns, cormorants, herons, geese, and gulls.

Resume the service road tour, ignoring a foot trail that branches left. Travel now is on two-track through wildflower grassland. Reach a T-junction (1.8 miles) and turn right to explore the western refuge and its loop. A left completes the impoundment loop for a 3.8-mile hike.

Noisy I–95 companions westbound travel through an edge community of woods and field. At 2.25 miles, bear right onto a foot trail to the next blind. A jungle growth of vegetation pinches the trail, but the path remains good. Fox or rabbit may be spied, while a bench seat offers looks across the marsh to the Philadelphia city skyline. At 2.4 miles is the wildlife blind.

Continue west past the blind, still on a vegetation-squeezed footpath. View open water, textured marsh, a sea of phragmites, and perhaps an egret flying low in the distance. A few silver maple and willow partially shade the dike. At a bridge crossing at 2.9 miles, enjoy unobstructed looks at an open-water channel. Rustles betray wildlife, and a muskrat may part the water.

Marsh observation platform, John Heinz National Wildlife Refuge at Tinicum.

By 3.5 miles, look for the trail to clear and widen for easier walking. The wetland landscape likewise undergoes change. At 4.1 miles, cross a tiered bridge over a second channel, coming to a junction. Bear left to complete the western loop and selected hike; the right leads to a parking area on PA 420.

Ahead, the trail bends left to parallel I–95 east back across the refuge. Find the next observation blind on the left; it overlooks open water and a pond lily marsh. Beyond the blind stretches shadeless travel. At 4.9 miles and 5.7 miles, pass through gates. Scattered nesting platforms and boxes facilitate nature.

At 5.75 miles, proceed forward to close the western refuge loop. Then, at 6.2 miles (the 1.8-mile junction), proceed forward to complete the impoundment loop. Gradually trees return, bringing partial shade to the service road. Remain on the service road to return along the wooded east shore of the impoundment pond. Avoid foot trails that branch left. A few wetland views sign off the refuge tour, which ends at 8.2 miles.

Appendix A: Hiker's Checklist

Not every item on this checklist will be needed for every trip, so customize the list based on your needs and comforts, the duration of the outing, weather, and the unexpected. Use this list as an organizing tool for planning, packing, and minimizing oversights. Feel free to pencil in items that you find critical to a successful trip.

Ten Essentials
- [ ] extra food
- [ ] extra clothing
- [ ] sunglasses
- [ ] knife
- [ ] fire starter
- [ ] matches in waterproof container
- [ ] first-aid kit and manual
- [ ] flashlight
- [ ] map(s) for the trail
- [ ] compass

Clothing
- [ ] lightweight underwear
- [ ] long johns
- [ ] undersocks
- [ ] wool boot socks
- [ ] long pants
- [ ] shorts
- [ ] long-sleeve shirt
- [ ] T-shirts
- [ ] wool sweater or shirt
- [ ] wool hat and gloves
- [ ] visor or cap
- [ ] raingear
- [ ] warm coat or parka
- [ ] belt
- [ ] bandanna
- [ ] swimsuit or trunks
- [ ] hiking boots
- [ ] sneakers or camp shoes

Personal Items
- [ ] prescriptions
- [ ] contacts or eyeglasses
- [ ] watch
- [ ] wallet and keys
- [ ] emergency medical information
- [ ] sunscreen and lip balm
- [ ] insect repellent
- [ ] toilet paper and trowel
- [ ] biodegradable soap/towelettes
- [ ] comb
- [ ] toothpaste and brush
- [ ] towel
- [ ] nail clipper and tweezers
- [ ] facial tissue or handkerchief

Gear
- [ ] water bottles
- [ ] pack(s)
- [ ] tent, with required poles and pegs
- [ ] ground cloth
- [ ] sleeping bag and foam pad
- [ ] stove and fuel
- [ ] pots and eating utensils
- [ ] can opener
- [ ] rope
- [ ] stuff bags
- [ ] large trash bags for emergency shelter for self or gear
- [ ] plastic bags for trash
- [ ] zipper-seal bags for foodstuffs
- [ ] aluminum foil

Food
- [ ] 3 meals, plus snacks, for each day
- [ ] extra food for delays
- [ ] salt/pepper
- [ ] vegetable oil
- [ ] drink mixes

Health & Safety Items
- [ ] emergency blanket
- [ ] water pump or purification tablets
- [ ] whistle
- [ ] pencil and paper
- [ ] picture wire for emergency repairs

Miscellaneous
- [ ] mosquito netting
- [ ] binoculars
- [ ] camera and film
- [ ] guidebooks
- [ ] identification books
- [ ] fishing gear and valid license

Appendix B: Further Reading

Appalachian Hiker II by Ed Garvey. Appalachian Books.

Appalachian Trail Guide to Pennsylvania, Ninth Edition edited by Maurice J. Forrester Jr. Keystone Trails Association.

Backpacking One Step at a Time, Fourth Edition by Harvey Manning. Random House.

The Basic Essentials of Map and Compass by Cliff Jacobson. The Globe Pequot Press.

Be Expert with Map and Compass by Bjorn Kjellstrom. Charles Scribner's Sons.

A Child's Introduction to the Outdoors by David Richey. Pagurian Press Limited.

The Complete Walker III by Colin Fletcher. Alfred A. Knopf.

A Field Guide to the Birds by Roger Tory Peterson. Houghton Mifflin Co.

Fifty Hikes in Central Pennsylvania by Tom Thwaites. Backcountry Publications.

Fifty Hikes in Eastern Pennsylvania by Tom Thwaites. Backcountry Publications.

Fifty Hikes in Western Pennsylvania by Tom Thwaites. Backcountry Publications.

Finding Your Way in the Outdoors by Robert L. Mooers Jr. E. P. Hutton Co.

A Guide to Field Identification: Wildflowers of North America by Frank D. Venning. Golden Press.

Guide to the National Wildlife Refuges by Laura and William Riley. Collier Books.

Guide to the Susquehannock Trail System, Second Edition by Chuck Dillon. Pine Creek Press, Publisher.

Guide to the West Rim Trail by Chuck Dillon. Pine Creek Press, Publisher.

Mountaineering First Aid, Third Edition by Martha J. Lentz, Steven C. Macdonald, and Jan D. Carline. The Mountaineers.

Mountaineering Medicine by Fred T. Darvill. Wilderness Press.

Pennsylvania Hiking Trails, Twelfth Edition—1998. Keystone Trails Association.

The Shrub Identification Book by George W. D. Symonds. William Morrow and Co.

Travel Light Handbook by Judy Keene. Contemporary Books.

Wild Country Companion: The Ultimate Guide to No-trace Outdoor Recreation and Wilderness Safety (FalconGuide) by Will Harmon. The Globe Pequot Press.

Wilderness Basics: The Complete Handbook for Hikers and Backpackers, Second Edition by the San Diego Chapter of the Sierra Club. The Mountaineers.

Appendix C: Where to Find Maps

For trail maps produced by the managing agencies, contact the information source indicated in the trail summary. The complete address and phone number for each source are listed in appendix D.

For copies of U.S. Geological Survey topographic quadrangles (USGS quads), check at libraries, at most backpacking and mountaineering stores, or at specialty maps and publications stores. Study the Pennsylvania state index to identify the name of the quad(s) that covers the area of interest. Or contact the U.S. Geological Survey Map Distribution Center, Box 25286 Federal Center, Building 41, Denver, CO 80225; ask for the Pennsylvania index and price list.

To obtain a variety of state maps and books on the state's geology and natural history, contact the Pennsylvania State Book Store, Department of General Services, 1825 Stanley Drive, Harrisburg, PA 17103; 717-787-5109.

The Keystone Trails Association (KTA) monitors government action and proposals that relate to or impact trails or the sport of hiking. The organization publishes a number of maps and guides and helps coordinate trail maintenance and hiking club activities throughout the state.

For information on becoming a member or for ordering the Keystone Trails Association maps or books, including the most current edition of *Pennsylvania Hiking Trails*, contact Keystone Trails Association, P.O. Box 251, Cogan Station, PA 17728-0251.

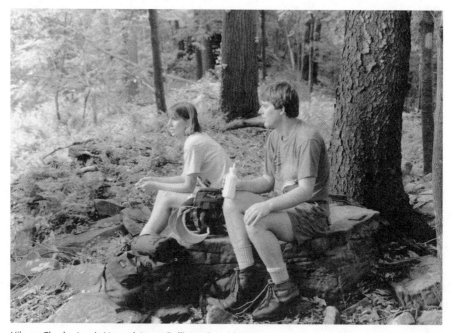

Hikers, Charles Lewis Natural Area, Gallitzen State Forest.

Appendix D: Land Management Listings

Allegheny National Forest
P.O. Box 847
222 Liberty Street
Warren, PA 16365
814-723-5150

Allegheny Valley Trails Association
Box 264
Franklin, PA 16323
http://eagle.clarion.edu/ ~ grads/avta

Appalachian Trail Conference
P.O. Box 807
Washington and Storer
College Place
Harpers Ferry, WV 25425
304-535-6331
For orders only, 1-888-ATSTORE

Beechwood Farms Nature Reserve
614 Dorseyville Road
Pittsburgh, PA 15238
412-963-6100

Bradford Ranger District
Allegheny National Forest
Star Route 1, Box 88
Bradford, PA 16701
814-362-4613

Buchanon State Forest
 District Headquarters
R.R. 2, Box 3
McConnellsburg, PA 17233
717-485-3148

Caledonia State Park
40 Rocky Mountain Road
Fayetteville, PA 17222
717-352-2161

Colonel Denning State Park
1599 Doubling Gap Road
Newville, PA 17241
717-776-5272

Cook Forest State Park
P.O. Box 120 (River Road)
Cooksburg, PA 16217
814-744-8407

Cowans Gap State Park
H.C. 17266
Fort Loudon, PA 17224-9801
717-485-3948

Delaware Canal State Park
11 Lodi Hill Road
Upper Black Eddy, PA 18972
610-982-5560

Delaware State Forest District Hdqrts.
HC 1, Box 95A
Swiftwater, PA 18370-9723
570-895-4000

Delaware Water Gap National
 Recreation Area
Bushkill, PA 18324
570-588-2451

Drake Well Museum
R.D. 3
Titusville, PA 16354
814-827-2797

Elk State Forest
 District Headquarters
R.R. 4, Box 212, Suite 1
Emporium, PA 15834
814-486-3353

Erie National Wildlife Refuge
11296 Wood Duck Lane
Guys Mills, PA 16327
814-789-3585

Fairmount Park Commission
Memorial Hall
West Park
P.O. Box 21601
Philadelphia, PA 19131-0901
215-685-0000

Forbes State Forest District Office
P.O. Box 519
Laughlintown, PA 15655
412-238-9533

French Creek State Park
843 Park Road
Elverson, PA 19520
610-582-9680

Friendship Hill National Historic Site
1 Washington Parkway
Farmington, PA 15437
724-725-9190

Gallitzin State Forest District
 Headquarters
155 Hillcrest Drive
P.O. Box 506
Ebensburg, PA 15931
814-472-1862

Hawk Mountain Sanctuary Association
1700 Hawk Mountain Road
Kempton, PA 19529-9449
610-756-6961
www.hawkmountain.org

Hopewell Furnace National
 Historic Site
2 Mark Bird Lane
Elverson, PA 19520
610-582-8773

Jennings Environmental Education
 Center
2951 Prospect Road
Slippery Rock, PA 16057-8701
724-794-6011

John Heinz National Wildlife Refuge at
 Tinicum
Refuge Headquarters
Scott Plaza II
Suite 104
Philadelphia, PA 19113
610-521-0662

Keystone Trails Association
P.O. Box 251
Cogan Station, PA 17728

Kings Gap Environmental Education
 and Training Center
500 Kings Gap Road
Carlisle, PA 17013
717-486-5031

Lackawanna State Forest District
 Headquarters
401 Samters Building
101 Penn Avenue
Scranton, PA 18503
570-963-4561

Lake Wallenpaupack
Pennsylvania Power and Light
 Company
P.O. Box 122
Hawley, PA 18428-0122
570-226-3702

Laurel Ridge State Park
1117 Jim Mountain Road
Rockwood, PA 15557
724-455-3744

Lehigh Gorge State Park
c/o Hickory Run State Park
R.R. 1, Box 81
White Haven, PA 18661
570-443-0400

Linn Run/Laurel
 Mountain Complex
P.O. Box 50
Rector, PA 15677-0030
724-238-6623

Little Pine State Park
H.C. 63, Box 100
4205 Little Pine Creek Road
Waterville, PA 17776-9705
570-753-6000

Marienville Ranger District
Allegheny National Forest
H.C. 2, Box 130
Marienville, PA 16239
814-927-6628

McConnell's Mill State Park
R.R. 2, Box 16
Portersville, PA 16051-9401
724–368–8091 or 368–8811

Michaux State Forest
10099 Lincoln Way East
Fayetteville, PA 17222
717–352–2211

Mid State Trail Association
P.O. Box 167
Boalsburg, PA 16827

Middle Creek Wildlife Management
 Area
P.O. Box 110
Kleinfeltersville, PA 17039
717–733–1512

Montour Preserve
R.R. 1, Box 292
Turbotville, PA 17772-9500
570–437–3131

Nolde Forest Environmental Education
 Center
2910 New Holland Road
Reading, PA 19607
610–775–1411

Northcentral Region Headquarters
Pennsylvania Game Commission
P.O. Box 5038
Jersey Shore, PA 17740
717–398–4774 or 1–800–422–7551

Ohiopyle State Park
P.O. Box 105
Ohiopyle, PA 15470-0105
724–329–8591

Oil Creek State Park
R.R. 1, Box 207
Oil City, PA 16301-9733
814–676–5915

Oil Creek State Park Bike Rentals
814–677–4684

Oil Creek and Titusville Railroad
P.O. Box 68
Oil City, PA 16301
814–676–1733

Pennsylvania Power and Light
 Company
Holtwood Land Management Office
9 New Village Road
Holtwood, PA 17532
717–284–2278

Pennypack Ecological
 Restoration Trust
2955 Edge Hill Road
Huntingdon Valley, PA 19006-5099
215–657–0830

Pine Creek Outfitters
R.R. 4, Box 130B
Wellsboro, PA 16901
717–724–3003

Pocono Environmental Education
 Center (PEEC)
R.D. 2, Box 1010
Dingmans Ferry, PA 18328-9614
570–828–2319

Potomac Appalachian Trail Club
118 Park Street Southeast
Vienna, VA 22180
703–242–0693

Presque Isle State Park
Department of Conservation and
 Natural Resources
P.O. Box 8510
Erie, PA 16505-0510
814–833–7424

Promised Land State Park
R.R. 1, Box 96
Greentown, PA 18426
717–676–3428

Raccoon Creek State Park
3000 State Route 18
Hookstown, PA 15050
park office: 724–899–2200
nature center: 724–899–3611

Rails-to-Trails of Central Pennsylvania
P.O. Box 592
Hollidaysburg, PA 16648-0592
814–832–2400

Raystown Lake
U.S. Army Corps of Engineers
R.R. 1, Box 222
Hesston, PA 16647
814–658–3405

Ricketts Glen State Park
R.R. 2, Box 130
Benton, PA 17814–8900
570–477–5675

Rothrock State Forest District
  Headquarters
Rothrock Lane
P.O. Box 403
Huntingdon, PA 16652
814–643–2340

Ryerson Station State Park
R.D. 1, Box 77
Wind Ridge, PA 15380
724–428–4254

S. B. Elliott State Park
c/o Parker Dam State Park
R.D. 1, Box 165
Penfield, PA 15849-9799
814–765–0630

Sproul State Forest District
  Headquarters
H.C.R. 62, Box 90
Renovo, PA 17764
570–923–6011

Stone Valley Recreation Area
The Pennsylvania State University
108 Business Services Building
University Park, PA 16802-1002
814–863–0762
http://www.psu.edu/Stone_Valley

Susquehanna Riverlands
R.R. 1, Box 1797
Berwick, PA 18603
570–542–2306

Susquehannock State Forest District
  Headquarters
P.O. Box 673
Coudersport, PA 16915
814–274–3600

The Susquehannock Trail Club
P.O. Box 643
Coudersport, PA 16915

Tiadaghton State Forest District
  Headquarters
423 East Central Avenue
South Williamsport, PA 17701
570–327–3450

Tioga State Forest District
  Headquarters
1 Nessmuk Lane
Wellsboro, PA 16901
570–724–2868

Tuscarora State Forest District
  Headquarters
R.D. 1, Box 42-A
Blain, PA 17006
717–536–3191

U.S. Army Corps of Engineers
Tioga–Hammond Lakes
R.R. 1, Box 65
Tioga, PA 16946-9733
570–835–5281

Worlds End State Park
P.O. Box 62
Forksville, PA 18616-0062
570–924–3287

Wyoming State Forest District
  Headquarters
R.D. 2, Box 47
Bloomsburg, PA 17815
717–387–4255

The Yough River Trail Council
P.O. Box 988
Connellsville, PA 15425
724–628–5500

About the Authors

Over the past twenty years, the Ostertags, Rhonda (a writer) and George (a photographer), have collaborated on a dozen outdoor guidebooks; sold hundreds of articles on topics of nature, travel, and outdoor recreation; and participated in environmental impact studies. They have returned once again to Pennsylvania to update *Hiking Pennsylvania* and revisit some of their favorite wilds.

After hiking more than a couple of thousand of miles on Pennsylvania trails, wearing through a few pairs of boots, and writing a second book on the state's scenic drives, the couple has an intimate knowledge and respect for the state's superb offerings and speak from firsthand knowledge.

Other titles by this team include *Scenic Driving Pennsylvania, Hiking New York, Hiking Southern New England,* and *Camping Oregon,* all FalconGuides with The Globe Pequot Press, and *California State Parks: A Complete Recreation Guide, Second Edition* and *100 Hikes in Oregon, Second Edition,* among their titles with The Mountaineers Books, Seattle, Washington.

American Hiking Society (AHS)

is the only national nonprofit organization dedicated to establishing, protecting, and maintaining America's foot trails—the same trails that are detailed in this book and around the country.

As a trail user, your support of AHS is important to ensure trails are forever protected and continually maintained.

Join American Hiking Society today and you will learn about trails to hike, their history, their importance, and how you can help protect them. American Hiking Society is:

A strong voice. With increasing threats to our treasured open space and wilderness, American Hiking Society exists to actively represent hikers' interests to safeguard these areas. To protect the hiking experience, AHS affects federal legislation, shapes public lands policy, collaborates with grassroots trail organizations, and partners with federal land managers. As a member of AHS, feel assured that while you are hiking, AHS is going *the extra mile* for you.

A helping hand. With more than 200,000 miles of trails in America, AHS steps in with needed maintenance for trail managers and hiking clubs. Through our Volunteer Vacations program, we provide more than 24,000 hours of trail work annually to help preserve some of the most scenic places in America. As an AHS Member, you can take advantage of this opportunity to give back to the trails that you use and love.

A critical resource. Each year, crucial trail funding continually falls behind trail maintenance demands. Your favorite trail will **not** be next, thanks to American Hiking Society! Our National Trails Fund annually awards financial grants to local and regional hiking clubs for land acquisition, volunteer recruitment, and trail maintenance. As you support AHS, you share in the satisfaction of helping grassroots trails clubs nationwide.

Join TODAY!

American Hiking Society

1422 Fenwick Lane · Silver Spring, MD 20910 · (301) 565–6704
www.AmericanHiking.org · info@AmericanHiking.org